CLIFFS

Graduate Record Examination

General Test

PREPARATION GUIDE

by

Jerry Bobrow, Ph.D.

Peter Z Orton, M.Ed.

William A. Covino, Ph.D.

Contributing Authors

Bernard V. Zandy, M.A.

David A. Kay, M.S.

Howard Horwitz, M.A.

LINCOLN, NEBRASKA 68501

ACKNOWLEDGMENTS

We would like to thank Cliffs Notes editor Michele Spence for her meticulous editing of the manuscript and her relentless determination in working all the problems.

We would also like to extend our sincere appreciation to the following authors and publications for permission to use excerpts from their writings:

Dr. Albert Upton for the use of excerpts from his outstanding book *Design for Thinking.*

"Sharks" by Sy Montgomery, *Los Angeles Times,* February 23, 1991, p. B-3.

"Opinions and Social Pressure," *Scientific American,* New York, November 1955.

ISBN 0-8220-2073-4

FIFTH EDITION

Printed in U.S.A.

CONTENTS

PART III: PRACTICE-REVIEW-ANALYZE-PRACTICE THREE FULL-LENGTH PRACTICE TESTS

PREFACE

YOUR GRE SCORES MAKE THE DIFFERENCE! And better scores result from thorough preparation. Therefore, your study time must be used most effectively. You need the most comprehensive test preparation guide that you can realistically complete in a reasonable time. It must be thorough, direct, precise, and easy to use, giving you all the information you need to do your best on the GRE.

In keeping with the fine tradition of Cliffs Notes, this guide was developed by leading experts in the field of test preparation as part of a series to specifically meet these standards. The testing strategies, techniques, and materials have been researched, tested, and evaluated, and are presently used at GRE preparation programs at many leading colleges and universities. This guide features the PATTERNED PLAN OF ATTACK for each section and focuses on six major areas:

1. The Ability Tested
2. The Basic Skills Necessary
3. Understanding Directions
4. Analysis of Directions
5. Suggested Approaches with Samples
6. Practice-Review-Analyze-Practice

These major areas include important mathematical symbols, terminology, and formulas, and a helpful list of prefixes, suffixes, and roots. Three complete practice exams follow with answers and *in-depth* explanations.

This guide was written to give you the edge in doing your best by maximizing your effort in the minimum amount of time. If you take the time to follow the Study Guide Checklist in this book, you will get the best preparation possible.

STUDY GUIDE CHECKLIST

If you're going to take the computerized version of the GRE, read "Taking the GRE on Computer" (page 441) before you start working through this checklist.

___ 1. Read the GRE Information Bulletin.
___ 2. Become familiar with the Test Format, page 3.
___ 3. Familiarize yourself with the answers to Questions Commonly Asked about the GRE, page 6.
___ 4. Learn the techniques of Two Successful Overall Approaches, page 9.
___ 5. Carefully read Part II, Analysis of Exam Areas, beginning on page 13.
___ 6. Review math Symbols, Terminology, Formulas, and General Information, page 56.
___ 7. Strictly observing time allotments, take Practice Test 1, section by section (review answers after each section), page 81.
___ 8. Check your answers and analyze your results, page 148.
___ 9. Fill out the Tally Sheet for Problems Missed to pinpoint your mistakes, page 154.
___ 10. While referring to each item of Practice Test 1, study ALL the Answers and Explanations that begin on page 157.
___ 11. Review as necessary Basic Skills, Symbols, Terminology, Formulas, and General Information given in Part II of this book.
___ 12. Strictly observing time allotments, take Practice Test 2, page 201.
___ 13. Check your answers and analyze your results, page 269.
___ 14. Fill out the Tally Sheet for Problems Missed to pinpoint your mistakes, page 275.

____ 15. While referring to each item of Practice Test 2, study ALL the Answers and Explanations that begin on page 279.
____ 16. Again, selectively review materials as needed.
____ 17. Carefully reread Part II, Analysis of Exam Areas, beginning on page 13.
____ 18. Strictly observing time allotments, take Practice Test 3, page 317.
____ 19. Check your answers and analyze your results, page 386.
____ 20. Fill out the Tally Sheet for Problems Missed to pinpoint your mistakes, page 392.
____ 21. While referring to each item of Practice Test 3, study ALL the Answers and Explanations that begin on page 395.
____ 22. Spend a little time reviewing the possible new question type, Analysis of Explanations, page 449.
____ 23. Again, selectively review materials as needed.
____ 24. Go over "FINAL PREPARATION" on page 440.

Part I: Introduction

FORMAT OF A RECENT GRE GENERAL TEST

Section I	**Verbal Ability**	**35–40 Questions**
30 Minutes	Sentence Completion	6–8 Questions
	Analogies	8–10 Questions
	Reading Comprehension (2 passages)	10–12 Questions
	Antonyms	10–12 Questions

Section II	**Quantitative Ability**	**Approximately 30 Questions**
30 Minutes	Quantitative Comparison	15 Questions
	Math Ability (with graphs)	15 Questions

Section III	**Analytical Ability**	**Approximately 25 Questions**
30 Minutes	Analytical Reasoning	19 Questions
	Logical Reasoning	6 Questions

Section IV	**Verbal Ability**	**35–40 Questions**
30 Minutes	Sentence Completion	6–8 Questions
	Analogies	8–10 Questions
	Reading Comprehension (2 passages)	10–12 Questions
	Antonyms	10–12 Questions

Section V	**Quantitative Ability**	**Approximately 30 Questions**
30 Minutes	Quantitative Comparison	15 Questions
	Math Ability (with graphs)	15 Questions

Section VI	**Analytical Ability**	**Approximately 25 Questions**
30 Minutes	Analytical Reasoning	19 Questions
	Logical Reasoning	6 Questions

Section VII 30 Minutes	**Either Verbal, Quantitative, Analytical, or Experimental**	**Approximately 30 Questions**

NOTE: The *order* in which the sections appear and the number of questions in each section may *vary* because there are several forms of the GRE. The actual test will contain a seventh section of experimental questions; *this section may appear at any point in the test.*

THE EXPERIMENTAL OR "PRETEST" SECTION

You should be aware that one of the seven sections on your GRE will be experimental. Your performance on this entire section will have no effect on your score. Your answers are being used by the testing company to pretest possible questions for future exams.

Typically the experimental section on a GRE will be a third section of either quantitative, verbal, or analytical ability. You know that two sections of each of these will be totaled to provide you with three scores, from 200 to 800. If you encounter, say, three verbal sections, then you can be sure that one of those sections is experimental and does not count in figuring your 200–800 score. *However,* you will not know whether it is the first, second, or third verbal. The experimental section could be any of the three.

On occasion, the testing company develops a new problem type, unlike any of the questions appearing on the three typical test sections. Recently, a new question type was Analysis of Explanations, which may no longer be experimental. This question type was explained in the directions but otherwise completely unfamiliar to the test taker. See page 449 for a discussion and sample questions.

Should you encounter a GRE section with question types that appear unusual or unlike any you have encountered in your preparation or mentioned in the official GRE Bulletin, chances are that that complete section is experimental. However, you should still try your best and keep your momentum going so you won't have to gear back up for the next section that will count toward your score.

GENERAL DESCRIPTION

The GRE General Test is used along with other information about your college achievements in order to assess your potential for success in graduate school. The test lasts approximately three and a half hours and consists entirely of multiple-choice questions.

The verbal section tests your reading comprehension and the breadth of your vocabulary. The quantitative section presents problems in arithmetic, algebra, and geometry. The analytical section tests your ability to read closely and reason logically from given information. All questions have the same point value.

QUESTIONS COMMONLY ASKED ABOUT THE GRE

Q: WHO ADMINISTERS THE GRE?

A: The GRE is administered by Educational Testing Service (ETS), which is located in Princeton, New Jersey. If you wish any information not covered in this book, write to ETS at Box 1502 Berkeley, California 94701 or at Box 955, Princeton, New Jersey 08540.

Q: CAN I TAKE THE GRE MORE THAN ONCE?

A: Yes. But be aware that your scores from each testing will appear on your score report. Therefore, even when you take the test for "practice," the results can have a real impact on your record.

Q: WHAT MATERIALS MAY I BRING TO THE GRE?

A: Bring your registration form, positive identification (check the bulletin for number and type), a watch, three or four sharpened Number 2 pencils, and a good eraser. You may not bring scratch paper, calculators, or books. You may do your figuring in the space provided in the test booklet.

Q: IF NECESSARY, MAY I CANCEL MY SCORE?

A: Yes. You may cancel your score on the day of the test by telling the test center supervisor, or you may write or telegraph ETS; your cancellation request must reach ETS within four days of the test date. Your GRE score report will note that you have canceled a score.

Q: SHOULD I GUESS ON THE GRE?

A: Yes! There is no penalty for guessing on the GRE. Before taking a wild guess, remember that eliminating one or more of the choices increases your chances of choosing the right answer.

Q: HOW SHOULD I PREPARE FOR THE GRE?

A: Understanding and practicing test-taking strategies will help a great deal, especially on the verbal and analytical sections. Subject-matter review is particularly useful for the math section. Both subject matter and strategies are fully covered in this book.

Q: WHEN IS THE GRE ADMINISTERED?

A: The GRE is administered nationwide five times during the school year, in October, December, February, April, and June, on Saturdays. The General Test is given in the morning, and the Advanced Tests are given in the afternoon There are special summer administrations, given in limited locations, in July, August, and September. Check with your regional testing office for other special administrations.

Q: WHERE IS THE GRE ADMINISTERED?

A: The GRE is administered at hundreds of schools and colleges in and out of the United States. A list of testing centers is included in the GRE information bulletin published by ETS. The testing or placement office at your college or university should have information about local administrations.

Q: HOW AND WHEN SHOULD I REGISTER?

A: A registration packet, complete with return envelope, is attached to the GRE information bulletin published by ETS. Mailing in the forms provided, plus the appropriate fees, completes the registration process. You should register about six weeks prior to the exam date.

Q: IS WALK-IN REGISTRATION PROVIDED?

A: Yes, on a limited basis. If you are unable to meet regular registration deadlines, you may attempt to register on the day of the test (an additional fee is required). You will be admitted only if space remains after preregistered students have been seated.

Q: WHAT IS THE DIFFERENCE BETWEEN THE GENERAL TEST AND THE ADVANCED TEST?

A: Your general scholastic ability is measured by the General Test; the questions on this section presume a broad, general college background. The Advanced Test deals with specific subject matter corresponding to your specific graduate study; the questions measure your undergraduate knowledge of the discipline you wish to pursue in graduate school.

Q: SHOULD I PREPARE DIFFERENTLY FOR THE ADVANCED TEST THAN FOR THE GENERAL TEST?

A: The test-taking strategies which help on the General Test will also help on the Advanced Test because it too consists entirely of multiple-choice questions. A short sample Advanced Test is sent to Advanced Test registrants by ETS; its questions are the most reliable indication of the level and range of questions you can expect. A general review of the material covered by the courses in your undergraduate major will be helpful insofar as it refreshes your memory of key facts, concepts, and personalities. Constructing multiple-choice questions of your own, based on what you have learned, is an ideal way to prepare.

Q: WHAT ARE THE SECTIONS OF THE GRE?

A: The GRE is composed of seven sections, each 30 minutes in length: two sections of Verbal Ability (35–40 questions each section), two sections of Quantitative Ability (Quantitative Comparison/Math Ability, 30 questions each section), two sections of Analytical Ability (Analytical Reasoning/Logical Reasoning, 25 questions each section), and one section that is experimental.

Q: HOW WILL COLLEGES USE MY SCORE ON THE ANALYTICAL SECTION?

A: The use of this section varies from college to college. Many colleges still discount the analytical score and emphasize the verbal and quantitative scores, simply because the analytical section is relatively new. For some schools, the analytical score is considered quite seriously; for others, it is used to substitute for possible weaknesses in your verbal or quantitative scores. Consult the graduate school to which you are applying to find out precisely how they consider your analytical score.

TAKING THE GRE
TWO SUCCESSFUL OVERALL APPROACHES

The "Plus-Minus" System

Many who take the GRE don't get their best possible score because they spend too much time on difficult questions, leaving insufficient time to answer the easy questions. Don't let this happen to you. Since every question within each section is worth the same amount, use the following system.

1. Answer easy questions immediately.
2. When you come to a question that seems "impossible" to answer, mark a large minus sign ("–") next to it on your test booklet.
3. Then mark a "guess" answer on your answer sheet and move on to the next question.
4. When you come to a question that seems solvable but appears too time consuming, mark a large plus sign ("+") next to that question in your test booklet and register a guess answer on your answer sheet. Then move on to the next question.

Since your time allotment is just over one minute per question, a "time-consuming" question is a question that you estimate will take you more than several minutes to answer. But don't waste time deciding whether a question is a "+" or a "–." Act quickly, as the intent of this strategy is, in fact, to save you valuable time.

After you work all the easy questions, your *booklet* should look something like this:

1.
+ 2.
3.
– 4.
+ 5.
etc.

5. After working all the problems you can do immediately in that section (the easy ones), go back and work your "+" problems. Change your "guess" on your answer sheet, if necessary, for those problems you are able to work.
6. If you finish working your "+" problems and still have time left, you can either
   (A) Attempt those "−" questions—the ones that you considered "impossible." Sometimes a problem later in that section will "trigger" your memory and you'll be able to go back and answer one of the earlier "impossible" problems.

   or

   (B) Don't bother with those "impossible" questions. Rather, spend your time reviewing your work to be sure you didn't make any careless mistakes on the questions you thought were easy to answer.

REMEMBER: You do not have to erase the pluses and minuses you made on your *question booklet.* And be sure to fill in all your answer spaces—if necessary, with a guess. As there is no penalty for wrong answers, it makes no sense to leave an answer space blank. And, of course, remember that you may work only in one section of the test at a time.

The Elimination Strategy

Take advantage of being allowed to mark in your testing booklet. As you eliminate an answer choice from consideration, make sure to *mark it out in your question booklet* as follows:

~~(A)~~
?(B)
~~(C)~~
~~(D)~~
?(E)

Notice that some choices are marked with question marks, signifying that they may be possible answers. This technique will help you avoid reconsidering those choices you have already eliminated. It will also help you narrow down your possible answers.

Again, these marks you make on your *question booklet* do not need to be erased.

Part II: Analysis of Exam Areas

This section is designed to introduce you to each GRE area by carefully reveiwing the

1. Ability Tested
2. Basic Skills Necessary
3. Directions
4. Analysis of Directions
5. Suggested Approach with Samples

This section features the PATTERNED PLAN OF ATTACK for each subject area and emphasizes important test-taking techniques and strategies and how to apply them to a variety of problem types. It also includes valuable symbols, terminology, formulas, basic math information, and a compact list of prefixes, suffixes, and roots to assist you in the verbal section.

INTRODUCTION TO VERBAL ABILITY

There are two Verbal Ability sections on the GRE, each 30 minutes in length. The two sections contain a total of about 80 questions (35–40 questions each). Each Verbal Ability section consists of four types of questions: Antonyms, Analogies, Sentence Completion, and Reading Comprehension. The total of the two sections is scaled from 200 to 800, with an average score of about 480.

A CAREFUL ANALYSIS OF EACH TYPE OF VERBAL ABILITY QUESTION FOLLOWS.

ANTONYMS

Ability Tested

The Antonym section tests your vocabulary—your ability to understand the meanings of words and to distinguish between fine shades of meaning.

Basic Skills Necessary

This section requires a strong college- or graduate-level vocabulary. A strong vocabulary cannot be developed instantly; it grows over a long period of time spent reading widely and learning new words. Knowing the meanings of prefixes, suffixes, and roots will help you to derive word meanings on the test.

Directions

Each word in CAPITAL LETTERS is followed by five words or phrases. The correct choice is the word or phrase whose meaning is most nearly *opposite* to the meaning of the word in capitals. You may be required to distinguish fine shades of meaning. Look at all choices before marking your answer.

Analysis

Although your choice may not be a "perfect" opposite, it must be the *most nearly opposite* of the five choices provided.

You should consider all the choices, keeping in mind that in most cases *three* of the five choices can be quickly eliminated as not at all opposite to the original word.

Suggested Approach with Samples

- **The prefix, root, and (sometimes) suffix of the original word may help you locate its opposite.** Sample:

1. PROFUSION
   (A) deficiency
   (B) certainty
   (C) proliferation
   (D) largeness
   (E) maximum

The prefix *pro-* has several meanings, and all of them have "positive" connotations; here it means *forward.* Of the five choices, the prefix most opposite to the meaning of *pro-* is *de-*. The connotations of *de-* are usually "negative"; most often, it means *away from, off,* or *down.*

Profusion means *abundance,* and *deficiency* refers to an *inadequacy* or *incompleteness.* Given these definitions, we see that these two terms are the most nearly opposite of those given. However, even without your knowing the definitions, the prefixes, in this case, provide strong clues.

- **Without considering the parts of the original word, you may be able to detect whether it is positive or negative in meaning. If the original word is positive, your choice must be negative, and vice versa.** Sample:

2. GHASTLY
   (A) stupendous
   (B) infectious
   (C) lovely
   (D) acceptable
   (E) standard

Ghastly is a strongly negative word. Although *acceptable* is a positive word, and therefore opposite to *ghastly, lovely* is a better choice. *Lovely* is more strongly positive than *acceptable* and therefore suits the strongly negative meaning of *ghastly.*

- **Working from the answer choices and looking for a single choice that "stands out" can be a useful strategy.** Sample:

3. DILAPIDATED
   (A) ruined
   (B) unconscionable
   (C) renovated
   (D) bizarre
   (E) hasty

Assessing the choices for positive or negative meaning, notice that only *renovated* is not clearly a negative word; thus, it "stands out" among the other choices. In this case, *renovated* (made good as new) is the opposite of *dilapidated,* which means *falling apart.*

- **Don't choose an antonym that is too broad or too limited to be an opposite.** Sample:

4. GARRULOUS
   (A) edited
   (B) speechless
   (C) censored
   (D) narrow minded
   (E) unyielding

Garrulous means *talking much.* Although choices (A), (C), (D), and (E) are all partial opposites because they contain the idea of restricting language, only (B) specifically refers to speech.

- **Try using the given word in a short clear sentence; try to think of how you've heard the word used before. You may discover a context for it that will help you make a choice.** Sample:

5. PATHOLOGICAL
   (A) unsteady
   (B) cured
   (C) predictable
   (D) stubborn
   (E) selective

Sentence: "One of my friends is a *pathological* liar." Since *pathological* here refers to a negative characteristic, the correct choice is positive, (B).

- **Occasionally, you may be uncertain as to the particular part of speech of a word. You can identify the part of speech of the root word by looking at the answer choices.** For example:

  Suppose the word in question is MINUTE. Is this the noun meaning *a unit of time equaling sixty seconds* (pronounced **min**-ut)? Or is it the adjective meaning *extremely small* (pronounced my-**noot**)? If the answer choices are all nouns, then the root word must also be a noun (indicating the former meaning of *minute*). If the answer choices are all adjectives, the root word is an adjective. All the answer choices in a particular question will represent the same part of speech. By scanning the answer choices, you can help identify the part of speech of the root word.

A PATTERNED PLAN OF ATTACK

Antonyms

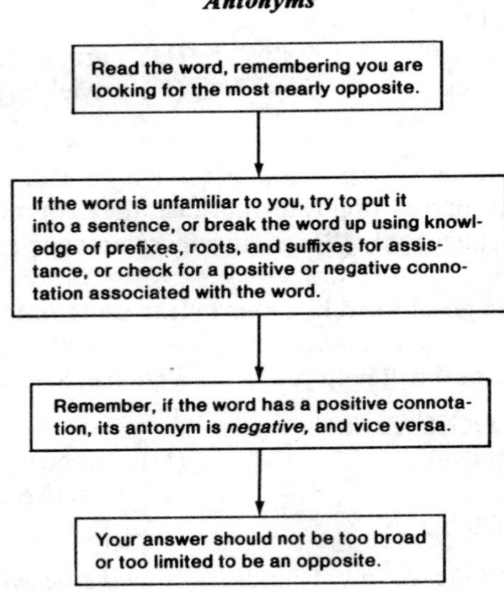

Read the word, remembering you are looking for the most nearly opposite.
If the word is unfamiliar to you, try to put it into a sentence, or break the word up using knowledge of prefixes, roots, and suffixes for assistance, or check for a positive or negative connotation associated with the word.
Remember, if the word has a positive connotation, its antonym is negative, and vice versa.
Your answer should not be too broad or too limited to be an opposite.

ANALOGIES

Ability Tested

The Analogy section tests your ability to understand logical relationships between pairs of words. Your vocabulary—your ability to understand the meanings of words—is also tested.

Basic Skills Necessary

The basic skills necessary for this section are, once again, a strong college- or graduate-level vocabulary and the ability to distinguish similarities and differences between words or ideas.

Directions

In each following sample, you are given a related pair of words or phrases. Select the lettered pair that *best* expresses a relationship similar to that in the original pair of words.

Analysis

It is important that you focus on understanding the *relationship* between the original pair because this is really what you are trying to parallel.

Notice that you are to select the *best* answer or most similar relationship; therefore, the correct answer may not be directly parallel. The use of the word *best* also implies that there may be more than one good answer.

Categories of Relationship

- **Opposites and Synonyms**

  Although a pair of analogies may not be *exact* opposites or *exact* synonyms, a number of pairs may have a roughly opposite or synonymous relationship.

  ERASE : RECORD :: RELINQUISH : ACQUIRE

  PRESENT : INTRODUCE :: SUCCEED : ACCOMPLISH

- **Action/Activity**

  Relationship between action and its meaning:

  YAWN : FATIGUE :: SOB : SORROW

  Relationship between action and its performer:

  ORATORY : CANDIDATE :: SOLILOQUY : ACTOR

  Relationship between action and its object:

  HATE : VILLAINY :: WORSHIP : DEITY

  Relationship between action and its recipient:

  DRAMA : AUDIENCE :: WRITING : READER

- **Characteristic/Condition**

  Relationship between a characteristic and a related action:

  OPPRESSED : LIBERATE :: MELANCHOLY : CHEER

  Relationship between a characteristic and a related person:

  CRAFTSMANSHIP : ARTISAN :: STATESMANSHIP : GOVERNOR

  Relationship between a characteristic and a related result:

  DISSATISFACTION : COMPLAINT :: CURIOSITY : QUESTIONING

- **Effect**

  Relationship between an effect and its cause:

  VERDICT : DELIBERATION :: DEFICIT : OVERSPENDING

  Relationship between an effect and its object

  OXIDATION : PAINT :: PHOTOSYNTHESIS : PLANT

- **Time and Space**

  Relationship between specific and general:

  SONNET : LITERATURE :: FOOTBALL : SPORT

Relationship between larger and smaller:

SKYLIGHT : PORTHOLE :: TOME : PAMPHLET

Relationship between younger and older:

SAPLING : TREE :: NEW STAR : NOVA

Relationship between container and contained:

PHOTOGRAPH : IMAGES :: LIBRARY : BOOKS

Relationship between part and whole:

MOVEMENT : SYMPHONY :: CHAPTER : NOVEL

Relationship between concrete and abstract:

STORY : HEIGHT :: DEGREE : TEMPERATURE

NOTE: Many of these relationships can be presented in a negative rather than a positive sequence. For instance, instead of a pair of words denoting an effect and its cause, you might encounter the *negation* of this relationship, an effect coupled with something that *cannot* be its cause. For example:

HAPPINESS : INJURY :: PEACEFULNESS : STRESS

"*Happiness* is not the effect of *injury* in the same way as *peacefulness* is not the effect of *stress.*" The relationship here may be represented as EFFECT : (−)CAUSE, using the minus sign to indicate the negative element in the pair.

- **As with Antonym questions, here, too, the parts of speech in the answer choices will exactly duplicate those in the root words.** For example:

  Suppose the root words are AMUSE : LAUGHTER :: The first word, *amuse,* is a verb; the second word, *laughter,* is a noun. All the choices will duplicate that structure—verb : noun :: Therefore, if you are in doubt about a choice, you can use this structure to clarify the word. Suppose choice (A) is *damage : destruction.* You now know that *damage* is a verb, meaning to *harm* or *cause destruction to,* rather than its meaning as a noun. And you may help yourself determine the parts of speech of the root words by examining the words in the answer choices.

Suggested Approach with Samples

- **To determine the relationship between the original pair of words, try to construct a sentence with words that link the pair.** Sample:

1. ORATORY : COMMUNICATION ::
   (A) key : ignition
   (B) concept : paragraph
   (C) dancing : recreation
   (D) stalling : conversation
   (E) cursing : crime

In this case, you might say to yourself, "*Oratory* is a specific kind of *communication*" and thus recognize that the relationship here is between specific and general.

- **Narrow your choice to a pair of words that demonstrates most precisely the same relationship as the original pair.**

Test the precision of the relationship by applying the sentence "A is to B in the same way as C is to D." In the example above, you would say to yourself, "*Oratory* is a specific kind of *communication* in the same way as . . . (A) a *key* is a specific kind of *ignition*?, (B) a *concept* is a specific kind of *paragraph*?, (C) *dancing* is a specific kind of *recreation*?, (D) *stalling* is a specific kind of *conversation*?, (E) *cursing* is a specific kind of *crime*?" After following this procedure, the best choices, those that demonstrate the relationship of the original pair, are (C) and (E.

To make your final choice, decide which pair of words expresses a "specific to general" relationship that is either *necessary* or *typical.* For instance, *cursing* is not *necessarily* or *typically* a specific kind of *crime*; however *dancing* is *necessarily* and *typically* a specific kind of *recreation.* Therefore, (C) is the best choice.

- **Often you will need to consider not only the *primary* relationship between the original words, but also a *secondary* relationship.** Sample:

2. PERJURY : TRUTH ::
   (A) attorney : client
   (B) treason : loyalty
   (C) courage : cowardice
   (D) sorcery : witchcraft
   (E) patience : indecision

"*Perjury* is the opposite of *truth.* This sentence tells us that the primary relationship between the original words is one of opposites.

Beyond this primary relationship, there are secondary relationships to consider. First, notice that *perjury* is an *unlawful* act. Second, notice that, considering more specifically the relationship of *perjury* to *truth*, we may conclude that *perjury* is a *violation* of *truth*. Scanning the answer choices, you see that *treason* is the opposite of *loyalty* and that *courage* is the opposite of *cowardice*. However, only choice (B) presents a relationship in which the first term is an *unlawful* act and in which the first term is a *violation* of the second. Thus, taking the secondary relationships of the original pair fully into account, you should conclude that (B) is the best choice.

To sum up this effective approach to analogies: (1) Determine the relationship between the original pair or words by using them in a sentence. (2) Narrow your choices to pairs that typically or necessarily express a similar relationship. (3) Choose the pair that expresses the original relationship most precisely by taking into account the secondary relationship(s) between the words in the original pair.

A PATTERNED PLAN OF ATTACK

Analogies

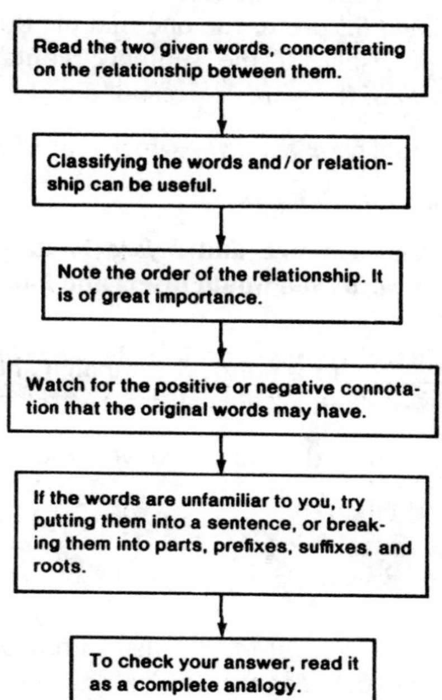

Read the two given words, concentrating on the relationship between them.
Classifying the words and/or relationship can be useful.
Note the order of the relationship. It is of great importance.
Watch for the positive or negative connotation that the original words may have.
If the words are unfamiliar to you, try putting them into a sentence, or breaking them into parts, prefixes, suffixes, and roots.
To check your answer, read it as a complete analogy.

SENTENCE COMPLETION

Ability Tested

This section tests your ability to complete sentences with a word or words that retain the meaning of the sentence and are compatible with given syntax and grammar cues.

Basic Skills Necessary

Good reading comprehension skills help in this section, as does a good college- or graduate-level vocabulary.

Directions

Each blank in the following sentences indicates that something has been omitted. Considering the lettered words beneath the sentence, choose the word or set of words that best fits the whole sentence.

Analysis

Note that you must choose the *best* word or words. In cases where several choices *might* fit, prefer the one that fits the meaning of the sentence most precisely. If the sentence contains two blanks, remember that *both* of the words corresponding to your choice must fit.

Suggested Approach with Samples

- ***After* reading the sentence and *before* looking at the answer choices, think of words you would insert and look for synonyms to them.** Sample:

1. Money ________ to a political campaign should be used for political purposes and nothing else.

How would you fill in the blank? Maybe with the word *given* or *donated*?

- **Now look at the choices and find a synonym for *given* or *donated:***

(A) used
(B) forwarded
(C) contributed
(D) spent
(E) channeled

The best choice is (C), *contributed;* it is the nearest synonym to *given* or *donated* and makes good sense in the sentence.

- **Look for signal words. Some signal words are *however, although, on the other hand,* and *but*.** Sample:

2. Most candidates spend _________ they can raise on their campaigns, but others wind up on election day with a _________.
   (A) so . . . bankroll
   (B) time . . . vacation
   (C) everything . . . surplus
   (D) every cent . . . deficit
   (E) nothing . . . war chest

But signals that the first half of the sentence *contrasts* with the second half. The fact that most candidates spend *everything* (and end up with nothing) contrasts with those who end up with a *surplus.* (C) is the correct answer.

- **Watch for contrasts between positive and negative words. Look for words like *not, never,* and *no*.** Sample:

3. A virtuous person will not shout _________ in public; he or she will respect the _________ of other people.

The first blank is obviously a negative word, something a good person would *not* shout; the second blank is a positive word, something that a good person *would* respect. Here are the choices:

(A) obscenities . . . feelings
(B) loudly . . . comfort
(C) anywhere . . . presence
(D) blessings . . . cynicism
(E) insults . . . threat

Choice (B) is neutral-positive; (C) is neutral-neutral; (D) is positive-negative; (E) is negative-negative. Only choice (A) offers a negative- positive pair of words; (A) is the best choice.

- **Sometimes it is more efficient to work from the second blank first.** Sample:

4. The merger will eliminate ________ and provide more ________ cross-training of staff.
   (A) profit . . . and more
   (B) paperwork . . . or less
   (C) duplication . . . effective
   (D) bosses . . . wasteful
   (E) competitors . . . aggressive

The second blank is something that is *provided.* Chances are that something *provided* is a positive word, and *effective* seems like a good choice. Reading choice (C) into the sentence, we find that it makes good sense and is stylistically and structurally correct.

- **What "sounds wrong" should be eliminated.** Sample:

5. High school students should not be ________ as being immature or naive.
   (A) helped
   (B) shoved
   (C) directed
   (D) categorized
   (E) taught

The only word that sounds right with *as* is *categorized;* (D) is the best choice.

A PATTERNED PLAN OF ATTACK

Sentence Completion

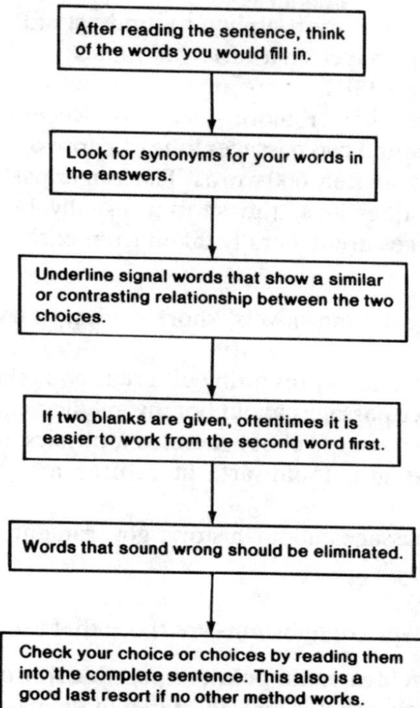

After reading the sentence, think of the words you would fill in.
Look for synonyms for your words in the answers.
Underline signal words that show a similar or contrasting relationship between the two choices.
If two blanks are given, oftentimes it is easier to work from the second word first.
Words that sound wrong should be eliminated.
Check your choice or choices by reading them into the complete sentence. This also is a good last resort if no other method works.

READING COMPREHENSION

Ability Tested

This section tests your ability to understand, interpret, and analyze reading passages on a variety of topics.

In each complete GRE, there are three or more reading passages, each followed by two or more questions. Recently, each verbal section has contained two passages, one of approximately 200 words and one of approximately 600 words. The longer passage is followed by six to eight questions, the shorter usually by three to four questions. Passages are generally taken from each of the following categories:

Narrative passages from novels, short stories, essays, and biographies
Argumentative passages presenting different points of view
Biological Science passages about botany, medicine, or zoology
Physical Science passages about chemistry, physics, or astronomy
Humanities passages about art, literature, music, folklore, or philosophy
Social Studies passages about history, government, economics, or sociology

The common types of questions are those that ask you

—about the **main idea, main point,** or **possible title** of the passage
—about **information** that is directly **stated** in the passage
—about **information** that is **implied, suggested,** or **can be inferred**
—to recognize **applications** of the author's **opinions** or **ideas**
—to evaluate how the author **develops** and **presents** the passage
—to recognize the **style** or **tone** of the passage

Basic Skills Necessary

Students who have read widely and know how to read and mark a passage actively and efficiently tend to do well on this section.

Directions

Each passage in this group is followed by questions based on its content. After reading a passage, choose the best answer to each question and blacken the corresponding space on the answer sheet. Answer all questions following a passage on the basis of what is *stated* or *implied* in that passage. You may refer back to the passage.

Analysis

Answer all the questions for one passage before moving on to the next one. If you don't know the answer, take an educated guess.

Use only the information given or implied in a passage. Do not consider outside information, even if it seems more accurate than the given information.

Suggested Approach with Sample Passages

- **Skim the questions first, marking words which give you a clue about what to look for when you read the passage.**

- **Read the passage actively, marking main points and other items you feel are important such as conclusions, names, definitions, places, and/or numbers. Make only a few marks per paragraph. Remember, these marks are to help you understand the passage.**

Short Passage

*By the time a child starts school, he has mastered the major part of the rules of his grammar. He has managed to accomplish this remarkable feat in such a short time by experimenting with and generalizing the rules all by himself. Each child, in effect, rediscovers language in the first few years of his life.

When it comes to vocabulary growth, it is a different story. Unlike grammar, the chief means through which vocabulary is learned is memorization. And some people have a hard time learning and remembering new words.

(The * indicates portions of the passage which refer directly to a question you've skimmed. Also marked are main points and key terms.)

1. A child has mastered many rules of grammar by about the age of
   (A) 3
   (B) 5
   (C) 8
   (D) 10
   (E) 18

The first sentence of the passage contains several words from this question, so it is likely to contain the correct answer. *By the time a child starts school* tells us that the answer is 5. Before choosing (B), you should look at all the answers and cross out those which seem incorrect.

2. Although vocabulary growth involves memorization and grammar-learning doesn't, we may conclude that both vocabulary and grammar make use of
   (A) memorization
   (B) study skills
   (C) words
   (D) children
   (E) teachers

The question asks you to simply use your common sense. Choice (A) is incorrect; it contradicts both the passage and the question itself. (D) and (E) make no sense. (B) is a possibility, but (C) is better because grammar-learning in young children does not necessarily involve study skills but does involve words.

3. The last sentence in the passage implies that
   (A) some people have little difficulty learning and remembering new words
   (B) some people have a hard time remembering new words
   (C) grammar does not involve remembering words
   (D) old words are not often remembered
   (E) learning and remembering are kinds of growth

Implies tells us that the answer is something suggested but not explicitly stated in the passage. Choice (B) is explicitly stated in the passage, so it may be eliminated. But (B) implies the opposite: If *some* people have a hard time, then it must be true that *some* people don't. (A) is therefore the correct choice. Choices (C), (D), and (E) are altogether apart from the meaning of the last sentence.

Long Passage

Woodrow Wilson is usually ranked among the country's great presidents in spite of his failures to win Senate approval of the League of Nations. Wilson had yearned for a political career all his life; he won his first office in 1910 when he was elected governor of New Jersey. Two years later he was elected president in one of the most rapid political rises in our history. For a while Wilson had practiced law but found it both boring and unprofitable; then he became a political scientist of great renown and finally president of Princeton University. He did an outstanding job at Princeton but lost out in a battle with Dean Andrew West for control of the graduate school. When he was asked by the Democratic boss of New Jersey, Jim Smith, to run for governor, Wilson readily accepted because his position at Princeton was becoming untenable.

Until 1910 Wilson seemed to be a conservative Democrat in the Grover Cleveland tradition. He had denounced Bryan in 1896 and had voted for the National Democratic candidate who supported gold. In fact, when the Democratic machine first pushed Wilson's nomination in 1912, the young New Jersey progressives wanted no part of him. Wilson later assured them that he would champion the progressive cause, and so they decided to work for his election. It is easy to accuse Wilson of political expediency, but it is entirely possible that by 1912 he had changed his views as had countless other Americans. While governor of New Jersey, he carried out his election pledges by enacting an impressive list of reforms.

Wilson secured the Democratic nomination on the forty-sixth ballot after a fierce battle with Champ Clark of Missouri and Oscar W. Underwood of Alabama. Clark actually had a majority of votes but was unable to attract the necessary two-thirds. In the campaign, Wilson emerged as the middle-of-the-road candidate—between the conservative William H. Taft and the more radical Theodore Roosevelt. Wilson called his program the New Freedom, which he said was the restoration of free competition as it had existed before the growth of the trusts. In contrast, Theodore Roosevelt was advocating a New Nationalism, which seemed to call for massive federal intervention in the economic life of the nation. Wilson felt that the trusts should be destroyed, but he made a distinction between a trust and a legitimately successful big business. Theodore Roosevelt, on the other hand, accepted the trusts as inevitable but said that the government should regulate them by establishing a new regulatory agency. The former president also felt that a distinction should be made between the "good" trusts and the "bad" trusts.

Questions

4. The author's main purpose in writing this passage is to
   (A) argue that Wilson is one of the great U.S. presidents
   (B) survey the differences between Wilson, Taft, and Roosevelt
   (C) explain Wilson's concept of the New Freedom
   (D) discuss some major events of Wilson's career
   (E) suggest reasons that Wilson's presidency may have started World War I

5. The author implies which of the following about the New Jersey progressives?
   (A) They did not support Wilson after he was governor.
   (B) They were not conservative Democrats.
   (C) They were more interested in political expediency than in political causes or reforms.
   (D) Along with Wilson, they were supporters of Bryan in 1896.
   (E) They particularly admired Wilson's experience as president of Princeton University.

6. The passage supports which of the following conclusions about the progress of Wilson's political career?
   (A) Few politicians have progressed so rapidly toward the attainment of higher office.
   (B) Failures late in his career caused him to be regarded as a president who regressed instead of progressed.
   (C) Wilson encountered little opposition once he determined to seek the presidency.
   (D) The League of Nations marked the end of Wilson's reputation as a strong leader.
   (E) Wilson's political progress was aided by Champ Clark and Oscar Underwood.

7. In the statement "Wilson readily accepted because his position at Princeton was becoming untenable," the meaning of "untenable" is probably which of the following?
   (A) unlikely to last for ten years
   (B) filled with considerably less tension
   (C) difficult to maintain or continue
   (D) filled with achievements that would appeal to voters
   (E) something he did not have a tenacious desire to continue

8. According to the passage, which of the following was probably true about the presidential campaign of 1912?
   (A) Woodrow Wilson won the election by an overwhelming majority.
   (B) The inexperience of Theodore Roosevelt accounted for his radical position.
   (C) Wilson was unable to attract two-thirds of the votes but won anyway.
   (D) There were three nominated candidates for the presidency.
   (E) Wilson's New Freedom did not represent Democratic interests.

Answers and Explanations

4. (D) Choices (A) and (E) are irrelevant to the information in the passage, and choices (B) and (C) mention *secondary* purposes rather than the primary one.

5. (B) In the second paragraph, Wilson's decision to *champion the progressive cause* after 1912 is contrasted with his earlier career, when *he seemed to be a conservative Democrat.* Thus, we may conclude that the progressives, whom Wilson finally joined, were not conservative Democrats, as was Wilson earlier in his career. Choices (A) and (D) contradict information in the paragraph, while choices (C) and (E) are not suggested by any information given in the passage.

6. (A) This choice is explicitly supported by the third sentence in paragraph one in which we are told that Wilson was *elected president in one of the most rapid political rises in our history.*

7. (C) On any reading comprehension test, it is best to be alert to the positive and negative connotations of words and phrases in each passage as well as in the questions themselves. In the case of *untenable,* the prefix *un-* suggests that the word has a negative connotation. The context in which the word occurs does so as well. Wilson *left* his position at Princeton; therefore, we may conclude that the position was somehow unappealing. Only two of the answer choices, (C) and (E), provide a negative definition. Although choice (E) may attract your attention because *tenacious* looks similar to *tenable,* the correct choice is (C), which is the conventional definition of *untenable.*

8. (D) Choices (A), (B), and (C) contain information that is not addressed in the passage. We may eliminate them as irrelevant. Choice (E) contradicts the fact that Wilson was a Democratic candidate. The discussion of Taft and Roosevelt as the candidates who finally ran against Wilson for the presidency supports choice (D).

A PATTERNED PLAN OF ATTACK

Reading Comprehension

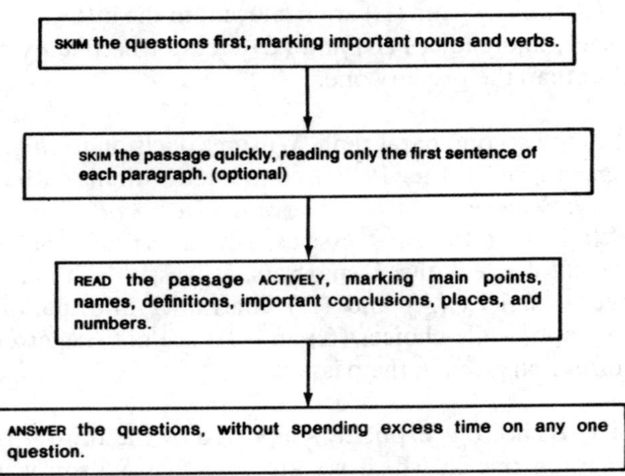

SKIM the questions first, marking important nouns and verbs.
SKIM the passage quickly, reading only the first sentence of each paragraph. (optional)
READ the passage ACTIVELY, marking main points, names, definitions, important conclusions, places, and numbers.
ANSWER the questions, without spending excess time on any one question.

COMMON PREFIXES, SUFFIXES, AND ROOTS

The following list should help you to arrive at definitions of unfamiliar words on the Verbal Section of the GRE. These prefixes, suffixes, and roots apply to thousands of words.

Prefixes

Prefix	Meaning	Example
pre-	before	precede
de-	away, from	deter
inter-	between	interstate
ob-	against	objection
in-	into	instruct
mono-	alone, one	monolith
epi-	upon	epilogue
mis-	wrong	mistake
sub-	under	submarine
trans-	across, beyond	transcend
over-	above	overbearing
ad-	to, toward	advance
non-	not	nonentity
com-	together, with	composite
re-	back, again	regress
ex-	out of	expel
in-	not	insufficient
pro-	forward	propel
anti-	against	antidote
omni-	all, everywhere	omniscient
equi-	equal, equally	equivalent
homo-	same, equal, like	homogenized
semi-	half, partly	semicircle
un-	not	unneeded
bi-	two	bicycle
poly-	many	polymorphous
retro-	backward	retrograde
mal-	bad	malfunction
hyper-	over, too much	hyperactive
hypo-	under, too little	hypodermic

Suffixes

Suffix	Meaning	Example
-able, -ible	able to	usable
-er, -or	one who does	competitor
-ism	the practice of	rationalism
-ist	one who is occupied with	feminist
-less	without, lacking	meaningless
-ship	the art or skill of	statesmanship
-fy	to make	dignify
-ness	the quality of	aggressiveness
-tude	the state of	rectitude
-logue	a particular kind of speaking or writing	prologue

Roots

Root	Meaning	Example
arch	to rule	monarch
belli	war, warlike	belligerent
bene	good	benevolent
chron	time	chronology
dic	to say	indicative
fac	to make, to do	artifact
graph	writing	telegraph
mort	to die	mortal
port	to carry	deport
vid, vis	to see	invisible

INTRODUCTION TO QUANTITATIVE ABILITY

There are two Quantitative Ability sections on the GRE, each 30 minutes in length. The two sections contain a total of about 60 questions (30 questions each). Each Quantitative Ability section consists of two basic types of questions: Quantitative Comparison and regular Math Ability, multiple-choice questions. The total of the two sections generates a scaled score that ranges from 200 to 800, with an average score of about 560.

A CAREFUL ANALYSIS OF EACH TYPE OF QUANTITATIVE ABILITY QUESTION FOLLOWS.

QUANTITATIVE COMPARISON

Ability Tested

Quantitative Comparison tests your ability to use mathematical insight, approximation, simple calculation, or common sense to quickly compare two given quantities.

Basic Skills Necessary

This section requires twelfth-grade competence in high school arithmetic, algebra, and intuitive geometry. Skills in approximating, comparing, and evaluating are also necessary. No advanced mathematics is necessary.

Directions

In this section you will be given two quantities, one in column A and one in column B. You are to determine a relationship between the two quantities and mark

(A) if the quantity in column A is greater than the quantity in column B
(B) if the quantity in column B is greater than the quantity in column A
(C) if the two quantities are equal
(D) if the comparison cannot be determined from the information given

Analysis

The purpose here is to make a comparison; therefore, exact answers are not always necessary. (Remember that you can tell whether you are taller than someone in many cases without knowing that person's height. Comparisons such as this can be made with only partial information—just enough to compare.) (D) is not a possible answer if there are values in each column because you can always compare values.

If you get different relationships, depending on the values you choose for variables, then the answer is always (D). Notice that there are only four possible choices here. *Never* mark (E) on your answer sheet for Quantitative Comparison.

Note that you can add, subtract, multiply, and divide both columns by the same value and the relationship between them will not change. EXCEPTION—You should not multiply or divide each column by negative numbers because then the relationship reverses. Squaring both columns is permissible, as long as each side is positive.

Suggested Approach with Sample Problems

- **This section emphasizes shortcuts, insight, and quick techniques. Long and/or involved mathematical computation is unnecessary and is contrary to the purpose of this section.** Sample:

Column A	Column B
$21 \times 43 \times 56$	$44 \times 21 \times 57$

Canceling (or dividing) 21 from each side leaves

43×56	44×57

The rest of this problem should be done by inspection because it is obvious that column B is greater than column A without doing any multiplication. You could have attained the correct answer by actually multiplying out each column, but you would then not have enough time to finish the section. The correct answer is (B).

- **The use of partial comparisons can be valuable in giving you insight into finding a comparison. If you cannot simply make a complete comparison, look at each column part by part.** Sample:

Column A	Column B
$\frac{1}{57} - \frac{1}{65}$	$\frac{1}{58} - \frac{1}{63}$

Since finding a common denominator would be too time consuming, you should first compare the first fraction in each column (partial comparison). Notice that $1/57$ is greater than $1/58$. Now compare the second fractions and notice that $1/65$ is less than $1/63$. Using some common sense and insight, if you start with a larger number and subtract a smaller number, it must be greater than starting with a smaller number and subtracting a larger number, as pointed out below.

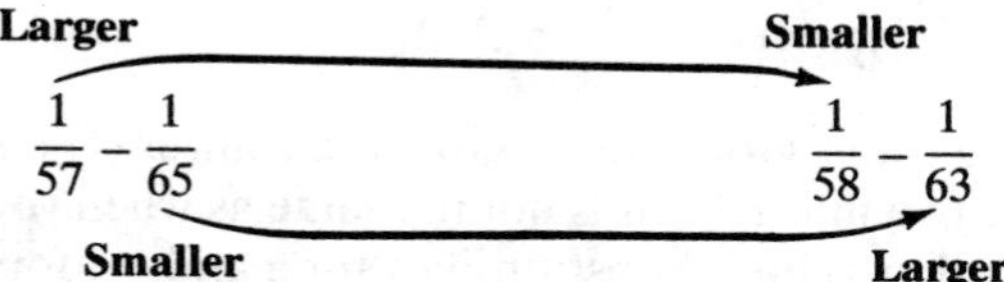

The correct answer is (A).

- **Always keep the columns in perspective before starting any calculations. Take a good look at the value in each column before starting to work on one column.** Sample:

Column A	Column B
$\sqrt[3]{7^6}$	2^8

After looking at each column (note that the answer could not be (D) because there are values in each column), compute the value on the left. Since you are taking a cube root, simply divide the power of 7 by 3 leaving 7^2, or 49. There is no need to take 2 out to the 8th power; just do as little as necessary:

$$2^2 = 4$$
$$2^3 = 8$$
$$2^4 = 16$$
$$2^5 = 32$$

STOP

It is evident that 2^8 is much greater than 49; the correct answer is (B). Approximating can also be valuable while remembering to keep the columns in perspective.

- **If a problem involves variables (without an equation), substitute in the numbers 0, 1, and −1. Then try ½, and 2 if necessary. Using 0, 1, and −1 will often tip off the answer.** Sample:

Column A		Column B
a + b		ab

Substituting 0 for a and 0 for b gives:

0 + 0		0(0)
Therefore, 0	=	0

Using these values for a and b gives the answer (C). But anytime you multiply two numbers, it is not the same as when you add them, so try some other values. Substituting 1 for a and −1 for b gives:

1 + (−1)		1(−1)
Therefore, 0	>	−1

and the answer is now (A).

Anytime you get more than one comparison (different relationships), depending on the values chosen, the correct answer must be (D), the relationship cannot be determined. Notice that if you had substituted the values a = 4, b = 5; or a = 6, b = 7; or a = 7, b = 9; and so on, you would repeatedly have gotten the answer (B) and might have chosen the incorrect answer.

- **Often, simplifying one or both columns can make an answer evident.** Sample:

Column A		Column B
	a, b, c, all greater than 0	
a(b + c)		ab + ac

Using the distributive property on column A to simplify, gives ab and ac; therefore, the columns are equal.

- **Sometimes you can solve for a column directly, in one step, without solving and substituting. If you have to solve an equation or equations to give the columns values, take a second and see if there is a very simple way to get an answer before going through all of the steps.** Sample:

Column A		Column B
	$4x + 2 = 10$	
$2x + 1$		4

Hopefully, you would spot that the easiest way to solve for $2x + 1$ is directly by dividing $4x + 2 = 10$ by 2, leaving $2x + 1 = 5$. Therefore,

5	>	4

Solving for x first in the equation and then substituting would also have worked but would have been more time consuming. The correct answer is (A).

- **Marking diagrams can be very helpful for giving insight into a problem. Remember that figures and diagrams are meant for positional information only. Just because something "looks" larger is not enough reason to choose an answer.** Sample:

Column A		Column B

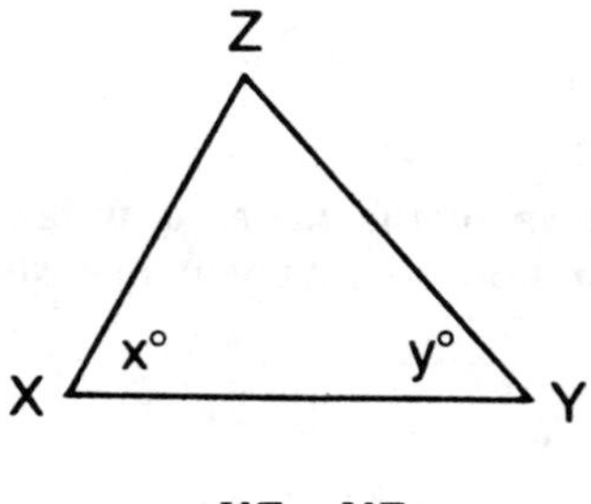

$XZ = YZ$

x	y

Even though x appears larger, this is not enough. Mark in the diagram as shown.

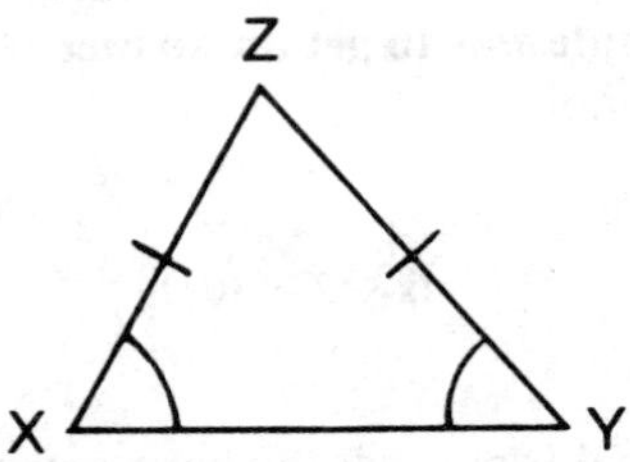

Notice that you should mark things of equal measure with the same markings, and since angles opposite equal sides in a triangle are equal, x = y. The correct answer is (C).

- **If you are given information that is unfamiliar to you and difficult to work with, change the number slightly (but remember what you've changed) to something easier to work with.** Sample:

Column A | **Column B**

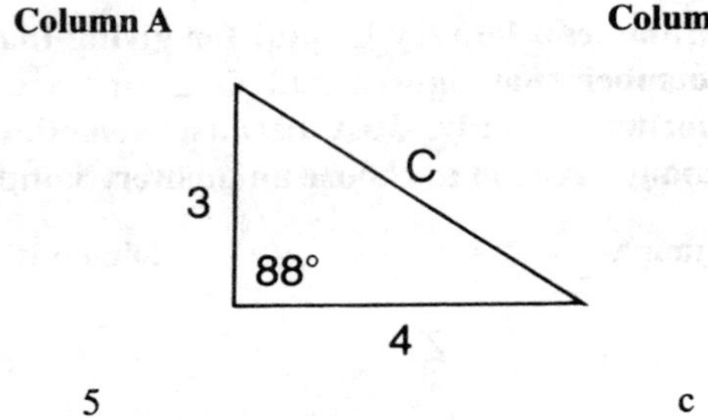

5 | c

Since the 88° shown in the figure is unfamiliar to work with, change it to 90° for now so that you may use the Pythagorean theorem to solve for c.

$$a^2 + b^2 = c^2$$

Solve for c as follows:

$$(3)^2 + (4)^2 = c^2$$
$$9 + 16 = c^2$$
$$25 = c^2$$

Therefore, $5 = c$

But since you used 90° instead of 88°, you should realize that the side opposite the 88° will be slightly smaller, or less than 5. The correct answer is then (A), $5 > c$. (Some students may have noticed the 3:4:5 triangle relationship and not have needed the Pythagorean theorem.)

A PATTERNED PLAN OF ATTACK

Quantitative Comparison

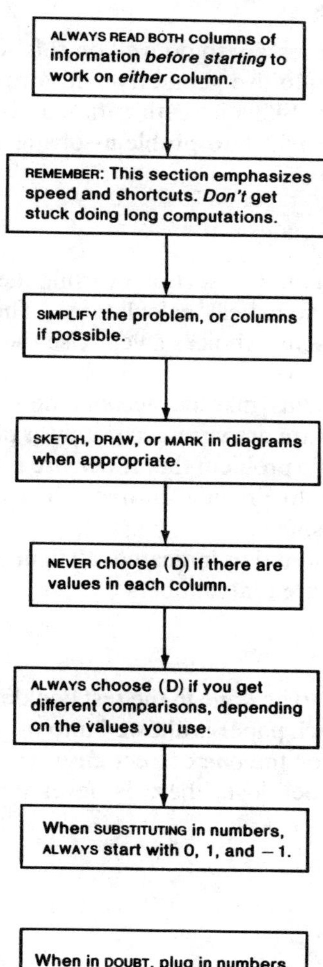

ALWAYS READ BOTH columns of information *before starting* to work on *either* column.
REMEMBER: This section emphasizes speed and shortcuts. *Don't* get stuck doing long computations.
SIMPLIFY the problem, or columns if possible.
SKETCH, DRAW, or MARK in diagrams when appropriate.
NEVER choose (D) if there are values in each column.
ALWAYS choose (D) if you get different comparisons, depending on the values you use.
When SUBSTITUTING in numbers, ALWAYS start with 0, 1, and −1.
When in DOUBT, plug in numbers.

MATH ABILITY

Ability Tested

The Math Ability section tests your ability to solve mathematical problems involving arithmetic, algebra, geometry, and word problems by using problem-solving insight, logic, and application of basic skills.

Basic Skills Necessary

The basic skills necessary to do well on this section include high school algebra and intuitive geometry—no formal trigonometry or calculus is necessary. Skills in arithmetic and basic algebra, along with some logical insight into problem-solving situations, are also necessary.

Directions

Solve each problem in this section by using the information given and your own mathematical calculations. Then select the *one* correct answer of the five choices given. Use the available space on the page for scratchwork.

Note: Some problems may be accompanied by figures or diagrams. These figures are drawn as accurately as possible *except* when it is stated in a specific problem that the figure is not drawn to scale. The figure is meant to provide information useful in solving the problem or problems.

Unless otherwise stated or indicated, all figures lie in a plane.

All numbers used are real numbers.

Analysis

All scratchwork is to be done in the test booklet; get used to doing this because no scratch paper is allowed into the testing area.

You are looking for the *one* correct answer; therefore, although other answers may be close, there is never more than one right answer.

Suggested Approach with Samples

- **Take advantage of being allowed to mark on the test booklet by always underlining or circling what you are looking for. This will ensure that you are answering the right question.** Sample:

1. If $x + 6 = 9$, then $3x + 1 =$
   (A) 3
   (B) 9
   (C) 10
   (D) 34
   (E) 46

You should first circle or underline $3x + 1$ because this is what you are solving for. Solving for x leaves $x = 3$, and then substituting into $3x + 1$ gives $3(3) + 1$, or 10. The most common mistake is to solve for x, which is 3, and *mistakenly choose* (A) as your answer. But remember, you are solving for $3x + 1$, not just x. You should also notice that most of the other choices would all be possible answers if you made common or simple mistakes. The correct answer is (C). *Make sure that you are answering the right question.*

- **Substituting numbers for variables can often be an aid to understanding a problem. Remember to substitute simple numbers, since *you* have to do the work.** Sample:

2. If $x > 1$, which of the following decreases as x decreases?

   I. $x + x^2$ II. $2x^2 - x$ III. $\frac{1}{x + 1}$

   (A) I only
   (B) II only
   (C) III only
   (D) I and II only
   (E) II and III only

This problem is most easily solved by taking each situation and substituting simple numbers. However, in the first situation (I. $x + x^2$), you should recognize that this expression will decrease as x decreases. Trying $x = 2$ gives $2 + (2)^2 = 6$. Now, trying $x = 3$ gives $3 + (3)^2 = 12$. Notice that choices (B), (C), and (E) are already eliminated because they do not contain I. You should also realize that now you need to try only the values in II. Since III is not paired with I as a possible choice, III cannot be one of the answers.

Trying $x = 2$ in the expression $2x^2 - x$ gives $2(2)^2 - 2$, or $2(4) - 2 = 6$. Now, trying $x = 3$ gives $2(3)^2 - 3$, or $2(9) - 3 = 15$. This expression also decreases as x decreases. Therefore, the correct answer is (D). Once again, notice that III was not even attempted because it was not one of the possible choices.

- **Sometimes you will immediately recognize the proper formula or method to solve a problem. If this is not the situation, try a reasonable approach and then work from the answers.** Sample:

3. Barney can mow the lawn in 5 hours, and Fred can mow the lawn in 4 hours. How long will it take them to mow the lawn together?
   (A) 5 hours
   (B) 4½ hours
   (C) 4 hours
   (D) 2²⁄₉ hours
   (E) 1 hour

Suppose that you are unfamiliar with the type of equation for this problem. Try the "reasonable" method. Since Fred can mow the lawn in 4 hours by himself, it will take less than 4 hours if Barney helps him. Therefore, choices (A), (B), and (C) are ridiculous. Taking this method a little further, suppose that Barney could also mow the lawn in 4 hours. Then together it would take Barney and Fred 2 hours. But since Barney is a little slower than this, the total time should be a little more than 2 hours. The correct answer is (D), $2\frac{2}{9}$ hours.

Using the equation for this problem would give the following calculations:

$$\frac{1}{5} + \frac{1}{4} = \frac{1}{x}$$

In 1 hour, Barney could do $\frac{1}{5}$ of the job, and in 1 hour, Fred could do $\frac{1}{4}$ of the job. Unknown $\frac{1}{x}$ is that part of the job they could do together in one hour. Now solving, you calculate as follows:

$$\frac{4}{20} + \frac{5}{20} = \frac{1}{x}$$

$$\frac{9}{20} = \frac{1}{x}$$

Cross multiplying gives $9x = 20$

Therefore, $x = \frac{20}{9}$ or $2\frac{2}{9}$

- **"Pulling" information out of the word problem structure can often given you a better look at what you are working with; therefore, you gain additional insight into the problem.** Sample:

4. If a mixture is $\frac{3}{7}$ alcohol by volume and $\frac{4}{7}$ water by volume, what is the ratio of the volume of alcohol to the volume of water in this mixture?
   (A) $\frac{3}{7}$
   (B) $\frac{4}{7}$
   (C) $\frac{3}{4}$
   (D) $\frac{4}{3}$
   (E) $\frac{7}{4}$

The first bit of information that should be pulled out should be what you are looking for: "ratio of the volume of alcohol to the volume of water." Rewrite it as A:W and then into its working form: A/W. Next, you should pull out the volumes of each : $A = \frac{3}{7}$ and $W = \frac{4}{7}$.

Now the answer can be easily figured by inspection or substitution. Using $(\frac{3}{7})$ $(\frac{4}{7})$, invert the bottom fraction and multiply to get $\frac{3}{7} \times \frac{7}{4} = \frac{3}{4}$. The ratio of the volume of alcohol to the volume of water is 3 to 4. The correct answer is (C).

When pulling out information, actually write out the numbers and/or letters to the side of the problem, putting them into some helpful form and eliminating some of the wording.

- **Sketching diagrams or simple pictures can also be very helpful in problem solving because the diagram may tip off either a simple solution or a method for solving the problem.** Sample:

5. What is the maximum number of pieces of birthday cake of size 4″ by 4″ that can be cut from a cake 20″ by 20″?
   (A) 5
   (B) 10
   (C) 16
   (D) 20
   (E) 25

Sketching the cake and marking in as shown makes this a fairly simple problem.

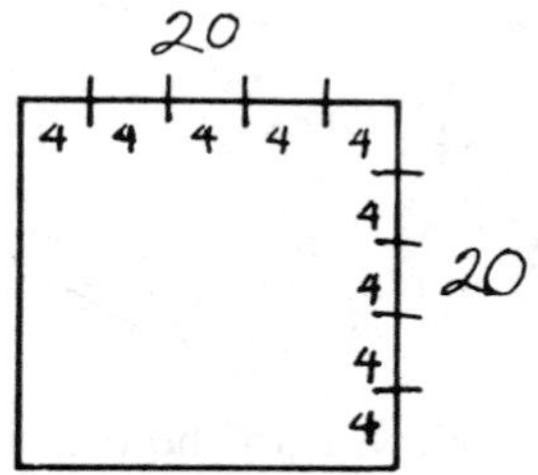

Notice that 5 pieces of cake will fit along each side.

Therefore $5 \times 5 = 25$. The correct answer is (E). Finding the total area of the cake and dividing it by the area of one of the 4×4 pieces would also have given you the correct answer, but beware of this method because it may *not* work if the pieces do not fit evenly into the original area.

- **Marking in diagrams as you read the questions can save you valuable time. Marking can also give you insight into how to solve a problem because you will have the complete picture clearly in front of you.** Sample:

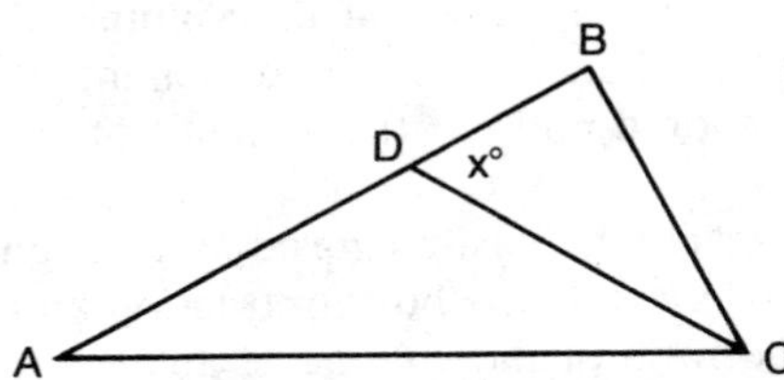

6. In the triangle above, CD is an angle bisector, angle ACD is 30°, and angle ABC is a right angle. What is the measurement of angle x in degrees?
   (A) 30°
   (B) 45°
   (C) 60°
   (D) 75°
   (E) 80°

You should have read the problem and marked as follows: In the triangle above, CD is an angle bisector (STOP AND MARK IN THE DRAWING), angle ACD is 30° (STOP AND MARK IN THE DRAWING), and angle ABC is a right angle (STOP AND MARK IN THE DRAWING). What is the measurement of angle x in degrees? (STOP AND MARK IN OR CIRCLE WHAT YOU ARE LOOKING FOR IN THE DRAWING).

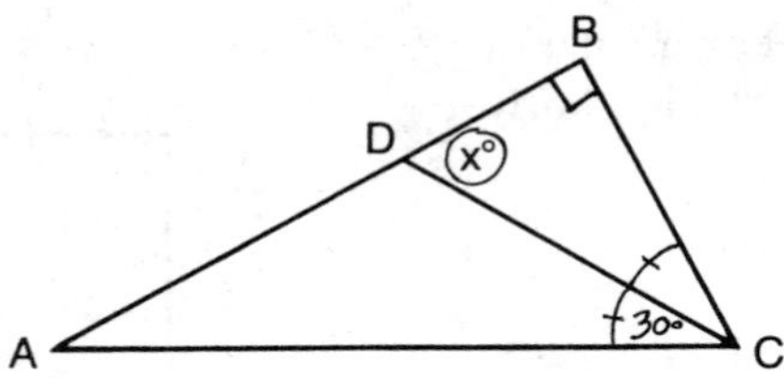

Now, with the drawing marked in, it is evident that, since angle ACD is 30°, then angle BCD is also 30° because they are formed by an angle bisector (divides an angle into two equal parts). Since angle ABC is 90° (right angle) and angle BCD is 30°, then angle x is 60° because there are 180° in a triangle.

$$180 - (90 + 30) = 60$$

The correct answer is (C). ALWAYS MARK IN DIAGRAMS AS YOU READ DESCRIPTIONS AND INFORMATION ABOUT THEM. THIS INCLUDES WHAT YOU ARE LOOKING FOR.

- **If it appears that extensive calculations are going to be necessary to solve a problem, check to see how far apart the choices are and then approximate. The reason for checking the answers first is to give you a guide to how freely you can approximate.** Sample:

7. The value for (.889 × 55)/9.97 to the nearest tenth is
   (A) 49.1
   (B) 7.7
   (C) 4.9
   (D) 4.63
   (E) .5

Before starting any computations, take a glance at the answers to see how far apart they are. Notice that the only close answers are (C) and (D). But (D) is not possible, since it is to the nearest hundredth, not tenth. Now, making some quick approximations, .889 = 1 and 9.97 = 10, which leaves the problem in this form:

$$\frac{1 \times 55}{10} = \frac{55}{10} = 5.5$$

The closest answer is (C). Therefore, it is the correct answer. Notice that choices (A) and (E) are not reasonable.

- **In some instances, it will be easier to work from the answers. Do not disregard this method because it will at least eliminate some of the choices and could give you the correct answer.** Sample:

8. What is the counting number that is less than 15, when divided by 3 has a remainder of 1, and when divided by 4 has a remainder of 2?
   (A) 5
   (B) 8
   (C) 10
   (D) 12
   (E) 13

By working from the answers, you eliminate wasting time on the other numbers from 1 to 14. Choices (B) and (D) can be immediately eliminated because they are divisible by 4, leaving no remainder. Choices (A) and (E) can also be eliminated because they leave a remainder of 1 when divided by 4. Therefore, the correct answer is (C); 10 leaves a remainder of 1 when divided by 3 and a remainder of 2 when divided by 4.

A PATTERNED PLAN OF ATTACK

Math Ability

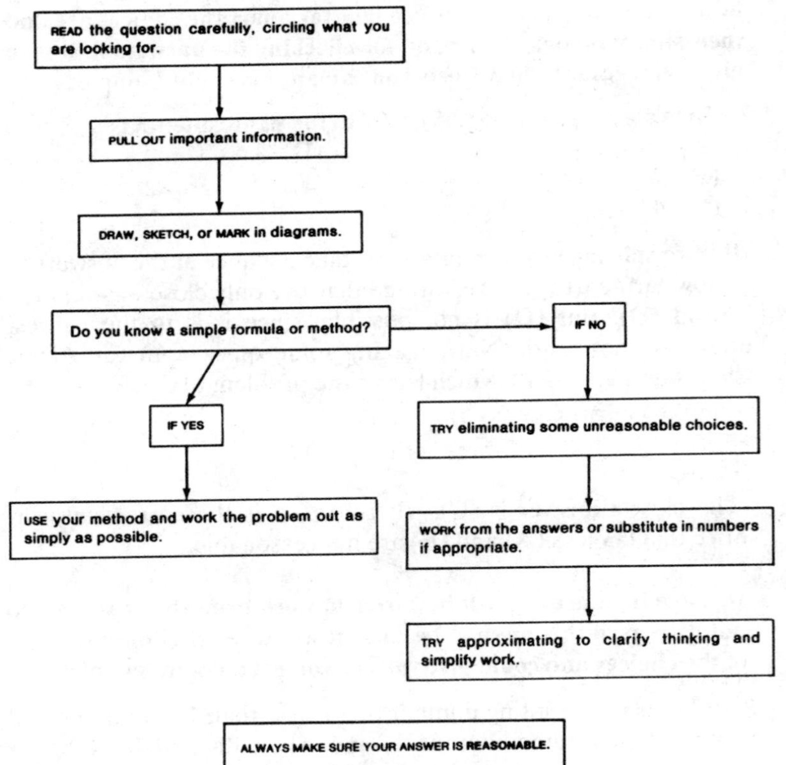

GRAPHS AND CHARTS

Graphs and charts are included in the Quantitative Comparison and/or Math Ability sections of the GRE.

Ability Tested

You will need to understand and to derive information from charts, tables, and graphs. Many of the problems require brief calculations based on the data, so your mathematical ability is also tested.

Basic Skills Necessary

The mathematics associated with graphs and charts does not go beyond high-school level. Your familiarity with a wide range of chart and graph types will help you feel comfortable with these problems and read the data accurately.

Directions

You are given data represented in chart or graph form. Following each set of data are questions based on that data. Select the *best* answer to each question by referring to the appropriate chart or graph and mark your choice on the answer sheet. Use only the given or implied information to determine your answer.

Analysis

Remember that you are looking for the *best* answer, not necessarily the perfect answer. Often, graph questions ask you for an *approximate* answer. If this happens, don't forget to round off numbers to make your work easier.

Use only the information given. Never "read into" the information on a graph.

Suggested Approach with Samples

Here are some helpful strategies for extracting accurate information, followed by some sample graph questions.

- **Skim the questions and quickly examine the whole graph before starting to work problems. This sort of prereading will tell you what to look for.**

- **Use your answer sheet as a straightedge in order to align points on the graph with their corresponding number values.**
- **Sometimes the answer to a question is available in supplementary information given with a graph (headings, scale factors, legends, etc.). Be sure to read this information.**
- **Look for the obvious: dramatic trends, high points, low points, etc. Obvious information often leads directly to an answer.**

Graph and Chart Questions

Questions 1-3 refer to the graph.

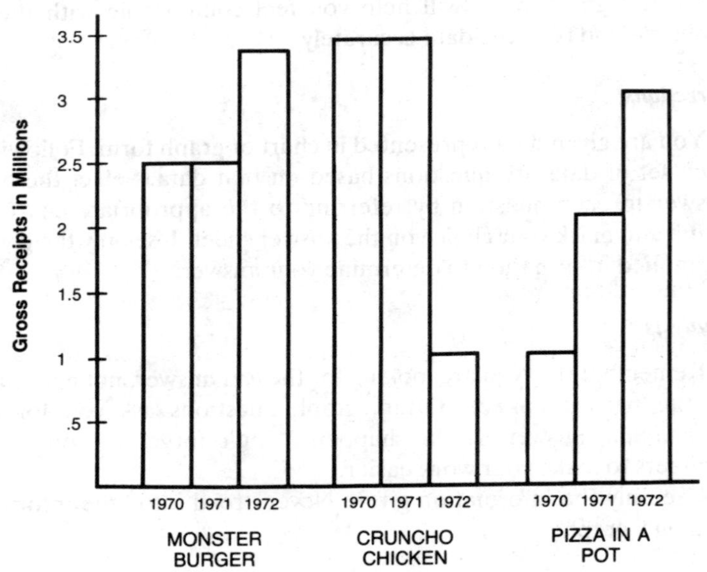

1. The 1970-72 gross receipts for Monster Burger exceeded those of Pizza In A Pot by approximately how much?
   (A) 0.2 million
   (B) 2 million
   (C) 8.2 million
   (D) 8.4 million
   (E) 17 million

2. From 1971 to 1972, the percent increase in receipts for Pizza In A Pot exceeded the percent increase of Monster Burger by approximately how much?
   (A) 0%
   (B) 2%
   (C) 10%
   (D) 15%
   (E) 43%

3. The 1972 decline in Cruncho Chicken's receipts may be attributed to
   (A) an increase in the popularity of burgers
   (B) an increase in the popularity of pizza
   (C) a decrease in the demand for chicken
   (D) a predictable slump attributable to the deceleration of the Vietnam War
   (E) cannot be determined from the information given

Answers and Explanations

This is a bar graph. Typically, this type of graph has a number scale along one edge and individual categories along another edge. Here we have multiple bars representing each fast-food category. Each single bar stands for the receipts from a single year.

You may be tempted to write out the numbers as you do your arithmetic (3.5 million = 3,500,000). This is unnecessary, as it often is on graphs which use large numbers. Since *all* measurements are in millions, adding zeros does not add precision to the numbers.

1. (B) Referring to the Monster Burger bars, we see that gross receipts are as follows: 1970 = 2.5, 1971 = 2.5, 1972 = 3.4 (use your answer sheet as a straightedge to determine this last number). Totaling the receipts for all three years, we get 8.4.

   Referring to the Pizza in A Pot bars, we see that gross receipts are as follows: 1970 = 1, 1971 = 2.1, 1972 = 3 (once again, use your straightedge, but do not designate numbers beyond the nearest tenth, since the graph numbers and the answer choices prescribe no greater accuracy than this). Totaling the receipts for all three years, we get 6.1.

   So Monster Burger exceeds Pizza In A Pot by 2.3 million. The answer which best approximates this figure is (B).

2. (C) Several graph and chart questions on the GRE may ask you to calculate percent increase or percent decrease. The formula for figuring either of these is the same:

$$\frac{\text{amount of change}}{\text{“starting” amount (follows the word } \textit{from}\text{)}}$$

In this case, we may first calculate the percent increase for Monster Burger:

Gross receipts in 1971 = 2.5

Gross receipts in 1972 = 3.4

Amount of change = .9

The 1971 amount is the "starting" or "from" amount.

$$\frac{\text{amount of change}}{\text{“starting” amount}} = \frac{.9}{2.5} = .36 = 36\%$$

Percent increase for Pizza In A Pot:

Gross receipts in 1971 = 2.1

Gross receipts in 1972 = 3

Amount of change = .9

$$\frac{\text{amount of change}}{\text{“starting” amount}} = \frac{.9}{2.1} = .428 \cong 43\%$$

So Pizza In A Pot exceeds Monster Burger by 7% (43% − 36%). The answer which best approximates this figure is (C).

3. (E) Never use information that you know is not given. In this case, the multiple factors which could cause a decline in receipts are not represented by the graph. All choices except (E) require you to speculate beyond the information given.

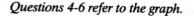

Questions 4-6 refer to the graph.

Gross Receipts of All Major
Fast-Food Restaurants
1971–1973

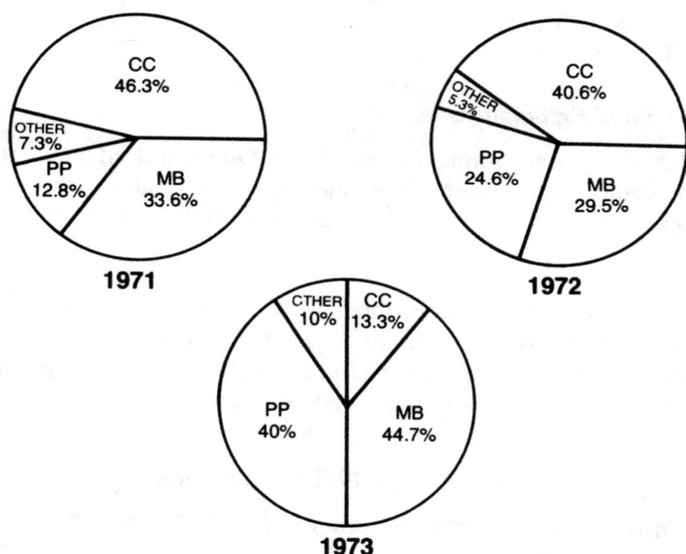

Gross Receipts for 1971: $7,500,000
Gross Receipts for 1972: $8,550,000
Gross Receipts for 1973: $8,100,000

MB—Monster Burger
CC—Cruncho Chicken
PP—Pizza In A Pot

4. The gross receipts for 1971 are approximately what percent of the gross receipts for all three years?
   (A) 30%
   (B) 46.3%
   (C) 46.7%
   (D) 50%
   (E) cannot be determined

5. Over all three years, the average percentage of gross receipts for Cruncho Chicken exceeds the average percentage of gross receipts for Pizza In A Pot by approximately how much?
   (A) 53%
   (B) 30%
   (C) 23%
   (D) 8%
   (E) 4%

6. The gross receipts earned by other restaurants in 1973 amount to precisely how much?
   (A) $453,150
   (B) $547,500
   (C) $810,000
   (D) $1,810,650
   (E) cannot be determined

Answers and Explanations

This is a circle graph, or pie chart. One hundred percent is represented by the whole circle, and the various "slices" represent portions of that 100%. The larger the slice, the higher the percentage.

4. (A) You can solve this problem without referring to the graphs. The necessary information is available in the list of gross receipts below the graphs. Don't write out all the zeros when calculating with these large figures; brief figures are easier to work with.

$$\text{Gross receipts for 1971} = 7.5 \text{ million}$$

$$\text{Gross receipts for all three years} = 7.5 + 8.6 + 8.1$$

$$= 24.2 \text{ million}$$

$$\frac{7.5}{24.2} = 31\%$$

The answer which best approximates 31% is 30%, (A). Notice that even without doing the calculations, you may approximate 30% by realizing that the gross receipts for any one year are about one-third of the total.

5. (D) To calculate the average percentage for Cruncho Chicken, add the percentages for each year and divide by 3.

$$46.3 + 40.6 + 13.3 = 100.2 \div 3 = 33.4\%$$

Do the same for Pizza In A Pot.

$$12.8 + 24.6 + 40 = 77.4 \div 3 = 25.8\%$$

Cruncho Chicken exceeds Pizza In A Pot by 33.4 − 25.8 = 7.6. Choice (D), 8%, best approximates this figure.

6. (C) In 1973, other restaurants earned precisely 10%. And 10% of $8,100,000 = $810,000, choice (C).

A PATTERNED PLAN OF ATTACK

Graphs and Charts

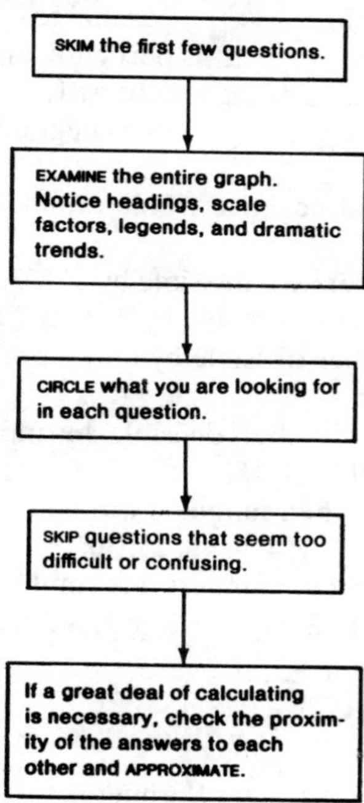

SKIM the first few questions.
EXAMINE the entire graph. Notice headings, scale factors, legends, and dramatic trends.
CIRCLE what you are looking for in each question.
SKIP questions that seem too difficult or confusing.
If a great deal of calculating is necessary, check the proximity of the answers to each other and APPROXIMATE.

IMPORTANT SYMBOLS, TERMINOLOGY, FORMULAS, AND GENERAL MATHEMATICAL INFORMATION

COMMON MATH SYMBOLS AND TERMS

Symbol References:

$=$ is equal to	$\geq$ is greater than or equal to
$\neq$ is not equal to	$\leq$ is less than or equal to
$>$ is greater than	$\parallel$ is parallel to
$<$ is less than	$\perp$ is perpendicular to

Natural numbers—the counting numbers: 1, 2, 3, . . .

Whole numbers—the counting numbers beginning with zero: 0, 1, 2, 3, . . .

Integers—positive and negative whole numbers and zero: . . . -3, -2, -1, 0, 1, 2, . . .

Odd numbers—numbers not divisible by 2: 1, 3, 5, 7, . . .

Even numbers—numbers divisible by 2: 0, 2, 4, 6, . . .

Prime number—number divisible by only 1 and itself: 2, 3, 5, 7, 11, 13, . . .

Composite number—number divisible by more than just 1 and itself: 4, 6, 8, 9, 10, 12, 14, 15, . . .

Squares—the results when numbers are multiplied by themselves, $(2 \cdot 2 = 4)$ $(3 \cdot 3 = 9)$: 1, 4, 9, 16, 25, 36, . . .

Cubes—the result when numbers are multiplied by themselves twice, $(2 \cdot 2 \cdot 2 = 8)$, $(3 \cdot 3 \cdot 3 = 27)$: 1, 8, 27, . . .

MATH FORMULAS

Triangle	Perimeter $= s_1 + s_2 + s_3$ Area $= \frac{1}{2}bh$
Square	Perimeter $= 4s$ Area $= s \cdot s$, or s^2
Rectangle	Perimeter $= 2(b + h)$, or $2b + 2h$ Area $= bh$, or lw
Parallelogram	Perimeter $= 2(l + w)$, or $2l + 2w$ Area $= bh$

Trapezoid — Perimeter = $b_1 + b_2 + s_1 + s_2$

Area = $\frac{1}{2}h(b_1 + b_2)$, or $h\left(\frac{b_1 + b_2}{2}\right)$

Circle — Circumference = $2\pi r$, or πd

Area = πr^2

Pythagorean theorem (for right triangles) $a^2 + b^2 = c^2$

The sum of the squares of the legs of a right triangle equals the square of the hypotenus.

Cube — Volume = $s \cdot s \cdot s = s^3$

Surface area = $s \cdot s \cdot 6$

Rectangular Prism — Volume = $l \cdot w \cdot h$

Surface area = $2(lw) + 2(lh) + 2(wh)$

IMPORTANT EQUIVALENTS

Memorizing the following can eliminate unnecessary computations:

$\frac{1}{100} = .01 = 1\%$
$\frac{1}{10} = .1 = 10\%$
$\frac{1}{5} = \frac{2}{10} = .2 = .20 = 20\%$
$\frac{3}{10} = .3 = .30 = 30\%$
$\frac{2}{5} = \frac{4}{10} = .4 = .40 = 40\%$
$\frac{1}{2} = \frac{5}{10} = .5 = .50 = 50\%$
$\frac{3}{5} = \frac{6}{10} = .6 = .60 = 60\%$
$\frac{7}{10} = .7 = .70 = 70\%$
$\frac{4}{5} = \frac{8}{10} = .8 = .80 = 80\%$
$\frac{9}{10} = .9 = .90 = 90\%$
$\frac{1}{4} = \frac{25}{100} = .25 = 25\%$
$\frac{3}{4} = \frac{75}{100} = .75 = 75\%$

$\frac{1}{3} = .33\frac{1}{3} = 33\frac{1}{3}\%$
$\frac{2}{3} = .66\frac{2}{3} = 66\frac{2}{3}\%$
$\frac{1}{8} = .125 = .12\frac{1}{2} = 12\frac{1}{2}\%$
$\frac{3}{8} = .375 = .37\frac{1}{2} = 37\frac{1}{2}\%$
$\frac{5}{8} = .625 = .62\frac{1}{2} = 62\frac{1}{2}\%$
$\frac{7}{8} = .875 = .87\frac{1}{2} = 87\frac{1}{2}\%$
$\frac{1}{6} = .16\frac{2}{3} = 16\frac{2}{3}\%$
$\frac{5}{6} = .83\frac{1}{3} = 83\frac{1}{3}\%$
$1 = 1.00 = 100\%$
$2 = 2.00 = 200\%$
$3\frac{1}{2} = 3.5 = 3.50 = 350\%$

MEASURES

Customary System, or English System

Length

12 inches (in) = 1 foot (ft)
3 feet = 1 yard (yd)
36 inches = 1 yard
1760 yards = 1 mile (mi)
5280 feet = 1 mile

Area

144 square inches (sq in) = 1 square foot (sq ft)
9 square feet = 1 square yard (sq yd)

Weight

16 ounces (oz) = 1 pound (lb)
2000 pounds = 1 ton (T)

Capacity

2 cups = 1 pint (pt)
2 pints = 1 quart (qt)
4 quarts = 1 gallon (gal)
4 pecks = 1 bushel

Time

365 days = 1 year
52 weeks = 1 year
10 years = 1 decade
100 years = 1 century

Metric System, or The International System of Units

Length—meter

Kilometer (km) = 1000 meters (m)
Hectometer (hm) = 100 meters
Dekameter (dam) = 10 meters

Meter
10 decimeters (dm) = 1 meter
100 centimeters (cm) = 1 meter
1000 millimeters (mm) = 1 meter

Volume—liter

Common measures
1000 milliliters (ml, or mL) = 1 liter (l, or L)
1000 liters = 1 kiloliter (kl, or kL)

Mass—gram

Common measures
1000 milligrams (mg) = 1 gram (g)
1000 grams = 1 kilogram (kg)
1000 kilograms = 1 metric ton (t)

PROBLEM-SOLVING WORDS AND PHRASES

Words that signal an operation:

ADDITION

- Sum
- Total
- Plus
- Increase
- More than
- Greater than

MULTIPLICATION

- Of
- Product
- Times
- At (Sometimes)
- Total (Sometimes)

SUBTRACTION

- Difference
- Less
- Decreased
- Reduced
- Fewer
- Have left

DIVISION

- Quotient
- Divisor
- Dividend
- Ratio
- Parts

GEOMETRY TERMS AND BASIC INFORMATION

Angles

Vertical angles—Formed by two intersecting lines, across from each other, always equal
Adjacent angles—Next to each other, share a common side and vertex
Right angle—Measures 90 degrees
Obtuse angle—Greater than 90 degrees

Acute angle—Less than 90 degrees
Straight angle, or line—Measures 180 degrees
Angle bisector—Divides an angle into two equal angles
Supplementary angles—Two angles whose total is 180 degrees
Complementary angles—Two angles whose total is 90 degrees

Lines

Two points determine a line
Parallel lines—Never meet
Perpendicular lines—Meet at right angles

Polygons

Polygon—A many-sided (more than two sides) closed figure
Regular polygon—A polygon with all sides and all angles equal
Triangle—Three-sided polygon; the interior angles total 180 degrees
  Equilateral triangle—All sides equal
  Isosceles triangle—Two sides equal
  Scalene triangle—All sides of different lengths
  Right triangle—A triangle containing a right angle
In a triangle—Angles opposite equal sides are equal
In a triangle—The longest side is across from the largest angle, and the shortest side is across from the smallest angle
In a triangle—The sum of any two sides of a triangle is larger than the third side
In a triangle—An exterior angle is equal to the sum of the remote two angles
Median of a triangle—A line segment that connects the vertex and the midpoint of the opposite side
Quadrilateral—Four-sided polygon; the interior angles total 360 degrees
  Parallelogram—A quadrilateral with opposite sides parallel
    Rectangle—A parallelogram with all right angles
    Rhombus—A parallelogram with equal sides
    Square—A parallelogram with equal sides and all right angles
    Trapezoid—A quadrilateral with two parallel sides

Pentagon—A five-sided polygon
Hexagon—A six-sided polygon
Octagon—An eight-sided polygon

Circles

Radius of a circle—A line segment from the center of the circle to the circle itself
Diameter of a circle—A line segment that starts and ends on the circle and goes through the center
Chord—A line segment that starts and ends on the circle
Arc—A part of the circle
Circle—Composed of 360°

INTRODUCTION TO ANALYTICAL ABILITY

The GRE has two 30-minute Analytical Ability sections, each containing about 25 questions. The total of the two sections is scaled from 200 to 800, with an average score of about 500. Each section usually consists of two types of questions: Analytical Reasoning and Logical Reasoning (but see "Analysis of Explanations," page 449).

ANALYTICAL REASONING

Ability Tested

You will need to draw reasoned conclusions from complex statements or situations.

Basic Skills Necessary

No knowledge of formal logic is required. Familiarity with constructing logical and spatial relationships from a given situation is valuable.

Directions

The general directions are as follows: The following questions or group of questions are based on a passage or set of statements. Choose the best answer for each question and blacken the corresponding space on your answer sheet. It may be helpful to draw rough diagrams or simple charts in attempting to answer these question types.

Analysis

Analytical Reasoning sets are composed of conditions followed by questions. Use only what is presented or implied by the conditions. Don't bring in more information than is warranted. For example, if a condition states that "Sarah is taller than Andy," it cannot necessarily be deduced that because Sarah is taller than Andy she is also heavier than Andy (unless such information also is given). Rely on common sense.

Suggested Approach with Samples

- **Use "rule breakers" as an effective elimination technique.** For example, suppose a set of conditions includes "Sam is taller than Jim" among its statements. Questions like this one will follow:

1. Which of the following is a possible list of children from shortest to tallest?
   (A) Bob, Jane, Tom, Cal, Sam, Jim
   (B) Jane, Bob, Jim, Cal, Tom, Sam
   (C) Bob, Jane, Tom, Sam, Cal, Jim
   (D) Jim, Bob, Jane, Cal, Sam, Tom
   (E) Sam, Bob, Cal, Jane, Jim, Sam

Notice that choices (A) and (C) "break the rule" of the condition stated above (Sam is taller than Jim). And two of the remaining choices (B), (D), and (E) will "break the rule" of one of the other conditions in the problem set (not listed above). As you can see, using "rule breakers" can be an effective technique to quickly knock out incorrect answer choices.

Occasionally a question will be phrased in the negative. For example, "All of the following are possible lists of children, from shortest to tallest, EXCEPT" . . . In this case, the one choice containing the "rule breaker" will be the correct answer to the question. Once you find it, mark that answer on your answer sheet and move to the next question.

- **Learn the common types of diagrams and symbols. Knowing how to quickly set up rough diagrams with simple symbols can be helpful.** For example, try this set of conditions and questions:

Questions 2–4

Seven people are seated in the front row of a theater.

There is a woman at either end.

A man is seated in the middle of the group.

No man is seated next to another man.

The man in the middle is flanked by women.

Two other men are also flanked by women.

2. How many women are seated in the front row?
   (A) 2
   (B) 3
   (C) 4
   (D) 5
   (E) 6

3. The man in the middle must have
   (A) no other men to his right
   (B) no women to his left
   (C) a man to his right and to his left
   (D) other men next to him
   (E) no women to his right

4. Without violating the given information, wishing to change seats with a man, a woman must
   (A) be initially seated at either end
   (B) remain where she is
   (C) switch with the man in the middle
   (D) ask another woman to also switch her seat
   (E) add more people to the row

Answers and Explanations

For this type of question, *draw* diagrams or make charts to gather information for your answers. Even a partial chart will help more than no chart at all. For this problem, we first number seven spaces.

1	2	3	4	5	6	7

Then place a woman at either end.

1	2	3	4	5	6	7
W						W

Then place a man in the middle.

1	2	3	4	5	6	7
W			M			W

Then flank the middle man with women.

1	2	3	4	5	6	7
W		W	M	W		W

Then add two more men who are also flanked by women.

1	2	3	4	5	6	7
W	M	W	M	W	M	W

Notice that no man is seated next to another man. The chart is complete. Now you may answer the questions as follows:

2. (C) By referring to the chart, it is evident that there are four women in the front row.

3. (C) By referring to the chart, you can see that the man in the middle has a man to his left and to his right but not next to him.

4. (B) Every choice except (B) violates the original information.

Now try the following set.

Questions 5–7

Four stamp dealers (Abby, Baker, Carmen, and David) each attend a different day of a stamp convention, held Thursday through Sunday of one week.

Carmen attends earlier than Abby.

David attends later than Baker.

5. Which of the following is a possible order of attendance at the convention?
   (A) Carmen, David, Abby, and Baker
   (B) Baker, Carmen, David, and Abby
   (C) David, Carmen, Abby, and Baker
   (D) Abby, Baker, David, and Carmen
   (E) Abby, Carmen, David, and Baker

6. If Carmen attends the convention on Saturday, who must attend on Thursday?
   (A) Abby
   (B) Baker
   (C) David
   (D) either Abby or David
   (E) either Baker or David

7. Each of the following is possible EXCEPT
   (A) Baker attends the convention on Thursday
   (B) Carmen attends the convention on Thursday
   (C) Abby attends the convention on Sunday
   (D) David attends the convention on Saturday
   (E) Baker attends the convention on Sunday

Answers and Explanations

You may wish to draw a simple diagram symbolizing the information contained in the conditions. Since you know that Carmen attends earlier than Abby, you might wish to put Carmen somewhere to the left of Abby. (Note that "earlier" does not mean exactly one day earlier, but rather "sometime earlier"):

```
Thursday   Friday   Saturday   Sunday
   C ←─────────────────────────→ A
```

And since David attends later than Baker:

```
Thursday   Friday   Saturday   Sunday
   C ←─────────────────────────→ A
   B ←─────────────────────────→ D
```

Notice that while no exact days can be determined from the information, you do know that C must be somewhere to the left of A and that B must be somewhere to the left of D. You can, if you wish, eliminate some possibilities as impossible, or "rule breakers":

```
  A̸ D̸                           B̸ C̸
Thursday   Friday   Saturday   Sunday
   C ←─────────────────────────→ A
   B ←─────────────────────────→ D
```

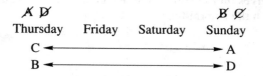

5. (B) This choice conforms to the conditions. Choices (D) and (E) violate the first condition. Choices (A) and (C) violate the second condition.

6. (B) Questions that use conditional information (*if, suppose, given that, assume,* etc.) intend that you use that information but *only* for that particular question. So, for this question only, if

Carmen attends on Saturday, Abby must attend on Sunday, since the first condition states that Carmen attends earlier than Abby. Since David attends later than Baker, of the remaining two days, Baker must attend on Thursday, and David must attend on Friday. Now that you have used the conditional information included in that question, return to the information contained only in the original conditions. (Disregard the information added in the previous question.)

7. (E) Since David attends later than Baker, Baker cannot attend the convention on Sunday.

Now try this set.

Questions 8–10

Five people are to serve on a committee to choose a new school principal. W, X, Y, and Z are teachers. S, T, U, and R are parents. The committee must have at least two parents and at least two teachers. The committee must conform to the following conditions:

If either W or X serves on the committee, Z will not serve on the committee.

If S serves on the committee, U will not serve on the committee.

If U serves on the committee, R must serve on the committee.

8. If Z serves on the committee, which of the following must also serve on the committee?

I. S
II. U
III. Y

(A) I only
(B) II only
(C) III only
(D) I and II only
(E) I, II, and III

9. Which of the following groups could serve as members of the committee?
   (A) S, U, R, W, X
   (B) S, U, W, X, Y
   (C) S, R, W, X, Y
   (D) S, R, W, X, Z
   (E) S, T, R, X, Z

10. If Z is chosen to serve on the committee, each of the following lists could comprise the other committee members EXCEPT

    I. Y, S, T, R
    II. Y, S, U, R
    III. Y, T, U, R

   (A) I only
   (B) II only
   (C) III only
   (D) I and III only
   (E) I, II, and III

Answers and Explanations

From the information given in the conditions, the following diagram can be drawn to help you answer the questions:

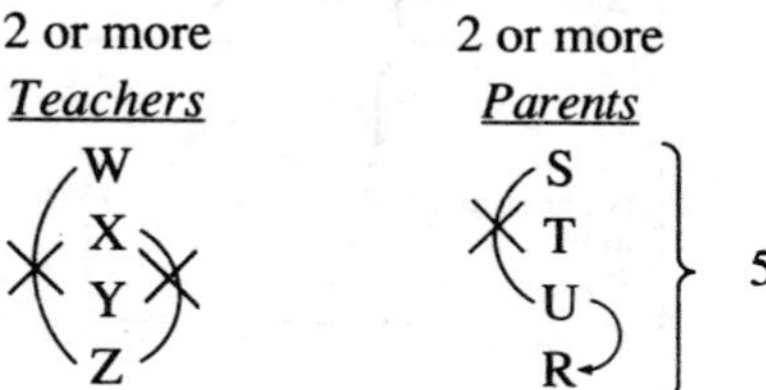

8. (C) III only. If Z serves on the committee, that eliminates W and X from serving, which leaves Y to serve as the second teacher on the committee.

9. (C) Choices (A) and (B) violate the second condition. Choices (D) and (E) violate the first condition.

10. (B) II only. Option II contains S with U, which is a violation of the second condition. Since the question is phrased in the negative (EXCEPT), choice (B) is the correct choice.

Some Analytical Reasoning problems are variations of the types illustrated thus far. These variations occur in the practice tests in this book and are fully explained in the answers section. *Review them carefully.*

A PATTERNED PLAN OF ATTACK

Analytical Reasoning

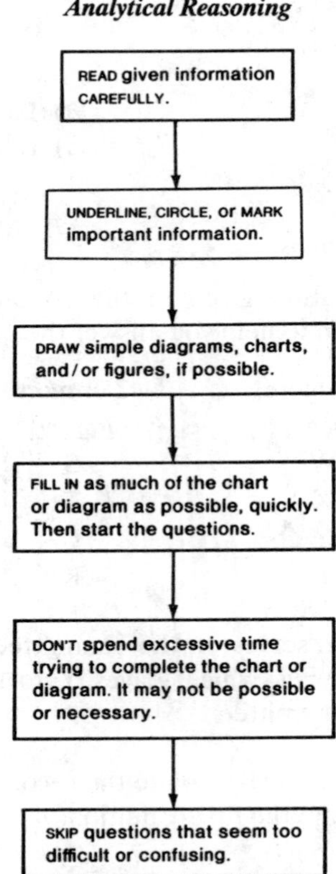
READ given information CAREFULLY.
UNDERLINE, CIRCLE, or MARK important information.
DRAW simple diagrams, charts, and/or figures, if possible.
FILL IN as much of the chart or diagram as possible, quickly. Then start the questions.
DON'T spend excessive time trying to complete the chart or diagram. It may not be possible or necessary.
SKIP questions that seem too difficult or confusing.

LOGICAL REASONING

There are usually six logical reasoning questions included within each Analytical Ability section.

Ability Tested

These questions test your ability to read and understand the logic presented in brief passages, statements, or conversations.

Basic Skills Necessary

Candidates who read critically and understand simple logic and reasoning do well on these questions. The ability to isolate the key point and to be able to identify supporting, weakening, and irrelevant issues is important.

Directions

The general directions are as follows: The following questions or group of questions are based on a passage or set of statements. Choose the best answer for each question and blacken the corresponding space on your answer sheet. It may be helpful to draw rough diagrams or simple charts in attempting to answer these question types.

Analysis

As you read the brief passage, you must follow the line of reasoning using only common-sense standards of logic. No knowledge of formal logic is required. Then you must choose the best answer, realizing that several choices may be possible, but only one will be best.

Rely on common sense. No special expertise is necessary.

Use only what is presented or implied by the passage. Do not make "large leaps in logic" in order to arrive at an answer choice. Don't "read in" what isn't there.

Choose the best answer choice. The test makers strongly imply that there may be more than one good answer.

Suggested Approach with Samples

- **Read the questions first, but don't preread the answer choices.**

  Each brief passage will be followed by a question or questions. Reading the question first, before reading the passage, enables you to focus on the elements of the passage essential to the question. Don't, however, preread the answer choices. Since four of the five choices are incorrect, scanning the choices introduces material 80% of which is irrelevant and/or inconsistent and therefore incorrect. Prereading the *choices* is not only a waste of time and energy, it probably will confuse you. Try prereading the question to the following passage and then reading the passage.

1. That seniors in the inner cities have inadequate health care available to them is intolerable. The medical facilities in the urban ghetto rarely contain basic medical supplies, and the technology in these hospitals is reflective of the 1960s, if that. Seniors living in the affluent suburbs, however, have available to them state-of-the-art technology and the latest in medical advances, drugs, and procedures.

   Which of the following best expresses the primary point of the passage?

   (A) Inner-city and suburban seniors should be cared for in hospitals equidistant from both.
   (B) Inner-city seniors should be transported to suburban hospitals.
   (C) Doctors should treat inner-city and suburban seniors equally.
   (D) Better medical care and facilities should be provided for inner-city seniors.
   (E) Inner-city seniors should have the same health care as that available to suburban seniors.

Prereading the question helps you to read the passage with a focus. That is, what is the author's point? The main point will be the overall thrust of the entire passage.

The major issue here is health care, and the author's point is that inner-city seniors should have health care better than that available to them now. The heavily charged word *intolerable* in the first sentence indicates that the author feels strongly that inadequate health care for inner-city seniors is not sufficient. Better (to be precise, adequate) care should be provided. Choice (D) is the best answer.

Notice that while a comparison is made to suburban seniors having superior health care, no direct argument is made that inner-city seniors should have the *same* health care as suburban seniors. While the superior, *state-of-the-art* quality of suburban health care is presented in order to contrast with that of inner-city health care, it does so simply for that reason: to show how abysmal inner-city health care is in comparison. But nothing in the passage directly indicates that health care for inner-city seniors should necessarily be equivalent with that provided suburban seniors. Inferring this would be beyond the scope of the passage; choice (E) as the author's primary point is incorrect.

Choices (A) and (B) are incorrect because the issues of hospital relocation and transportation are never raised by the passage. And choice (C) not only raises the problematic issue of "equal" treatment (which, as stated above, is not directly indicated in the passage) but also alters the focus simply to *doctors,* which in the context of a passage noting medical facilities, technology, supplies, etc., is far too narrow.

- **Read and analyze all the choices.**

  Our analysis of this question critically assessed each of the answer choices. As you work each Logical Reasoning question, you should be assessing *all* the choices, eliminating (marking out) those that are off topic, irrelevant, inconsistent, or beyond the scope of the passage and retaining (using question marks or circling the choice's letter) those you think apply. As mentioned above, frequently several choices will appear to be correct. You are to choose the one that answers the question best, that is, the most directly relevant to the passage.

- **Know the common question types.**

  Many Logical Reasoning questions fall into one of the following common categories. Identifying a common question type and being familiar with its demands make it easier for you to quickly cut through the morass of words and assess what's being asked in each question.

MAIN IDEA

What is the author's point? As you've obseverd, *main idea* can be expressed as *primary point of the passage* or *author's primary point.* As in the above example of inner-city health care, you should derive only what is most directly indicated by the passage. A jump beyond the scope of the passage will result in an incorrect choice.

Other (but not all the) ways this question type can be asked are:

- In the passage above, the author argues that . . .
- The most appropriate title for the passage above is . . .
- The author's argument is best expressed as . . .

IMPLICATION/INFERENCE/CONCLUSION/DEDUCTION

The definition of an inference is *the next logical step in a line of reasoning.* For example, the statement that *only a minority of children under the age of six have visited a dentist* implies that *a majority of children under the age of six have not visited a dentist.* Questions asking for a conclusion or a deduction of an argument require you to find what necessarily will follow, what *must* be true, not just what could be true.

Some other ways this question may be expressed:

- Which of the following may be inferred from the passage?
- If the passage above is true, what must logically follow?
- The passage above implies which of the following?
- Based upon the passage above, what can be concluded?
- Which of the following is the best completion of the statement? (with a blank following the passage)

HOW MORE INFORMATION AFFECTS THE STATEMENT

Usually phrased as *strengthens, weakens,* or *which of the following is relevant,* this type asks how new information in the answer choices would affect the argument. For example:

2. Research finds that children of smoking parents have lower test scores than do children of nonsmokers. Therefore, second-hand cigarette smoke is a cause of lower test scores.

   Which of the following, if true, would weaken the conclusion above?

   (A) A disproportionately high number of cigarette-smoking parents live in states where the school systems are considered inferior.

Notice how this choice would weaken the conclusion. A similar question might have asked for information that would strengthen the argument (instead of weaken) or for information that would be relevant to the argument (either strengthen or weaken).

Notice that this question type may contain the words *if true*. That means that you should accept all the answer choices as being true; do not challenge their reasonableness or the possibility of their truthfulness. Rather, accept all choices as true and, from there, decide which would strengthen or weaken the argument, whichever the question requires.

Some other ways this question type may be expressed:

- Which of the following, if true, would damage the logic of the passage?
- Which of the following, if true, would support the argument?
- Which of the following would confirm the author's conclusion?
- Which of the following would undermine the argument?

METHOD OF ARGUMENT

What technique does the author use to make the point? For example, the passage may use a generalization to prove a specific point. Or vice versa. Or it may use an analogy (comparison). Or it may present a conclusion without adequately supporting it. Or it may contradict its original premise within the passage. There are endless variations in ways a line of reasoning can be correctly, or incorrectly, structured.

You should be aware that for this type of question, the correctness of the reasoning may be unimportant. You are being asked simply to describe in structural terms how the author has set up the argument.

Some of the ways this type may be expressed;

- The author makes his or her point primarily by . . .
- The author uses which of the following methods of persuasion?
- In the passage above, the author does which of the following?

OTHER TYPES

Other Logical Reasoning questions may appear on your Analytical Ability section (*identify a flaw, best completion to the passage,* etc.). The list above of major types does not imply that these are the only types appearing on the test.

A PATTERNED PLAN OF ATTACK

Logical Reasoning

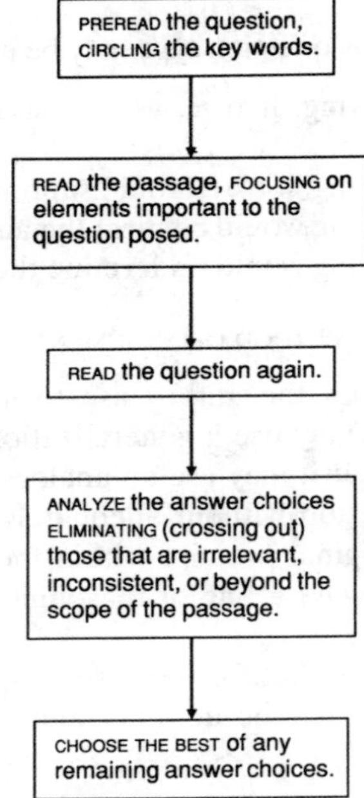

PREREAD the question, CIRCLING the key words.
READ the passage, FOCUSING on elements important to the question posed.
READ the question again.
ANALYZE the answer choices ELIMINATING (crossing out) those that are irrelevant, inconsistent, or beyond the scope of the passage.
CHOOSE THE BEST of any remaining answer choices.

Part III: Practice-Review-Analyze-Practice

Three Full-Length Practice Tests

This section contains three full-length practice simulation GREs. The practice tests are followed by complete answers, explanations, and analysis techniques. The format, levels of difficulty, question structure, and number of questions are similar to those on the actual GRE. The actual GRE is copyrighted and many not be duplicated and these questions are not taken directly from the actual tests.

When taking these exams, try to simulate the test conditions by following the time allotments carefully. Remember the total testing time for each practice test is approximately 3½ hours and each section is 30 minutes.

PRACTICE TEST 1

Section I:	Verbal Ability—30 Minutes; 39 Questions
Section II:	Quantitative Ability—30 Minutes; 30 Questions
Section III:	Analytical Ability—30 Minutes; 25 Questions
Section IV:	Quantitative Ability—30 Minutes; 30 Questions
Section V:	Verbal Ability—30 Minutes; 37 Questions
Section VI:	Analytical Ability—30 Minutes; 25 Questions
Section VII:	Quantitative Ability—30 Minutes; 30 Questions

CUT HERE

ANSWER SHEET FOR PRACTICE TEST 1
(Remove This Sheet and Use It to Mark Your Answers)

SECTION I

1	Ⓐ	Ⓑ	Ⓒ	Ⓓ	Ⓔ
2	Ⓐ	Ⓑ	Ⓒ	Ⓓ	Ⓔ
3	Ⓐ	Ⓑ	Ⓒ	Ⓓ	Ⓔ
4	Ⓐ	Ⓑ	Ⓒ	Ⓓ	Ⓔ
5	Ⓐ	Ⓑ	Ⓒ	Ⓓ	Ⓔ
6	Ⓐ	Ⓑ	Ⓒ	Ⓓ	Ⓔ
7	Ⓐ	Ⓑ	Ⓒ	Ⓓ	Ⓔ
8	Ⓐ	Ⓑ	Ⓒ	Ⓓ	Ⓔ
9	Ⓐ	Ⓑ	Ⓒ	Ⓓ	Ⓔ
10	Ⓐ	Ⓑ	Ⓒ	Ⓓ	Ⓔ
11	Ⓐ	Ⓑ	Ⓒ	Ⓓ	Ⓔ
12	Ⓐ	Ⓑ	Ⓒ	Ⓓ	Ⓔ
13	Ⓐ	Ⓑ	Ⓒ	Ⓓ	Ⓔ
14	Ⓐ	Ⓑ	Ⓒ	Ⓓ	Ⓔ
15	Ⓐ	Ⓑ	Ⓒ	Ⓓ	Ⓔ
16	Ⓐ	Ⓑ	Ⓒ	Ⓓ	Ⓔ
17	Ⓐ	Ⓑ	Ⓒ	Ⓓ	Ⓔ
18	Ⓐ	Ⓑ	Ⓒ	Ⓓ	Ⓔ
19	Ⓐ	Ⓑ	Ⓒ	Ⓓ	Ⓔ
20	Ⓐ	Ⓑ	Ⓒ	Ⓓ	Ⓔ
21	Ⓐ	Ⓑ	Ⓒ	Ⓓ	Ⓔ
22	Ⓐ	Ⓑ	Ⓒ	Ⓓ	Ⓔ
23	Ⓐ	Ⓑ	Ⓒ	Ⓓ	Ⓔ
24	Ⓐ	Ⓑ	Ⓒ	Ⓓ	Ⓔ
25	Ⓐ	Ⓑ	Ⓒ	Ⓓ	Ⓔ
26	Ⓐ	Ⓑ	Ⓒ	Ⓓ	Ⓔ
27	Ⓐ	Ⓑ	Ⓒ	Ⓓ	Ⓔ
28	Ⓐ	Ⓑ	Ⓒ	Ⓓ	Ⓔ
29	Ⓐ	Ⓑ	Ⓒ	Ⓓ	Ⓔ
30	Ⓐ	Ⓑ	Ⓒ	Ⓓ	Ⓔ
31	Ⓐ	Ⓑ	Ⓒ	Ⓓ	Ⓔ
32	Ⓐ	Ⓑ	Ⓒ	Ⓓ	Ⓔ
33	Ⓐ	Ⓑ	Ⓒ	Ⓓ	Ⓔ
34	Ⓐ	Ⓑ	Ⓒ	Ⓓ	Ⓔ
35	Ⓐ	Ⓑ	Ⓒ	Ⓓ	Ⓔ
36	Ⓐ	Ⓑ	Ⓒ	Ⓓ	Ⓔ
37	Ⓐ	Ⓑ	Ⓒ	Ⓓ	Ⓔ
38	Ⓐ	Ⓑ	Ⓒ	Ⓓ	Ⓔ
39	Ⓐ	Ⓑ	Ⓒ	Ⓓ	Ⓔ

SECTION II

1	Ⓐ	Ⓑ	Ⓒ	Ⓓ	Ⓔ
2	Ⓐ	Ⓑ	Ⓒ	Ⓓ	Ⓔ
3	Ⓐ	Ⓑ	Ⓒ	Ⓓ	Ⓔ
4	Ⓐ	Ⓑ	Ⓒ	Ⓓ	Ⓔ
5	Ⓐ	Ⓑ	Ⓒ	Ⓓ	Ⓔ
6	Ⓐ	Ⓑ	Ⓒ	Ⓓ	Ⓔ
7	Ⓐ	Ⓑ	Ⓒ	Ⓓ	Ⓔ
8	Ⓐ	Ⓑ	Ⓒ	Ⓓ	Ⓔ
9	Ⓐ	Ⓑ	Ⓒ	Ⓓ	Ⓔ
10	Ⓐ	Ⓑ	Ⓒ	Ⓓ	Ⓔ
11	Ⓐ	Ⓑ	Ⓒ	Ⓓ	Ⓔ
12	Ⓐ	Ⓑ	Ⓒ	Ⓓ	Ⓔ
13	Ⓐ	Ⓑ	Ⓒ	Ⓓ	Ⓔ
14	Ⓐ	Ⓑ	Ⓒ	Ⓓ	Ⓔ
15	Ⓐ	Ⓑ	Ⓒ	Ⓓ	Ⓔ
16	Ⓐ	Ⓑ	Ⓒ	Ⓓ	Ⓔ
17	Ⓐ	Ⓑ	Ⓒ	Ⓓ	Ⓔ
18	Ⓐ	Ⓑ	Ⓒ	Ⓓ	Ⓔ
19	Ⓐ	Ⓑ	Ⓒ	Ⓓ	Ⓔ
20	Ⓐ	Ⓑ	Ⓒ	Ⓓ	Ⓔ
21	Ⓐ	Ⓑ	Ⓒ	Ⓓ	Ⓔ
22	Ⓐ	Ⓑ	Ⓒ	Ⓓ	Ⓔ
23	Ⓐ	Ⓑ	Ⓒ	Ⓓ	Ⓔ
24	Ⓐ	Ⓑ	Ⓒ	Ⓓ	Ⓔ
25	Ⓐ	Ⓑ	Ⓒ	Ⓓ	Ⓔ
26	Ⓐ	Ⓑ	Ⓒ	Ⓓ	Ⓔ
27	Ⓐ	Ⓑ	Ⓒ	Ⓓ	Ⓔ
28	Ⓐ	Ⓑ	Ⓒ	Ⓓ	Ⓔ
29	Ⓐ	Ⓑ	Ⓒ	Ⓓ	Ⓔ
30	Ⓐ	Ⓑ	Ⓒ	Ⓓ	Ⓔ

ANSWER SHEET FOR PRACTICE TEST 1
(Remove This Sheet and Use It to Mark Your Answers)

SECTION III

1 Ⓐ Ⓑ Ⓒ Ⓓ Ⓔ
2 Ⓐ Ⓑ Ⓒ Ⓓ Ⓔ
3 Ⓐ Ⓑ Ⓒ Ⓓ Ⓔ
4 Ⓐ Ⓑ Ⓒ Ⓓ Ⓔ
5 Ⓐ Ⓑ Ⓒ Ⓓ Ⓔ

6 Ⓐ Ⓑ Ⓒ Ⓓ Ⓔ
7 Ⓐ Ⓑ Ⓒ Ⓓ Ⓔ
8 Ⓐ Ⓑ Ⓒ Ⓓ Ⓔ
9 Ⓐ Ⓑ Ⓒ Ⓓ Ⓔ
10 Ⓐ Ⓑ Ⓒ Ⓓ Ⓔ

11 Ⓐ Ⓑ Ⓒ Ⓓ Ⓔ
12 Ⓐ Ⓑ Ⓒ Ⓓ Ⓔ
13 Ⓐ Ⓑ Ⓒ Ⓓ Ⓔ
14 Ⓐ Ⓑ Ⓒ Ⓓ Ⓔ
15 Ⓐ Ⓑ Ⓒ Ⓓ Ⓔ

16 Ⓐ Ⓑ Ⓒ Ⓓ Ⓔ
17 Ⓐ Ⓑ Ⓒ Ⓓ Ⓔ
18 Ⓐ Ⓑ Ⓒ Ⓓ Ⓔ
19 Ⓐ Ⓑ Ⓒ Ⓓ Ⓔ
20 Ⓐ Ⓑ Ⓒ Ⓓ Ⓔ

21 Ⓐ Ⓑ Ⓒ Ⓓ Ⓔ
22 Ⓐ Ⓑ Ⓒ Ⓓ Ⓔ
23 Ⓐ Ⓑ Ⓒ Ⓓ Ⓔ
24 Ⓐ Ⓑ Ⓒ Ⓓ Ⓔ
25 Ⓐ Ⓑ Ⓒ Ⓓ Ⓔ

SECTION IV

1 Ⓐ Ⓑ Ⓒ Ⓓ Ⓔ
2 Ⓐ Ⓑ Ⓒ Ⓓ Ⓔ
3 Ⓐ Ⓑ Ⓒ Ⓓ Ⓔ
4 Ⓐ Ⓑ Ⓒ Ⓓ Ⓔ
5 Ⓐ Ⓑ Ⓒ Ⓓ Ⓔ

6 Ⓐ Ⓑ Ⓒ Ⓓ Ⓔ
7 Ⓐ Ⓑ Ⓒ Ⓓ Ⓔ
8 Ⓐ Ⓑ Ⓒ Ⓓ Ⓔ
9 Ⓐ Ⓑ Ⓒ Ⓓ Ⓔ
10 Ⓐ Ⓑ Ⓒ Ⓓ Ⓔ

11 Ⓐ Ⓑ Ⓒ Ⓓ Ⓔ
12 Ⓐ Ⓑ Ⓒ Ⓓ Ⓔ
13 Ⓐ Ⓑ Ⓒ Ⓓ Ⓔ
14 Ⓐ Ⓑ Ⓒ Ⓓ Ⓔ
15 Ⓐ Ⓑ Ⓒ Ⓓ Ⓔ

16 Ⓐ Ⓑ Ⓒ Ⓓ Ⓔ
17 Ⓐ Ⓑ Ⓒ Ⓓ Ⓔ
18 Ⓐ Ⓑ Ⓒ Ⓓ Ⓔ
19 Ⓐ Ⓑ Ⓒ Ⓓ Ⓔ
20 Ⓐ Ⓑ Ⓒ Ⓓ Ⓔ

21 Ⓐ Ⓑ Ⓒ Ⓓ Ⓔ
22 Ⓐ Ⓑ Ⓒ Ⓓ Ⓔ
23 Ⓐ Ⓑ Ⓒ Ⓓ Ⓔ
24 Ⓐ Ⓑ Ⓒ Ⓓ Ⓔ
25 Ⓐ Ⓑ Ⓒ Ⓓ Ⓔ

26 Ⓐ Ⓑ Ⓒ Ⓓ Ⓔ
27 Ⓐ Ⓑ Ⓒ Ⓓ Ⓔ
28 Ⓐ Ⓑ Ⓒ Ⓓ Ⓔ
29 Ⓐ Ⓑ Ⓒ Ⓓ Ⓔ
30 Ⓐ Ⓑ Ⓒ Ⓓ Ⓔ

SECTION V

1 Ⓐ Ⓑ Ⓒ Ⓓ Ⓔ
2 Ⓐ Ⓑ Ⓒ Ⓓ Ⓔ
3 Ⓐ Ⓑ Ⓒ Ⓓ Ⓔ
4 Ⓐ Ⓑ Ⓒ Ⓓ Ⓔ
5 Ⓐ Ⓑ Ⓒ Ⓓ Ⓔ

6 Ⓐ Ⓑ Ⓒ Ⓓ Ⓔ
7 Ⓐ Ⓑ Ⓒ Ⓓ Ⓔ
8 Ⓐ Ⓑ Ⓒ Ⓓ Ⓔ
9 Ⓐ Ⓑ Ⓒ Ⓓ Ⓔ
10 Ⓐ Ⓑ Ⓒ Ⓓ Ⓔ

11 Ⓐ Ⓑ Ⓒ Ⓓ Ⓔ
12 Ⓐ Ⓑ Ⓒ Ⓓ Ⓔ
13 Ⓐ Ⓑ Ⓒ Ⓓ Ⓔ
14 Ⓐ Ⓑ Ⓒ Ⓓ Ⓔ
15 Ⓐ Ⓑ Ⓒ Ⓓ Ⓔ

16 Ⓐ Ⓑ Ⓒ Ⓓ Ⓔ
17 Ⓐ Ⓑ Ⓒ Ⓓ Ⓔ
18 Ⓐ Ⓑ Ⓒ Ⓓ Ⓔ
19 Ⓐ Ⓑ Ⓒ Ⓓ Ⓔ
20 Ⓐ Ⓑ Ⓒ Ⓓ Ⓔ

21 Ⓐ Ⓑ Ⓒ Ⓓ Ⓔ
22 Ⓐ Ⓑ Ⓒ Ⓓ Ⓔ
23 Ⓐ Ⓑ Ⓒ Ⓓ Ⓔ
24 Ⓐ Ⓑ Ⓒ Ⓓ Ⓔ
25 Ⓐ Ⓑ Ⓒ Ⓓ Ⓔ

26 Ⓐ Ⓑ Ⓒ Ⓓ Ⓔ
27 Ⓐ Ⓑ Ⓒ Ⓓ Ⓔ
28 Ⓐ Ⓑ Ⓒ Ⓓ Ⓔ
29 Ⓐ Ⓑ Ⓒ Ⓓ Ⓔ
30 Ⓐ Ⓑ Ⓒ Ⓓ Ⓔ

31 Ⓐ Ⓑ Ⓒ Ⓓ Ⓔ
32 Ⓐ Ⓑ Ⓒ Ⓓ Ⓔ
33 Ⓐ Ⓑ Ⓒ Ⓓ Ⓔ
34 Ⓐ Ⓑ Ⓒ Ⓓ Ⓔ
35 Ⓐ Ⓑ Ⓒ Ⓓ Ⓔ

36 Ⓐ Ⓑ Ⓒ Ⓓ Ⓔ
37 Ⓐ Ⓑ Ⓒ Ⓓ Ⓔ

CUT HERE

ANSWER SHEET FOR PRACTICE TEST 1
(Remove This Sheet and Use It to Mark Your Answers)

SECTION VI

1 Ⓐ Ⓑ Ⓒ Ⓓ Ⓔ
2 Ⓐ Ⓑ Ⓒ Ⓓ Ⓔ
3 Ⓐ Ⓑ Ⓒ Ⓓ Ⓔ
4 Ⓐ Ⓑ Ⓒ Ⓓ Ⓔ
5 Ⓐ Ⓑ Ⓒ Ⓓ Ⓔ

---

6 Ⓐ Ⓑ Ⓒ Ⓓ Ⓔ
7 Ⓐ Ⓑ Ⓒ Ⓓ Ⓔ
8 Ⓐ Ⓑ Ⓒ Ⓓ Ⓔ
9 Ⓐ Ⓑ Ⓒ Ⓓ Ⓔ
10 Ⓐ Ⓑ Ⓒ Ⓓ Ⓔ

---

11 Ⓐ Ⓑ Ⓒ Ⓓ Ⓔ
12 Ⓐ Ⓑ Ⓒ Ⓓ Ⓔ
13 Ⓐ Ⓑ Ⓒ Ⓓ Ⓔ
14 Ⓐ Ⓑ Ⓒ Ⓓ Ⓔ
15 Ⓐ Ⓑ Ⓒ Ⓓ Ⓔ

---

16 Ⓐ Ⓑ Ⓒ Ⓓ Ⓔ
17 Ⓐ Ⓑ Ⓒ Ⓓ Ⓔ
18 Ⓐ Ⓑ Ⓒ Ⓓ Ⓔ
19 Ⓐ Ⓑ Ⓒ Ⓓ Ⓔ
20 Ⓐ Ⓑ Ⓒ Ⓓ Ⓔ

---

21 Ⓐ Ⓑ Ⓒ Ⓓ Ⓔ
22 Ⓐ Ⓑ Ⓒ Ⓓ Ⓔ
23 Ⓐ Ⓑ Ⓒ Ⓓ Ⓔ
24 Ⓐ Ⓑ Ⓒ Ⓓ Ⓔ
25 Ⓐ Ⓑ Ⓒ Ⓓ Ⓔ

SECTION VII

1 Ⓐ Ⓑ Ⓒ Ⓓ Ⓔ
2 Ⓐ Ⓑ Ⓒ Ⓓ Ⓔ
3 Ⓐ Ⓑ Ⓒ Ⓓ Ⓔ
4 Ⓐ Ⓑ Ⓒ Ⓓ Ⓔ
5 Ⓐ Ⓑ Ⓒ Ⓓ Ⓔ

---

6 Ⓐ Ⓑ Ⓒ Ⓓ Ⓔ
7 Ⓐ Ⓑ Ⓒ Ⓓ Ⓔ
8 Ⓐ Ⓑ Ⓒ Ⓓ Ⓔ
9 Ⓐ Ⓑ Ⓒ Ⓓ Ⓔ
10 Ⓐ Ⓑ Ⓒ Ⓓ Ⓔ

---

11 Ⓐ Ⓑ Ⓒ Ⓓ Ⓔ
12 Ⓐ Ⓑ Ⓒ Ⓓ Ⓔ
13 Ⓐ Ⓑ Ⓒ Ⓓ Ⓔ
14 Ⓐ Ⓑ Ⓒ Ⓓ Ⓔ
15 Ⓐ Ⓑ Ⓒ Ⓓ Ⓔ

---

16 Ⓐ Ⓑ Ⓒ Ⓓ Ⓔ
17 Ⓐ Ⓑ Ⓒ Ⓓ Ⓔ
18 Ⓐ Ⓑ Ⓒ Ⓓ Ⓔ
19 Ⓐ Ⓑ Ⓒ Ⓓ Ⓔ
20 Ⓐ Ⓑ Ⓒ Ⓓ Ⓔ

---

21 Ⓐ Ⓑ Ⓒ Ⓓ Ⓔ
22 Ⓐ Ⓑ Ⓒ Ⓓ Ⓔ
23 Ⓐ Ⓑ Ⓒ Ⓓ Ⓔ
24 Ⓐ Ⓑ Ⓒ Ⓓ Ⓔ
25 Ⓐ Ⓑ Ⓒ Ⓓ Ⓔ

---

26 Ⓐ Ⓑ Ⓒ Ⓓ Ⓔ
27 Ⓐ Ⓑ Ⓒ Ⓓ Ⓔ
28 Ⓐ Ⓑ Ⓒ Ⓓ Ⓔ
29 Ⓐ Ⓑ Ⓒ Ⓓ Ⓔ
30 Ⓐ Ⓑ Ⓒ Ⓓ Ⓔ

SECTION I: VERBAL ABILITY

Time: 30 Minutes
39 Questions

In this section, choose the best answer for each question and blacken the corresponding space on the answer sheet.

Sentence Completion

DIRECTIONS

Each blank in the following sentences indicates that something has been omitted. Considering the lettered words beneath the sentence, choose the word or set of words that best fits the whole sentence.

1. Although the thirteen-year-old boys grew __________ under the teacher's new discipline policy, the girls seemed __________ by it.
   (A) anxious . . . intimidated
   (B) argumentative . . . frustrated
   (C) restive . . . unperturbed
   (D) remorseful . . . enchanted
   (E) taciturn . . . attracted

2. The New Testament was written in the Greek language, and ideas derived from Greek philosophy were __________ in many parts of it.
   (A) altered
   (B) criticized
   (C) incorporated
   (D) nullified
   (E) translated

3. President Eisenhower was widely __________ for refusing to __________ the excesses of the loathed Senator McCarthy.
   (A) applauded . . . implement
   (B) chagrined . . . prevent
   (C) criticized . . . curb
   (D) condemned . . . promote
   (E) supported . . . ostracize

4. During the *Pax Romana* the _________ of material prosperity in the ancient world was reached.
   (A) simplification
   (B) stratification
   (C) majority
   (D) depth
   (E) pinnacle

5. With her customary _________, the Queen replied to reporters only with a smile, but the President _________ happily about what a good time he was having.
   (A) aplomb . . . objected
   (B) reticence . . . exclaimed
   (C) choler . . . spoke
   (D) tact . . . grumbled
   (E) volubility . . . gushed

6. *Rite of Passage* is a good novel by any standards; _________, it should rank high on any list of science fiction.
   (A) consistently
   (B) invariably
   (C) lingeringly
   (D) consequently
   (E) fortunately

7. After years of unchecked exploitation of its natural resources, the state, predictably, has _________ the population of its native plants and animals.
   (A) stymied
   (B) increased
   (C) reduced
   (D) normalized
   (E) decimated

8. When finishing an essay, do not end with a(n) _________ for not having said anything, or with a(n) _________ statement about the unfairly small time period.
   (A) flourish . . . unwarranted
   (B) ellipsis . . . analogical
   (C) apology . . . indignant
   (D) smirk . . . silly
   (E) excuse . . . political

Analogies

DIRECTIONS

In each question below, you are given a related pair of words or phrases. Select the lettered pair that *best* expresses a relationship similar to that in the original pair of words.

9. INITIATE : END ::
   (A) attend : ignore
   (B) inure : harden
   (C) remain : retreat
   (D) infer : imply
   (E) require : insure

10. CHEF : RECIPE ::
   (A) carpenter : tool
   (B) farmer : seed
   (C) saleswoman : pitch
   (D) novelist : story
   (E) musician : score

11. PHOTOSYNTHESIS : OXYGEN ::
   (A) camera : photograph
   (B) combustion : heat
   (C) past : present
   (D) plant : light
   (E) inhalation : health

12. PLAN : SCHEME ::
   (A) antiquity : age
   (B) avoidance : evasion
   (C) statesman : politician
   (D) assignment : task
   (E) prison : jail

13. TAPESTRY : LOOM ::
   (A) film : screen
   (B) map : legend
   (C) painting : easel
   (D) watercolor : mat
   (E) symphony : orchestra

14. OSSIFY : BONE ::
   (A) refine : ore
   (B) evaporate : water
   (C) pulverize : dust
   (D) swear : allegiance
   (E) petrify : fear

15. TEDIOUS : BOREDOM ::
   (A) garrulous : misunderstanding
   (B) sinuous : obscenity
   (C) enigmatic : uncertainty
   (D) tendentious : uplift
   (E) youthful : rejuvenation

16. GROVEL : SERVILE ::
   (A) boast : opportunistic
   (B) risk : fortuitous
   (C) denigrate : ironic
   (D) foresee : prescient
   (E) neglect : indiscriminate

17. BANTER : PERSIFLAGE ::
   (A) similarity : analogy
   (B) ambiquity : anticlimax
   (C) simile : euphemism
   (D) talk : poetry
   (E) cliche : epigram

Reading Comprehension

DIRECTIONS

Questions follow each of the passages below. Using only the stated or implied information in each passage, answer the questions.

I saw the spot where a cluster of trees once waved their branches on the shores of the Atlantic, when that ocean (now driven back seven hundred miles) came to the foot of the Andes. I saw that they had sprung from a volcanic soil which had been raised above the level of the sea, and that subsequently this dry land, with its upright trees, had been let down into the depths of the ocean. In these depths the formerly dry land was covered by sedimentary beds, and these again by enormous streams of submarine lava—one such mass attaining the thickness of a thousand feet; and these deluges of molten stone and aqueous deposits five times alternately had been spread out. The ocean which received such thick masses must have been profoundly deep; but again the subterranean volcanic forces exerted themselves, and I now beheld the bed of that ocean, forming a chain of mountains more than seven thousand feet in height. The great piles of strata had been intersected by many wide valleys, and the trees, now changed into silica, were exposed projecting from the volcanic soil, now changed into rock, whence formerly, in a green and budding state, they had raised their lofty heads. Now, all is utterly irreclaimable and desert; even the lichen cannot adhere to the stony casts of former trees. Vast as such changes must ever appear, yet they have all occurred within a period recent when compared with many of the fossiliferous strata of Europe and America.

18. The author is primarily concerned with
    (A) formulating a theory to account for the formation of petrified trees
    (B) describing the geography of South America
    (C) describing the formation of the Andes mountains
    (D) attesting to the power of volcanic action
    (E) explaining the history of fossils

19. According to the passage, which of the following is (are) true of the Andes?

    I. They were once located on the shores of the ocean.
    II. They were once part of the ocean floor.
    III. They are among the most ancient of the earth's mountain ranges.

    (A) I only
    (B) II only
    (C) III only
    (D) I and II only
    (E) II and III only

20. That this passage was written in the nineteenth century rather than by a contemporary scientist is suggested by the
    (A) use of figurative language in such phrases as *trees . . . had raised their lofty heads*
    (B) oblique references to religion throughout the passage
    (C) use of reasoning from cause and effect
    (D) comparison of one geological area with another as in the last sentence
    (E) use of such terms as *volcanic, sedimentary,* and *strata*

21. The speaker's response to the geological events described in this passage may be best described as
    (A) cooly scientific
    (B) uncomprehending bafflement
    (C) studied indifference
    (D) genuine astonishment
    (E) guarded skepticism

When the new discipline of social psychology was born at the beginning of this century, its first experiments was essentially adaptations of the suggestion demonstration. The technique generally followed a simple plan. The subjects, usually college students, were asked to give their opinions or preferences concerning various matters; some time later they were again asked to state their choices, but now they were also informed of the opinions held by authorities or large groups of their peers on the same matters. (Often the alleged consensus was fictitious.) Most of these studies had substantially the same result: confronted with opinions contrary to their own, many subjects apparently shifted their judgments in the direction of the views of the majorities or the experts. The late psychologist Edward L. Thorndike reported that he had succeeded in modifying the esthetic preferences of adults by this procedure. Other psychologists reported that people's evaluations of the merit of a literary passage could be raised or lowered by ascribing the passage to different authors. Apparently the sheer weight of numbers or authority sufficed to change opinions, even when no arguments for the opinions themselves were provided.

Now the very ease of success in these experiments arouses suspicion. Did the subjects actually change their opinions, or were the experimental victories scored only on paper? On grounds of common sense, one must question whether opinions are generally as watery as these studies indicate. There is some reason to wonder whether it was not the investigators who, in their enthusiasm for a theory, were suggestible, and whether the ostensibly gullible subjects were not providing answers which they thought good subjects were expected to give.

The investigations were guided by certain underlying assumptions, which today are common currency and account for much that is thought and said about the operations of propaganda and public opinion. The assumptions are that people submit uncritically and painlessly to external manipulation by suggestion or prestige, and that any given idea or value can be "sold" or "unsold" without reference to its merits. We should be skeptical, however, of the supposition that the power of social pressure necessarily implies uncritical submission to it; independence and the capacity to rise above group passion are also open to human beings. Further, one may question on psychological grounds whether it is possible as a rule to change a person's judgment of a situation or an object without first changing his knowledge or assumptions about it.

22. The first experiments in social psychology appeared to demonstrate all of the following EXCEPT
    (A) that many people will agree with what they believe to be the opinion held by the majority of their peers
    (B) that many people will agree with what they believe to be the opinion of experts
    (C) that many people change their opinions given good arguments for doing so
    (D) that an individual's evaluation of a literary work can be altered by ascribing the work to a different writer
    (E) that college students' opinions can be changed

23. According to the second paragraph, persons who first claimed to dislike a poem but changed their opinion when told the poem had been written by Shakespeare
    (A) may really like the poetry better because Shakespeare wrote it
    (B) may like the poetry better because Shakespeare is a highly regarded writer
    (C) are likely to be equally insecure in their evaluation of paintings or sculpture
    (D) may have changed their minds because they think the answer is expected
    (E) may be saying they have changed their minds though, in fact, they have no opinion

24. The author cites the work of Edward L. Thorndike as an example of

    I. an alleged instance of the selling of an idea
    II. a pioneering social psychology study confirmed by the work of contemporary research
    III. the studies that demonstrated the willingness of subjects to change their views on matters of esthetic preference

    (A) II only
    (B) I and II only
    (C) I and III only
    (D) II and III only
    (E) I, II, and III

25. The author implies that persons who altered their opinion on a controversial topic have most likely done so because they
    (A) have been influenced by overt social pressures
    (B) have been influenced by covert external manipulation
    (C) have learned more about the topic
    (D) have learned how experts judge the topic
    (E) are incapable of independent thought

26. The main point of the passage is to
    (A) question some assumptions about the influence of social pressures
    (B) show that a judgment of a situation cannot change without a change in the knowledge of the situation
    (C) demonstrate the gullibility of psychological investigators and their subjects
    (D) question the notion that any idea can be "sold" or "unsold"
    (E) support investigations into ideas of propaganda

27. With which of the following ideas would the author be most likely to agree?
    (A) Human beings can be programmed like machines.
    (B) Women are more likely to agree with men than with other women.
    (C) Women are more likely to agree with other women than with men.
    (D) Like men, women are capable of independent thought.
    (E) Like women, men submit uncritically to external manipulation.

28. Which of the following best describes how the passage is organized?
    (A) The ideas of the first paragraph are supported in the second and third paragraphs.
    (B) The ideas of the first paragraph are questioned in the second and third paragraphs.
    (C) The specific details of the first and second paragraphs are generalized in the third paragraph.
    (D) The first paragraph is concrete, while the second and third paragraphs are abstract.
    (E) Only the first paragraph uses figurative language.

Antonyms

DIRECTIONS

Each word in CAPITAL LETTERS is followed by five words or phrases. The correct choice is the word or phrase whose meaning is most nearly *opposite* to the meaning of the word in capitals. You may be required to distinguish fine shades of meaning. Look at all choices before marking your answer.

29. MITIGATED
    (A) repeated
    (B) aggravated
    (C) terminated
    (D) raised
    (E) declined

30. PROSELYTE
    (A) neophyte
    (B) electrolyte
    (C) delegate
    (D) apostate
    (E) renegade

31. CLOY
    (A) deny
    (B) refuse
    (C) club
    (D) flay
    (E) glut

32. RESUSCITATE
    (A) succumb
    (B) crush
    (C) flatten
    (D) kill
    (E) succeed

33. RUSTICATED
    (A) deteriorated
    (B) urban
    (C) domesticated
    (D) repatriated
    (E) emaciated

34. PENURY
    (A) wealth
    (B) penance
    (C) pensiveness
    (D) impenetrability
    (E) indifference

35. LACONIC
    (A) compendious
    (B) obtrusive
    (C) verbose
    (D) lethargic
    (E) creative

36. MORIBUND
    (A) spiritual
    (B) eternal
    (C) extant
    (D) progressive
    (E) faded

37. INEFFABLE
    (A) dictatable
    (B) separable
    (C) cogent
    (D) definable
    (E) ethereal

38. ERSATZ
    (A) serious
    (B) separate
    (C) stable
    (D) genuine
    (E) modest

39. ESTHETICISM
    (A) tastelessness
    (B) formlessness
    (C) pragmatism
    (D) resolution
    (E) enthusiasm

STOP. IF YOU FINISH BEFORE TIME IS CALLED, CHECK YOUR WORK ON THIS SECTION ONLY. DO NOT WORK ON ANY OTHER SECTION IN THE TEST.

SECTION II: QUANTITATIVE ABILITY

Time: 30 Minutes
30 Questions

Quantitative Comparison

DIRECTIONS

In this section you will be given two quantities, one in column A and one in column B. You are to determine a relationship between the two quantities and mark

(A) if the quantity in column A is greater than the quantity in column B
(B) if the quantity in column B is greater than the quantity in column A
(C) if the quantities are equal
(D) if the comparison cannot be determined from the information that is given

Common Information:

Information centered above both columns refers to one or both columns.
All numbers used are real numbers.
Figures are intended to provide useful positional information, but are not necessarily drawn to scale and should not be used to estimate sizes by measurement.
Lines that appear straight can be assumed to be straight.

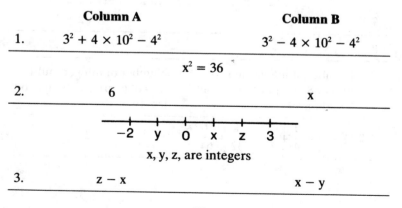

	Column A		**Column B**
1.	$3^2 + 4 \times 10^2 - 4^2$		$3^2 - 4 \times 10^2 - 4^2$
		$x^2 = 36$	
2.	6		x
		−2 y 0 x z 3 (number line)	
		x, y, z, are integers	
3.	z − x		x − y

	Column A		Column B

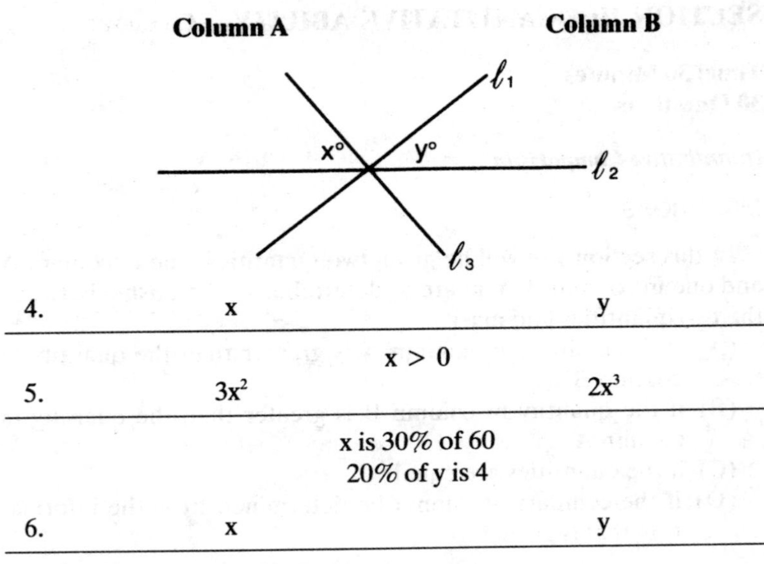

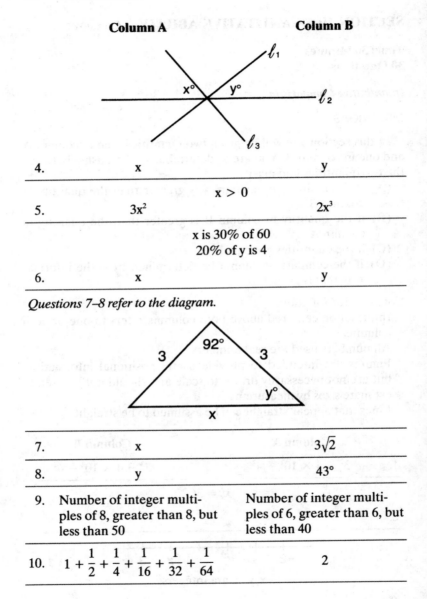

	Column A		Column B
4.	x		y
		$x > 0$	
5.	$3x^2$		$2x^3$
		x is 30% of 60 20% of y is 4	
6.	x		y

Questions 7–8 refer to the diagram.

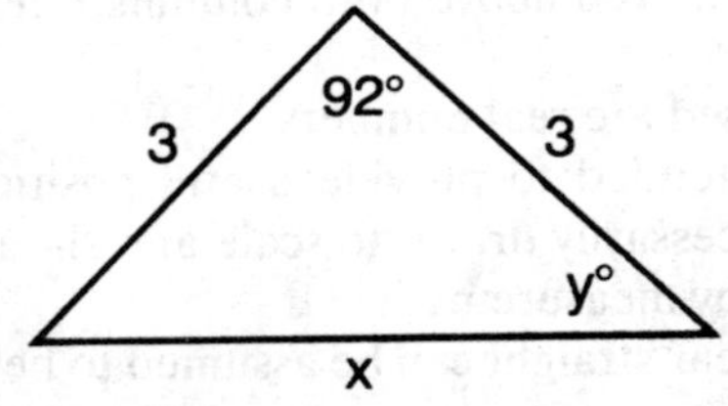

	Column A	Column B
7.	x	$3\sqrt{2}$
8.	y	43°
9.	Number of integer multiples of 8, greater than 8, but less than 50	Number of integer multiples of 6, greater than 6, but less than 40
10.	$1 + \frac{1}{2} + \frac{1}{4} + \frac{1}{16} + \frac{1}{32} + \frac{1}{64}$	2

	Column A	**Column B**
	$0 < x + y < 2$	
11.	x	y
12.	Volume of cube with side 6	Volume of rectangular prism with two dimensions less than 6
	$x^2 + 2x + 1 - 0$	$y^2 - 2y + 1 = 0$
13.	x	y
14.	$8^{29} - 8^{28}$	8^{28}
	$x > y > 0$	
15.	$\sqrt{x} - \sqrt{y}$	$\sqrt{x - y}$

Math Ability

DIRECTIONS

Solve each problem in this section by using the information given and your own mathematical calculations. Then select the *one* correct answer of the five choices given. Use the available space on the page for scratchwork. NOTE: Some problems may be accompanied by figures or diagrams. These figures are drawn as accurately as possible, *except* when it is stated in a specific problem that the figure is not drawn to scale. The figure is meant to provide information useful in solving the problem or problems. Unless otherwise stated or indicated, all figures lie in a plane. All numbers used are real numbers.

16. What is .25% of 12?
(A) $\frac{3}{100}$
(B) $\frac{3}{10}$
(C) $\frac{1}{3}$
(D) 3
(E) 300

17. If $2/x = 4$ and if $2/y = 8$, then $x - y =$
(A) ⅛
(B) ¼
(C) ¾
(D) 4
(E) 24

18. Bob is older than Jane, but he is younger than Jim. If Bob's age is b, Jane's age is c, and Jim's age is d, then which of the following is true?
(A) $c < b < d$
(B) $b < c < d$
(C) $b < d < c$
(D) $c < d < b$
(E) $d < c < b$

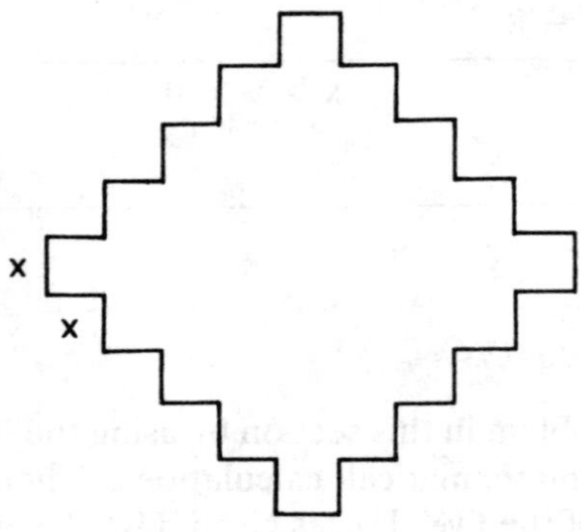

19. In the figure, all line segments meet at right angles, and each segment has a length of x. What is the area of the figure in terms of x?
(A) $25x^2$
(B) $35x^2$
(C) $36x^2$
(D) $41x^2$
(E) $45x^2$

20. What is the area of a square inscribed in a circle whose circumference is 16π?
(A) 8
(B) 32
(C) 64
(D) 128
(E) 256

Questions 21–25 refer to the graph.

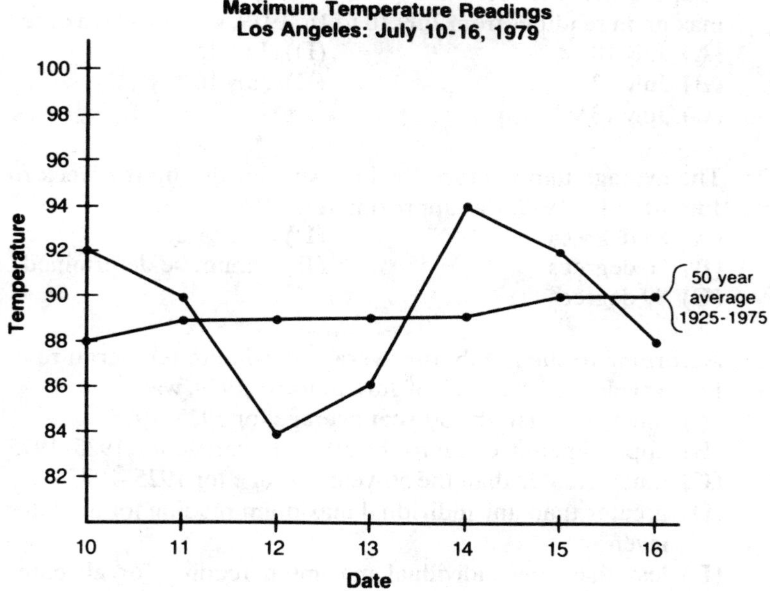

21. Of the seven dates shown, what percent of the days did the maximum readings for 1979 exceed the 50-year average temperature?
    (A) 3
    (B) 4
    (C) 7
    (D) 43
    (E) 57

22. What was the percent increase in the maximum temperature from July 12 to July 14, 1979?
    (A) 10
    (B) 10.6
    (C) 11.9
    (D) 84
    (E) 94

23. Of the following, the greatest difference in Los Angeles temperatures between the 50-year average (1925–1975) and the maximum readings from July 10 to 16, 1979, was on which date?
(A) July 10
(B) July 12
(C) July 13
(D) July 15
(E) July 16

24. The average temperature for Los Angeles during the week of July 10 to 16, 1979, was approximately
(A) 84 degrees
(B) 86 degrees
(C) 89 degrees
(D) 92 degrees
(E) cannot be determined

25. According to the graph, the average maximum temperature in Los Angeles for the week of July 10 to 16, 1979, was
(A) much less than the 50-year average for 1925–1975
(B) approximately equal to the 50-year average for 1925–1975
(C) much greater than the 50-year average for 1925–1975
(D) greater than any individual maximum reading for all dates given
(E) less than any individual maximum reading for all dates given

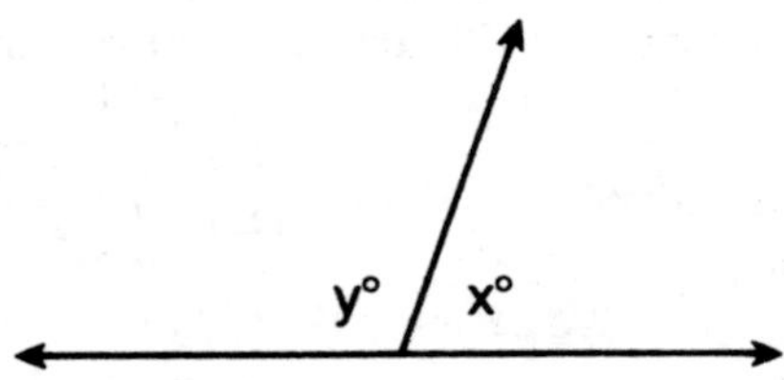

26. If in the figure $x = \frac{2}{3}y$, then $y =$
(A) 36
(B) 72
(C) 108
(D) 144
(E) cannot be determined

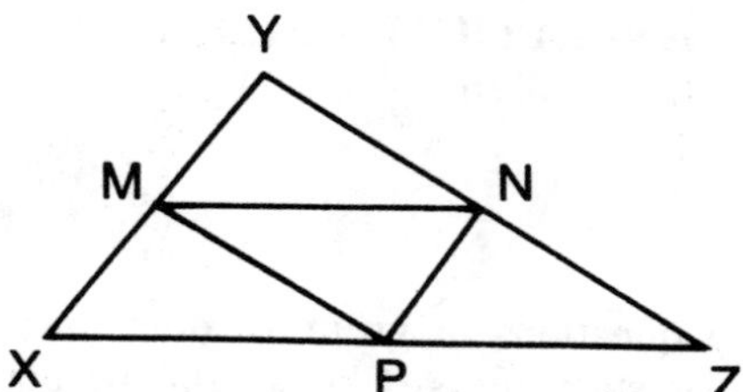

27. In △ XYZ, points M, N, and P are midpoints. If XY = 10, YZ = 15, and XZ = 17, what is the perimeter of △ MNP?
    (A) 10⅔
    (B) 14
    (C) 16
    (D) 21
    (E) cannot be determined

28. If a and b are integers, which of the following conditions is sufficient for $\frac{a^2 - b^2}{a - b} = a + b$ to be true?
    (A) $a > 0$
    (B) $a < 0$
    (C) $a > b$
    (D) $b > 0$
    (E) $b < 0$

29. A bus leaves from Burbank at 9:00 A.M., traveling east at 50 miles per hour. At 1:00 P.M. a plane leaves Burbank traveling east at 300 miles per hour. At what time will the plane overtake the bus?
    (A) 12:45 P.M.
    (B) 1:10 P.M.
    (C) 1:40 P.M.
    (D) 1:48 P.M.
    (E) 1:55 P.M.

30. If the average of two numbers is y, and one of the numbers is equal to z, then the other number is equal to
    (A) $2z - y$
    (B) $\frac{y + z}{2}$
    (C) $z - y$
    (D) $2y - z$
    (E) $y + 2z$

STOP. IF YOU FINISH BEFORE TIME IS CALLED, CHECK YOUR WORK ON THIS SECTION ONLY. DO NOT WORK ON ANY OTHER SECTION IN THE TEST.

SECTION III: ANALYTICAL ABILITY

Time: 30 Minutes
25 Questions

DIRECTIONS

The following questions or group of questions are based on a passage or set of statements. Choose the best answer for each question and blacken the corresponding space on your answer sheet. It may be helpful to draw rough diagrams or simple charts in attempting to answer these question types.

Questions 1–6

Results were posted in 1975 and 1990 for eight dental patients: Quincy, Sonntag, Tav, Ulmer, Vinton, Waud, Yu, and Zimino.

In 1975, Ulmer's cavities outnumbered Vinton's cavities and outnumbered Yu's cavities; in 1990, Vinton's cavities outnumbered Zimino's cavities and outnumbered Tav's cavities.

In 1975, Zimino's cavities outnumbered Tav's cavities; in 1990, Zimino's cavities outnumbered Waud's cavities.

In 1975, Yu's cavities outnumbered Sonntag's cavities; in 1990, Waud's cavities outnumbered Yu's cavities.

In 1975, Waud's cavities outnumbered Ulmer's cavities and outnumbered Zimino's cavities; in 1990; Tav's cavities outnumbered Sonntag's cavities and outnumbered Ulmer's cavities.

1. Of the following, who could NOT have had the fewest number of cavities in either year, 1975 or 1990?
   (A) Tav
   (B) Ulmer
   (C) Vinton
   (D) Yu
   (E) Zimino

2. A complete and accurate listing of those who could have had the fourth lowest number of cavities in 1990 would include
   (A) Quincy, Sonntag, and Waud
   (B) Quincy, Sonntag, Ulmer, and Waud
   (C) Quincy, Sonntag, Tav, Ulmer, and Waud
   (D) Quincy, Sonntag, Ulmer, Waud, Yu, and Zimino
   (E) Quincy, Sonntag, Tav, Ulmer, Waud, Yu, and Zimino

3. Ulmer's number of cavities must have been greater than Yu's in 1990 if, in 1990,
   (A) Quincy had more cavities than Waud
   (B) Waud had more cavities than Sonntag
   (C) Tav had more cavities than Waud
   (D) Waud had more cavities than Ulmer
   (E) Ulmer had more cavities than Waud

4. Which of the following must be true?

   I. Waud's cavities in 1975 and 1990 outnumbered Ulmer's cavities in those years.
   II. Waud's cavities in 1975 and 1990 outnumbered Yu's cavities in those years.
   III. Quincy's cavities in 1975 and 1990 outnumbered Sonntag's cavities in those years.

   (A) I only
   (B) II only
   (C) III only
   (D) I and II only
   (E) I, II, and III

5. Suppose each patient's cavities are totaled for the two years, 1975 and 1990. Which must be true?
   (A) Waud's total cavities are more than Quincy's total.
   (B) Ulmer's total cavities are more than Sonntag's total.
   (C) Tav's total cavities are more than Sonntag's total.
   (D) Waud's total cavities are more than Yu's total.
   (E) Zimino's total cavities are more than Yu's total.

6. Disregarding Quincy, suppose three patients had the same number for the fewest cavities in 1975, and three patients had the same number for the fewest cavities in 1990. Who must have had the fewest total cavities in 1975 and 1990 combined?
   (A) Sonntag
   (B) Tav
   (C) Ulmer
   (D) Vinton
   (E) Yu

Questions 7–9

Five men (Frank, George, Harry, Irving, and Jack) and five women (Karla, Laurie, Marie, Olivia, and Polly) are seated at a round table with eleven seats.

None of the women are sitting in a seat adjacent to another woman.

Karla sits between Frank and George, and next to each of them.

Jack does not sit next to Irving.

7. Which of the following is a possible seating order around the table?
   (A) empty seat, Frank, Karla, George, Laurie, Olivia, Harry, Irving, Polly, Jack, Marie
   (B) empty seat, Frank, Karla, George, Laurie, Jack, Polly, Olivia, Irving, Marie, Harry
   (C) empty seat, Frank, Karla, George, Laurie, Olivia, Jack, Polly, Irving, Marie, Harry
   (D) empty seat, Olivia, Frank. Karla, George, Laurie, Jack, Irving, Polly, Harry, Marie
   (E) empty seat, Marie, Frank, Karla, George, Laurie, Jack, Polly, Irving, Olivia, Harry

8. If Laurie, Harry, Marie, Jack, and George are seated in that order, which of the following is a correct completion of the seating order after George?
   (A) Karla, Frank, Olivia, Irving, Polly, empty seat
   (B) Karla, Frank, Irving, Olivia, empty seat, Polly
   (C) Frank, Polly, Karla, Irving, Olivia, empty seat
   (D) Karla, Frank, Polly, Irving, empty seat, Olivia
   (E) Karla, Frank, Olivia, Jack, Polly, Irving

9. If no man is sitting next to another man and all original conditions remain the same, which of the following is a possible seating order?
   (A) Laurie, Jack, Marie, Harry, Karla, Frank, Polly, George, Olivia, empty seat, Irving
   (B) Laurie, Jack, Marie, empty seat, Karla, Frank, Polly, Irving, George, Olivia, Harry
   (C) Laurie, Jack, Marie, empty seat, Harry, Karla, Frank, Polly, Irving, Olivia, George
   (D) Laurie, Jack, Marie, George, Karla, Frank, Polly, Irving, Olivia, empty seat, Harry
   (E) Laurie, Jack, Marie, Harry, Frank, Karla, George, Polly, Irving, Olivia, empty seat

10. Studies on animals done in the 1930s indicate that stomach juices were the controlling cue for eating. However, this was later contested by researchers noting that animals without stomachs have normal eating habits. Subsequent work done in the 1960s indicated that an "eating center" in the brain controls hunger. More recent work suggests the presence of specific hungers for materials lacking in a given diet; for example, wolves put on low-calcium diets will seek out and eat bones.

    In the passage above, the author

    I. favors one theory over two others by citing specific evidence to show its superiority
    II. cites no important differences among the major findings cited and their implications
    III. presents conflicting information from different studies without favoring any particular theory

    (A) I only
    (B) II only
    (C) III only
    (D) I and II only
    (E) II and III only

11. The United Greetings Company has discovered that 85% of the artists in a randomly chosen group who worked a ten-hour-per-day, four-day week produced 20% more greeting cards in a month than those employees who worked the traditional five-day, eight-hour-per-day schedule. The same 85% who produced more greeting cards were those in the group who preferred the four-day schedule. The other 15% produced fewer cards per month than those on the five-day schedule.

    On the basis of these results, which of the following is likely to produce the greatest increase in the productivity of the workers?

    (A) The company will use only a ten-hour, four-day work schedule for 85% of its workers.
    (B) The company will use a ten-hour, four-day work schedule for 85% of its workers.
    (C) The company will use only eight-hour, five-day work schedules.
    (D) The company will allow workers to choose between a four-day and a five-day schedule.
    (E) The company will use a four-day and a five-day work schedule in alternate weeks.

12. Superpersonal awareness (SA) refers to the extraordinary ability of some persons to apparently circumvent normal intellectual and informational techniques and instead acquire knowledge by intuitive means. The three phenomena identified as components of SA are recognition (familiarity with the object), intuition (knowledge of information not directly through the five senses), and abstraction (the ability to realize concrete elements based upon other symbolic elements). All evidence for these components of SA is for the most part dependent upon unusual statistical information that requires a great number of trials for weak returns under nonreproducible conditions.

    The author of the passage above assumes which of the following?

(A) Superpersonal awareness may consist of more than the three phenomena mentioned.
(B) Perception-cognition studies are normally conducted under rigorous controls and specifications.
(C) Much evidence has been gathered from unusual events to support the existence of superpersonal awareness.
(D) Large numbers of trials have produced evidence which circumvents normal sensory channels.
(E) A basis for scientific proof requires significant results from repeatable, controlled experiments.

Questions 13–17

Six commuter trains depart, one every hour on the hour. Of the six, three are express trains (the Streamliner, the Coast, and the Flyer) and three are local trains (the Arrow, the Beamer, and the Zephyr). Four commuters (Jackson, Klein, Landau, and Morris) each ride a different train. The following is always true:

The first train departs at 5 A.M. and the last train departs at 10 A.M.

Each train departs at a different hour, and the express trains depart only at odd-numbered hours.

The Zephyr departs earlier than the Coast.

If the Coast departs at 7 A.M., then the Streamliner departs at 5 A.M.

Klein's train departs at 7 A.M.; Morris rides the Beamer, which departs at 10 A.M.

Jackson's train departs before Klein's, and Landau's train departs after Klein's.

13. Which of the following time intervals is possible between the departure of Jackson's train and the departure of Landau's train?

I. exactly two hours
II. exactly three hours
III. exactly four hours

(A) I only
(B) I and II only
(C) I and III only
(D) II and III only
(E) I, II, and III

14. Of the following, which could be the daily schedule of departures, from earliest to latest?
    (A) Coast, Arrow, Streamliner, Zephyr, Flyer, Beamer
    (B) Streamliner, Zephyr, Coast, Arrow, Flyer, Beamer
    (C) Flyer, Zephyr, Coast, Arrow, Streamliner, Beamer
    (D) Streamliner, Zephyr, Arrow, Coast, Flyer, Beamer
    (E) Beamer, Arrow, Coast, Zephyr, Streamliner, Flyer

15. Given the information that Klein rides the Streamliner, then which must be true?
    (A) Jackson rides the Flyer.
    (B) Landau rides the Coast.
    (C) The Arrow departs at 8 A.M.
    (D) The Zephyr departs at 6 A.M.
    (E) The Coast departs at 9 A.M.

16. Which of the following is a complete and accurate listing of the trains which CANNOT be scheduled for 6 A.M.?
    (A) Arrow, Zephyr, Beamer
    (B) Arrow, Streamliner, Beamer
    (C) Flyer, Zephyr, Beamer
    (D) Flyer, Streamliner, Coast, Beamer
    (E) Flyer, Streamliner, Coast, Zephyr, Beamer

17. Suppose the schedule is altered and trains depart two hours apart, with Morris departing on the final train, the Beamer, at 3 P.M. If all other restrictions remain the same, all of the following would be possible EXCEPT
    (A) Klein rides the Coast
    (B) Landau's train departs at 9 A.M.
    (C) Landau's train departs at 11 A.M.
    (D) Landau's train departs at 1 P.M.
    (E) Jackson rides the Zephyr

Questions 18–22

In order to reduce serious injuries, the Boxing Commission establishes new rules for a boxing match:

Two boxers begin with the first round and fight until all ten rounds are fought or until someone wins the match.

A total of three points is awarded in each round. The winner of each round is the boxer to score at least two of the three points awarded in that round.

A boxer cannot receive a fraction of a point, so a tie score in any one round is not possible.

If a fighter wins three consecutive rounds, the fight is over and the winner of those three rounds wins the match.

If no fighter wins three consecutive rounds, whoever has the most points after the tenth round wins the match.

In any match between Stuart and Riley, it is observed that the winner of any round always earns at least one point in the next round.

18. Suppose Stuart wins the first and second rounds. If Riley wins the sixth round, it must be true that Riley wins
    (A) exactly three points in the fourth round
    (B) at least two points in the fourth round
    (C) at least one point in the fourth round
    (D) exactly one point in the fourth round
    (E) no points in the fourth round

19. Suppose Stuart loses in the eighth round and the match is therefore over. What is the greatest total number of points that he could have won in all the rounds fought?
    (A) 13
    (B) 14
    (C) 15
    (D) 16
    (E) 17

20. Suppose Stuart loses the fourth round and the match is therefore over. What is the least number of points that Stuart must have won in all the rounds fought?
    (A) 1
    (B) 2
    (C) 3
    (D) 4
    (E) 5

21. Suppose Stuart wins the first and third rounds and Riley wins the sixth and seventh rounds. If Stuart wins the match, then Riley could NOT have had a total of

(A) 10
(B) 11
(C) 12
(D) 13
(E) 14

22. If Stuart wins only three of the rounds but the match goes the full ten rounds, it must be true that Stuart wins

I. the third round
II. the sixth round
III. the ninth round

(A) I only
(B) II only
(C) III only
(D) I, II, and III
(E) none of these

23. For more than a hundred years, entomologists have believed that viceroy butterflies mimic the coloration of the queen and monarch butterflies to avoid being eaten by birds which avoid the bad-tasting queens and monarchs. But recent experiments have demonstrated that the monarch and the viceroy are equally repellent to birds, while the queen butterfly is somewhat more palatable.

All of the following would be logical conclusions of this passage EXCEPT

(A) scientists are now wondering why the belief that the viceroy imitated the monarch and queen butterflies was never tested before
(B) the conclusions astonished those entomologists who believed that an unprotected species will develop its own defenses rather than simply imitate the appearance of another
(C) the results support the scientists who believe mimicry is rare
(D) mimicry of the sort the viceroy was supposed to exemplify is probably less common than has been believed
(E) the many textbooks that use the viceroy butterfly to illustrate protective mimicry will have to be revised

24. American toothpaste recently conducted a survey to determine how well American was doing in comparison with its nearest competitor, National toothpaste. The results of the survey found that of the 2135 polled, 70% of the respondents regularly purchase American toothpaste, 28% of the respondents regularly purchase American's nearest competitor, National toothpaste, and 18% of the respondents regularly purchase a third brand and distant competitor, Brighten toothpaste.

If the survey conducted by American toothpaste is correct, it can be inferred that

(A) not all the respondents questioned in the poll regularly purchase toothpaste
(B) some of the brands of toothpaste that were regularly purchased must have been both American and National
(C) some of the respondents of the poll must have answered incorrectly or dishonestly
(D) some of those who regularly purchase American toothpaste also regularly purchase National toothpaste
(E) some of the respondents who regularly purchase one brand of toothpaste also regularly purchase another brand of toothpaste

25. Research was recently undertaken in which subjects were required to indicate which of two sounds was the loudest. In this simple test, associates of the experimenter, posing as other subjects, gave a clearly incorrect answer. This provided the real subject with a dilemma between his or her perception and desire to conform to the group. The results were dramatic: yielding to an obviously incorrect answer increased as the number of opposing persons increased up to five, after which there was little effect. But when a minimum one of the associates agreed with the subject, yielding behavior sharply declined, even though the majority was still overwhelmingly against the subject.

Which of the following best expresses the point of the passage above?

(A) As more and more people disagree with a research subject, he or she becomes more and more inclined to agree with the group.
(B) Uncertain tasks often cause confusion in the minds of subjects faced with uncertain parameters.
(C) Associates should not be allowed to confuse a subject's judgment in research studies.
(D) Subjects are seldom sure of their judgment when evaluating loudness of sounds.
(E) Group pressure may be a strong factor on individual judgment in situations requiring perception.

STOP. IF YOU FINISH BEFORE TIME IS CALLED, CHECK YOUR WORK ON THIS SECTION ONLY. DO NOT WORK ON ANY OTHER SECTION IN THE TEST.

SECTION IV: QUANTITATIVE ABILITY

Time: 30 Minutes
30 Questions

Quantitative Comparison

DIRECTIONS

In this section you will be given two quantities, one in column A and one in column B. You are to determine a relationship between the two quantities and mark

(A) if the quantity in column A is greater than the quantity in column B
(B) if the quantity in column B is greater than the quantity in column A
(C) if the quantities are equal
(D) if the comparison cannot be determined from the information that is given

Common Information:

Information centered above both columns refers to one or both columns.
All numbers used are real numbers.
Figures are intended to provide useful positional information, but are not necessarily drawn to scale and should not be used to estimate sizes by measurement.
Lines that appear straight can be assumed to be straight.

	Column A		**Column B**
1.	$\frac{1}{3} \times \frac{2}{5} \times \frac{1}{8}$		$.33 \times .4 \times .125$
2.	Area of rectangle with length 8		Area of rectangle with width 7
3.	35% of 50		50% of 35
		$a = 3b$ $b = -2$	
4.	$\frac{a^2 + b}{ab}$		$\frac{a + b^2}{ab}$

	Column A	Column B
5.	Number of ways to arrange four books on a shelf	12

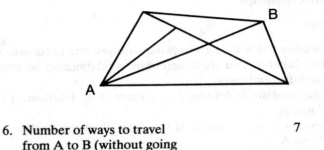

	Column A	Column B
6.	Number of ways to travel from A to B (without going over a line more than once on any one attempt)	7
7.	$(x^2y^3)^8$	$(x^4y^6)^4$

Questions 8–9 refer to the diagram.

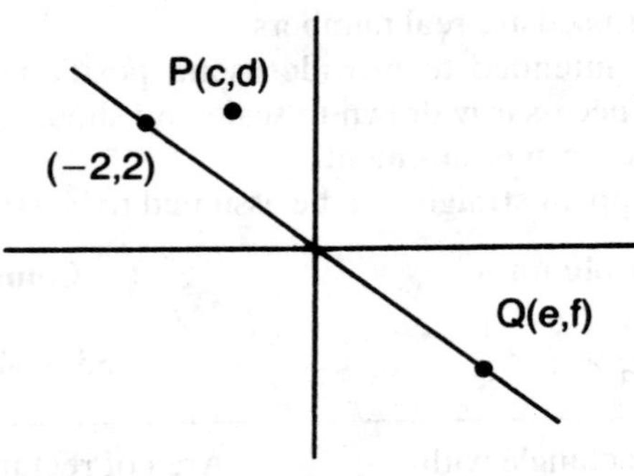

	Column A	Column B
8.	c	d
9.	c + d	e + f

$x > 0$

	Column A	Column B
10.	$x(x + 2) + (x + 2)$	$(x + 1)(x + 3)$

	Column A	Column B
11.	Number of seconds in two hours	Number of hours in 50 weeks
12.	$\sqrt{3^{18}}$	$(\sqrt{27^3})^2$

Questions 13–14 refer to the diagram.

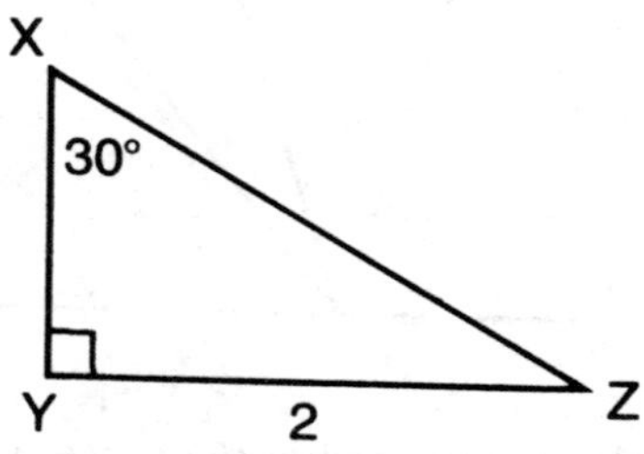

	Column A	Column B
13.	XY	YZ
14.	XY	$3\sqrt{2}$
15.	$\frac{\sqrt{3}}{3}$	$\frac{1}{\sqrt{3}}$

Math Ability

DIRECTIONS

Solve each problem in this section by using the information given and your own mathematical calculations. Then select the *one* correct answer of the five choices given. Use the available space on the page for scratchwork. NOTE: Some problems may be accompanied by figures or diagrams. These figures are drawn as accurately as possible, *except* when it is stated in a specific problem that the figure is not drawn to scale. The figure is meant to provide information useful in solving the problem or problems. Unless otherwise stated or indicated, all figures lie in a plane. All numbers used are real numbers.

16. If $x = -2$, then $x^3 - x^2 - x - 1 =$
    (A) -15
    (B) -11
    (C) -3
    (D) 0
    (E) 13

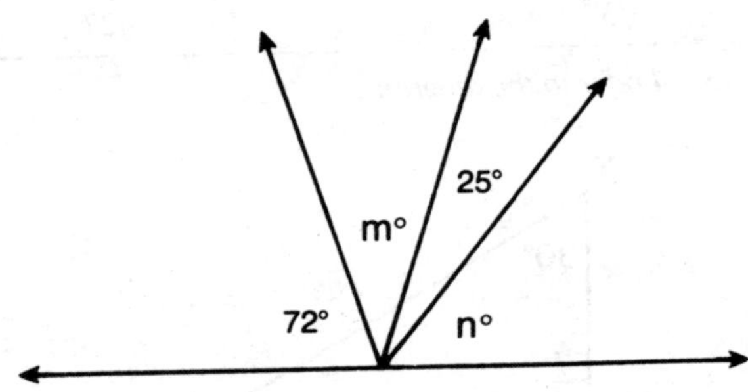

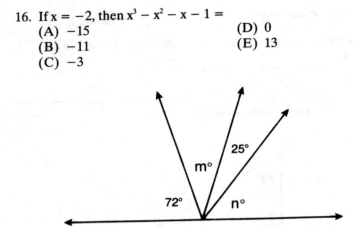

17. In the figure, what is the number of degrees in the sum of $m + n$?
    (A) 83
    (B) 93
    (C) 97
    (D) 103
    (E) cannot be determined

18. If x is between 0 and 1, which of the following statements is (are) true?

    I. $x^2 > 1$
    II. $x^2 > 0$
    III. $x^2 > x$

    (A) I only
    (B) II only
    (C) III only
    (D) I and II only
    (E) II and III only

19. If 15 students in a class average 80% on an English exam and 10 students average 90% on the same exam, what is the average in percent for all 25 students?
    (A) $86\frac{2}{3}\%$
    (B) 85%
    (C) 84%
    (D) $83\frac{1}{2}\%$
    (E) 83%

20. If a pipe can drain a tank in t hours, what part of the tank does it drain in 3 hours?
(A) 3t
(B) t/3
(C) t + 3
(D) 3/t
(E) t − 3

Questions 21–25 refer to the graph.

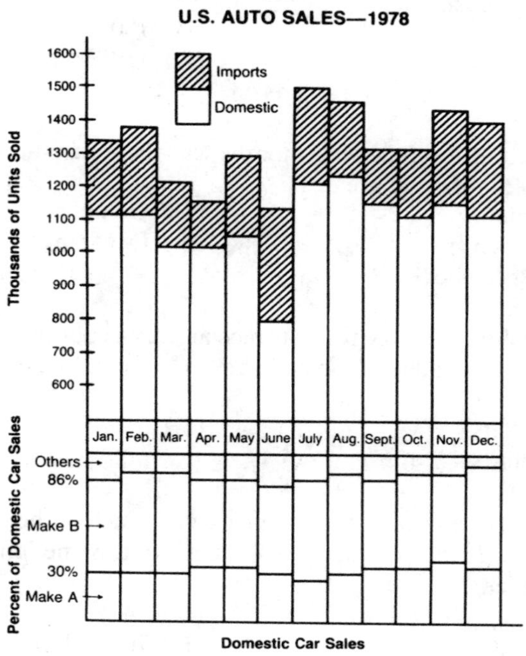

21. Approximately how many cars of make B were sold in July?
(A) 732,000
(B) 800,000
(C) 900,000
(D) 1,049,200
(E) 1,290,000

22. During which month(s) did imports outsell domestics?
(A) August
(B) June
(C) May
(D) April
(E) no months

23. What were the average monthly domestic sales (in millions) for the given year?
(A) .6–1.8
(B) .8–1.0
(C) 1.0–1.2
(D) 1.2–1.4
(E) 1.4–1.6

24. What is the approximate percent increase in total sales from June to December?
(A) 10%
(B) 30%
(C) 60%
(D) 100%
(E) 150%

25. In which of the following months was the domestic-to-imports auto sales ratio the greatest?
(A) January
(B) March
(C) September
(D) October
(E) December

26. If the volume and the total surface area of a cube are equal, how long must the edge of the cube be?
(A) 2 units
(B) 3 units
(C) 4 units
(D) 5 units
(E) 6 units

27. The base of an isosceles triangle exceeds each of the equal sides by 8 feet. If the perimeter is 89 feet, what is the length of the base in feet?
(A) 27
(B) $29\frac{2}{3}$
(C) 35
(D) 54
(E) 70

28. If two numbers have only the number 1 as a common divisor, then they are called "relatively prime." Which of the following are NOT relatively prime?

I. 3 II. 4 III. 7 IV. 12

(A) I and II, I and III
(B) I and IV, II and IV
(C) II and III, II and IV
(D) II and IV, III and IV
(E) I and II, I and IV

29. If (a,b) ⊗ (c,d) = (ac − bd,ad) then (−2,3) ⊗ (4,−1) =
(A) (−5,2)
(B) (−5,−2)
(C) (−11,2)
(D) (−11,−2)
(E) (−5,−3)

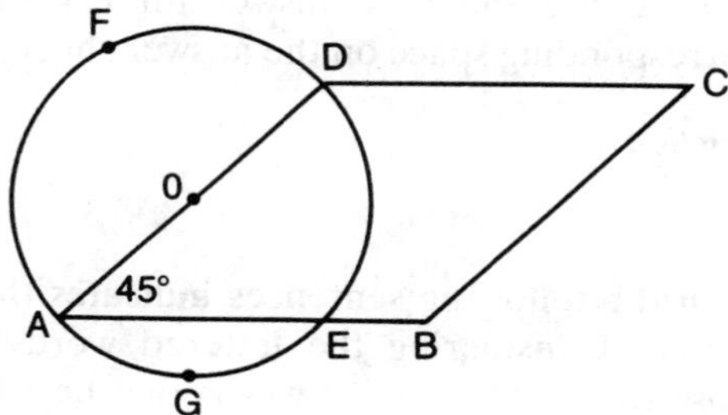

30. In the rhombus, BC = 6, AE ≃ 4, and angle DAE = 45°. AD is the diameter of the circle. If a man started at C and followed around the outer edge of this figure to D, F, A, G, E, B, and back to C, approximately how far did he travel?
(A) $14 + 6\pi$
(B) $14 + 9\pi/2$
(C) $14 + 27\pi/4$
(D) $12 + 6\pi$
(E) $12 + 9\pi/2$

STOP. IF YOU FINISH BEFORE TIME IS CALLED, CHECK YOUR WORK ON THIS SECTION ONLY. DO NOT WORK ON ANY OTHER SECTION IN THE TEST.

SECTION V: VERBAL ABILITY

Time: 30 Minutes
37 Questions

In this section, choose the best answer for each question and blacken the corresponding space on the answer sheet.

Sentence Completion

DIRECTIONS

Each blank in the following sentences indicates that something has been omitted. Considering the lettered words beneath the sentence, choose the word or set of words that best fits the whole sentence.

1. The horrifying _________ of the fire was reported on all the news stations, and the arson squad worked later through the week to uncover the _________ of the tragedy.
   (A) scene . . . rumble
   (B) result . . . jeopardy
   (C) aftermath . . . cause
   (D) cost . . . liability
   (E) origin . . . reality

2. Although the seemingly _________ nature of the task appeared fundamental, further application of the principles seemed _________.
   (A) facile . . . awkward
   (B) complex . . . easy
   (C) redundant . . . impossible
   (D) parallel . . . obvious
   (E) devious . . . ambiguous

3. Feeling restless and unhappy, he left the house to take a quiet stroll, hoping the tone of the day would not decline further into _________ and uncertainty.
   (A) dissonance
   (B) ardor
   (C) perversity
   (D) pretense
   (E) reticence

4. If the patriotic legend revealed the hard ________ of Roman culture, the love story tended to show its ________ belly.
   (A) facts . . . fictitious
   (B) backbone . . . vulnerable
   (C) times . . . easygoing
   (D) stubbornness . . . abdominal
   (E) paternalism . . . maternal

5. When the war ended, the king ________ all claims for damages, but he is now demanding ________ that will cost millions of dollars.
   (A) relinquished . . . expenses
   (B) questioned . . . repayments
   (C) waived . . . reparations
   (D) accepted . . . funds
   (E) reviewed . . . indemnity

6. The population of a species at any given time is determined by the ratio of the biotic ________ to environmental resistance.
   (A) jeopardy
   (B) potential
   (C) excitement
   (D) lexicon
   (E) annoyance

7. There has been a large amount of ________ and lack of ________ in the description of such categories as ethnic, and especially racial, groups.
   (A) disagreement . . . consensus
   (B) bias . . . prejudice
   (C) agreement . . . harmony
   (D) violence . . . lawfulness
   (E) indoctrination . . . malaise

8. Brandon Smith's penetrating criticism of the new play, *Zoot Suit,* was as ________ as a surgeon's scalpel.
   (A) truthful
   (B) catty
   (C) succinct
   (D) trenchant
   (E) verbose

9. The decline of ________ forms was hastened by the discovery of global trade routes, which soon produced basic ________ in the supply of money and price structure, thus dooming land as the basic element of wealth and preferment.
(A) feudal . . . alterations
(B) oligarchical . . . change
(C) democratic . . . remedies
(D) monarchical . . . alternatives
(E) barbaric . . . reductions

Analogies

DIRECTIONS

In each question below, you are given a related pair of words or phrases. Select the lettered pair that *best* expresses a relationship similar to that in the original pair of words.

10. SCOWL : SMILE ::
(A) antidote : serum
(B) square : circle
(C) cost : discount
(D) stock : bond
(E) despair : hope

11. DOLLAR : DIME ::
(A) pound : rubble
(B) century : decade
(C) ewe : lamb
(D) bracelet : necklace
(E) bus : automobile

12. CLARIFY : CONFUSION ::
(A) retreat : victory
(B) declare : bankruptcy
(C) criticize : euphoria
(D) mediate : altercation
(E) extend : ephemera

13. LECHER : LUST ::
(A) burglar : swag
(B) glutton : greed
(C) archer : bow
(D) manager : expertise
(E) factor : merchant

14. MOAT : CASTLE ::
(A) cummerbund : waist
(B) shoe : foot
(C) root : earth
(D) elevator : skyscraper
(E) drawbridge : river

15. FINCH : ORNITHOLOGY ::
(A) fetus : etymology
(B) rain : geology
(C) potsherd : archeology
(D) mind : philology
(E) word : sociology

16. SPANGLE : DARKEN ::
(A) hug : abjure
(B) seek : find
(C) inquire : question
(D) negotiate : haggle
(E) command : request

17. NYMPH : FAUN ::
(A) sheep : goat
(B) temple : altar
(C) duck : drake
(D) cowboy : horse
(E) cat : kitten

18. RUNE : ALPHABET ::
(A) cairn : stone
(B) team : contest
(C) mystery : puzzle
(D) forest : mountain
(E) star : constellation

Reading Comprehension

DIRECTIONS

Questions follow each of the passages below. Using only the stated or implied information in each passage, answer the questions.

People pondering the origin of language for the first time usually arrive at the conclusion that it developed gradually as a system of conventionalized grunts, hisses, and cries and must have been a very simple affair in the beginning. But when we observe the language behavior of what we regard as primitive cultures, we find it strikingly elaborate and complicated. Steffanson, the explorer, said that "in order to get along reasonably well an Eskimo must have at the tip of his tongue a vocabulary of more than 10,000 words, much larger than the active vocabulary of an average businessman who speaks English." Moreover, a single noun can be spoken or written in several hundred different forms. The Eskimo language is one of the most difficult to learn, with the result that almost no traders or explorers have even tried to learn it. Consequently, there has grown up, in intercourse between Eskimos and whites, a jargon similar to the pidgin English used in China, with a vocabulary of from 300 to 600 uninflected words, most of them derived from Eskimo but some derived from English, Danish, Spanish, Hawaiian and other languages. It is the jargon which is usually referred to by travelers as the "Eskimo language."

19. The size of the Eskimo language spoken by most whites is
    (A) about one third the size of the language spoken by the Eskimos
    (B) less than one tenth the size of the language spoken by Eskimos
    (C) determined by the number of inflections
    (D) more than 10,000 words
    (E) smaller than the jargon travelers call the "Eskimo language"

20. It can be inferred that pidgin English used in China
    (A) includes many words derived from English, Danish, Spanish, and Hawaiian
    (B) was invented by explorers from Europe
    (C) was developed because of the difficulty of the Chinese
    (D) has a large vocabulary of inflected words
    (E) has many words derived from Eskimo

21. Which of the following may plausibly be inferred from the passage?

    I. The language of primitive cultures other than the Eskimos is simple.
    II. Our notion of what is primitive is subject to revision.
    III. The complexity of a language is determined by the complexity of the civilization in which it arises.

    (A) I only
    (B) II only
    (C) III only
    (D) I and III only
    (E) I, II, and III

22. The overall point of the passage is that
    (A) languages may reflect cultural attitudes
    (B) most "primitive" languages are similar to one another
    (C) all languages are subject to change and development
    (D) comparison of "primitive" languages may reveal the origin of language
    (E) a "primitive" language may be large and complex

Many people seem to think that science fiction is typified by the covers of some of the old pulp magazines; the Bug-Eyed Monster, embodying every trait and feature that most people find repulsive, is about to grab, and presumably ravish, a sweet, blonde, curvaceous, scantily clad Earth girl. This is unfortunate because it demeans and degrades a worthwhile and even important literary endeavor. In contrast to this unwarranted stereotype, science fiction rarely emphasizes sex, and when it does, it is more discreet than other contemporary fiction. Instead, the basic interest of science fiction lies in the relation between man and his technology and between man and the universe. Science fiction is a literature of change and a literature of the future, and while it would be foolish to claim that science fiction is a major literary genre at this time, the aspects of human life that it considers make it well worth reading and studying—for no other literary form does quite the same things.

What is science fiction? To begin, the following definition should be helpful: science fiction is a literary sub-genre which postulates a change (for human beings) from conditions as we know them and follows the implications of these changes to a conclusion. Although this definition will necessarily be modified and expanded, it covers much of the basic groundwork and provides a point of departure.

The first point—that science fiction is a literary sub-genre—is a very important one, but one which is often overlooked or ignored in most discussions of science fiction. Specifically, science fiction is either a short story or a novel. There are only a few dramas which could be called science fiction, with Karel Capek's *RUR* (Rossum's Universal Robots) being the only one that is well known; the body of poetry that might be labeled science fiction is only slightly larger. To say that science fiction is a sub-genre of prose fiction is to say that it has all the basic characteristics and serves the same basic functions in much the same way as prose fiction in general—that is, it shares a great deal with all other novels and short stories.

Everything that can be said about prose fiction, in general, applies to science fiction. Every piece of science fiction, whether short story or novel, must have a narrator, a story, a plot, a setting, characters, language, and theme. And like any prose, the themes of science fiction are concerned with interpreting man's nature and experience in relation to the world around him. Themes in science fiction are constructed and presented in exactly the same ways that themes are dealt with in any other kind of fiction. They are the result of a particular combination of narrator, story, plot, character, setting, and language. In short, the reasons for reading and enjoying science fiction, and the ways of studying and analyzing it, are basically the same as they would be for any other story or novel.

23. Although a few examples of science fiction written before 1900 exist, we can infer that it has been most popular in the twentieth century because
    (A) with the growth of literacy, the size of the reading public has increased
    (B) competition from television and film has created a demand for more exciting fiction
    (C) science fiction is easier to understand than other kinds of fiction
    (D) the increased importance of technology in our lives has given science fiction an increased relevance
    (E) other media have captured the large audience that read novels in the nineteenth century

24. According to the definition in the passage, a fictional work that places human beings in a prehistoric world inhabited by dinosaurs
    (A) cannot properly be called science fiction because it does not deal with the future
    (B) cannot properly be called science fiction because it does not deal with technology
    (C) can properly be called science fiction because it is prose fiction
    (D) can properly be called science fiction because it places people in an environment different from the one we know
    (E) can properly be called science fiction because it deals with man's relation to the world around him

25. Science fiction is called a literary sub-genre because
    (A) it is not important enough to be a literary genre
    (B) it cannot be made into a dramatic presentation
    (C) it has its limits
    (D) it shares characteristics with other types of prose fiction
    (E) to call it a "genre" would subject it to literary jargon

26. From the passage, we can infer that science fiction films based upon ideas that have orginally appeared in other media are chiefly adaptions of
    (A) short stories
    (B) plays
    (C) novels
    (D) poems
    (E) folk tales

27. The emphasis on theme in the final paragraph of the passage suggests that the author regards which of the following as an especially important reason for reading science fiction?
    (A) the discovery of meaning
    (B) the display of character
    (C) the beauty of language
    (D) the psychological complexity
    (E) the interest of setting

28. One implication of the final sentence in the passage is that
    (A) the reader should turn next to commentaries on general fiction
    (B) there is no reason for any reader not to like science fiction
    (C) the reader should compare other novels and stories to science fiction
    (D) there are reasons for enjoying science fiction
    (E) those who can appreciate prose fiction can appreciate science fiction

29. An appropriate title for this passage would be
    (A) On the Inaccuracies of Pulp Magazines
    (B) Man and the Universe
    (C) Toward a Definition of Science Fiction
    (D) A Type of Prose Fiction
    (E) Beyond the Bug-Eyed Monster

Antonyms

DIRECTIONS

Each word in CAPITAL LETTERS is followed by five words or phrases. The correct choice is the word or phrase whose meaning is most nearly *opposite* to the meaning of the word in capitals. You may be required to distinguish fine shades of meaning. Look at all choices before marking your answer.

30. LUXURIANT
    (A) profound
    (B) curious
    (C) small
    (D) miserly
    (E) peeling

31. TYRO
    (A) factotum
    (B) instigator
    (C) virtuoso
    (D) investigator
    (E) dilettante

32. UBIQUITOUS
    (A) hiding
    (B) localized
    (C) jailed
    (D) bilious
    (E) exhaustive

33. ABSTEMIOUS
    (A) punctual
    (B) vainglorious
    (C) gluttonous
    (D) finicky
    (E) disdainful

34. SOPORIFIC
    (A) exciting
    (B) terrific
    (C) specific
    (D) vapid
    (E) sophomoric

35. FACTOTUM
    (A) idol
    (B) amateur
    (C) specialist
    (D) tyro
    (E) investigator

36. ESCHEW
    (A) hasten
    (B) grant
    (C) swallow
    (D) decide
    (E) court

37. MULCT
    (A) deprecate
    (B) award
    (C) send
    (D) impute
    (E) fertilize

STOP. IF YOU FINISH BEFORE TIME IS CALLED, CHECK YOUR WORK ON THIS SECTION ONLY. DO NOT WORK ON ANY OTHER SECTION IN THE TEST.

SECTION VI: ANALYTICAL ABILITY

Time: 30 Minutes
25 Questions

DIRECTIONS

The following questions or group of questions are based on a passage or set of statements. Choose the best answer for each question and blacken the corresponding space on your answer sheet. It may be helpful to draw rough diagrams or simple charts in attempting to answer these question types.

Questions 1–7

A gambler enters a wagering game consisting of four rounds of betting (Deals 1, 2, 3, and 4) in which coins and currency are bet. The gambler has the following coins and currency: one silver-dollar coin ($), two half-dollar coins (H), four quarters (Q), and one dollar bill (D). The following is observed:

The gambler bets exactly $1.00 during each deal.

The silver dollar is bet before Deal 3.

Two quarters begin the betting of the deal immediately after the deal in which the silver dollar is bet.

The dollar bill is not bet prior to betting any coin.

1. Suppose the silver dollar is NOT bet in Deal 2. Which of the following is NOT a sequence of betting for Deals 2 and 3?

	Deal 2	*Deal 3*
(A)	Q Q H	H Q Q
(B)	Q Q H	Q H Q
(C)	Q Q H	Q Q H
(D)	Q Q Q Q	H H
(E)	Q H Q	H Q Q

2. Suppose a quarter is the last bet before the silver dollar is bet. Which of the following is a possible sequence of betting for the first three deals?

	Deal 1	*Deal 2*	*Deal 3*
(A)	H H	Q Q Q Q	$
(B)	H Q Q	$	Q Q H
(C)	Q H Q	$	Q H Q
(D)	Q H Q	$	H Q Q
(E)	H Q Q	H Q Q	$

3. Suppose two of the deals each end with a bet of the same demonination coin. Which of the following must be true?
(A) The two deals are Deal 2 and Deal 3.
(B) The two deals are Deal 1 and Deal 3.
(C) The two deals are Deal 1 and Deal 2.
(D) The two deals end with half-dollar bets.
(E) The two deals end with quarter bets.

4. Which of the following is a possible betting sequence?

	Deal 1	*Deal 2*	*Deal 3*	*Deal 4*
(A)	$	Q Q H	Q H Q	D
(B)	$	H Q Q	Q Q H	D
(C)	H H	$	Q Q H	D
(D)	Q H Q	$	Q H Q	D
(E)	H Q Q	Q Q H	Q H Q	D

5. Assume the betting sequence in Deal 3 is exactly the same as in Deal 2. Which of the following CANNOT be true?

I. Deals 2 and 3 each end with a quarter bet.
II. Deals 2 and 3 each begin with a half-dollar bet.
III. Deals 2 and 3 each begin with a quarter bet.

(A) I only
(B) II only
(C) III only
(D) I and II only
(E) II and III only

6. The betting sequence of "quarter then half dollar then quarter" CANNOT appear in which of the following deals?

I. Deal 1
II. Deal 2
III. Deal 3
IV. Deal 4

(A) II and IV only
(B) III only
(C) I, II, and IV only
(D) II, III, and IV only
(E) I, II, III, and IV

7. If the gambler exchanges one of the half dollars for two quarters, which of the following is now a possible sequence of betting?

	Deal 1	*Deal 2*	*Deal 3*	*Deal 4*
(A)	$	Q Q Q Q	H H Q	D
(B)	D	H Q Q	Q Q Q Q	$
(C)	H Q Q	$	Q Q Q Q	D
(D)	H H Q	$	Q Q Q Q	D
(E)	Q Q Q Q	H Q	$ Q	D

8. When growing redwoods, a forester must thoroughly douse young saplings each morning until the first sign of new growth appears. Douglas firs, on the other hand, are not redwoods. Therefore, a thorough dousing each morning of young Douglas fir saplings is hardly necessary.

The reasoning in the above passage is flawed because

(A) a thorough dousing of water each morning will not adversely affect Douglas fir saplings
(B) redwoods and Douglas firs are two different trees and, as such, cannot be compared
(C) many young Douglas fir saplings have been known to thrive given thorough dousing each morning
(D) what is necessary for one tree sapling may be necessary for another sapling, even though they may be different trees
(E) redwoods are typically found in old-growth forests, whereas Douglas firs rarely are

9. The once vast regions of South American rain forest are fast dwindling in number and size. As a result, species extinction is fifty times more rapid today than two decades ago. Despite the outcries of environmentalists to halt the destruction of species-rich and oxygen-producing forest regions, little is being done to protect these wildernesses, so vital to the well-being and continuation of earth's fragile ecological system.

   Which of the following is an implication of the passage above?

   (A) The continued existence and health of rain forests is imperative for the survival of future generations.
   (B) Environmentalists are unnecessarily concerned about threats to the rain forest.
   (C) The number of wilderness areas should be increased beyond those that presently exist.
   (D) Radical action is necessary in order to reverse the environmental damage incurred by wilderness regions.
   (E) The legal system is slow to effect change but will eventually respond to the ecological needs of the people.

10. Results of recent studies conducted on three breeds of laboratory rats indicate that overfeeding leads to a diminished capacity in locomotive activity as well as a decrease in specific mating behaviors. One can therefore conclude that when human beings overeat, they not only will feel lethargic but also will demonstrate less inclination toward the opposite sex.

    Which of the following is an unstated assumption necessary to the passage above?

    (A) Rats normally have overactive sex lives, and it requires a change in environment to affect their drive.
    (B) Conclusions about human behavior can be derived from studies observing rat behavior.
    (C) It is neither immoral nor irresponsible to do experiments that may potentially harm laboratory animals.
    (D) Human beings typically are lethargic, and when they overeat, they become significantly more so.
    (E) All other species of rats will demonstrate the same behaviors demonstrated by the laboratory rats.

Questions 11–17

A county five miles long and five miles wide is divided into 25 equal one-mile-square regions. Each region is controlled by one of five district leaders, Alicia, Barker, Capshaw, Descarte, or Escargo. The regions are either wilderness or plains.

Home region, in the center, is controlled by Barker.

North Plain is to the immediate north of Home; East Plain is to the immediate east of Home; and so forth.

Only the regions along the outer edge of the county are wilderness, and are all controlled by Escargo, who controls no plains.

No two plains regions with a common side are controlled by the same leader.

Northeast Plain is controlled by Descarte; Southeast Plain is controlled by Alicia; Northwest Plain is not controlled by Capshaw; Southwest Plain is controlled by neither Barker nor Capshaw.

11. How many regions are controlled by Escargo?
    (A) 20
    (B) 19
    (C) 18
    (D) 17
    (E) 16

12. If Alicia controls as few regions as possible, how many regions must Alicia control?
    (A) 1
    (B) 2
    (C) 3
    (D) 4
    (E) 5

13. Suppose Descarte controls only the Northeast Plain. Which of the following CANNOT be true?
    (A) South Plain is controlled by Capshaw.
    (B) Northwest Plain is controlled by Alicia.
    (C) Northwest Plain is controlled by Barker.
    (D) West Plain is controlled by Capshaw.
    (E) West Plain is controlled by Alicia.

14. Which one of the following statements must be false?
(A) West Plain is controlled by Descarte, and South Plain is controlled by Descarte.
(B) West Plain is controlled by Descarte, and South Plain is controlled by Capshaw.
(C) West Plain is controlled by Capshaw, and South Plain is controlled by Descarte.
(D) West Plain is controlled by Alicia, and South Plain is controlled by Descarte.
(E) West Plain is controlled by Alicia, and South Plain is controlled by Capshaw.

15. Assume Southwest Plain is controlled by Descarte. If so, the control of which of the following can be determined?
I. North Plain
II. West Plain
III. South Plain

(A) I only
(B) II only
(C) III only
(D) I and III only
(E) II and III only

16. Assume Capshaw controls as many regions as possible. How many of the regions must be controlled by Capshaw?
(A) 2
(B) 3
(C) 4
(D) 5
(E) 6

17. All of the following can be true EXCEPT
(A) South Plain is controlled by Descarte
(B) Northwest Plain is controlled by Alicia
(C) West Plain is controlled by Alicia
(D) South Plain is controlled by Alicia
(E) Northwest Plain is controlled by Barker

Questions 18–22

Five blue pennants and four yellow pennants are flown on a mast from top to bottom, numbered 1 through 9, respectively.

A solid yellow pennant flies in place 7.

Four of the pennants are solid in color; the others are striped.

Two pennants are triangular.

One triangular pennant flies in place 2, and the other flies next to it.

No fewer than four of the blue pennants are always flying next to each other.

18. Suppose blue pennants fly in the topmost and bottommost places. Then it must be true that
    (A) all the yellow pennants do not fly adjacent to each other
    (B) a yellow pennant flies in place 8
    (C) a yellow pennant flies in place 3
    (D) a blue pennant flies in place 5
    (E) there is a yellow triangular pennant

19. If a yellow pennant flies in place 2, it could be true that a yellow pennant also flies in which place?

    I. place 1
    II. place 8
    III. place 9

    (A) I only
    (B) III only
    (C) I and II only
    (D) II and III only
    (E) I, II, and III

20. If a blue, striped pennant flies between and next to each of two yellow pennants, in which of the following places it it possible for this blue, striped pennant to fly?
    (A) place 1
    (B) place 2
    (C) place 3
    (D) place 6
    (E) place 7

21. Given all the yellow pennants flying next to one another, each of the following is possible EXCEPT
    (A) there is only one striped, blue, triangular pennant
    (B) there are two striped, blue, triangular pennants
    (C) there are three solid, yellow pennants
    (D) there are three striped, yellow pennants
    (E) there is one striped, triangular, yellow pennant

22. Suppose all the solid pennants fly next to each other. Which of the following CANNOT be true?
    (A) Two yellow pennants are triangular.
    (B) Two blue pennants are solid.
    (C) Two triangular pennants are blue.
    (D) Two triangular pennants are yellow.
    (E) Two triangular pennants are solid.

23. A young man with a spotless driving record drove his automobile cautiously whenever he was within the city limits of Dobbsville, but upon leaving Dobbsville, he threw all caution to the wind and drove in a careless manner. When questioned by a passenger in his automobile as to why his driving style changed so radically, the young man declared, "The National Safety Council reports that statistics over the past twenty years show that 97% of all automobile accidents occur within ten miles of home. Since I live exactly ten miles within the borders of Dobbsville, I don't have to worry whenever I drive outside of town."

    The young man's logic is faulty because

    (A) he could easily be involved in an accident with a resident of a neighboring town
    (B) his actions may be related to percentages recently computed, but not as far back as twenty years
    (C) statistics of overall numbers of accidents may tell nothing about any one individual's chances of having an accident
    (D) his driving record was spotless because, being so young, he has been driving only a few years
    (E) statistics from the National Safety Council are occasionally disputed by reputable researchers

24. A college catalogue states the following: Every student receiving a diploma at graduation after four years of undergraduate study will have demonstrated a competency of at least one particular skill. Some students will have learned skills of research methodology in a particular field of endeavor. Others will have shown excellence in teaching and/or imparting cognitive information. Still others will have demonstrated their ability to write original material, whether fiction or nonfiction.

    If the above passage is true, which of the following statements must also be true?

    (A) All of the skills demonstrated by undergraduates will have been learned at the university.
    (B) Not all of the skills taught at the university will have been learned by undergraduates.
    (C) One of the skills demonstrated by undergraduates will be the ability to write original material.
    (D) Some of the skills learned by undergraduates will not be research methodology, excellence in teaching, or ability to write original material.
    (E) Not all the skills demonstrated by undergraduates will be learned at the end of four years.

25. After auditioning for a role in a college play, a student-actor was told the following by the faculty advisor: I'm sorry to have to tell you that the play's producers passed on you for the role for which you auditioned. Because of the ethnic nature of all the roles and their requirement that the performers have a flawless Hungarian accent and be able to speak Russian, it was necessary to deny parts to many capable actors.

Taken at face value, which of the following can be deduced from the faculty advisor's statement?

(A) Very few of the student-actors auditioning for the play actually were given parts in the play.
(B) Except for the lack of Hungarian accent and inability to speak Russian, the student-actor was otherwise capable for the role.
(C) Only those students who were capable actors were given roles in the play.
(D) Whether the auditioners were capable actors was only one consideration in assigning roles for the play.
(E) None of the actors who were accepted for roles in the play were capable actors.

STOP. IF YOU FINISH BEFORE TIME IS CALLED, CHECK YOUR WORK ON THIS SECTION ONLY. DO NOT WORK ON ANY OTHER SECTION IN THE TEST.

SECTION VII: QUANTITATIVE ABILITY

Time: 30 Minutes
30 Questions

Quantitative Comparison

DIRECTIONS

In this section you will be given two quantities, one in column A and one in column B. You are to determine a relationship between the two quantities and mark

(A) if the quantity in column A is greater than the quantity in column B
(B) if the quantity in column B is greater than the quantity in column A
(C) if the quantities are equal
(D) if the comparison cannot be determined from the information that is given

Common Information:

Information centered above both columns refers to one or both columns.
All numbers used are real numbers.
Figures are intended to provide useful positional information, but are not necessarily drawn to scale and should not be used to estimate sizes by measurement.
Lines that appear straight can be assumed to be straight.

	Column A	**Column B**
1.	Number of ones in 48	Number of tens in 68
2.	$\sqrt{48}$	7
3.	$x + 4$	$y - 3$
4.	40% of 60	60% of 40
5.	$.05 - .125$	.1

	Column A	Column B
	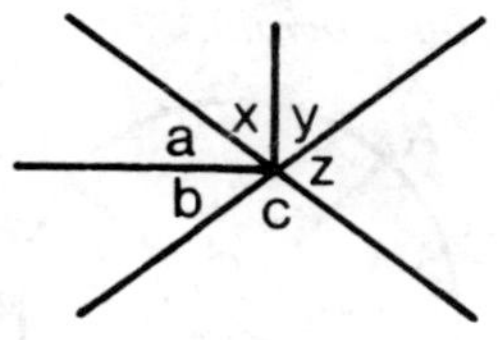	
6.	x + y + c	a + z + b

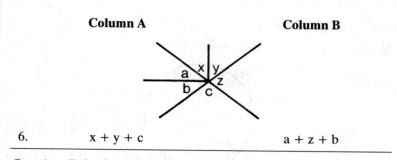

Questions 7–8 refer to the diagram.

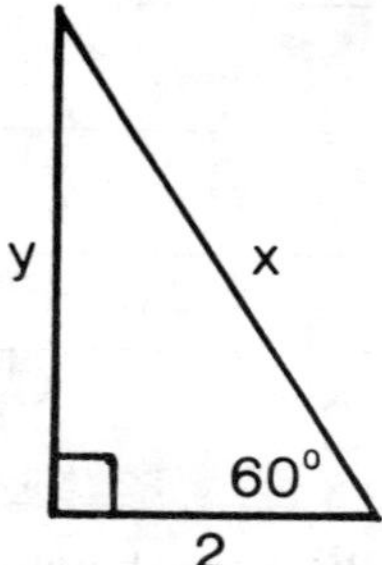

	Column A	Column B
7.	x	y
8.	2	$\frac{x}{2}$
9.	5%	$\frac{1}{20}$

	Column A	Column B

Questions 10–12 refer to the diagram.

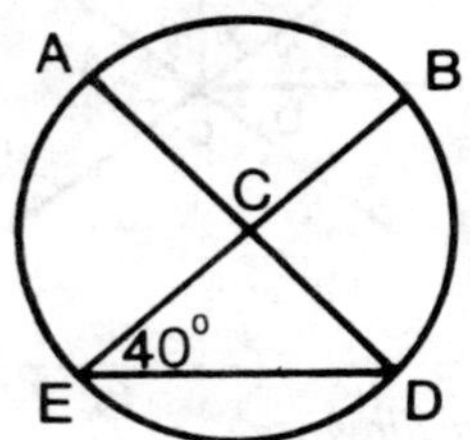

	Column A	Column B
10.	∠CED	½$\overparen{BD}$
11.	$\overparen{AB}$	$\overparen{AE}$
12.	∠BCD	∠CDE
13.	Number of diagonals in a hexagon	Number of sides of a hexagon

ABCD is a rhombus with height 4 and area 20

	Column A	Column B
14.	Length of side AB	Length of diagonal AC

$T > x$
$y < m$
$x < y$

	Column A	Column B
15.	$x + y$	$T + m$

Math Ability

DIRECTIONS

Solve each problem in this section by using the information given and your own mathematical calculations. Then select the *one* correct answer of the five choices given. Use the available space on the page for scratchwork. NOTE: Some problems may be accompanied by figures or diagrams. These figures are drawn as accurately as possible, *except* when it is stated in a specific problem that the figure is not drawn to scale. The figure is meant to provide information useful in solving the problem or problems. Unless otherwise stated or indicated, all figures lie in a plane. All numbers used are real numbers.

16. If $x - 4 = y$, what must $(y - x)^3$ equal?
(A) -64
(B) -12
(C) 12
(D) 64
(E) cannot be determined

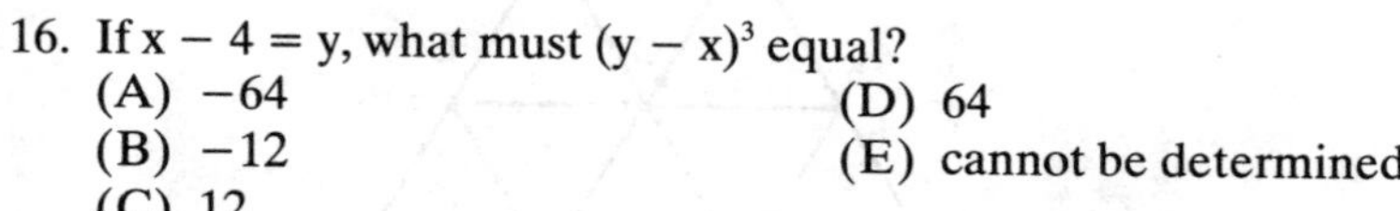

17. If $a/b = c/d$ and a, b, c, and d are positive integers, then which of the following is true?
(A) $a/b = d/c$
(B) $ac = bd$
(C) $a + d = b + c$
(D) $d/b = c/a$
(E) $a/d = c/b$

18. There are 36 students in a certain geometry class. If two-thirds of the students are boys and three-fourths of the boys are under six feet tall, how many boys in the class are under six feet tall?
(A) 6
(B) 12
(C) 18
(D) 24
(E) 27

19. When a certain integer J is divided by 5, the remainder is 1. When integer J is divided by 3, the remainder is 2. The value for J is
(A) 6
(B) 11
(C) 12
(D) 16
(E) 21

20. A bag contains 20 gumballs. If there are 8 red, 7 white, and 5 green, what is the minimum number of gumballs one must pick from the bag to be assured of one of each color?

(A) 16
(B) 9
(C) 8
(D) 6
(E) 3

Questions 21–25 refer to the graphs.

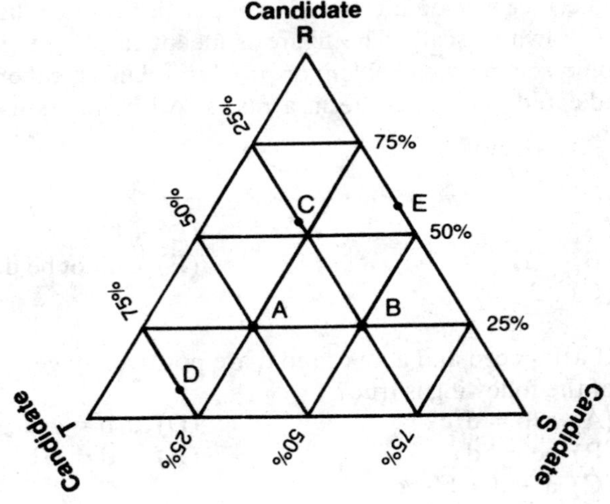

The above graph shows the distribution of votes among three candidates in five different cities in a statewide election.

The graph below shows the total votes cast for these three candidates in these five cities.

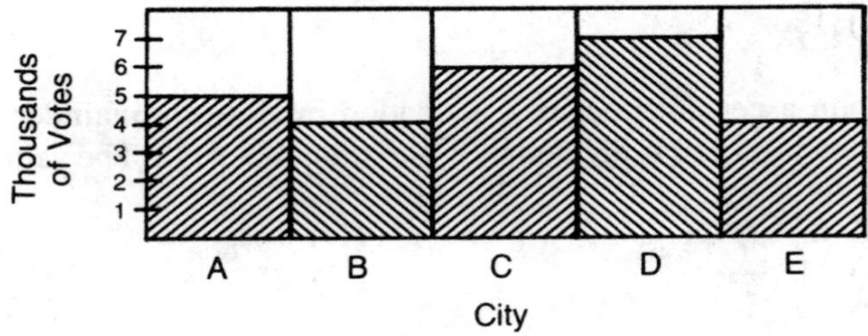

21. Which city cast the most votes for candidate R?
(A) A
(B) B
(C) C
(D) D
(E) E

22. How many cities cast more votes for candidate S than for candidate T?
(A) 0
(B) 1
(C) 2
(D) 3
(E) 4

23. Which cities cast the same number of votes for candidate R?
(A) A and B
(B) B and C
(C) C and D
(D) A and C
(E) all cities were different

24. About how many votes did candidate T receive total in the five cities?
(A) 2000–4000
(B) 4000–6000
(C) 6000–8000
(D) 8000–10,000
(E) 10,000–12,000

25. How many cities cast over two-thirds of their votes for one candidate?
(A) 0
(B) 1
(C) 2
(D) 3
(E) 4

26. If the ratio of x to y is $\frac{3}{4}$ and the ratio of y to z is $\frac{12}{13}$, the ratio of x to z is
(A) $\frac{3}{13}$
(B) $\frac{4}{13}$
(C) $\frac{1}{3}$
(D) $\frac{9}{13}$
(E) $\frac{12}{13}$

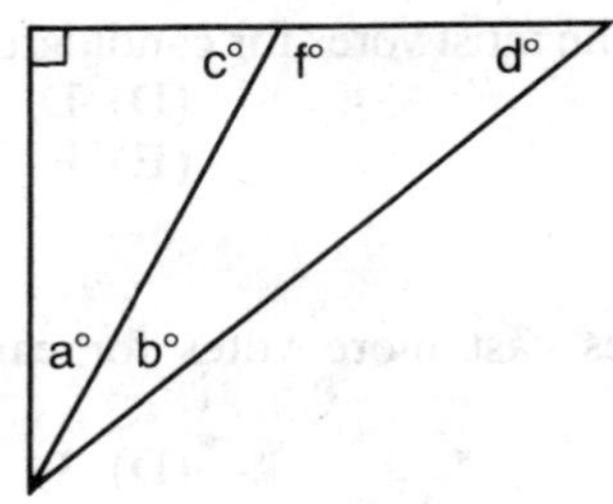

27. In the right triangle, c = 2a and d > 2b; therefore, which of the following must be true?
(A) c > b + d
(B) angle a is greater than angle b
(C) angle a equals angle b
(D) angle b is greater than angle a
(E) angle d equals twice angle a

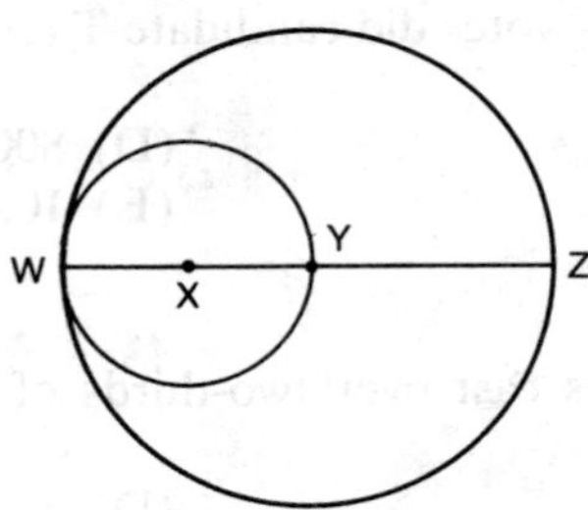

28. In the figure, X and Y are the centers of the two circles. If the area of the larger circle is 144π, what is the area of the smaller circle?
(A) 72π
(B) 36π
(C) 24π
(D) 12π
(E) 12

29. How many pounds of tea worth 93¢ per pound must be mixed with tea worth 75¢ per pound to produce 10 pounds worth 85¢ per pound?
(A) $2\frac{2}{9}$
(B) $3\frac{1}{2}$
(C) $4\frac{4}{9}$
(D) $5\frac{5}{9}$
(E) $9\frac{1}{2}$

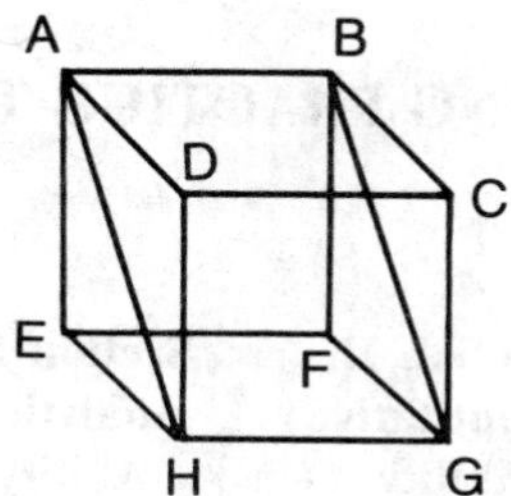

30. In the cube above, AH and BG are diagonals and the surface area of side ABFE is 16. What is the area of rectangle ABGH?
(A) $4\sqrt{2}$
(B) 16
(C) $16 + \sqrt{2}$
(D) $16\sqrt{2}$
(E) $15\sqrt{3}$

STOP. IF YOU FINISH BEFORE TIME IS CALLED, CHECK YOUR WORK ON THIS SECTION ONLY. DO NOT WORK ON ANY OTHER SECTION IN THE TEST.

SCORING PRACTICE TEST 1

ANSWER KEY

Section I Verbal Ability		Section II Quantitative Ability	Section III Analytical Ability	Section IV Quantitative Abiltiy
1. C	31. A	1. A	1. E	1. A
2. C	32. D	2. D	2. E	2. D
3. C	33. B	3. B	3. E	3. C
4. E	34. A	4. D	4. B	4. A
5. B	35. C	5. D	5. D	5. A
6. D	36. B	6. B	6. A	6. A
7. E	37. D	7. A	7. E	7. C
8. C	38. D	8. A	8. A	8. B
9. A	39. A	9. C	9. D	9. A
10. E		10. B	10. C	10. B
11. B		11. D	11. D	11. B
12. C		12. D	12. E	12. C
13. C		13. B	13. E	13. A
14. C		14. A	14. B	14. B
15. C		15. B	15. E	15. C
16. D		16. A	16. D	16. B
17. A		17. B	17. A	17. A
18. C		18. A	18. C	18. B
19. D		19. D	19. C	19. C
20. A		20. D	20. C	20. D
21. D		21. E	21. A	21. A
22. C		22. C	22. E	22. E
23. D		23. B	23. B	23. C
24. C		24. E	24. E	24. B
25. C		25. B	25. E	25. C
26. A		26. C		26. E
27. D		27. D		27. C
28. B		28. C		28. B
29. B		29. D		29. A
30. D		30. D		30. B

ANSWER KEY

Section V Verbal Ability		Section VI Analytical Ability	Section VII Quantitative Ability
1. C	31. C	1. E	1. A
2. A	32. B	2. B	2. B
3. A	33. C	3. D	3. D
4. B	34. A	4. A	4. C
5. C	35. C	5. D	5. B
6. B	36. E	6. A	6. D
7. A	37. B	7. C	7. A
8. D		8. D	8. C
9. A		9. A	9. C
10. E		10. B	10. C
11. B		11. E	11. D
12. D		12. A	12. A
13. B		13. E	13. A
14. A		14. D	14. D
15. C		15. C	15. B
16. A		16. C	16. A
17. C		17. D	17. D
18. E		18. B	18. C
19. B		19. E	19. B
20. C		20. D	20. A
21. B		21. E	21. C
22. E		22. E	22. C
23. D		23. C	23. E
24. D		24. C	24. E
25. D		25. D	25. B
26. C			26. D
27. A			27. B
28. E			28. B
29. C			29. D
30. C			30. D

SCORE RANGE APPROXIMATORS

The following charts are designed to give you only an approximate score range, not an exact score. When you take the GRE General Test, you will have questions that are similar to those in this book; however, some questions may be slightly easier or more difficult. Needless to say, this may affect your scoring range.

Because one section of the GRE is experimental (it doesn't count toward your score), for the purposes of this approximation, do not count Section VII. Remember, on the actual test the experimental section could appear anywhere on your test.

Verbal Ability

To approximate your verbal score:

1. Total the number of questions you answered correctly in sections I and V. No points are subtracted for incorrect answers.
2. Use the following table to match the total number of correct answers in those two sections and the corresponding approximate score range.

Number Right	Approximate Score Range
65–75	710–800
55–64	590–700
45–54	490–580
35–44	400–480
25–34	320–390
15–24	220–310
0–14	200–220

Average score is approximately 480.

Quantitative Ability

To approximate your quantitative score:

1. Total the number of questions you answered correctly in Sections II and IV. No points are subtracted for incorrect answers.
2. Use the following table to match the total number of correct answers in those two sections and the corresponding approximate score range.

Number Right	Approximate Score Range
50–60	700–800
40–49	570–690
30–39	450–560
20–29	330–440
10–19	220–320
0–9	200–210

Average score is approximately 560.

Analytical Ability

To approximate your analytical score:

1. Total the number of questions you answered correctly in Sections III and VI. No points are subtracted for incorrect answers.
2. Use the following table to match the total number of correct answers in those two sections and the corresponding approximate score range.

Number Right	Approximate Score Range
40–50	700–800
30–39	560–690
20–29	410–550
10–19	240–400
0–9	200–230

Average score is approximately 540.

Remember, these are *approximate* score ranges.

ANALYZING YOUR TEST RESULTS

The charts on the following pages should be used to carefully analyze your results and spot your strengths and weaknesses. The complete process of analyzing each subject area and each individual problem should be completed for each practice test. These results should then be reexamined for trends in types of errors (repeated errors) or poor results in specific subject areas. THIS REEXAMINATION AND ANALYSIS IS OF TREMENDOUS IMPORTANCE TO YOU IN ASSURING MAXIMUM TEST PREPARATION BENEFIT.

VERBAL ABILITY ANALYSIS SHEET

SECTION I

	Possible	Completed	Right	Wrong
Sentence Completion	8			
Analogies	9			
Reading Comprehension	11			
Antonyms	11			
SUBTOTALS	39			

SECTION V

	Possible	Completed	Right	Wrong
Sentence Completion	9			
Analogies	9			
Reading Comprehension	11			
Antonyms	8			
SUBTOTALS	37			
OVERALL VERBAL ABILITY TOTALS	76			

QUANTITATIVE ABILITY ANALYSIS SHEET

SECTION II

	Possible	Completed	Right	Wrong
Quantitative Comparison	15			
Math Ability	15			
SUBTOTALS	30			

SECTION IV

	Possible	Completed	Right	Wrong
Quantitative Comparison	15			
Math Ability	15			
SUBTOTALS	30			
OVERALL QUANTITATIVE ABILITY TOTALS	60			

SECTION VII

NOTE: For this practice test, do not include Section VII in your overall Quantitative Ability score.

	Possible	Completed	Right	Wrong
Quantitative Comparison	15			
Math Ability	15			
TOTALS	30			

ANALYTICAL ABILITY ANALYSIS SHEET

	Possible	Completed	Right	Wrong
Section III	25			
Section VI	25			
OVERALL ANALYTICAL ABILITY TOTALS	50			

ANALYSIS: TALLY SHEET FOR PROBLEMS MISSED

One of the most important parts of test preparation is analyzing WHY! you missed a problem so that you can reduce the number of mistakes. Now that you have taken the practice test and corrected your answers, carefully tally your mistakes by marking them in the proper column.

REASON FOR MISTAKE

	Total Missed	Simple Mistake	Misread Problem	Lack of Knowledge
SECTION I: VERBAL ABILITY				
SECTION V: VERBAL ABILITY				
SUBTOTALS				
SECTION II: QUANTITATIVE ABILITY				
SECTION IV: QUANTITATIVE ABILITY				
SUBTOTALS				
SECTION III: ANALYTICAL ABILITY				
SECTION VI: ANALYTICAL ABILITY				
SUBTOTALS				
TOTAL VERBAL, QUANTITATIVE, AND ANALYTICAL				

Reviewing the above data should help you determine WHY you are missing certain problems. Now that you have pinpointed the type of error, take the next practice test focusing on avoiding your most common type.

COMPLETE ANSWERS AND EXPLANATIONS FOR PRACTICE TEST 1

SECTION I: VERBAL ABILITY

Sentence Completion

1. (C) The answer here is *restive . . . unperturbed. Although* signals a contrast between the boys' behavior and the girls'. The correct pair of words then must be opposite in meaning. Choices (A) and (B) are synonymous pairs and can be eliminated on that basis. Choices (D) and (E) are not contrasts—*remorseful* (sad) and *enchanted* (charmed) and *tactiturn* (silent) and *attracted* (drawn to) are not opposite in meaning. (C) is left as the only pair which satisfies the context and the contrast indicated by the rest of the sentence.

2. (C) The correct answer is *incorporated.* The conjunction *and* indicates that the ideas from Greek philosophy are considered as parallel to Greek language in the first half of the sentence. With crucial derivative ideas one would not *nullify, criticize,* or *alter* them.

3. (C) The answer is *criticized . . . curb.* The idiomatic expression in the second part of the sentence calls for a verb. *Excesses* are *curbed* not *implemented, promoted,* or *ostracized.* Choice (B) is an incorrect use of the word *chagrined,* leaving (C) as the best choice.

4. (E) The signal word here is *reached;* the only choice which one can *reach* is *pinnacle.* If you had asked yourself, "What was reached?" this answer should have occurred to you.

5. (B) The noun associated with the Queen must accord with her silence, so (C) and (E) cannot be right. The President's verb must go with *happily* so (A) and (D) will not work.

6. (D) The best choice is *consequently.* The semicolon is needed to connect the two clauses. The second part of the sentence positively extends the quality of the novel stated in the first part. The connecting word *consequently* provides the direction needed to extend the meaning of the first part of the sentence.

7. (E) The required verb must follow logically the exploitation of resources. Choice (C) is possible, but *unchecked exploitation* suggests a stronger verb, such as *decimated.*

8. (C) A remark to explain not having written a substantial essay would be an *apology,* and a remark about unfairness would tend to be *indignant.*

Analogies

9. (A) *Initiate* (to begin) and *end* (to conclude) are verbs with opposite meanings. *Attend* (pay attention to) is the opposite of *ignore.*

10. (E) The *recipe* is the written set of directions from which the *chef* produces a dish; the *score* is the written account of the piece upon which a *musician* depends.

11. (B) *Photosynthesis* is a process, the product of which is *oxygen.* Similarly, *heat* is the product of the process of *combustion.* A *camera* is not a process.

12. (C) A *scheme* is a *plan* with sinister connotations. Of the choices here, the closest is the *statesman/politician.*

13. (C) The *loom* is the frame upon which a *tapestry* is woven. The *easel* is the support of the canvas upon which a painting is made.

14. (C) To *ossify* is to turn to *bone;* to *pulverize* is to reduce to *dust.*

15. (C) A *tedious* conversation or person will produce *boredom* as that which is *enigmatic* will produce *uncertainty.*

16. (D) A person who *grovels* (fawns) may be described by the adjective *servile.* A person who *foresees* is *prescient* (knowing before).

17. (A) *Banter* (playful language) is a synonym for *persiflage* as *similarity* is a synonym for *analogy.*

Reading Comprehension

18. (C) Though the paragraph begins with the mention of petrified trees, the central issue is how the Andes mountains were formed.

19. (D) Both I and II are confirmed in the paragraph, but the last sentence asserts that the Andes are the product of changes that have occurred within a comparatively *recent* period.

20. (A) Modern scientific discourse is likely to be less personal and use fewer figures such as this. There are no religious references in the passage (B), while reasoning from cause and effect (C), comparing geological areas (D), and terms like *volcanic* or *strata* are common in both nineteenth- and twentieth-century scientific writings.

21. (D) The adjectives and adverbs of the passage suggest the awe or astonishment of the speaker as he or she contemplates the evidence.

22. (C) The first paragraph supports answers (A), (B), (D), and (E). One of the points of the experiments described is to show that people will change their opinions *without* being given good reasons to do so.

23. (D) The second paragraph (and the third) questions the validity of the conclusions of the experiments described in the first paragraph.

24. (C) Thorndike's claims to have altered his subjects' esthetic preferences are instances of selling an idea and studies of change of esthetic preference, but the passage does not assert that contemporary research confirms these claims.

25. (C) The passage concludes that a change of judgment is likely to be based on a change of knowledge or assumptions about the topic.

26. (A) Though the passage refers to ideas in choices (B), (C), and (D), only (A) is the main point of the *whole* passage.

27. (D) The passage gives us no information on the author's views of men as opposed to women. Answer (D), referring to both men and women, is clearly implied by the last paragraph.

28. (B) The first paragraph (the claims of early social psychologists) presents ideas that are questioned in the second and third paragraphs.

Antonyms

29. (B) Something *mitigated* has become less severe or painful. Something *aggravated* has become worse. *Raised* merely indicates a direction of movement, but not whether the movement is for better or worse.

30. (D) A *proselyte* is one who has been convinced to adopt a new religion, politcal party, or opinion. An *apostate* (*apo* = from; *sta* = stand) is one who forsakes a former system of beliefs. A *renegade* is a deserter from an army or tribe; since a *renegade* does not necessarily desert beliefs, the word is not a near opposite of *proselyte.*

31. (A) To *cloy* is to oversatisfy, or surfeit. Its opposite is *deny.*

32. (D) *Resuscitate* (*re* = again; *cit* = to put into motion) means to revive, bring back to life. Its opposite is *kill.* To *succumb* may mean to die, but could be an opposite only if *resuscitate* meant to live.

33. (B) To *rusticate* is to spend time in the country (*rus* = country); being *urban* means spending time in the city.

34. (A) *Penury* is abject poverty, the opposite of *wealth.*

35. (C) *Laconic* refers to a response which is very short. Its opposite is *verbose,* which refers to using many words. *Compendious* refers to saying much in a few words.

36. (B) *Moribund* means dying, passing out of existence (*mori* = death). So the direct opposite is *eternal,* never- dying.

37. (D) *Ineffable* (*in* = not; *fab* = to speak) describes something which is inexpressible or indescribable. Its opposite is *definable,* which means capable of being described exactly. *Cogent* refers to something which is convincingly to the point.

38. (D) The adjective *ersatz* means substitute, artificial, false. Its opposite is *genuine.*

39. (A) *Estheticism* is a strong liking for art, beauty, and good taste. Its opposite is *tastelessness.*

SECTION II: QUANTITATIVE ABILITY

Quantitative Comparison

1. (A) By inspection both sides are exactly the same, *except* in column A you are adding 4×10^2 and in column B you are subtracting 4×10^2. Therefore, column A is greater. Solving for values would give

$$
\begin{array}{lcl}
3^2 + 4 \times 10^2 - 4^2 & & 3^2 - 4 \times 10^2 - 4^2 \\
9 + 4 \times 100 - 16 & & 9 - 4 \times 100 - 16 \\
9 + 400 - 16 & & 9 - 400 - 16 \\
409 - 16 & & -391 - 16 \\
393 & > & -407
\end{array}
$$

2. (D) Solving $x^2 = 36$ gives $+6$ and -6. Therefore, x can be equal to 6 or less than 6, making no comparison possible.

3. (B) On the number line, if x, y, and z are integers, then by inspection $x = 1$, $y = -1$, and $z = 2$. Substituting these values into each column gives

$$2 - 1 \quad \text{and} \quad 1 - (-1)$$

$$\text{hence} \quad 1 \quad < \quad 2$$

Therefore the correct answer is (B).

4. (D) Since x and y are not vertical angles and no other information is given, no comparison can be made. The correct answer is (D).

5. (D) Trying some small values is required here, keeping in mind that x must be greater than 0. Let $x = 1$ then

$$
\begin{array}{lcl}
3(1)^2 & & 2(1)^3 \\
3(1) & & 2(1) \\
3 & > & 2
\end{array}
$$

In this case column A is greater. Now try another value for x. Let $x = 2$ then

$3(2)^2$		$2(2)^3$
$3(4)$		$2(8)$
12	<	16

In this case column B is greater. Since there are different comparisons depending on the values chosen, the correct answer is (D)—cannot be determined.

6. (B) Solve the first problem as follows:

x is 30% of 60

Replacing "=" for "is" and "·" for "of" (30% = 3/10)
then $x = (3/10) \cdot 60$
then $x = 18$

Solve the second problem as follows:

$$20\% \text{ of } y \text{ is } 4$$
$$(20\% = 1/5)$$
$$(1/5) \cdot y = 4$$
$$(1/5)y = 4$$

Multiplying by 5/1 gives $(5/1) \cdot (1/5)y = 4 \cdot (5/1)$; then $y = 20$.

7. (A) If the top angle was 90°, then x would be $3\sqrt{2}$. This could be calculated using the Pythagorean theorem.

$$a^2 + b^2 = c^2$$
$$3^2 + 3^2 = x^2$$
$$9 + 9 = x^2$$
$$18 = x^2$$

Therefore $\sqrt{18} = x$

which simplified is $3\sqrt{2}$. But since the angle was originally larger than 90°, then the side across from 92° must be larger than $3\sqrt{2}$. The correct answer is (A).

8. (A) Since there are 180° in a triangle and 92° in one angle, that leaves 88° to be split equally between two angles. Thus angle y is 44°. (The degrees must be split equally because angles across from equal sides are equal). And the triangle has two equal sides (isosceles). The correct answer is (A).

9. (C) The integer multiples of 8 greater than 8 but less than 50 are 16, 24, 32, 40, and 48. Column A is therefore 5. The integer multiples of 6 greater than 6 but less than 40 are 12, 18, 24, 30, 36. Therefore, column B is also 5. The correct answer is (C).

10. (B) The easiest method is by inspection (and/or addition). Column A is approaching 2, but will not get there. Mathematically getting a common denominator and adding gives

$1 + \frac{1}{2} + \frac{1}{4} + \frac{1}{16} + \frac{1}{32} + \frac{1}{64}$, or
$1 + \frac{32}{64} + \frac{16}{64} + \frac{4}{64} + \frac{2}{64} + \frac{1}{64}$
$1 + \frac{55}{64}$
and $1\frac{55}{64} < 2$

11. (D) Substituting 0 for x and 1 for y fits the condition $0 < x + y < 2$ $(0 < 0 + 1 < 2)$ and gives an answer of (B), column B is greater. Now substituting 1 for x and 0 for y also fits the condition $0 < x + y < 2$ $(0 < 1 + 0 < 2)$ but gives an answer of (A), column A is greater. Therefore the correct answer is (D). Since different values give different comparisons, no comparison can be made.

12. (D) Volume of cube with side 6 is $6 \times 6 \times 6 = 216$. Volume of rectangular prism with two dimensions less than 6 is not determinable because the third dimension is needed. Therefore no comparison can be made.

13. (B) Solve each equation as follows

	$x^2 + 2x + 1 = 0$		$y^2 - 2y + 1 = 0$
Factoring gives	$(x + 1)(x + 1) = 0$		$(y - 1)(y - 1) = 0$
then	$x + 1 = 0$		$y - 1 = 0$
leaves	$x = -1$		$y = 1$
Therefore	x	<	y

14. (A) To make this comparison it is necessary to factor column A.

$8^{29} - 8^{28}$
$8^{28}(8^1 - 8^0)$
$8^{28}(8 - 1)$
$8^{28}(7) \quad > \quad 8^{28}$

15. (B) Substitute x = 9 and y = 4 (note these are square numbers and they can make solving easier when dealing with square roots).

	$\sqrt{x} - \sqrt{y}$		$\sqrt{x - y}$
	$\sqrt{9} - \sqrt{4}$		$\sqrt{9 - 4}$
	$3 - 2$		$\sqrt{5}$
then	1	<	2.23

Now try two other numbers. You will find that column B will always be greater.

Math Ability

16. (A) $\dfrac{\text{percent}}{100} = \dfrac{\text{is number}}{\text{of number}}$

$$\frac{.25}{100} = \frac{x}{12} \text{ (cross multiplying)}$$

$$100x = 3.00$$

$$\frac{100x}{100} = \frac{3.00}{100}$$

$$x = .03, \text{ or } \frac{3}{100}$$

17. (B) Solving the first equation for x as follows:

$$\frac{2}{x} = 4$$

$$2 = 4x$$

$$\frac{2}{4} = x$$

Therefore $\frac{1}{2} = x$

Now solving the second equation for y,

$\frac{2}{y} = 8$

$2 = 8y$

$\frac{2}{8} = y$

Therefore $\frac{1}{4} = y$

Substituting these values for $x - y$ gives $\frac{1}{2} - \frac{1}{4} = \frac{2}{4} - \frac{1}{4} = \frac{1}{4}$

Therefore, $x - y = \frac{1}{4}$, and the correct answer is (B).

18. (A) b = Bob's age
    c = Jane's age
    d = Jim's age

Since Bob is older than Jane, we have $c < b$.
Since Bob is younger than Jim, we have $b < d$.
Hence, $c < b$ and $b < d$, or $c < b < d$.

19. (D) Breaking the figure into squares of side x by adding lines gives

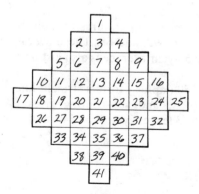

1
2 3 4
5 6 7 8 9
10 11 12 13 14 15 16
17 18 19 20 21 22 23 24 25
26 27 28 29 30 31 32
33 34 35 36 37
38 39 40
41

Remember each square has area x^2. Then the total area is $41x^2$.

20. (D) Circumference = πd

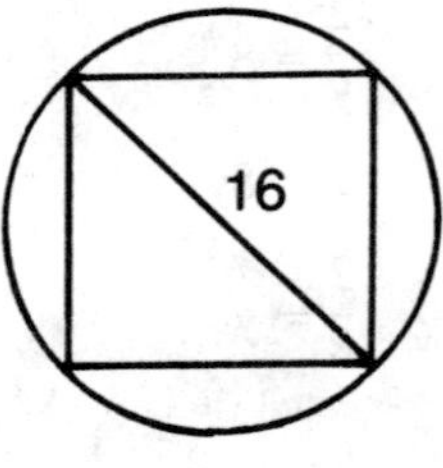

$16\pi = \pi d$
$d = 16$

diameter of circle = diagonal of square
area of square = ½ (product of diagonals)

$= \frac{1}{2} d_1 \times d_2$
$= \frac{1}{2}(16)(16) = 128$

21. (E) There were 4 days where the maximum temperature exceeded the average, thus 4/7 is approximately 57%.

22. (C) The increase was 94 − 84 = 10. The percent increase is found by dividing the increase by the *original* or *from* amount. Thus 10/84 = 11.9%.

23. (B) The greatest difference between the maximum for 1979 and the 50-year average was 5 degrees, which occurred on July 12.

24. (E) The chart gives only the *maximum* temperature readings for these days in 1979. While one can determine an average *maximum* temperature, or a 50-year average, there is not enough information to determine an *average* temperature for these days in 1979.

25. (B) The maximum temperatures for July 10 to 16, 1979, were 92, 90, 84, 86, 94, 92, and 88. These average to just under 90 degrees. The 50-year average is also just under 90 degrees.

26. (C) $x + y = 180$ (x plus y form a straight line, or straight angle) since $x = (\frac{2}{3})y$, and substituting gives $(\frac{2}{3})y + y = 180$. Multiplying by 3 leaves $2y + 3y = 540$, and solving

$5y = 540$
$y = 108$

27. (D) Perimeter of $\triangle$MNP = ½ (perimeter of $\triangle$XYZ)
= ½ (XY + YZ + XZ)
= ½ (10 + 15 + 17)
= ½ (42)

Perimeter of $\triangle$MNP = 21

28. (C) For $(a^2 - b^2)/(a - b) = a + b$ to be true, the denominator $a - b$ cannot equal zero, therefore a cannot equal b; $a > b$ is sufficient for this.

29. (D) Set up the equation as follows: Let t be the length of time it will take the plane to overtake the bus; then $t + 4$ is the time that the bus has traveled before the plane starts. The distance that the bus has traveled by 1:00 P.M. is $50(t + 4)$, since distance equals rate times time ($d = rt$). The distance the plane will travel is $300t$. Now equating these two (they will have to travel the same distance for one to overtake the other), gives $50(t + 4) = 300t$.

Solve the equation as follows:

$$50(t + 4) = 300t$$
$$50t + 200 = 300t$$
$$200 = 250t$$

Therefore $\frac{4}{5} = t$

⅘ of an hour (⅘ × 60) is 48 minutes. Hence it will take 48 minutes for the plane to overtake the bus; and since the plane is starting at 1:00 P.M., it will overtake the bus at 1:48 P.M.

30. (D) Let x = the missing number.
Since the average of x and z is y, we have

$\frac{1}{2}(x + z) = y$
$2 \cdot \frac{1}{2}(x + z) = 2y$
$x + z = 2y$
$x + z - z = 2y - z$
$x = 2y - z$

SECTION III: ANALYTICAL ABILITY

Using the information in the conditions for questions 1–6, the following charts could be drawn:

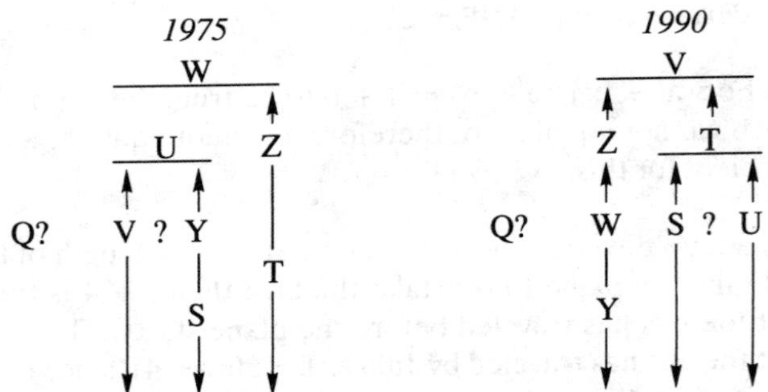

1. (E) In 1975 Zimino's cavities outnumbered Tav's; in 1990 Zimino's cavities outnumbered Waud's. Therefore, Zimino could not have had the fewest number of cavities in either of those years.

2. (E) Since we have no information about Quincy, Quincy could have been fourth lowest, or lowest, second lowest, third lowest, fifth lowest, etc. That allows all but Vinton the possibility of being fourth lowest in 1990. Vinton could have been only the highest or second highest (if Quincy was the highest).

3. (E) If Ulmer had more cavities than Waud, then Ulmer must also have more cavities than Yu.

4. (B) II only. The only definitive information in both years can be drawn between Waud and Yu. Waud had more cavities than Yu in both 1975 and 1990.

5. (D) Only Waud's cavities definitely outnumbered Yu's cavities in each of the years; therefore, Waud's total must be greater than Yu's.

6. (A) Disregarding Quincy, if three patients had the same number of fewest cavities in 1975, those three patients must have been Vinton, Sonntag, and Tav, since those are the only three who could be tied with the fewest number in that year. Disregarding Quincy, if three patients had the same number of fewest cavities in

1990, those patients must have been Yu, Sonntag, and Ulmer. Since Sonntag is the only patient who had fewest in both years, Sonntag must have had the fewest total cavities in both years.

7. (E) Choices (A), (B), and (C) have two women sitting in adjacent seats. Choice (D) has Jack sitting next to Irving.

8. (A) Choices (B), (C), and (D) have two women sitting in adjacent seats. (Note how the woman at the end of the list is next to Laurie.) In addition, Choice (C) does not have Karla sitting between George and Frank. Choice (E) has Jack listed a second time with no empty seat.

9. (D) Choices (A), (B), and (C) do not have Karla sitting next to both George and Frank. Choice (E) has two men sitting in adjacent seats.

10. (C) III only. Three distinct and opposing theories are presented, but the author takes no position favoring any one of them.

11. (D) If workers are allowed to choose, those workers who prefer the four-day schedule and work well on it will not be joined by those who prefer the five-day schedule and work better in those hours. If the randomly chosen sample is a true sample, the workers will be more productive when they select the schedule.

12. (E) While the passage appears to support SA, the final sentence repudiates the evidence by stating that weak results were generated from a great number of trials which were not conducted under reproducible conditions. Therefore, the author assumes that one basis for scientific proof requires significant results from reproducible conditions.

From the information contained in the conditions for questions 13–17, the following diagram can be drawn:

E	L	E	L	E	L
Jackson?	Jackson?	Klein	Landau?	Landau?	Morris
5 A.M.	6 A.M.	7 A.M.	8 A.M.	9 A.M.	10 A.M.
then Streamliner		*if Coast*		*then Flyer*	*Beamer*

Zephyr—— *before* —— Coast

13. (E) I, II, and III. Jackson's train departs at either 5 A.M. or 6 A.M.; Landau's train departs at either 8 A.M. or 9 A.M. Therefore, there may be two, three, or four hours between Jackson's and Landau's trains.

14. (B) Choices (A) and (E) are not possible because the Coast precedes the Zephyr. (D) is not possible because the Coast, an express, must depart at an odd-numbered hour. Choice (C) is not possible because if the Coast departs at 7 A.M., then the Streamliner, not the Flyer, must depart at 5 A.M.

15. (E) If Klein rides the Streamliner (at 7 A.M.), then the Coast must depart at 9 A.M. (in order for the Zephyr to depart before the Coast does), and the Flyer must depart at 5 A.M.

16. (D) None of the express trains (Flyer, Streamliner, and Coast) leave at an even-numbered hour, and we know the Beamer departs at 10 A.M.

17. (A) The chart now looks like this:

E	L	E	L	E	L
Jackson	Klein	Landau?	Landau?	Landau?	Morris
5 A.M.	7 A.M.	9 A.M.	11 A.M.	1 P.M.	3 P.M.

Beamer

It is not possible for Klein to ride the Coast, since this would make the Streamliner depart at 5 A.M. *and* make the Zephyr, which leaves before the Coast, also depart at 5 A.M.

18. (C) If Stuart wins the first and second rounds, and Riley wins the sixth round, then Riley must also have won the third round. (If Riley doesn't win the third round, the match will be over.) So the winners of the rounds are

①	②	③	④	⑤	⑥	⑦	⑧	⑨	⑩
S	S	R			R				

We don't know if Riley wins either the fourth or fifth round, but we do know that since he wins the third round, he must win at least one point in the fourth round.

19. (C) If Stuart loses the eighth round and the match is therefore over, then Riley must have won the sixth, seventh, and eighth rounds. Stuart therefore could have won the first, second, fourth, and fifth rounds:

①	②	③	④	⑤	⑥	⑦	⑧	⑨	⑩
S	S	R	S	S	R	R	R		

Stuart could have won all three points in the first and second rounds, must have won one point in the third round and two points in the fourth round (since Riley will have won one point in the fourth round), could have won all three points in the fifth round, and one point each in the sixth, seventh, and eighth rounds. Total: 15.

20. (C) Because Stuart loses in the fourth round and the match is over, Riley must have won the second, third, and fourth rounds. Therefore Stuart must have won the first round. The least number of points Stuart must have in all the rounds fought are: at least two from having won the first round and one for the second round—a minimum of three points.

21. (A) If Stuart wins the first and third rounds, and Riley wins the sixth and seventh rounds . . .

①	②	③	④	⑤	⑥	⑦	⑧	⑨	⑩
S		S			R	R			

Now we can deduce that Riley must have won the second round, and Stuart must have won the fifth and eighth:

①	②	③	④	⑤	⑥	⑦	⑧	⑨	⑩
S	R	S		S	R	R	S		

And therefore Riley must have won the fourth:

①	②	③	④	⑤	⑥	⑦	⑧	⑨	⑩
S	R	S	R	S	R	R	S		

At this point we know that Riley won exactly two points for each of the second, fourth, and sixth rounds, and exactly one point for each of the third, fifth, and eighth rounds, for a subtotal of nine points. Since Riley must have won at least two points for the seventh round, Riley has a minimum of eleven points through eight rounds.

22. (E) If Stuart won exactly three rounds of a match that goes the full ten rounds, then Stuart could have won:

①	②	③	④	⑤	⑥	⑦	⑧	⑨	⑩
R	R	S	R	R	S	R	R	S	R

OR

①	②	③	④	⑤	⑥	⑦	⑧	⑨	⑩
R	S	R	R	S	R	R	S	R	R

OR

①	②	③	④	⑤	⑥	⑦	⑧	⑨	⑩
R	R	S	R	S	R	R	S	R	R

OR

①	②	③	④	⑤	⑥	⑦	⑧	⑨	⑩
R	R	S	R	R	S	R	S	R	R

Etc.

You can see that Stuart could have won the second, fifth, and eighth, and the match would still have gone the full ten rounds.

23. (B) Choices (A), (C), (D), and (E) would be logical conclusions. But entomologists who are skeptical about mimicry will not be "astonished" by a finding that supports their ideas.

24. (E) Since the survey does not state that respondents regularly purchased *only* American toothpaste, *only* National toothpaste, or *only* Brighten toothpaste, the most reasonable inference that can be made is that some of the respondents questioned must have regularly purchased at least two different brands of toothpaste; exactly which ones we do not know. This would explain why the percentage totals more than 100%.

25. (E) While (A) is partially true, it is correct only up to a seven, after which it is no longer correct. Only (E) accurately expresses the point of the passage: that group pressure can alter a subject's judgment.

SECTION IV: QUANTITATIVE ABILITY

Quantitative Comparison

1. (A) Changing column A to decimals

$$\frac{1}{3} \times \frac{2}{5} \times \frac{1}{8}$$

gives $.33\frac{1}{3} \times .4 \times .125$ which by inspection is greater than column B. Another method would be to change column B to all fractions and then compare.

2. (D) Since two dimensions, length and width, are necessary to find the area of a rectangle, and only one dimension is given in each case, then no comparison is possible. The correct answer is (D).

3. (C) This comparison should be made without any actual computation as follows:

35% of 50	50% of 35
$.35 \times 50$	$.50 \times 35$

Since 35×50 is on each side, and each column's answer has two decimal places, the quantities are equal.

Or $35/100 \times 50$ $\quad$ $50/100 \times 35$

$1/100 \times 35 \times 50 = 1/100 \times 50 \times 35$

4. (A) Since $a = 3b$ and $b = -2$, then $a = 3(-2) = -6$, substituting into the numerator of each expression (since the denominators are positive and alike, they can be eliminated)

$$\frac{a^2 + b}{\cancel{ab}} \qquad \frac{a + b^2}{\cancel{ab}}$$

$$(-6)^2 + -2 \qquad -6 + (-2)^2$$

$$36 + -2 \qquad -6 + 4$$

Therefore $34 > -2$

5. (A) To find the number of ways four books can be arranged on a shelf, you multiply $4 \times 3 \times 2 \times 1$ and get 24, which is greater than column B.

6. (A) The following diagrams show eight ways of going from A to B, and there are more.

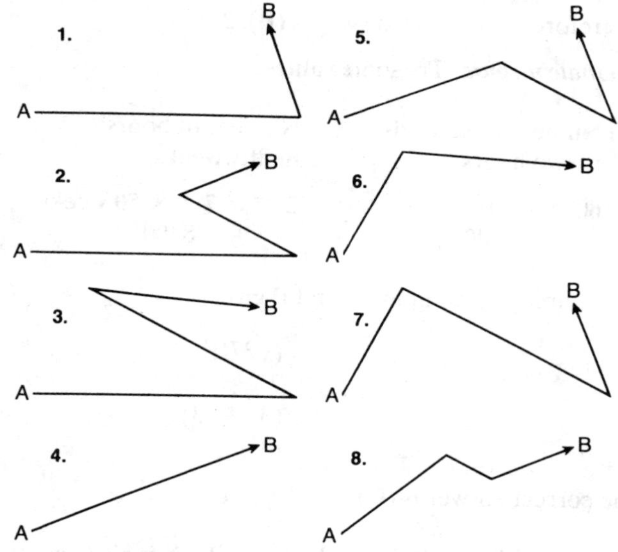

7. (C) Simplifying columns A and B leaves $x^{16}y^{24} = x^{16}y^{24}$. Note that when you have a number with an exponent to a power, you simply multiply the exponents together.

8. (B) Since d is above the x axis, it must be positive and c, being to the left of the y axis, must be negative. Therefore $c < d$, since all negatives are less than all positives.

9. (A) Since point P is above the line containing points $(-2, 2)$, then d (actual distance) is greater than $|c|$; therefore $c + d$ is a positive number. Point Q is on the line; therefore e and f are additive inverses of each other, totaling 0. All positive numbers are greater than 0, so $c + d > e + f$.

10. (B) Simplifying column A by using the distributing property, leaves

$(x + 1)(x + 2)$ and $(x + 1)(x + 3)$

Canceling $x + 1$ from each side, leaves $x + 2$ and $x + 3$. (This can be done because $x > 0$).
Then canceling x from each side gives 2 and 3.
Therefore the correct answer is (B), $2 < 3$.

Alternate method: Try some values.

11. (B) Number of seconds in two hours | Number of hours in fifty weeks

$60^{min} \times 60^{sec} \times 2$ hrs | $24^{hrs} \times 7^{days} \times 50$ weeks

7200 $<$ 8400

12. (C) Simplifying columns A and B gives

$$\sqrt{3^{18}} \qquad (\sqrt{27^3})^2$$
$$27^3$$
$$(3 \cdot 3 \cdot 3)^3$$
$$3^9 \quad = \quad (3^3)^3$$

The correct answer is (C).

13. (A) In the triangle $\angle Z$ must be 60° and $\angle X$ is given as 30°. Since the side across from the larger angle in a triangle is the longer side, then $XY > YZ$.

14. (B) The ratio of the sides of a 30-60-90 triangle is 1, 2, $\sqrt{3}$, and since the side across from 30° is 2, the side across from 60° is $2\sqrt{3}$. Compare each column by squaring the number outside and multiply by the numbers under the radical.

$$2\sqrt{3} \qquad 3\sqrt{2}$$
$$\sqrt{3 \cdot 4} \qquad \sqrt{2 \cdot 9}$$
$$\sqrt{12} \quad < \quad \sqrt{18}$$

15. (C) Cross multiplying the values in each column gives

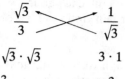

$$\frac{\sqrt{3}}{3} \quad \times \quad \frac{1}{\sqrt{3}}$$

$$\sqrt{3} \cdot \sqrt{3} \qquad\qquad 3 \cdot 1$$

Therefore $3 = 3$

Math Ability

16. (B) Substituting:

If $x = -2$, $x^3 - x^2 - x - 1 = (-2)^3 - (-2)^2 - (-2) - 1$

$$= -8 - 4 + 2 - 1$$
$$= -12 + 2 - 1$$
$$= -10 - 1$$
$$= -11$$

Hence $x^3 - x^2 - x - 1 = -11$

17. (A) Since the sum of the angles is 180° we have

$$m + n + 72 + 25 = 180$$
$$m + n + 97 = 180$$
$$m + n = 180 - 97$$
$$m + n = 83$$

Hence the sum of $m + n$ is 83°.

18. (B) Since the square of a positive number is a positive number, choice (B) is the correct answer.

19. (C) In this type of problem (weighted average) you must multiply the number of students times their respective scores and divide this total by the number of students as follows:

$$15 \times 80 = 1200$$
$$10 \times 90 = 900$$
$$\text{total} \quad 25 \qquad 2100$$

Now divide 25 into 2100. This leaves an average of 84%; therefore the correct answer is (C).

20. (D) Since it takes the pipe t hours to drain the tank completely, it will drain 1/t part of the tank each hour.
Hence in three hours, it will drain 3(1/t), or 3/t, part of the tank.

21. (A) From the bottom graph we see that make B amounted to about 60% of the total domestic sales in July. Thus, 60% of 1,220,000 is about 732,000.

22. (E) If you thought the answer was June, look again at the graph. The bottom of the graph is cut off, so the domestic portion of the column appears shorter than it really is.

23. (C) From the upper graph, we see that all the columns except one are more than 1,000,000, and all the columns except two are less than 1,200,000. Thus the average is between 1.0 and 1.2 million. Taking the time to add up all the months' totals and divide by 12 is not a good use of time.

24. (B) Percent increase is figured by dividing the difference of the two months' sales by the starting month's sales. June is approximately 1100 and December is approximately 1400, hence

$$\frac{1400 - 1100}{1100} = \frac{300}{1100} \cong 30\%$$

25. (C) In September, domestic auto sales were approximately 1150, and imports were approximately 175: 1150/175, or about 6½ to 1. None of the other choices is as high as this ratio.

26. (E) Let x equal the length of a side of the cube. The volume V = x^3 and the surface area S = $6x^2$.

Since V = S
$x^3 = 6x^2$
Hence x = 6

27. (C) Let

x = length of equal sides in feet
$x + 8$ = length of base in feet

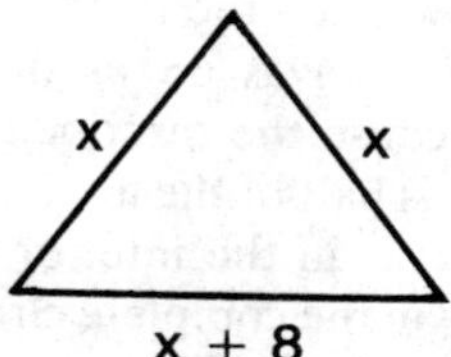

Since the perimeter is 89 feet, we have

$$x + x + (x + 8) = 89$$
$$3x + 8 = 89$$
$$3x + 8 - 8 = 89 - 8$$
$$3x = 81$$
$$\frac{3x}{3} = \frac{81}{3}$$
$$x = 27$$

Hence the length of the base is $x + 8$, or 35 feet.

28. (B) Check each possible pair of numbers for common divisions. For example:

I. 3 } Only common divisor 1;
II. 4 } these are relatively prime.

I. 3 } Only common divisor 1;
III. 7 } these are relatively prime.

I. 3 } Common divisors are 1 and 3;
IV. 12 } these are *not* relatively prime.

29. (A) $(-2, 3) \otimes (4, -1) = [(-2)(4) - (3)(-1), (-2)(-1)]$
$= [(-8) - (-3), (2)]$
$= (-5, 2)$

30. (B) Since ABCD is a rhombus, all sides are equal; therefore BC = CD = 6 and BC + CD = 12. AB = 6, minus AE ≅ 4, leaves 6 − 4 ≅ 2, which is the approximate length of BE. Adding 12 + 2 = 14, gives the distance around the rhombus that will be traveled. Now using the formula for circumference of a circle = $2\pi r$, or πd, leaves 6π as the circumference of the complete circle. Because the inscribed angle is 45°, arc DE is 90° (inscribed angle is half of the arc it intercepts). This 90° will not be traveled, as it is in the interior of the figure; therefore only 270° of the 360° in the complete circle will be traveled, or ¾ of the circle. $\frac{3}{4} \times 6\pi = 9\pi/2$. This added to the original 14 gives answer (B) $14 + 9\pi/2$.

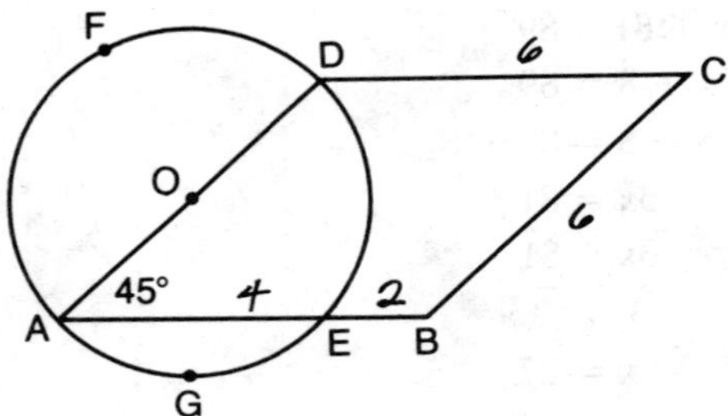

SECTION V: VERBAL ABILITY

Sentence Completion

1. (C) The correct choice is *aftermath . . . cause.* The best clue in this sentence comes from the second part of the sentence. The logical activity of an arson squad *after* a fire would be to *uncover* a *cause.* None of the other second word choices fit the context in this case. From this second word, work back to the first.

2. (A) The correct answer is *facile . . . awkward.* There is a definitional clue in this sentence in the word *fundamental.* The first blank requires a word which is somewhat synonymous with this word. The signal word *although* sets up a contrast construction so that a word opposite in meaning to the first blank is required for the second. The only pair with a word that fits the first blank's definition and has a contrasting second term is (A).

3. (A) The correct choice is *dissonance.* The clue words are *tone* and *decline.* The appropriate choice must be a term which both is negative and relates to *tone.*

4. (B) *Backbone* corresponds with *belly,* and *backbone* is to *belly* in the same way as *hard* is to *vulnerable.* The correspondences indicate (B).

5. (C) The *but* makes clear that the missing verb should oppose *demanding* in the second half of the sentence. Either *relinquished,* (A), or *waived,* (C), makes sense, but in the context (war), the noun *reparations* is more suitable than *expenses.*

6. (B) The best choice is *potential.* The clue words in this sentence are *ratio* and *resistance.* The word *resistance* has a negative connotation. *Ratio* suggests that the answer will need to contrast with *resistance.* The only positive words provided as choices are (B), *potential,* and (C), *excitement. Excitement* does not provide the sentence with proper contextual meaning.

7. (A) These two blanks contrast each other; the first tells what there has been, the second what there has not been (what has been lacking). The two choices which offer contrasts are (A) and (D), and

(D) may be eliminated because its terms are not appropriate to a *description.*

8. (D) The correct answer is *trenchant.* This sentence's clue lies in the comparison. The answer must be similar to a *surgeon's scalpel.* The sharpness and keenness connoted by *trenchant* satisfy the context of the comparison.

9. (A) The key phrase here is *land as the basic element of wealth;* land equals wealth in a *feudal* society. Thus (A) is indicated.

Analogies

10. (E) A *scowl* and a *smile* are expressions of opposite feelings. The paired opposites here are *despair* and *hope.*

11. (B) The relation here is of one hundred to ten: a *dollar* (one hundred cents) to a *dime* (ten cents) or a *century* (one hundred years) to a *decade* (ten years).

12. (D) The verb here will correct the condition the noun describes. To *clarify* may alleviate *confusion;* to *mediate* may correct an *altercation* (a quarrel or dispute).

13. (B) A *lecher* is a person characterized by the vice of *lust* as a *glutton* is a person characterized by *greed* for food.

14. (A) A *moat* surrounds a *castle;* a *cummerbund* is an article of dress that goes around the *waist.*

15. (C) A *finch* (type of bird) is an object of study in *ornithology* (the study of birds) as a potsherd (fragment of pottery) is likely to be an object of study in *archeology* (study of ancient peoples).

16. (A) To *spangle* is to glitter, the antonym of *darken.* To *hug* (to cling to or cherish) is the antonym of to *abjure* (to renounce). Both verbs might be used with a belief as object.

17. (C) The *nymph* and *faun* are female and male creatures of myth. The parallel here is *duck* and *drake.*

18. (E) A *rune* is a character in an ancient *alphabet,* a part of a whole, as a *star* is a part of a *constellation.*

Reading Comprehension

19. (B) The language spoken by Eskimos has more than 10,000 words, while the whites' version has between 300 and 600 words.

20. (C) Since the similar jargon was invented to avoid learning the difficult language of the Eskimos, it is logical to infer that the pidgin used in Asia was developed because of the difficulty of Chinese.

21. (B) The passage takes issue with the assumption that "primitive" cultures have simple languages. The first and third assertions are counter to what the passage suggests.

22. (E) The passage uses Eskimos to show how a "primitive" language may be large and complex.

23. (D) Choices (A), (B), and (E) do not apply to science fiction as opposed to other fiction genres. Choice (C) may or may not be true. Since science fiction is concerned wih the *relation between man and his technology,* it follows that as technology becomes more important, the fiction of technology would become more popular.

24. (D) Paragraph two defines science fiction as postulating a change from known to unknown conditions.

25. (D) The last sentence of the third paragraph explains why science fiction is called a sub-genre of fiction.

26. (C) Though short stories are a possible source, it is more probable that the longer novel is the source of science fiction films. The passage alludes to the scarcity of science fiction works in poetry or drama.

27. (A) The theme is the controlling idea or meaning of a work of literature.

28. (E) The final sentence presents a general comparison between *any other story or novel* and science fiction, emphasizing their similarities, and thus suggesting that the sub-genre of science fiction should be read as one reads fiction in general.

29. (C) The first paragraph leads up to the central question—*What is science fiction?* All of the passage is an attempt to answer that question. Choices (A) and (D) are too specific; (B) is too general; and (E) does not fit the tone of the passage.

Antonyms

30. (C) *Luxuriant* (*luxus* = extravagance) means plentiful and is usually used to describe something which is abundant in growth. The opposite is *small. Miserly* is also opposite to plentiful, but since it refers to hoarding money, it is more nearly opposite to the idea of abundant wealth, not abundant growth.

31. (C) A *tyro* is a beginner at some particular profession, occupation, or art. The best opposite is (C) because it descibes someone who is advanced and accomplished at a particular profession.

32. (B) Something *ubiquitous* is something found, or existing, everywhere (*ubique* = everywhere). (B) refers to one particular place, and is therefore more nearly opposite than (A), since *hiding* could refer to several locations.

33. (C) To be *abstemious* is to be moderate in the use of food or drink. (*ab* = from; *temetum* = strong drink). Clearly, the opposite is *gluttonous.*

34. (A) Something *soporific* induces sleep (*sopor* = sleep). The best opposite is *exciting,* (A). *Terrific,* (B), is a fair choice, but not so associated with stimulation and wakefulness as (A).

35. (C) A *factotum* is a handyman, jack-of-all-trades (*facere* = do; *totum* = all). The most nearly opposite, then, is the term which opposes the *factotum's* broad talent with narrow talent: *specialist.*

36. (E) The verb *eschew* means to avoid, to get away from; the antonym is *court,* to seek, to try to get.

37. (B) *Mulct* means to deprive of a possession unjustly. It is a negative word, so its opposite is a positive one; the only clearly positive choice is (B).

SECTION VI: ANALYTICAL ABILITY

From the conditions given for questions 1–7, we can deduce that the dollar bill must be the bet in Deal 4, since the bill cannot be bet prior to any coin.

1. (E) If the silver dollar is not bet in Deal 2, it must be bet in Deal 1 in order to be bet before Deal 3. Since the silver dollar is bet in Deal 1, Deal 2 must begin with a bet of two quarters. Only choice (E) does not begin Deal 2 with a bet of two quarters and is therefore the correct answer.

2. (B) If a quarter is the last bet before the silver dollar is bet, then the silver dollar is bet in Deal 2 and must be followed in the next deal (Deal 3) by two quarters. This is choice (B).

3. (D) Since the silver dollar is bet before Deal 3, it is bet in either Deal 1 or Deal 2. Therefore, two quarters will be bet at the beginning of Deal 2 or Deal 3:

Deal 1	*Deal 2*	*Deal 3*	*Deal 4*
$	Q Q		D

OR

Deal 1	*Deal 2*	*Deal 3*	*Deal 4*
	$	Q Q	D

Since two quarters are initiating either Deal 2 or Deal 3, a quarter cannot end each of two deals (and still have the bets in each deal equal $1.00). Therefore, the two deals each ending with a bet of the same denomination coin must end with half dollars:

Deal 1	*Deal 2*	*Deal 3*	*Deal 4*
$	Q Q H	Q Q H	D

OR

Deal 1	*Deal 2*	*Deal 3*	*Deal 4*
Q Q H	$	Q Q H	D

4. (A) Only (A) is possible. In choices (B) and (D), quarters do not immediately follow the silver-dollar bet. In (C) there are too many half dollars and not enough quarters; in (E) there are too many half dollars and quarters and no silver dollar.

5. (D) I and II only cannot be true. If the betting sequence in Deal 2 and Deal 3 are the same, the silver dollar is bet in Deal 1. That requires Deal 2 to begin with two quarters, and so the same is true with Deal 3.

6. (A) II and IV only. The betting sequence of "quarter than half dollar then quarter" cannot happen in Deal 4, which must be the dollar bill. Also "quarter then half dollar then quarter" cannot happen in Deal 2 because then the silver dollar must be bet in Deal 1 and would then not be immediately followed by a bet of two quarters.

7. (C) If one half dollar is exchanged for two quarters, choice (C) is possible. Choices (A) and (D) still contain two half dollars (and also total more than $1.00 in a single deal), (B) has the dollar bill bet prior to a coin, and (E) does not follow the silver dollar with a bet of two quarters.

8. (D) Because two trees are different, one may not therefore conclude that what is important for one tree will not necessarily be important for another. For example, two human beings may be different, yet food, oxygen, and shelter are important for each. The passage incorrectly assumes that a thorough dousing of water is important *only* for young redwood saplings.

9. (A) The author maintains, in the last sentence, that the rain forest is *vital to the well-being and continuation of earth's fragile ecological system.* Therefore, the author implies that future generations depend upon the continued health of the rain forests.

10. (B) For the author to make conclusions about human behavior based upon observations of rat behavior, the author must assume that conclusions about human behavior can be based upon what is learned from rat behavior. None of the other choices is an essential assumption for the author's argument.

For the information given for questions 11–17, the following diagram can be drawn:

E	E	E	E	E
E	~~C~~		D	E
E		B		E
E	~~B~~ ~~C~~		A	E
E	E	E	E	E

Since no two plains regions with a common side are controlled by the same leader, and since Escargo does not control any plains, East Plains must be controlled by Capshaw:

E	E	E	E	E
E	~~C~~		D	E
E		B	C	E
E	~~B~~ ~~C~~		A	E
E	E	E	E	E

11. (E) Escargo controls only the 16 border regions.

12. (A) If Alicia controls as few regions as possible, the map could look like this:

E	E	E	E	E
E	B	C	D	E
E	C	B	C	E
E	D	C	A	E
E	E	E	E	E

Alicia would control only the Southeast Plain.

13. (E) If Descarte controls only the Northeast, the West Plain cannot be controlled by Alicia because that would leave Descarte to also control the Southwest Plain:

E	E	E	E	E
E	~~C~~		D	E
E	A	B	C	E
E	~~B~~ ~~C~~		A	E
E	E	E	E	E

14. (D) If West Plain is controlled by Alicia and South Plain is controlled by Descarte, that eliminates all leaders from control of the Southwest Plain:

E	E	E	E	E
E	~~C~~		D	E
E	A	B	C	E
E	~~B~~ ~~C~~	D	A	E
E	E	E	E	E

15. (C) III only. If the Southwest Plain is controlled by Descarte, then the South Plain must be controlled by Capshaw:

E	E	E	E	E
E	Ȼ		D	E
E		B	C	E
E	D	C	A	E
E	E	E	E	E

16. (C) If Capshaw controls as many regions as possible, Capshaw would control the North, South, East, and West regions:

E	E	E	E	E
E	Ȼ	C	D	E
E	C	B	C	E
E	Ȼ Ƀ	C	A	E
E	E	E	E	E

17. (D) The South region cannot be controlled by Alicia, since the Southeast region is controlled by Alicia and those two plains regions have a common side.

From the information given in the conditions for questions 18–22, the following diagram can be drawn:

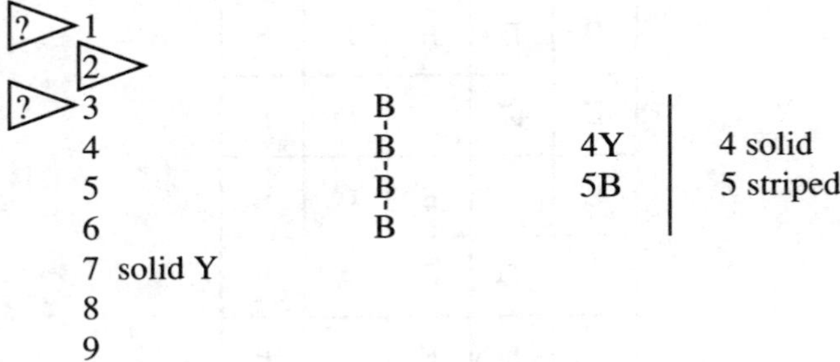

18. (B) If blue pennants fly at the top and bottom, and since we know 7 is yellow, then the four blue pennants which fly next to each other can be only in places 1 through 4. Since the remaining pennants are yellow, a yellow pennant flies in place 8.

19. (E) I, II, and III. If a yellow pennant flies in place 2, then the four blue pennants flying together must be in 3 through 6. That leaves each of places 1, 2, 8, and 9 to a yellow pennant or the final blue pennant.

20. (D) Of those places listed, only place 6 can have a blue pennant between two yellows and still allow the four blue pennants to fly next to each other. Place 8 is also possible, but that is not one of the choices listed.

21. (E) If all the yellow pennants fly next to each other, they will fly in places 5 through 8 or 6 through 9. Since the triangular pennants are either in places 1 and 2 or in places 2 and 3, it is not possible for a yellow pennant to be triangular.

22. (E) If all four solid pennants fly next to each other, they will be in places 6 through 9, 5 through 8, or 4 through 7. Since the two triangular pennants are in places 1 and 2 or places 2 and 3, none of the solid pennants will be triangular.

23. (C) General statistics for populations do not necessarily correlate to any one individual. For example, because 40% of the citizenry of the United States gives birth does not mean that every United States citizen (for example, a man) has a 40% chance to give birth.

24. (C) As stated in the catalogue, some undergraduates will, at the end of four years, have demonstrated the ability to write original material, either fiction or nonfiction. While the other choices are possible, only (C) necessarily follows from the passage.

25. (D) Choices (A), (B), (C), and (E) are each possible, but none of them can necessarily be deduced. The only choice that is deducible ("must follow" or "necessarily true") is (D).

SECTION VII: QUANTITATIVE ABILITY

Quantitative Comparison

1. (A) There are 8 ones in 48. There are 6 tens in 68. Thus there are more ones in 48 than tens in 68.

2. (B) $\sqrt{48}$ is slightly less than $\sqrt{49}$. $\sqrt{49}$ is actually 7. Thus 7 is greater than $\sqrt{48}$.

3. (D) There are no conditions on which values we may plug in for x or y. Thus, if we use 0 for x and 1000 for y, then column B is greater. But if we use 1000 for x and 0 for y, column A is greater. So the answer is (D).

4. (C) There is no need to do any calculations for this problem. Column A can be written $(40/100) \times 60$. Column B can be written $(60/100) \times 40$. You should then note that both columns have $(40 \times 60)/100$.

5. (B) Subtracting in Column A, we get $.05 - .125 = -.075$. Our difference is a negative number. Thus the positive value in column B must be greater.

6. (D) The angles in column A (x, y, c) sum to the total of both vertical angles running up and down. The angles in column B (a, z, b) sum to the total of both vertical angles running side to side.

   As the diagram is not drawn to scale, it may look like this, in which case column A would be greater.

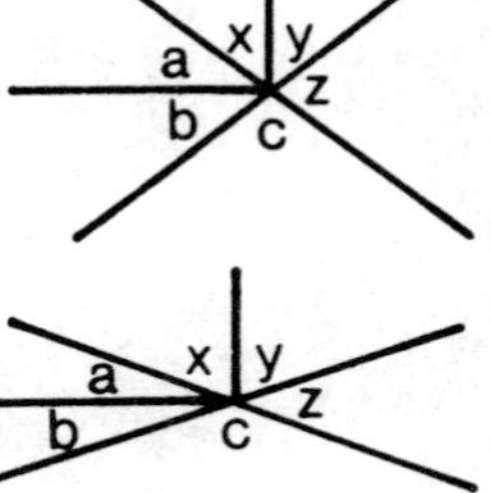

Or like this, in which case column B would be greater.

Or they could be equal.

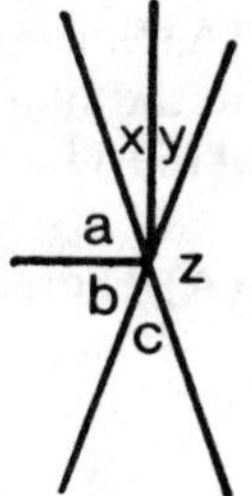

7. (A) In any triangle, the largest side is opposite the largest angle. Side x is opposite the right angle (90°), so it must be the largest side.

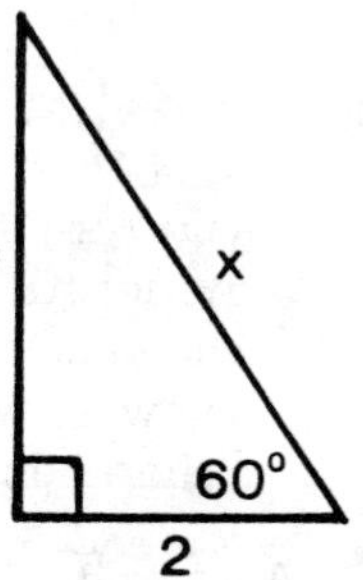

8. (C) The triangle is a 30°, 60°, 90° triangle, which mean its sides are in proportion 1, $\sqrt{3}$, 2. Since the smallest side (opposite the smallest angle, 30°) equals 2, then the other sides must be $2\sqrt{3}$ and 4. Thus x equals 4. So column B, x/2, equals 4/2 or 2.

9. (C) 1/20 equals 5/100, which is equal to 5%.

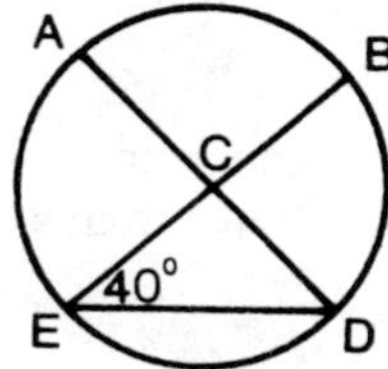

10. (C) $\angle$CED is given as 40°. Note that $\widehat{BD}$ is the arc that $\angle$CED intercepts. A rule in geometry states that any inscribed angle equals half the arc it intercepts, so column A equals column B.

11. (D) We have no way of knowing what the measures of the angles of the circle ($\angle$ACB or $\angle$ACE) are. Thus we cannot know the values of $\widehat{AE}$ or $\widehat{AB}$.

12. (A) Since ∠BCD is an exterior angle of △CED, then it is equal to the sum of the remote angles (∠CED + ∠CDE). Therefore, it must be greater than one of them.

13. (A) There are 9 diagonals in a hexagon, but only 6 sides.

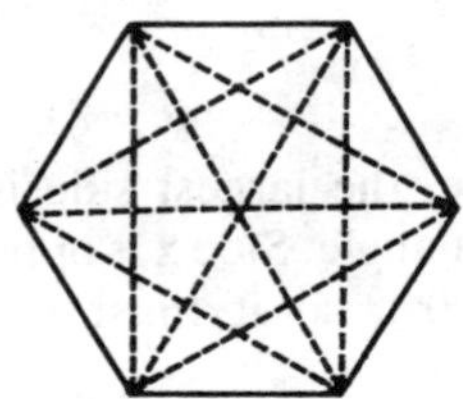

14. (D) A rhombus is a parallelogram with all sides equal. Column A (length of side AB) then equals 5 because the area of a rhombus equals *bh* ($20 = 4 \times$ base). But we have no way of knowing whether diagonal AC is the "long" diagonal or the "short" diagonal. (See the alternate drawings that follow.)

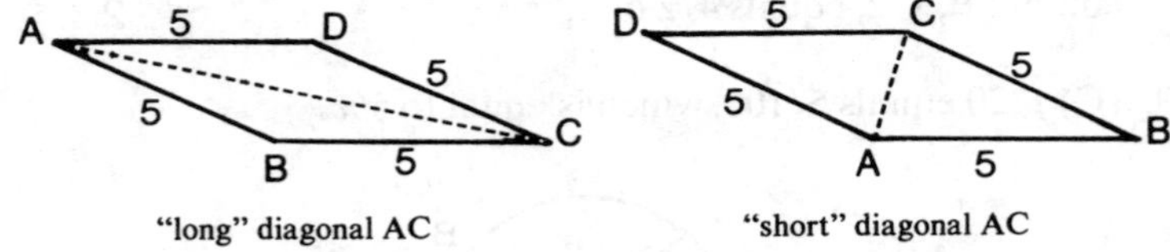

15. (B) Since T is greater than x, and m is greater than y, then T + m must always be greater than x + y.

Math Ability

16. (A) If $x - 4 = y$ then $y - x = -4$
Hence $(y - x)^3 = (-4)^3 = -64$

17. (D) If $a/b = c/d$ then, by cross multiplying, we get $ad = bc$.

If $d/b = c/a$ then we get the same result by cross multiplying, $ad = bc$.

Hence if $a/b = c/d$, then $d/b = c/a$

18. (C) Since two-thirds of the students are boys, we have $\frac{2}{3}(36) = 24$ boys in the class.
Out of the 24 boys in the class, three-fourths of them are under six feet tall or $\frac{3}{4}(24) = 18$ boys under six feet tall.

19. (B) This problem is most easily solved by working from the answers. Divide each of the answers by 5 and notice that choice (C) is eliminated, since it does not give a remainder of 1.

$$\frac{12}{5} = 2r2; \frac{16}{5} = 3r1; \frac{21}{5} = 4r1; \frac{6}{5} = 1r1; \frac{11}{5} = 2r1$$

Now dividing the remaining choices by 3 gives

$$\frac{16}{3} = 5r1; \frac{21}{3} = 7; \frac{6}{3} = 2; \frac{11}{3} = 3r2$$

The correct choice is (B), 11, which when divided by 5 has a remainder of 1 and when divided by 3 has a remainder of 2.

20. (A) If 15 gumballs are picked from the bag, it is possible that 8 of them are red and 7 are green. On the next pick however (the 16th), one is assured of having one gumball of each color.

21. (C) City E cast 60% of its 4000 votes (2400) for candidate R.
City C cast 55% of its 6000 votes (3300) for candidate R.

22. (C) City B and city E are closer to the 100% point of candidate S than candidate T.

23. (E) Cities A and B cast the same percentage of votes for candidate R but different numbers of votes.

24. (E) For city D, 75% of 7000 = 5250.
For city A, 50% of 5000 = 2500.
For city B, 25% of 4000 = 1000.
For city C, 25% of 6000 = 1500.
Therefore 5250 plus 2500 plus 1000 plus 1500 equals 10,250.

25. (B) Only city D cast *more* than two-thirds for one candidate.

26. (D) Since $x/y = 3/4$, and $y/z = 12/13$, cross multiplying gives $4x = 3y$ and $12z = 13y$. Now solving each for x and z, respectively, $x = 3y/4$ and $z = 13y/12$. Hence

$$\frac{x}{z} = \frac{3y/4}{13y/12} = \frac{9y}{13y} = 9/13$$

27. (B) In the right triangle, if c = 2a, then angle a = 30° and c = 60°. Since angle f is supplementary to angle c, angle f must be 120°. If angle f is 120°, then there are 60° left to be divided between angles d and b (remember there are 180° in a triangle). Since d > 2b, then b must be less than 30; therefore the correct answer is (B), angle a (30°) is greater than angle b (less than 30°). Notice the way you should have marked the diagram to assist you.

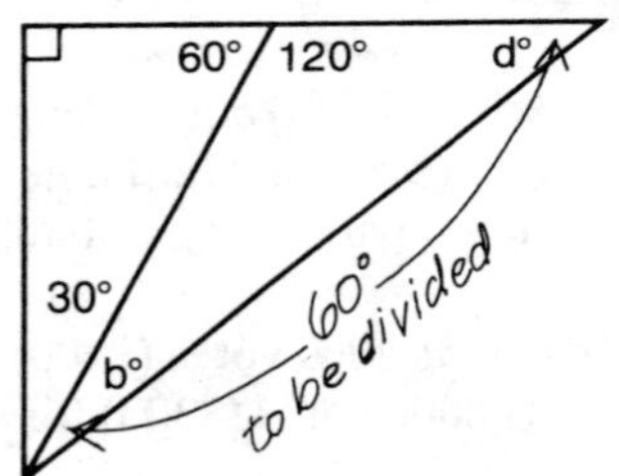

28. (B) Area of larger circle = 144π

Since area = πr^2, then

$\pi r^2 = 144\pi$
$r^2 = 144$
$r = 12$

Radius of larger circle = 12
Diameter of smaller circle = 12
Radius of smaller circle = 6

Area of smaller circle $= \pi r^2$
$= \pi(6)^2$
$= 36\pi$

29. (D) The only reasonable answer is $5\frac{5}{9}$ since 85¢ per pound is slightly closer to 93¢ per pound than 75¢ per pound, then slightly more than half of the 10 pounds must be 93¢ per pound.

Algebraically, let x stand for the pounds of 93¢ tea, then 10 − x is the 75¢ tea. This leads to the equation

$$.93x + .75\,(10 - x) = .85(10)$$

Solving gives $93x + 750 - 75x = 850$

$$18x = 100$$

$$x = \frac{100}{18}$$

Therefore $x = 5\frac{5}{9}$

30. (D) Since the surface area of side ABFE is 16, then each side is 4. Now use the Pythagorean theorem to find the length of the diagonal that is also the length of the rectangle.

$$4^2 + 4^2 = AH^2$$

$$16 + 16 = AH^2$$

$$32 = AH^2$$

$$\sqrt{32} = AH$$

Simplifying $\sqrt{32} = \sqrt{16 \times 2} = \sqrt{16} \times \sqrt{2} = 4\sqrt{2}$

Now multiplying length times width gives $4 \times 4\sqrt{2} = 16\sqrt{2}$

Notice you may have recognized the ratio of a 45°:45°:90° triangle as $1{:}1{:}\sqrt{2}$ and found the diagonal quickly using $4{:}4{:}4\sqrt{2}$.

PRACTICE TEST 2

Section I:	Quantitative Ability—30 Minutes; 30 Questions
Section II:	Verbal Ability—30 Minutes; 38 Questions
Section III:	Analytical Ability—30 Minutes; 25 Questions
Section IV:	Verbal Ability—30 Minutes; 39 Questions
Section V:	Quantitative Ability—30 Minutes; 30 Questions
Section VI:	Analytical Ability—30 Minutes; 25 Questions
Section VII:	Quantitative Ability—30 Minutes; 30 Questions

ANSWER SHEET FOR PRACTICE TEST 2
(Remove This Sheet and Use It to Mark Your Answers)

SECTION I

1 Ⓐ Ⓑ Ⓒ Ⓓ Ⓔ
2 Ⓐ Ⓑ Ⓒ Ⓓ Ⓔ
3 Ⓐ Ⓑ Ⓒ Ⓓ Ⓔ
4 Ⓐ Ⓑ Ⓒ Ⓓ Ⓔ
5 Ⓐ Ⓑ Ⓒ Ⓓ Ⓔ
6 Ⓐ Ⓑ Ⓒ Ⓓ Ⓔ
7 Ⓐ Ⓑ Ⓒ Ⓓ Ⓔ
8 Ⓐ Ⓑ Ⓒ Ⓓ Ⓔ
9 Ⓐ Ⓑ Ⓒ Ⓓ Ⓔ
10 Ⓐ Ⓑ Ⓒ Ⓓ Ⓔ
11 Ⓐ Ⓑ Ⓒ Ⓓ Ⓔ
12 Ⓐ Ⓑ Ⓒ Ⓓ Ⓔ
13 Ⓐ Ⓑ Ⓒ Ⓓ Ⓔ
14 Ⓐ Ⓑ Ⓒ Ⓓ Ⓔ
15 Ⓐ Ⓑ Ⓒ Ⓓ Ⓔ
16 Ⓐ Ⓑ Ⓒ Ⓓ Ⓔ
17 Ⓐ Ⓑ Ⓒ Ⓓ Ⓔ
18 Ⓐ Ⓑ Ⓒ Ⓓ Ⓔ
19 Ⓐ Ⓑ Ⓒ Ⓓ Ⓔ
20 Ⓐ Ⓑ Ⓒ Ⓓ Ⓔ
21 Ⓐ Ⓑ Ⓒ Ⓓ Ⓔ
22 Ⓐ Ⓑ Ⓒ Ⓓ Ⓔ
23 Ⓐ Ⓑ Ⓒ Ⓓ Ⓔ
24 Ⓐ Ⓑ Ⓒ Ⓓ Ⓔ
25 Ⓐ Ⓑ Ⓒ Ⓓ Ⓔ
26 Ⓐ Ⓑ Ⓒ Ⓓ Ⓔ
27 Ⓐ Ⓑ Ⓒ Ⓓ Ⓔ
28 Ⓐ Ⓑ Ⓒ Ⓓ Ⓔ
29 Ⓐ Ⓑ Ⓒ Ⓓ Ⓔ
30 Ⓐ Ⓑ Ⓒ Ⓓ Ⓔ

SECTION II

1 Ⓐ Ⓑ Ⓒ Ⓓ Ⓔ
2 Ⓐ Ⓑ Ⓒ Ⓓ Ⓔ
3 Ⓐ Ⓑ Ⓒ Ⓓ Ⓔ
4 Ⓐ Ⓑ Ⓒ Ⓓ Ⓔ
5 Ⓐ Ⓑ Ⓒ Ⓓ Ⓔ
6 Ⓐ Ⓑ Ⓒ Ⓓ Ⓔ
7 Ⓐ Ⓑ Ⓒ Ⓓ Ⓔ
8 Ⓐ Ⓑ Ⓒ Ⓓ Ⓔ
9 Ⓐ Ⓑ Ⓒ Ⓓ Ⓔ
10 Ⓐ Ⓑ Ⓒ Ⓓ Ⓔ
11 Ⓐ Ⓑ Ⓒ Ⓓ Ⓔ
12 Ⓐ Ⓑ Ⓒ Ⓓ Ⓔ
13 Ⓐ Ⓑ Ⓒ Ⓓ Ⓔ
14 Ⓐ Ⓑ Ⓒ Ⓓ Ⓔ
15 Ⓐ Ⓑ Ⓒ Ⓓ Ⓔ
16 Ⓐ Ⓑ Ⓒ Ⓓ Ⓔ
17 Ⓐ Ⓑ Ⓒ Ⓓ Ⓔ
18 Ⓐ Ⓑ Ⓒ Ⓓ Ⓔ
19 Ⓐ Ⓑ Ⓒ Ⓓ Ⓔ
20 Ⓐ Ⓑ Ⓒ Ⓓ Ⓔ
21 Ⓐ Ⓑ Ⓒ Ⓓ Ⓔ
22 Ⓐ Ⓑ Ⓒ Ⓓ Ⓔ
23 Ⓐ Ⓑ Ⓒ Ⓓ Ⓔ
24 Ⓐ Ⓑ Ⓒ Ⓓ Ⓔ
25 Ⓐ Ⓑ Ⓒ Ⓓ Ⓔ
26 Ⓐ Ⓑ Ⓒ Ⓓ Ⓔ
27 Ⓐ Ⓑ Ⓒ Ⓓ Ⓔ
28 Ⓐ Ⓑ Ⓒ Ⓓ Ⓔ
29 Ⓐ Ⓑ Ⓒ Ⓓ Ⓔ
30 Ⓐ Ⓑ Ⓒ Ⓓ Ⓔ
31 Ⓐ Ⓑ Ⓒ Ⓓ Ⓔ
32 Ⓐ Ⓑ Ⓒ Ⓓ Ⓔ
33 Ⓐ Ⓑ Ⓒ Ⓓ Ⓔ
34 Ⓐ Ⓑ Ⓒ Ⓓ Ⓔ
35 Ⓐ Ⓑ Ⓒ Ⓓ Ⓔ
36 Ⓐ Ⓑ Ⓒ Ⓓ Ⓔ
37 Ⓐ Ⓑ Ⓒ Ⓓ Ⓔ
38 Ⓐ Ⓑ Ⓒ Ⓓ Ⓔ

CUT HERE

ANSWER SHEET FOR PRACTICE TEST 2
(Remove This Sheet and Use It to Mark Your Answers)

SECTION III

1 Ⓐ Ⓑ Ⓒ Ⓓ Ⓔ
2 Ⓐ Ⓑ Ⓒ Ⓓ Ⓔ
3 Ⓐ Ⓑ Ⓒ Ⓓ Ⓔ
4 Ⓐ Ⓑ Ⓒ Ⓓ Ⓔ
5 Ⓐ Ⓑ Ⓒ Ⓓ Ⓔ

6 Ⓐ Ⓑ Ⓒ Ⓓ Ⓔ
7 Ⓐ Ⓑ Ⓒ Ⓓ Ⓔ
8 Ⓐ Ⓑ Ⓒ Ⓓ Ⓔ
9 Ⓐ Ⓑ Ⓒ Ⓓ Ⓔ
10 Ⓐ Ⓑ Ⓒ Ⓓ Ⓔ

11 Ⓐ Ⓑ Ⓒ Ⓓ Ⓔ
12 Ⓐ Ⓑ Ⓒ Ⓓ Ⓔ
13 Ⓐ Ⓑ Ⓒ Ⓓ Ⓔ
14 Ⓐ Ⓑ Ⓒ Ⓓ Ⓔ
15 Ⓐ Ⓑ Ⓒ Ⓓ Ⓔ

16 Ⓐ Ⓑ Ⓒ Ⓓ Ⓔ
17 Ⓐ Ⓑ Ⓒ Ⓓ Ⓔ
18 Ⓐ Ⓑ Ⓒ Ⓓ Ⓔ
19 Ⓐ Ⓑ Ⓒ Ⓓ Ⓔ
20 Ⓐ Ⓑ Ⓒ Ⓓ Ⓔ

21 Ⓐ Ⓑ Ⓒ Ⓓ Ⓔ
22 Ⓐ Ⓑ Ⓒ Ⓓ Ⓔ
23 Ⓐ Ⓑ Ⓒ Ⓓ Ⓔ
24 Ⓐ Ⓑ Ⓒ Ⓓ Ⓔ
25 Ⓐ Ⓑ Ⓒ Ⓓ Ⓔ

SECTION IV

1 Ⓐ Ⓑ Ⓒ Ⓓ Ⓔ
2 Ⓐ Ⓑ Ⓒ Ⓓ Ⓔ
3 Ⓐ Ⓑ Ⓒ Ⓓ Ⓔ
4 Ⓐ Ⓑ Ⓒ Ⓓ Ⓔ
5 Ⓐ Ⓑ Ⓒ Ⓓ Ⓔ

6 Ⓐ Ⓑ Ⓒ Ⓓ Ⓔ
7 Ⓐ Ⓑ Ⓒ Ⓓ Ⓔ
8 Ⓐ Ⓑ Ⓒ Ⓓ Ⓔ
9 Ⓐ Ⓑ Ⓒ Ⓓ Ⓔ
10 Ⓐ Ⓑ Ⓒ Ⓓ Ⓔ

11 Ⓐ Ⓑ Ⓒ Ⓓ Ⓔ
12 Ⓐ Ⓑ Ⓒ Ⓓ Ⓔ
13 Ⓐ Ⓑ Ⓒ Ⓓ Ⓔ
14 Ⓐ Ⓑ Ⓒ Ⓓ Ⓔ
15 Ⓐ Ⓑ Ⓒ Ⓓ Ⓔ

16 Ⓐ Ⓑ Ⓒ Ⓓ Ⓔ
17 Ⓐ Ⓑ Ⓒ Ⓓ Ⓔ
18 Ⓐ Ⓑ Ⓒ Ⓓ Ⓔ
19 Ⓐ Ⓑ Ⓒ Ⓓ Ⓔ
20 Ⓐ Ⓑ Ⓒ Ⓓ Ⓔ

21 Ⓐ Ⓑ Ⓒ Ⓓ Ⓔ
22 Ⓐ Ⓑ Ⓒ Ⓓ Ⓔ
23 Ⓐ Ⓑ Ⓒ Ⓓ Ⓔ
24 Ⓐ Ⓑ Ⓒ Ⓓ Ⓔ
25 Ⓐ Ⓑ Ⓒ Ⓓ Ⓔ

26 Ⓐ Ⓑ Ⓒ Ⓓ Ⓔ
27 Ⓐ Ⓑ Ⓒ Ⓓ Ⓔ
28 Ⓐ Ⓑ Ⓒ Ⓓ Ⓔ
29 Ⓐ Ⓑ Ⓒ Ⓓ Ⓔ
30 Ⓐ Ⓑ Ⓒ Ⓓ Ⓔ

31 Ⓐ Ⓑ Ⓒ Ⓓ Ⓔ
32 Ⓐ Ⓑ Ⓒ Ⓓ Ⓔ
33 Ⓐ Ⓑ Ⓒ Ⓓ Ⓔ
34 Ⓐ Ⓑ Ⓒ Ⓓ Ⓔ
35 Ⓐ Ⓑ Ⓒ Ⓓ Ⓔ

36 Ⓐ Ⓑ Ⓒ Ⓓ Ⓔ
37 Ⓐ Ⓑ Ⓒ Ⓓ Ⓔ
38 Ⓐ Ⓑ Ⓒ Ⓓ Ⓔ
39 Ⓐ Ⓑ Ⓒ Ⓓ Ⓔ

CUT HERE

ANSWER SHEET FOR PRACTICE TEST 2
(Remove This Sheet and Use It to Mark Your Answers)

SECTION V	SECTION VI	SECTION VII
1 Ⓐ Ⓑ Ⓒ Ⓓ Ⓔ	1 Ⓐ Ⓑ Ⓒ Ⓓ Ⓔ	1 Ⓐ Ⓑ Ⓒ Ⓓ Ⓔ
2 Ⓐ Ⓑ Ⓒ Ⓓ Ⓔ	2 Ⓐ Ⓑ Ⓒ Ⓓ Ⓔ	2 Ⓐ Ⓑ Ⓒ Ⓓ Ⓔ
3 Ⓐ Ⓑ Ⓒ Ⓓ Ⓔ	3 Ⓐ Ⓑ Ⓒ Ⓓ Ⓔ	3 Ⓐ Ⓑ Ⓒ Ⓓ Ⓔ
4 Ⓐ Ⓑ Ⓒ Ⓓ Ⓔ	4 Ⓐ Ⓑ Ⓒ Ⓓ Ⓔ	4 Ⓐ Ⓑ Ⓒ Ⓓ Ⓔ
5 Ⓐ Ⓑ Ⓒ Ⓓ Ⓔ	5 Ⓐ Ⓑ Ⓒ Ⓓ Ⓔ	5 Ⓐ Ⓑ Ⓒ Ⓓ Ⓔ
6 Ⓐ Ⓑ Ⓒ Ⓓ Ⓔ	6 Ⓐ Ⓑ Ⓒ Ⓓ Ⓔ	6 Ⓐ Ⓑ Ⓒ Ⓓ Ⓔ
7 Ⓐ Ⓑ Ⓒ Ⓓ Ⓔ	7 Ⓐ Ⓑ Ⓒ Ⓓ Ⓔ	7 Ⓐ Ⓑ Ⓒ Ⓓ Ⓔ
8 Ⓐ Ⓑ Ⓒ Ⓓ Ⓔ	8 Ⓐ Ⓑ Ⓒ Ⓓ Ⓔ	8 Ⓐ Ⓑ Ⓒ Ⓓ Ⓔ
9 Ⓐ Ⓑ Ⓒ Ⓓ Ⓔ	9 Ⓐ Ⓑ Ⓒ Ⓓ Ⓔ	9 Ⓐ Ⓑ Ⓒ Ⓓ Ⓔ
10 Ⓐ Ⓑ Ⓒ Ⓓ Ⓔ	10 Ⓐ Ⓑ Ⓒ Ⓓ Ⓔ	10 Ⓐ Ⓑ Ⓒ Ⓓ Ⓔ
11 Ⓐ Ⓑ Ⓒ Ⓓ Ⓔ	11 Ⓐ Ⓑ Ⓒ Ⓓ Ⓔ	11 Ⓐ Ⓑ Ⓒ Ⓓ Ⓔ
12 Ⓐ Ⓑ Ⓒ Ⓓ Ⓔ	12 Ⓐ Ⓑ Ⓒ Ⓓ Ⓔ	12 Ⓐ Ⓑ Ⓒ Ⓓ Ⓔ
13 Ⓐ Ⓑ Ⓒ Ⓓ Ⓔ	13 Ⓐ Ⓑ Ⓒ Ⓓ Ⓔ	13 Ⓐ Ⓑ Ⓒ Ⓓ Ⓔ
14 Ⓐ Ⓑ Ⓒ Ⓓ Ⓔ	14 Ⓐ Ⓑ Ⓒ Ⓓ Ⓔ	14 Ⓐ Ⓑ Ⓒ Ⓓ Ⓔ
15 Ⓐ Ⓑ Ⓒ Ⓓ Ⓔ	15 Ⓐ Ⓑ Ⓒ Ⓓ Ⓔ	15 Ⓐ Ⓑ Ⓒ Ⓓ Ⓔ
16 Ⓐ Ⓑ Ⓒ Ⓓ Ⓔ	16 Ⓐ Ⓑ Ⓒ Ⓓ Ⓔ	16 Ⓐ Ⓑ Ⓒ Ⓓ Ⓔ
17 Ⓐ Ⓑ Ⓒ Ⓓ Ⓔ	17 Ⓐ Ⓑ Ⓒ Ⓓ Ⓔ	17 Ⓐ Ⓑ Ⓒ Ⓓ Ⓔ
18 Ⓐ Ⓑ Ⓒ Ⓓ Ⓔ	18 Ⓐ Ⓑ Ⓒ Ⓓ Ⓔ	18 Ⓐ Ⓑ Ⓒ Ⓓ Ⓔ
19 Ⓐ Ⓑ Ⓒ Ⓓ Ⓔ	19 Ⓐ Ⓑ Ⓒ Ⓓ Ⓔ	19 Ⓐ Ⓑ Ⓒ Ⓓ Ⓔ
20 Ⓐ Ⓑ Ⓒ Ⓓ Ⓔ	20 Ⓐ Ⓑ Ⓒ Ⓓ Ⓔ	20 Ⓐ Ⓑ Ⓒ Ⓓ Ⓔ
21 Ⓐ Ⓑ Ⓒ Ⓓ Ⓔ	21 Ⓐ Ⓑ Ⓒ Ⓓ Ⓔ	21 Ⓐ Ⓑ Ⓒ Ⓓ Ⓔ
22 Ⓐ Ⓑ Ⓒ Ⓓ Ⓔ	22 Ⓐ Ⓑ Ⓒ Ⓓ Ⓔ	22 Ⓐ Ⓑ Ⓒ Ⓓ Ⓔ
23 Ⓐ Ⓑ Ⓒ Ⓓ Ⓔ	23 Ⓐ Ⓑ Ⓒ Ⓓ Ⓔ	23 Ⓐ Ⓑ Ⓒ Ⓓ Ⓔ
24 Ⓐ Ⓑ Ⓒ Ⓓ Ⓔ	24 Ⓐ Ⓑ Ⓒ Ⓓ Ⓔ	24 Ⓐ Ⓑ Ⓒ Ⓓ Ⓔ
25 Ⓐ Ⓑ Ⓒ Ⓓ Ⓔ	25 Ⓐ Ⓑ Ⓒ Ⓓ Ⓔ	25 Ⓐ Ⓑ Ⓒ Ⓓ Ⓔ
26 Ⓐ Ⓑ Ⓒ Ⓓ Ⓔ		26 Ⓐ Ⓑ Ⓒ Ⓓ Ⓔ
27 Ⓐ Ⓑ Ⓒ Ⓓ Ⓔ		27 Ⓐ Ⓑ Ⓒ Ⓓ Ⓔ
28 Ⓐ Ⓑ Ⓒ Ⓓ Ⓔ		28 Ⓐ Ⓑ Ⓒ Ⓓ Ⓔ
29 Ⓐ Ⓑ Ⓒ Ⓓ Ⓔ		29 Ⓐ Ⓑ Ⓒ Ⓓ Ⓔ
30 Ⓐ Ⓑ Ⓒ Ⓓ Ⓔ		30 Ⓐ Ⓑ Ⓒ Ⓓ Ⓔ

SECTION I: QUANTITATIVE ABILITY

Time: 30 Minutes
30 Questions

Quantitative Comparison

DIRECTIONS

In this section you will be given two quantities, one in column A and one in column B. You are to determine a relationship between the two quantities and mark

(A) if the quantity in column A is greater than the quantity in column B
(B) if the quantity in column B is greater than the quantity in column A
(C) if the quantities are equal
(D) if the comparison cannot be determined from the information that is given

Common Information:

Information centered above both columns refers to one or both columns.
All numbers used are real numbers.
Figures are intended to provide useful positional information, but are not necessarily drawn to scale and should not be used to estimate sizes by measurement.
Lines that appear straight can be assumed to be straight.

	Column A	Column B
1.	$\frac{3}{7} \times \frac{2}{5} \times \frac{5}{8}$	$\frac{2}{5} \times \frac{4}{11} \times \frac{5}{8}$
	$x < y < z$	
2.	$x + y + z$	xyz
	a,b,c, all greater than 0	
3.	$(b + c)a$	$ac + ab$

	Column A		Column B
		$x\sqrt{.09} = 2$	
4.	7		x
5.	Number of degrees in the interior angles of a pentagon		500°
		$x < y$	
6.	$(x - y)^2$		$x^2 - y^2$
7.	$\frac{1}{71} - \frac{1}{151}$		$\frac{1}{65} - \frac{1}{153}$
		$a = b$ $a < c$	
8.	2a		b +c

Questions 9–12 refer to the diagram.

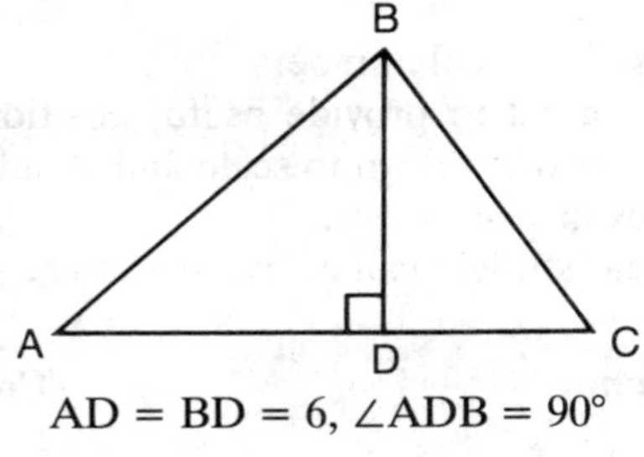

AD = BD = 6, ∠ADB = 90°

9.	AB	BC
10.	∠BAD	∠ABD
11.	∠DBC + ∠BCD	90°
12.	AB + BC	AC

	Column A	Column B
	$3x - 12y = 36$	
13.	$2x - 8y$	21
	$1 > x > 0$	
14.	x^{-2}	x^{-3}

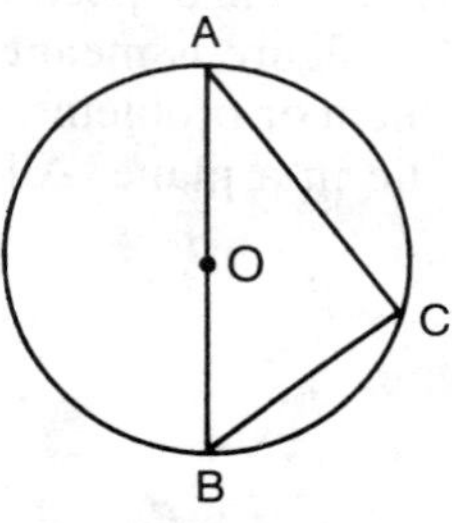

AB is a diameter

15.	$\angle ACB$	$180° - (\angle CAB + \angle ABC)$

Math Ability

DIRECTIONS

Solve each problem in this section by using the information given and your own mathematical calculations. Then select the *one* correct answer of the five choices given. Use the available space on the page for scratchwork. NOTE: Some problems may be accompanied by figures or diagrams. These figures are drawn as accurately as possible, *except* when it is stated in a specific problem that the figure is not drawn to scale. The figure is meant to provide information useful in solving the problem or problems. Unless otherwise stated or indicated, all figures lie in a plane. All numbers used are real numbers.

16. $\dfrac{2/3 - 1/2}{1/6 + 1/4 + 2/3} =$

(A) $2/13$
(B) $2/9$
(C) $13/20$
(D) $1\,1/13$
(E) $3\,1/4$

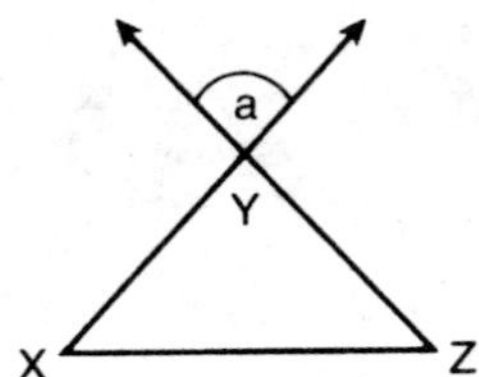

17. In $\triangle XYZ$, $XY = 10$, $YZ = 10$, and $\angle a = 84°$. What is the degree measure of $\angle Z$?

(A) 42°
(B) 48°
(C) 84°
(D) 96°
(E) cannot be determined

18. If it takes 18 minutes to fill ⅔ of a container, how long will it take to fill the rest of the container at the same rate?
(A) 6 minutes
(B) 9 minutes
(C) 12 minutes
(D) 27 minutes
(E) 36 minutes

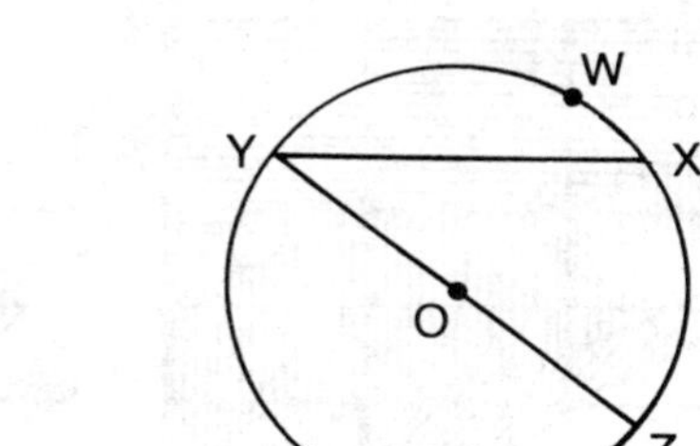

19. On the circle with center O, arc YWX equals 100°. What is the degree measure of ∠XYZ?
(A) 40°
(B) 50°
(C) 80°
(D) 100°
(E) 130°

20. The average of 9 numbers is 7, and the average of 7 other numbers is 9. What is the average of all 16 numbers?
(A) 8
(B) 7⅞
(C) 7½
(D) 7¼
(E) 7⅛

Questions 21–25 refer to the graphs.

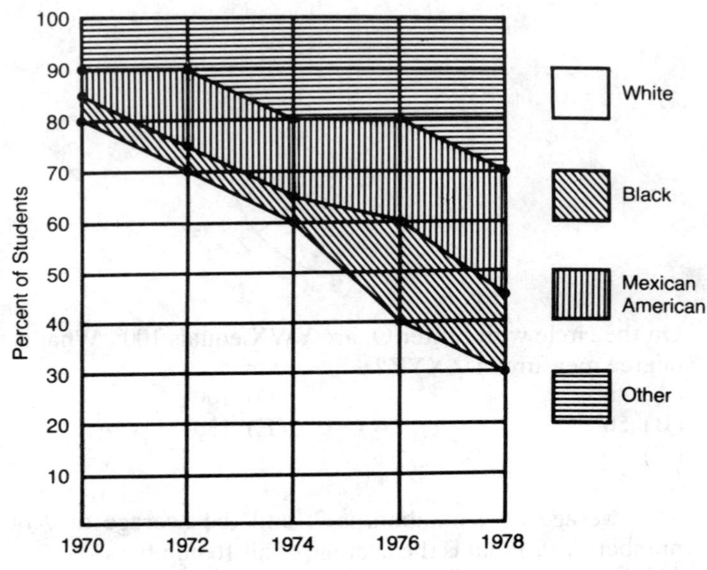

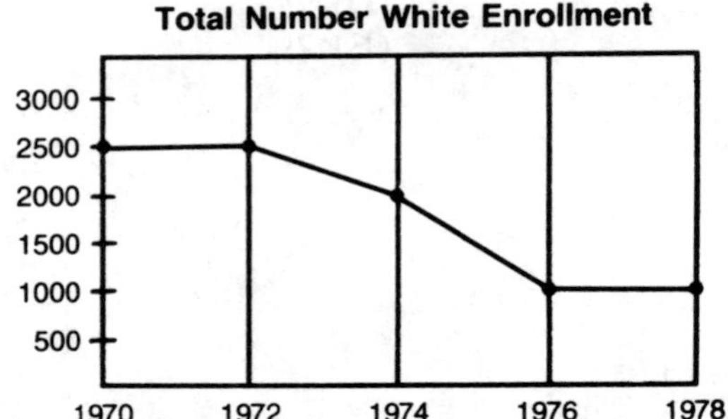

21. In which of the following years in the Northwood, California, School District did the number of white students exceed the number of students classified as "other"?

    I. 1974
    II. 1976
    III. 1978

    (A) I only
    (B) II only
    (C) III only
    (D) I and II only
    (E) I, II, and III

22. Approximately how many black students were enrolled in 1974?
    (A) 100
    (B) 167
    (C) 224
    (D) 300
    (E) 500

23. What was the total student enrollment in 1976?
    (A) 1000
    (B) 2400
    (C) 2500
    (D) 4000
    (E) 5000

24. Which of the indicated groups showed the largest percent change in percent breakdown from 1970 to 1978?
    (A) white
    (B) black
    (C) Mexican American
    (D) other
    (E) cannot be determined

25. What happened to the number of "other" students from 1974 to 1976?
    (A) same
    (B) up by less than 100
    (C) down by less than 100
    (D) up by more than 100
    (E) down by more than 100

26. If $n! = n \cdot (n-1) \cdot (n-2) \cdot (n-3) \ldots 2 \cdot 1$, what is the value of

$$\frac{(6!)(4!)}{(5!)(3!)}$$

(A) $\frac{5}{4}$
(B) $\frac{8}{5}$
(C) 10
(D) 24
(E) 1152

27. If x, y, and z are consecutive positive integers greater than 1, not necessarily in that order, then which of the following is (are) true?

I. $x > z$
II. $x + y > z$
III. $yz > xz$
IV. $xy > y + z$

(A) I only
(B) II only
(C) II and III only
(D) III and IV only
(E) II and IV only

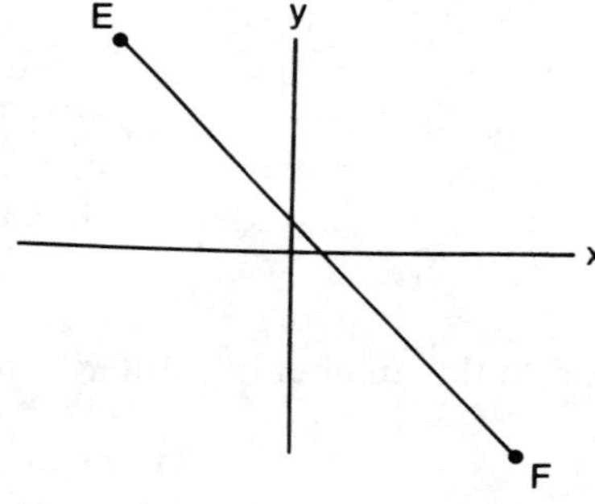

28. If point E has coordinates $(-3,5)$ and point F has coordinates $(6,-7)$, then length of EF =
(A) 21
(B) 15
(C) 7
(D) 5
(E) 3

29. What is the area of a square in square inches if its perimeter is 10 feet?
(A) 6.25
(B) 25
(C) 60
(D) 600
(E) 900

30. Mr. Smitherly leaves Beverly Hills at 8:00 A.M. and drives north on the highway at an average speed of 50 miles per hour. Mr. Dinkle leaves Beverly Hills at 8:30 A.M. and drives north on the same highway at an average speed of 60 miles per hour. Mr. Dinkle will
(A) overtake Mr. Smitherly at 9:30 A.M.
(B) overtake Mr. Smitherly at 10:30 A.M.
(C) overtake Mr. Smitherly at 11:00 A.M.
(D) be 30 miles behind at 8:35 A.M.
(E) never overtake Mr. Smitherly

STOP. IF YOU FINISH BEFORE TIME IS CALLED, CHECK YOUR WORK ON THIS SECTION ONLY. DO NOT WORK ON ANY OTHER SECTION IN THE TEST.

SECTION II: VERBAL ABILITY

Time: 30 Minutes
38 Questions

In this section, choose the best answer for each question and blacken the corresponding space on the answer sheet.

Sentence Completion

DIRECTIONS

Each blank in the following sentences indicates that something has been omitted. Considering the lettered words beneath the sentence, choose the word or set of words that best fits the whole sentence.

1. The thought of a nuclear ________ sparked by a misunderstanding poses an awesome ________.
   (A) device . . . reverberation
   (B) holocaust . . . specter
   (C) danger . . . spectacle
   (D) liaison . . . probability
   (E) explosion . . . calamity

2. Rural dwellers who hold ________ values may, at times, be altogether uncritical of various federal programs aimed at the regulation and ________ of agriculture.
   (A) rigorous . . . legalization
   (B) conventional . . . subsidization
   (C) ludicrous . . . obfuscation
   (D) rhythmic . . . communization
   (E) similarity . . . decimation

3. Truman tried to continue Roosevelt's ________ approach to the Soviet Union, but by 1946, he had adopted a much tougher policy toward the Russians.
   (A) cursory
   (B) strict
   (C) obligatory
   (D) uncompromising
   (E) conciliatory

4. As the controversial argument continued, the debaters became more ________ and their remarks became more ________.
   (A) subdued . . . hostile
   (B) vehement . . . acrimonious
   (C) reticent . . . cliche
   (D) affable . . . adverse
   (E) emotional . . . adroit

5. My wealthy aunt is more than economical; she is so ________ that she washes paper plates to be used again.
   (A) affluent
   (B) parsimonious
   (C) indigent
   (D) impoverished
   (E) selfish

6. In spite of competition, the newspaper ________ remains among the best ________ of communication between advertisers and customers.
   (A) cannot . . . medium
   (B) never . . . means
   (C) still . . . media
   (D) often . . . measure
   (E) consistently . . . standard

7. The primitivist assumption that the human disposition is naturally ________ is likely to depend on blaming institutions for all the ________ in the world.
   (A) innocent . . . happiness
   (B) corruptible . . . warfare
   (C) malleable . . . indifference
   (D) benevolent . . . corruption
   (E) untrustworthy . . . crime

8. _________ must be distinguished from _________, which is the recognition of different categories of people without the imputing of any differences in rank.
(A) Totalitarianism . . . brotherhood
(B) Modification . . . ossification
(C) Classification . . . ramification
(D) Stratification . . . differentiation
(E) Finitude . . . infinitude

Analogies

DIRECTIONS

In each question below, you are given a related pair of words or phrases. Select the lettered pair that *best* expresses a relationship similar to that in the original pair of words.

9. AMBIGUOUS : CLEAR ::
(A) few : plural
(B) ambivalent : dexterous
(C) synthetic : real
(D) impassioned : sympathetic
(E) poignant : acute

10. VIGILANTE : POLICE OFFICER ::
(A) posse : sheriff
(B) judge : jury
(C) villain : criminal
(D) lynching : execution
(E) intern : doctor

11. LARVA : ADULT ::
(A) spider : insect
(B) kid : goat
(C) tadpole : frog
(D) female : male
(E) fish : mammal

12. EXTRACT : QUOTATION ::
(A) radius : diameter
(B) forecast : prediction
(C) exile : solitude
(D) tropics : tundra
(E) longitude : latitude

13. CUPOLA : ROOF ::
(A) branch : tree
(B) building : story
(C) bishop : scepter
(D) airplane : propeller
(E) statue : pedestal

14. FELONY : MISDEMEANOR ::
(A) blunder : mistake
(B) zenith : nadir
(C) hurricane : typhoon
(D) agreement : contract
(E) pause : delay

15. FISH : FRY ::
(A) lion : whelp
(B) oatmeal : cookie
(C) whale : pod
(D) kitchen : cook
(E) beef : steak

16. SLOTHFUL : OVERWORK ::
(A) confused : overexplain
(B) mean : overspend
(C) average : overrate
(D) expensive : overcharge
(E) tired : overexert

17. ANACHRONISM : PERIOD ::
(A) calendar : year
(B) setting : scene
(C) fallacy : logic
(D) crime : property
(E) repetition : comma

Reading Comprehension

DIRECTIONS

Questions follow each of the passages below. Using only the stated or implied information in each passage, answer the questions.

Laboratory evidence indicates that life originated through chemical reactions in the primordial mixture (water, hydrogen, ammonia, and hydrogen cyanide) which blanketed the earth at its formation. These reactions were brought about by the heat, pressure, and radiation conditions then prevailing. One suggestion is that nucleosides and amino acids were formed from the primordial mixture, and the nucleosides produced nucleotides which produced the nucleic acids (DNA, the common denominator of all living things, and RNA). The amino acids became polymerized (chemically joined) into proteins, including enzymes, and lipids were formed from fatty acids and glycerol-like molecules. The final step appears to have been the gradual accumulation of DNA, RNA, proteins, lipids, and enzymes into a vital mass which began to grow, divide, and multiply.

The evolution of the various forms of life from this biochemical mass must not be considered a linear progression. Rather, the fossil record suggests an analogy between evolution and a bush whose branches go every which way. Like branches, some evolutionary lines simply end, and others branch again. Many biologists believe the pattern to have been as follows: bacteria emerged first and from them branched viruses, red algae, blue-green algae, and green flagellates. From the latter branched green algae, from which higher plants evolved, and colorless rhizoflagellates, from which diatoms, molds, sponges, and protozoa evolved. From ciliated protozoa (ciliophora) evolved multinucleate (syncytial) flatworms. These branched into five lines, one of which leads to the echinoderms and chordates. The remaining lines lead to most of the other phyla of the animal kingdom.

18. From the language of the first paragraph, we can assume that

I. some scientists do not accept the theories of the origin of life the passage presents
II. the reactions that produced life required a unique combination of heat, pressure, and radiation
III. some living forms are without DNA

(A) I only
(B) I and II only
(C) I and III only
(D) II and III only
(E) I, II, and III

19. Which of the following best expresses the analogy between evolution and a bush?
(A) species : evolution :: bush : branching
(B) species : branching :: bush : evolution
(C) evolution : species :: bush : branched viruses
(D) evolution : species :: bush : branches
(E) evolution : species :: branches : bush

20. Which of the following can we infer to be the least highly evolved?
(A) green algae
(B) blue-green algae
(C) molds
(D) flatworms
(E) ciliated protozoa

21. According to the passage, the evolutionary line of sponges in its proper order is
(A) bacteria–viruses–green algae–sponges
(B) bacteria–viruses–rhizoflagellates–sponges
(C) bacteria–red algae–blue-green algae–rhizoflagellates–sponges
(D) bacteria–blue-green algae–green flagellates–rhizoflagellates–sponges
(E) bacteria–green flagellates–rhizoflagellates–sponges

In economics, demand implies something slightly different from the common meaning of the term. The layman uses the term to mean the amount that is demanded of an item. Thus, if the price were to decrease and individuals wanted more of an item, it is commonly said that demand increases. To an economist, demand is a relationship between a series of prices and a series of corresponding quantities that are demanded at these prices. If one reads the previous sentence carefully, it should become apparent that there is a distinction between the quantity demanded and demand. This distinction is often a point of confusion. Demand is a relationship between price and quantities demanded, and therefore suggests the effect of one (e.g., price) on the other (e.g., quantity demanded). Therefore, knowledge of the demand for a product enables one to predict how much more of a good will be purchased if price decreases. But the increase in quantity demanded does not mean demand has increased, since the relationship between price and quantity demanded (i.e., the demand for the product) has not changed. Demand shifts when there is a change in income, expectations, taste, etc., such that a different quantity of the good is demanded at the same price.

In almost all cases, a consumer wants more of an item if the price decreases. This relationship between price and quantity demanded is so strong that it is referred to as the "law of demand." This "law" can be explained by the income and substitution effects. The income effect occurs because price increases reduce the purchasing power of the individual and, thus, the quantity demanded of goods must decrease. The substitution effect reflects the consumer's desire to get the "best buy." Accordingly, if the price of good A increases, the individual will tend to substitute another good and purchase less of good A. The negative correlation between price and quantity demanded is also explained by the law of diminishing marginal utility. According to this law, the additional utility the consumer gains from consuming a good decreases as successively more units of the good are consumed. Because the additional units yield less utility or satisfaction, the consumer is willing to purchase more only if the price of the good decreases.

Economists distinguish between individual and market demand. As the term implies, individual demand concerns the individual consumer and illustrates the quantities that individuals demand at different prices. Market demand includes the demand of all individuals for a particular good and is found by summing the quantities demanded by all individuals at the various prices.

22. Which of the following is an instance of a shift in demand as it is understood by economists?

    I. A market is selling two pounds of coffee for the price it usually charges for one pound; the *demand* for coffee has increased.
    II. The success of a television program featuring cartoon turtles has increased the *demand* for an oat cereal in turtle shapes.
    III. Because of the rail strike, California lettuce costs more in Chicago, and the *demand* for lettuce has fallen.

    (A) I only
    (B) II only
    (C) III only
    (D) I and III only
    (E) I, II, and III

23. Assume that as economists use the term, the demand for houses increases. Which of the following would most likely cause such a shift?

    (A) Prices are reduced on homes because of overbuilding.
    (B) The government predicts a large increase in the extent of unemployment.
    (C) A new government program provides jobs for a large number of workers.
    (D) A low-priced type of mobile home which is a good substitute for houses is announced.
    (E) The cost of lumber increases.

24. According to the passage, a change in demand, as economists use the term, would occur in which of the following situations.
    (A) The gasoline price increases, resulting in the increased sale of compact cars (whose price remains stable).
    (B) The gasoline price increases, resulting in the increased sale of compact cars (which go on sale in response to increased gas prices).
    (C) The gasoline price decreases on the same day that a new 43-mpg car enters the market.
    (D) A federal order imposes a price ceiling on gasoline.
    (E) A federal order lifts price regulations for gasoline.

25. Assume that firms develop an orange-flavored breakfast drink high in vitamin C that is a good substitute for orange juice but sells for less. Based upon assertions in the passage, which of the following would occur with respect to the demand for orange juice?
    (A) Health food stores would resurrect the law of diminishing marginal utility.
    (B) Assuming that the price of fresh orange juice remained constant, more orange juice would be consumed.
    (C) The law of demand would prevail.
    (D) Assuming that the price of fresh orange juice remained constant, the demand would not change.
    (E) There is not enough information in the passage to answer this question.

26. For eleven months, the Acme food chopper led all others in sales. Though the price and the product have remained unchanged and no competitive product has been introduced, sales have fallen sharply. Economists would describe this phenomenon as
    (A) an increase in quantity demanded
    (B) the income effect
    (C) the substitution effect
    (D) the law of diminishing marginal utility
    (E) individual demand

27. According to the passage, a group of individuals will
    (A) derive increasingly less satisfaction from a product
    (B) exert individual demand under appropriate conditions
    (C) employ the boycott to lower prices
    (D) constitute a market
    (E) emphasize supply over demand

28. The purpose of the passage is to
    (A) introduce several important definitions
    (B) outline the theory of supply on demand
    (C) correct the layman's economic misapprehensions about prices
    (D) introduce a student to a theory of marketing
    (E) question a popular misunderstanding of "demand"

Antonyms

DIRECTIONS

Each word in CAPITAL LETTERS is followed by five words or phrases. The correct choice is the word or phrase whose meaning is most nearly *opposite* to the meaning of the word in capitals. You may be required to distinguish fine shades of meaning. Look at all choices before marking your answer.

29. COVENANT
    (A) condemnation
    (B) breach
    (C) disillusion
    (D) inference
    (E) argument

30. PRECARIOUS
    (A) carnivorous
    (B) caring
    (C) equivocal
    (D) soluble
    (E) certain

31. CONTUMACIOUS
    (A) compliant
    (B) reciprocal
    (C) pertinacious
    (D) obdurate
    (E) dogged

32. WRANGLE
    (A) concord
    (B) ironing
    (C) protest
    (D) benefit
    (E) immunity

33. TRACTABLE
    (A) retractable
    (B) refractory
    (C) refreshing
    (D) retrainable
    (E) retrenched

34. VAPID
    (A) loquacious
    (B) engaging
    (C) remarkable
    (D) translatable
    (E) succinct

35. GLIB
    (A) plaintive
    (B) ominous
    (C) halting
    (D) didactic
    (E) disparaging

36. PROTOTYPE
    (A) individual
    (B) sycophant
    (C) facsimile
    (D) handwriting
    (E) opponent

37. PLETHORA
    (A) supply
    (B) alliance
    (C) enigma
    (D) modicum
    (E) shortage

38. MORBID
    (A) alive
    (B) hale
    (C) salutary
    (D) calm
    (E) enraged

STOP. IF YOU FINISH BEFORE TIME IS CALLED, CHECK YOUR WORK ON THIS SECTION ONLY. DO NOT WORK ON ANY OTHER SECTION IN THE TEST.

SECTION III: ANALYTICAL ABILITY

Time: 30 Minutes
25 Questions

DIRECTIONS

The following questions or group of questions are based on a passage or set of statements. Choose the best answer for each question and blacken the corresponding space on your answer sheet. It may be helpful to draw rough diagrams or simple charts in attempting to answer these question types.

Questions 1–6

Six films (*Quest to Hope, Rats, Sam, Terror, Victory,* and *Wellfleet*) are scheduled to be screened at a film festival. No more than two films may be screened during one day, but all of the films will be screened exactly once during the festival held Wednesday through Sunday. The screening schedule adheres to these parameters:

The producers of *Terror* will not allow it to be screened anytime prior to the screening of *Victory.*

Rats and *Sam* are complementary shorts and are to be screened the same day.

Quest to Hope and *Wellfleet* are both black-and-white films and should not be screened the same day.

1. If *Victory* and *Terror* are screened the same day, which of the following must be true about the film festival schedule if it conforms to its parameters?
   (A) *Quest to Hope* and *Wellfleet* will be screened the same day.
   (B) *Victory* cannot be screened on Sunday.
   (C) *Sam* and *Rats* will not be screened the same day.
   (D) Exactly one day of the schedule will not have any film screening.
   (E) Each day of the schedule will have at least one film screening.

2. Each of the following schedules are in accordance with festival parameters EXCEPT

	Wednesday	Thursday	Friday	Saturday	Sunday
(A)	*Victory*	*Quest to Hope*	*Sam/Rats*	*Terror*	*Wellfleet*
(B)	*Wellfleet*	*Sam/Rats*	*Victory*	*Quest to Hope*	*Terror*
(C)	*Quest to Hope*	*Rats/Sam*	*Wellfleet*	*Victory/Terror*	
(D)	*Wellfleet*	*Terror*	*Quest to Hope*	*Victory*	*Rats/Sam*
(E)	*Victory/Terror*		*Quest to Hope*	*Sam/Rats*	*Wellfleet*

3. All of the following conform to the parameters of the schedule EXCEPT
   (A) *Sam* and *Wellfleet* are both screened on Friday
   (B) *Wellfleet* and *Terror* are both screened on Thursday
   (C) *Victory* and *Wellfleet* are both screened on Saturday
   (D) *Quest to Hope* is not screened on Friday
   (E) *Rats* is not screened on Saturday

4. If *Quest to Hope, Rats,* and *Terror* are scheduled for Wednesday, Thursday, and Friday, respectively, and if the schedule conforms to the parameters, then it must be true that
   (A) *Victory* is screened on Wednesday
   (B) *Victory* is not screened on Friday
   (C) *Wellfleet* is screened on Friday
   (D) *Wellfleet* is screened on Wednesday
   (E) *Victory* is not screened on Saturday

5. If *Victory* is screened on Sunday, then which of the following would NOT conform to the parameters of the schedule?
   (A) *Wellfleet* is screened on Wednesday.
   (B) *Rats* is screened on Wednesday.
   (C) *Quest to Hope* is screened on Friday.
   (D) *Terror* is screened on Friday.
   (E) No film is screened on Thursday.

6. If *Wellfleet* is screened on Thursday and the schedule conforms to its parameters, which of the following could be true?
   (A) *Sam* is screened on Thursday.
   (B) *Quest to Hope* is screened on Thursday.
   (C) *Rats* is screened on Thursday.
   (D) *Rats* and *Terror* are screened on Friday.
   (E) *Victory* and *Terror* are screened on Friday.

Questions 7–12

Row	*Column* 1	2	3	4
I	hill	lock	team	step
II	pill	flock	seem	stop
III	dill	clock	ream	stand
IV	still	block	beam	strand
V	mill	stock	deem	store

Each word in the first three columns rhymes with the other words in that column.

There are no words with more than five letters.

Each word in a column except column 4 starts with a different letter.

Other rules can be drawn from words in the columns.

7. Which of the following words could NOT be in column 2?
   (A) mock
   (B) sock
   (C) knock
   (D) dock
   (E) rock

8. Which of the following words could be added to column 4 without breaking any rules?
   (A) subtle
   (B) stumped
   (C) simple
   (D) stove
   (E) steeple

9. Which of the columns does NOT follow all of the rules?
   (A) 1
   (B) 2
   (C) 3
   (D) 4
   (E) none

10. If column 1 must end in *ill,* which of the following words could NOT be added to column 1?

    I. fill II. will III. spill IV. instill

   (A) I and II
   (B) II and III
   (C) III and IV
   (D) I and III
   (E) II and IV

11. It can be deduced from the word chart
   (A) each word in column 3 ends in *am*
   (B) each word in column 2 includes the word *lock*
   (C) each word in column 4 has one vowel
   (D) each word in column 3 has two vowels
   (E) none of the above

12. Which of the following could be row VI?
   (A) kill, mock, fume, start
   (B) fill, soak, mean, still
   (C) mild, crock, seam, sold
   (D) spill, mock, steam, stone
   (E) bill, dock, cream, stow

13. To complain that the rich are unfairly treated by our tax laws is preposterous. It is the rich who rely most on tax-free income. It is the rich who make use of the loopholes in the tax laws. And it is the richest 5% of the population that controls 95% of the nation's wealth.

Which of the following, if true, best supports the claim above?

(A) A fundamental principal of wealth is the use of its power to maintain its wealth.
(B) The chances of an income tax audit are higher as taxable income increases.
(C) The tax upon capital gains has risen twice in the last decade.
(D) At least 80% of the money collected in taxes is used in some form to protect or enhance the nation's wealth.
(E) Only the taxable income, not the real income, of the most affluent Americans is known.

14. Conservative farmers in drought-stricken California have been reluctant to try drip irrigation systems. They complain about its high installation costs. But the systems will produce twice the grapes on half the water, using less fertilizer, herbicide, labor, and electric power. Drip irrigation can be used on row crops as well. But unless the government cuts off the water supply or provides low-interest loans for installation, California farms will continue to overconsume. And why not?

Which of the following is the most logical conclusion to this passage?

(A) Water costs are low, and water districts do not reward savings.
(B) The drought in California is already five years old and shows no signs of ending.
(C) Banks are ready to lend money for equipment that will aid conservation.
(D) Water rationing is expected to affect agricultural customers in the next few years.
(E) The acreage of crops that require very little water has remained unchanged for many years.

15. The crime rate in this city has reached new heights. As your police commissioner, I know that the only answer to this problem is to increase the quality of our police force. Therefore, I'm petitioning the city council to enact pay raises for municipal employees without delay.

    Which of the following is a presupposition essential to the above passage?

    (A) Crime is inversely proportional to the pay of civil servants.
    (B) A better-paid police officer is a police officer better able to reduce crime.
    (C) Crime can be controlled through bribery.
    (D) The city council is composed of scoundrels.
    (E) Police are paid far too little according to their worth.

Questions 16–20

Each player of a six-member team (Ali, Berti, Cap, Dani, Evan, and Fran) carries the ball and then passes it to another player. On one play, each member carried the ball exactly once. The following is true about that one play:

Cap passed the ball to Fran.

Berti received the ball from Ali.

Fran carried the ball after Evan carried it.

Dani carried the ball before Ali.

16. Which of the following could be the order in which the players carried the ball?

    (A) Evan, Dani, Ali, Cap, Fran, Berti
    (B) Evan, Dani, Cap, Fran, Ali, Berti
    (C) Cap, Fran, Evan, Dani, Ali, Berti
    (D) Ali, Berti, Evan, Dani, Cap, Fran
    (E) Evan, Fran, Cap, Dani, Ali, Berti

17. If Dani carried the ball second, who must have carried the ball first?
    (A) Ali
    (B) Berti
    (C) Cap
    (D) Fran
    (E) Evan

18. If Berti carried the ball fourth, which of the following must be true?
    (A) Evan passed the ball to Cap.
    (B) Evan passed the ball to Dani.
    (C) Dani passed the ball to Evan.
    (D) Berti passed the ball to Cap.
    (E) Dani passed the ball to Ali.

19. Which of the players could NOT have carried the ball second?

    I. Dani
    II. Berti
    III. Cap

    (A) I only
    (B) II only
    (C) III only
    (D) I and II only
    (E) I, II, and III

20. If Berti passed the ball to Evan, all of the following must be true EXCEPT
    (A) Fran carried the ball sixth
    (B) Dani carried the ball second
    (C) Cap carried the ball fifth
    (D) Dani passed the ball to Ali
    (E) Evan passed the ball to Cap

Questions 21–22

The Metropolitan Transit Company runs its van for shoppers every hour on the hour.

The van holds up to five passengers.

The van always starts at First Street and ends at Fifth Street.

Only three streets are between the van's start and end points: Second Street, Third Street, and Fourth Street, in that order.

On its run, the van always goes in one direction and never reverses.

On the 3 P.M. run, the van left First Street with three passengers aboard and arrived at Fifth Street with five passengers aboard.

On the 3 P.M. run, the van made exactly three stops, which included its final stop at Fifth Street.

On the 3 P.M. run, three passengers got on at Second Street.

21. Which of the following must be true about the 3 P.M. run?
    (A) At least one passenger got off the van at Second Street.
    (B) At least two passengers got off the van at Second Street.
    (C) No passenger got off the van at Third Street.
    (D) Only one passenger got off the van at Second Street.
    (E) At least one passenger got on the van at Third Street.

22. Which of the following must be false about the 3 P.M. run?

    I. The van stopped at Third Street.
    II. No passenger got off the van at Second Street.
    III. No passenger got on the van at Fourth Street.

    (A) I only
    (B) II only
    (C) III only
    (D) I and II only
    (E) II and III only

23. Prior to 1963, the ovens in most English homes were fueled by a highly poisonous gas derived from coal. In the last eighteen years, all but a few of these homes have been converted to a far less lethal natural gas. During the same period, suicides in Great Britain involving gas dropped from over 2300 to 11 per year, and the suicide rate fell by one third.

Which of the following may be inferred from this information?

(A) Suicide is probably anger directed at another but exercised upon oneself.
(B) If given the chance to delay, many potential suicide victims would change their minds.
(C) Suicide in Great Britain is no longer the expression of an ancient cultural tradition.
(D) Religious sanctions have always been the most important factor in preventing suicide.
(E) Suicide is increasingly predictable and preventable.

24. The swimming pool in little Jimmy Jones's neighborhood park is no longer open. The bond measure in the June ballot will provide money for the Parks and Recreation Department that will be used to repair city parks. Please support this measure so Jimmy and his friends can go swimming this summer.

The author's point is made by

(A) using analogy
(B) appealing to authority
(C) pointing out inconsistency
(D) exploiting an ambiguity
(E) arguing from a particular case

25. The breakup of the phone company in 1984 and the deregulation of long-distance rates have produced nothing but benefits. The American phone companies are no longer falling behind the rest of the world in technology. Long-distance rates have declined since deregulation. Telephone costs to businesses have remained the same or even declined slightly. And a legion of smaller telephone companies are showing high profits.

    Which of the following, if true, most seriously weakens the argument above?

    (A) The price of stock in the companies spun off from American Telephone has risen sharply since 1984.
    (B) The monthly charge for telephone service in the home has risen each year since 1985.
    (C) Sixty percent of the telephone service in African countries is dependent upon American technology.
    (D) Increased revenue earned by telephone companies leads to increased federal revenues by way of taxes on telephone calls and corporate profits.
    (E) Eighty percent of the consumers polled report better telephone services in 1990 than in 1980.

STOP. IF YOU FINISH BEFORE TIME IS CALLED, CHECK YOUR WORK ON THIS SECTION ONLY. DO NOT WORK ON ANY OTHER SECTION IN THE TEST.

SECTION IV: VERBAL ABILITY

Time: 30 Minutes
39 Questions

In this section, choose the best answer for each question and blacken the corresponding space on the answer sheet.

Sentence Completion

DIRECTIONS

Each blank in the following sentences indicates that something has been omitted. Considering the lettered words beneath the sentence, choose the word or set of words that best fits the whole sentence.

1. When thrust into an unknown world, people are careful to note the conditions in which they find themselves, _________ them with their _________.
   (A) bemusing . . . daydreams
   (B) refuting . . . expertise
   (C) congealing . . . observations
   (D) concurring . . . thoughts
   (E) comparing . . . expectations

2. When the Axel Corporation purchased the newspapers, their sales were at their _________ in both revenue and profit, but the recession has _________ the profitability of almost all media properties.
   (A) height . . . undermined
   (B) mean . . . improved
   (C) zenith . . . increased
   (D) bottom . . . destroyed
   (E) nadir . . . extended

3. Despite its staid appearance, the Mexican Stock Exchange is the most _________ in North America.
(A) inactive
(B) volatile
(C) obscure
(D) conservative
(E) efficient

4. Another _________ function of the political institution is the protection of the society from _________ forces.
(A) expendable . . . natural
(B) inherent . . . political
(C) conservative . . . governmental
(D) liberal . . . conservative
(E) salient . . . external

5. In _________ nature, myths use _________ reasoning, relating the unfamiliar to the familiar by means of likeness.
(A) observing . . . logical
(B) appreciating . . . irrational
(C) disclosing . . . metonymic
(D) interpreting . . . analogical
(E) seizing . . . fanciful

6. Phoenician seamen were primarily interested in commerce and may have been the first people to _________ Africa.
(A) circumnavigate
(B) demystify
(C) explore
(D) mispronounce
(E) expropriate

7. One cannot _________ to be impressed by the structural and _________ differences between the United States as a federal union in 1789 and the United States as a federal union today.
(A) refuse . . . legal
(B) stop . . . attitudinal
(C) begin . . . economic
(D) fail . . . operational
(E) start . . . classical

8. Generally, Babylonian mythology lacks the _________ quality of the myth of Osiris; it is more earthbound and more materialistic.
   (A) ancient
   (B) anthropological
   (C) artistic
   (D) experiential
   (E) transcendental

9. The _________ of Darwin's theory of evolution on Victorian religion was to create a bitter _________ of ideas and beliefs.
   (A) result . . . moderation
   (B) effect . . . conflict
   (C) extension . . . growth
   (D) origin . . . compromise
   (E) influence . . . solidarity

Analogies

DIRECTIONS

In each question below, you are given a related pair of words or phrases. Select the lettered pair that *best* expresses a relationship similar to that in the original pair of words.

10. CANDY : SUGAR ::
   (A) pickle : brine
   (B) distill : spirits
   (C) chicken : fricassee
   (D) harvest : crop
   (E) broil : lobster

11. HELMET : HEAD ::
   (A) glove : mitten
   (B) ring : finger
   (C) goggles : eyes
   (D) arrow : quiver
   (E) scarf : necklace

12. DOMINO : MASQUERADE ::
   (A) tango : dance
   (B) violin : concert
   (C) tuxedo : prom
   (D) taxi : limousine
   (E) dice : casino

13. INDISTINCT : MIST ::
    (A) impressionistic : painting
    (B) tidal : spray
    (C) refulgent : light
    (D) colorful : spectrum
    (E) bucolic : grass

14. ZEALOT : ENTHUSIASTIC ::
    (A) prisoner : sullen
    (B) lawyer : honest
    (C) banker : moneyed
    (D) idler : lazy
    (E) runner : speedy

15. BELLWETHER : FLOCK ::
    (A) lion : pride
    (B) election : plebiscite
    (C) preamble : afterthought
    (D) goose : gosling
    (E) foreman : crew

16. BIBLIOGRAPHER : LIBRARY ::
    (A) orange : grove
    (B) lawyer : jail
    (C) carpenter : wood
    (D) teacher : classroom
    (E) bishop : see

17. VERBIAGE : PROLIX ::
    (A) star : solar
    (B) fertility : fecund
    (C) environment : sullied
    (D) action : verbal
    (E) value : expensive

18. WANTON : ASCETIC ::
    (A) nervous : insecure
    (B) fervent : furtive
    (C) costly : unpaid
    (D) obstreperous : shy
    (E) hermetic : monkish

Reading Comprehension

DIRECTIONS

Questions follow each of the passages below. Using only the stated or implied information in each passage, answer the questions.

As Augustine contemplates his own nature as well as that of his fellow men, he sees wickedness and corruption on every hand. Man is a sinful creature and there is nothing that is wholly good about him. The cause is to be found in original sin, which mankind inherited from Adam. If Adam is regarded as a particular human being, it would make no sense at all to blame his descendants for the mistakes that he made. But Adam is interpreted to mean the universal man rather than a particular individual. Since the universal necessarily includes all of the particulars belonging to the class, they are involved in whatever the universal does.

The total corruption of human nature as taught by Augustine did not mean that man is incapable of doing any good deeds. It meant that each part of his nature is infected with an evil tendency. In contrast to the Greek notion of a good mind and an evil body, he held that both mind and body had been made corrupt as a result of the fall. This corruption is made manifest in the lusts of the flesh and also in the activities of the mind. So far as the mind is concerned, the evil tendency is present in both the intellect and in the will. In the intellect, it is expressed in the sin of pride, and in the will, there is the inclination to follow that which is pleasant at the moment rather than to obey the demands of reason.

19. According to the passage, in order for modern man to be guilty of original sin
    (A) he must be corrupt in both mind and body
    (B) he must be guilty of intellectual and physical errors
    (C) Adam must be regarded as a unique human being
    (D) Adam must be regarded as the universal man
    (E) Adam must be regarded as responsible for Eve's fall

20. Which of the following is a logical inference from this passage?
    (A) The earlier in history a man is born, the more sinful he is likely to be.
    (B) The later in history a man is born, the more sinful he is likely to be.
    (C) Augustine would not agree with the phrase "as innocent as a new-born child."
    (D) Augustine would agree that animals inherit original sin from Adam.
    (E) At birth, a female is less guilty of sin than a male.

21. Which of the following would Augustine be most likely to regard as a consequence of the infected will?
    (A) pride in one's ancestry
    (B) envy of another's wisdom
    (C) overeating
    (D) vanity about one's appearance
    (E) temper tantrums

22. According to the passage, the Greek idea of man differs from Augustine's because it believed that
    (A) man is incapable of performing good deeds
    (B) man possesses an evil body but a good mind
    (C) corruption proceeds from the infected will
    (D) man possesses a good body and a good mind
    (E) man is incapable of following the dictates of reason

The Amblyrhynchus, a remarkable genus of lizards, is confined to this archipelago. There are two species, resembling each other in general form, one being terrestrial and the other aquatic. This latter species with its short, broad head and strong claws of equal length, has habits of life that are different from those of its nearest ally, the iguana. It is extremely common on all the islands, throughout the group, and lives exclusively on the rocky sea beaches, being never found even ten yards in-shore. It is a hideous-looking creature, of a dirty black color, stupid, and sluggish in its movements. The usual length of a full-grown one is about a yard, but there are some even four feet long; a large one weighed twenty pounds: on the island of Albemarle they seem to grow to a greater size than elsewhere. Their tails are flattened sideways, and all four feet are partially webbed. They are occasionally seen some hundred yards from shore swimming about.

It must not, however, be supposed that they live on fish. I opened the stomachs of several and found them largely distended with a minced seaweed of a bright green or a dull red color. I do not recollect having observed this seaweed in any quanity on the tidal rocks; I believe it grows at the bottom of the sea, at some distance from the coast. If such be the case, the object of these animals occasionally going out to sea is explained. The stomach contained nothing but the seaweed. A piece of crab in one might have got in accidentally, in the same manner as I have seen a caterpillar, in the midst of some lichen, in the paunch of a tortoise. The intestines were large, as in other herbivorous animals. The nature of this lizard's food, as well as the structure of its tail and feet, and the fact of its having been seen voluntarily swimming out at sea, absolutely prove its aquatic habits.

Yet there is in this respect one strange anomaly—namely, that when frightened it will not enter the water. Hence, it is easy to drive these lizards down to any little point overhanging the sea, where they will sooner allow a person to catch hold of their tails than jump into the water. Perhaps this singular piece of apparent stupidity may be accounted for by the circumstance that this reptile has no enemy whatever on shore, whereas at sea it must often fall a prey to the numerous sharks. Hence, urged by a fixed and hereditary instinct that the shore is its place of safety, whatever the emergency may be, it there takes refuge.

23. According to the passage, the aquatic lizard

I. is more numerous than the land lizard of the same genus
II. spends more time at sea than on land
III. is a remarkably unattractive looking animal

(A) I only
(B) II only
(C) III only
(D) I and II only
(E) I and III only

24. Which of the following can we infer about the land species of Amblyrhynchus from information in the passage?

I. It is a hideous looking creature.
II. It can be found more than ten yards from the shore.
III. It has webbed feet.

(A) II only
(B) I and II only
(C) I and III only
(D) II and III only
(E) I, II, and III

25. The author's conclusion that the marine lizard lives only on seaweed is based upon

I. observation of the feeding habits
II. inferences from the size of its intestines
III. inferences from the content of its intestines

(A) II only
(B) I and II only
(C) I and III only
(D) II and III only
(E) I, II, and III

26. It can be inferred that the lizards seen swimming at some distance from the shore

(A) are attempting to escape from marine predators such as sharks
(B) are attempting to regulate the temperature of their bodies
(C) have attempted to migrate from one island in the archipelago to another
(D) have been feeding or are seeking food
(E) have been feeding upon edible shellfish found in those waters

27. Which of the following does the author cite as evidence that the lizard is an aquatic animal?

(A) its tail and foot structure
(B) its sluggish movement on land
(C) its fear of sharks
(D) the finding of a crab in its intestines
(E) its instinct that land is a place of refuge

28. A newly introduced, slow-moving land predator upon the marine lizards described in the passage would most likely

(A) initially be much less successful than a swiftly moving marine predator
(B) be about as successful as a swiftly moving marine predator
(C) be more successful than a swiftly moving marine predator
(D) have to depend, at first, upon preying on the very young or very old marine lizards
(E) be unable to survive on the archipelago

29. The main purpose of the passage is to
    (A) discriminate between marine lizards and land lizards
    (B) discuss the characteristics of herbivorous lizards
    (C) describe the author's visit to an archipelago
    (D) suggest a basis for an evolutionary theory
    (E) describe some notable features of a marine lizard

Antonyms

DIRECTIONS

Each word in CAPITAL LETTERS is followed by five words or phrases. The correct choice is the word or phrase whose meaning is most nearly *opposite* to the meaning of the word in capitals. You may be required to distinguish fine shades of meaning. Look at all choices before marking your answer.

30. OBSEQUIOUS
    (A) rough-hewn
    (B) rustic
    (C) antique
    (D) rude
    (E) parasitic

31. BELLICOSE
    (A) varicose
    (B) fretful
    (C) ringing
    (D) peaceful
    (E) calm

32. SPORADIC
    (A) constant
    (B) indifferent
    (C) internal
    (D) piglike
    (E) organized

33. RESERVE
    (A) buoyancy
    (B) revelry
    (C) action
    (D) loquacity
    (E) nostalgia

34. PIQUANT
(A) basic
(B) indigestible
(C) insipid
(D) strong
(E) svelt

35. INSOUCIANT
(A) condoned
(B) insistent
(C) slovenly
(D) concerned
(E) defaulted

36. SPRUCE
(A) tasteless
(B) squalid
(C) leafless
(D) obnoxious
(E) dapper

37. PERFIDY
(A) faithfulness
(B) treachery
(C) infidelity
(D) fallaciousness
(E) loving

38. PALINGENESIS
(A) devotion
(B) stability
(C) pleasantry
(D) vitality
(E) omnipotence

39. HIE
(A) undulate
(B) create
(C) saunter
(D) heave
(E) gnaw

STOP. IF YOU FINISH BEFORE TIME IS CALLED, CHECK YOUR WORK ON THIS SECTION ONLY. DO NOT WORK ON ANY OTHER SECTION IN THE TEST.

SECTION V: QUANTITATIVE ABILITY

Time: 30 Minutes
30 Questions

Quantitative Comparison

DIRECTIONS

In this section you will be given two quantities, one in column A and one in column B. You are to determine a relationship between the two quantities and mark

(A) if the quantity in column A is greater than the quantity in column B
(B) if the quantity in column B is greater than the quantity in column A
(C) if the quantities are equal
(D) if the comparison cannot be determined from the information that is given

Common Information:
Information centered above both columns refers to one or both columns.
All numbers used are real numbers.
Figures are intended to provide useful positional information, but are not necessarily drawn to scale and should not be used to estimate sizes by measurement.
Lines that appear straight can be assumed to be straight.

	Column A		Column B
1.	$\frac{.89 \times 57}{.919}$		58
		$x < 0$	
2.	$x^3 - 1$		0
3.	Number of prime numbers between 3 and 19		5

	Column A		Column B
		$\frac{a}{6} = \frac{b}{4}$	
4.	2a		3b

Questions 5–6 refer to the diagram.

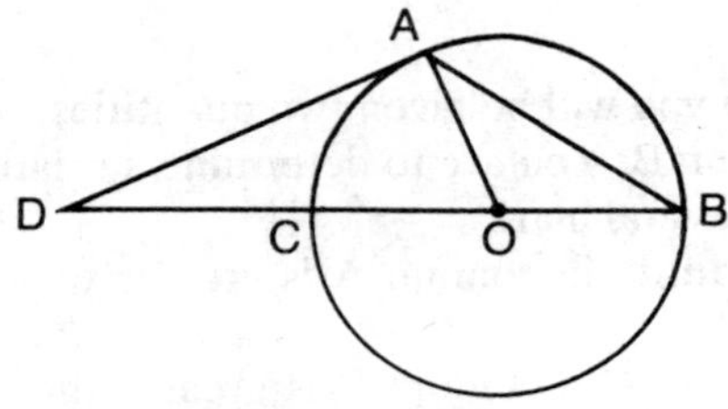

O is the center

	Column A		Column B
5.	$\overset{\frown}{AC}$		$2(\angle B)$
6.	$\angle AOB$		$\angle ADB$
		$2x + 5y > 4$	
7.	x		y
8.	Number of inches in one mile		Number of minutes in one year
9.	Area of circle with diameter 8		Area of square with side 7
10.	$3\sqrt{2}$		$\sqrt{17}$
		$5x + y = 2$ $x + 3y = 6$	
11.	x		y

	Column A	Column B
	$n \neq 0$ $n \neq -\frac{1}{2}$ $n \neq -1$	
12.	$\dfrac{1}{1 + \dfrac{1}{1 + 1/n}}$	$\dfrac{n + 1}{2n + 1}$

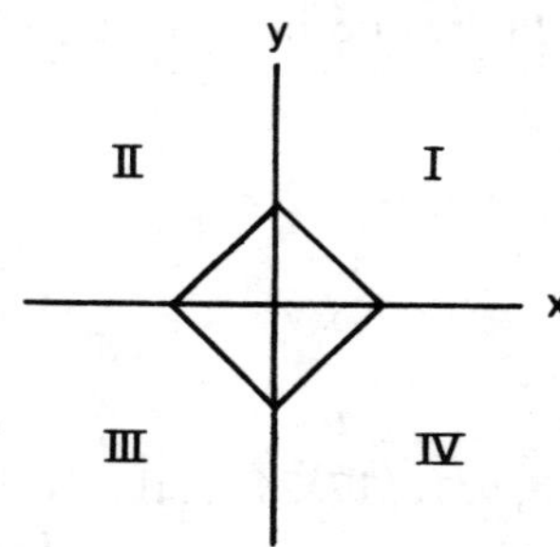

Point (x, y) is a point in quadrant II on the quadrilateral

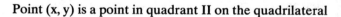

	Column A	Column B
13.	x	y
14.	$5 + 4 \cdot 10^2 + 8 \cdot 10^3$	8405

Alice is taller than Hilda, Joan is taller than Alice, and Jill is taller than Hilda

	Column A	Column B
15.	Jill's height	Joan's height

Math Ability

Solve each problem in this section by using the information given and your own mathematical calculations. Then select the *one* correct answer of the five choices given. Use the available space on the page for scratchwork. NOTE: Some problems may be accompanied by figures or diagrams. These figures are drawn as accurately as possible, *except* when it is stated in a specific problem that the figure is not drawn to scale. The figure is meant to provide information useful in solving the problem or problems. Unless otherwise stated or indicated, all figures lie in a plane. All numbers used are real numbers.

16. If $2x - 5 = 9$, then $3x + 2 =$
    (A) 7
    (B) 14
    (C) 16
    (D) 23
    (E) 44

17. In the series 8, 9, 12, 17, 24 . . . the next number would be
    (A) 29
    (B) 30
    (C) 33
    (D) 35
    (E) 41

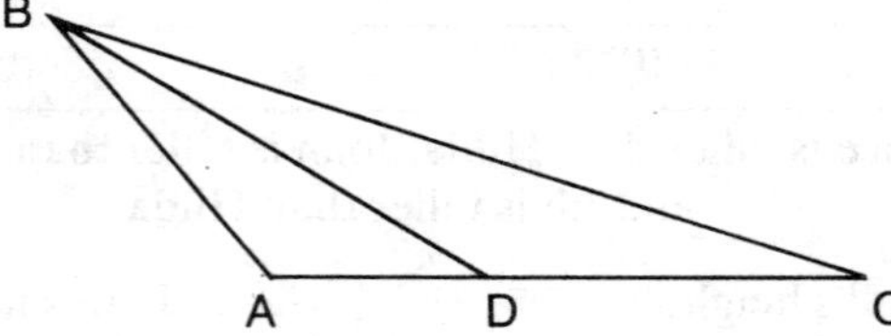

18. In the figure, AB = AD and BD = CD. If $\angle C$ measures 19°, what is the measure of $\angle A$ in degrees?
    (A) 75
    (B) 94
    (C) 104
    (D) 142
    (E) cannot be determined

19. What is the ratio of $\frac{3}{10}$ to $\frac{5}{8}$?
    (A) $\frac{3}{16}$
    (B) $\frac{12}{25}$
    (C) $\frac{37}{40}$
    (D) $\frac{25}{12}$
    (E) $\frac{16}{3}$

20. If it takes a machine ⅔ of a minute to produce one item, how many items will it produce in 2 hours?
(A) ⅓
(B) ⁴⁄₃
(C) 80
(D) 120
(E) 180

Questions 21–25 refer to the graph.

AVERAGE FAMILY'S EXPENSES

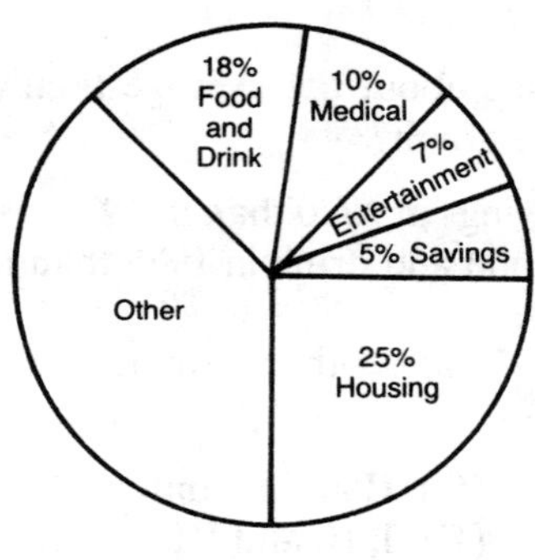

1970
Average Income $12,000

1975
Average Income $16,000

21. For the year in which the average family's housing expenses were $3000, what were the average family's medical expenses?
(A) $600
(B) $1000
(C) $1200
(D) $1920
(E) $2400

22. What was the approximate ratio of income spent on housing in 1970 to income spent on housing in 1975?
(A) 4 to 17
(B) 3 to 5
(C) 25 to 32
(D) 1 to 1
(E) 3 to 2

23. What was the percent increase from 1970 to 1975 in the percentage spent on food and drink?
(A) 4%
(B) 18%
(C) 22%
(D) 40%
(E) 50%

24. How much more did the average family spend on entertainment in 1975 than in 1970?
(A) $4000
(B) $1120
(C) $870
(D) $400
(E) $280

25. Which of the following statements about the average family's expenses can be inferred from the graph?

I. More money was put into savings in 1970 than in 1975.
II. More money was spent for food and drink in 1975 than for food and drink in 1970.
III. More money was spent in 1975 for "other" expenses than for "other" expenses in 1970.

(A) I only
(B) II only
(C) III only
(D) II and III only
(E) I, II, and III

26. If m and n are integers and $\sqrt{mn} = 10$, which of the following CANNOT be a value of m + n?
(A) 25
(B) 29
(C) 50
(D) 52
(E) 101

27. The denominator of a fraction is 5 greater than the numerator. If the numerator and the denominator are increased by 2, the resulting fraction is equal to $\frac{7}{12}$. What is the value of the original fraction?
(A) $\frac{5}{12}$
(B) $\frac{1}{2}$
(C) $\frac{9}{14}$
(D) $\frac{2}{3}$
(E) $\frac{12}{17}$

28. If a = p + prt, then r =
(A) (a − 1)/t
(B) (a − p)/pt
(C) a − p − pt
(D) a/t
(E) (a + p)/pt

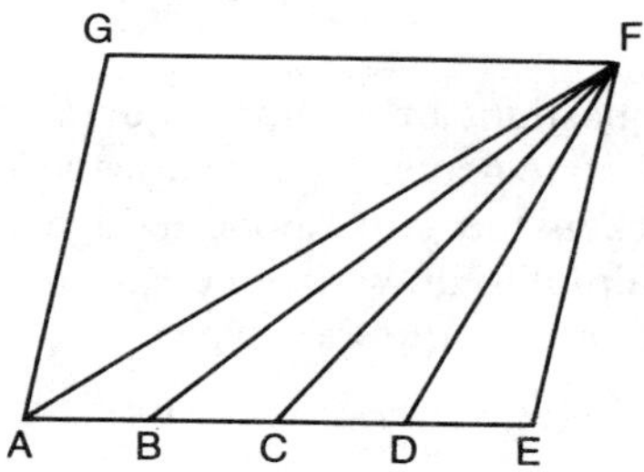

29. In the parallelogram, if AB = BC = CD = DE, what is the ratio of the area of triangle CDF to the area of triangle ABF?
(A) 1:4
(B) 1:1
(C) 2:1
(D) 4:1
(E) cannot be determined

30. The average of three numbers is 55. The second is 1 more than twice the first, and the third is 4 less than three times the first. What is the largest number?
(A) 165
(B) 88
(C) 80
(D) 57
(E) 55

STOP. IF YOU FINISH BEFORE TIME IS CALLED, CHECK YOUR WORK ON THIS SECTION ONLY. DO NOT WORK ON ANY OTHER SECTION IN THE TEST.

SECTION VI: ANALYTICAL ABILITY

Time: 30 Minutes
25 Questions

DIRECTIONS

The following questions or group of questions are based on a passage or set of statements. Choose the best answer for each question and blacken the corresponding space on your answer sheet. It may be helpful to draw rough diagrams or simple charts in attempting to answer these question types.

Questions 1–6

Eight seats face the stage of a small theater. Four seats (A1, A2, A3, and A4, in that order) are in row A, the first row from the stage. The four seats in row B (B1, B2, B3, and B4, in that order) are immediately behind row A. Six theater patrons attend the play, each sitting in a seat. The following is known about the seating arrangement:

Erkel sits exactly in front of Cabot.

Seat A2 is always empty.

Davis does not sit next to Forge.

Gabron sits in seat A4.

Harris does not sit in seat B4

1. If Davis sits in seat B3, then Forge must sit in seat
   (A) B1
   (B) B2
   (C) B4
   (D) A1
   (E) A3

2. Suppose Harris and Erkel are sitting in seats A1 and A3, respectively, then it CANNOT be true that seat
   (A) B1 is empty
   (B) B2 is empty
   (C) B4 is empty
   (D) B3 is occupied by Cabot
   (E) B1 is occupied by Davis

3. Which patrons must be in the same row no matter what the seating arrangement?
   (A) Cabot and Forge
   (B) Forge and Davis
   (C) Harris and Erkel
   (D) Gabron and Davis
   (E) Gabron and Erkel

4. If Harris sits next to Gabron, which of the following CANNOT be true?
   (A) Davis sits in B2.
   (B) Davis sits in B3.
   (C) Forge sits in B4.
   (D) Forge sits in B2.
   (E) Cabot sits in B1.

5. If Cabot sits next to Harris, then Harris must sit in
   (A) B1
   (B) B2
   (C) B3
   (D) B4
   (E) row A

6. If Forge sits in B3, then
   (A) Cabot must sit in A1
   (B) Gabron must sit in B4
   (C) Davis must sit in A3
   (D) Harris must sit in A2
   (E) Harris must sit in A3

Questions 7–10

Eight newly born puppies are purchased by Mrs. Gold.

Five of the puppies are female.
Seven of the puppies are brown.
Four of the puppies are spotted in color; the others are solid.

7. Which of the following must be true?

I. All of the females are brown.
II. At least one of the spotted puppies is female.
III. Three of the brown puppies are male.

(A) I only
(B) II only
(C) III only
(D) I and II only
(E) II and III only

8. Which of the following must be false?
(A) All the spotted females are brown.
(B) One of the females is not brown.
(C) One of the males is not brown.
(D) All the males are spotted and brown.
(E) All the females are spotted and brown.

9. Which of the following must be true?
(A) At least one spotted puppy is not brown.
(B) At least three spotted puppies are not male.
(C) At least three brown puppies are not female.
(D) At least three brown puppies are not spotted.
(E) At least one male puppy is not spotted.

10. Which of the following must be false?
(A) All the male puppies are brown and spotted.
(B) Four brown puppies are all female.
(C) All the nonspotted puppies are male.
(D) All the spotted puppies are female.
(E) All the nonspotted puppies are female.

11. Biff Bramley is a great baseball player. After all, he led the league in home runs last season.

The foregoing conclusion can be properly drawn if it is true that

(A) Biff Bramley did lead the league in home runs last season
(B) Biff Bramley also led the league in batting average
(C) great baseball players are home run hitters
(D) it takes a great baseball player to lead the league in home runs
(E) success is something that cannot be attained in one season

12. Following the publication of a report that the power steering on some 1992 Wombats locked at low speeds causing potential accidents, the chairman of Wombat Motors remarked, "This could really hurt our company."

The chairman assumes that

I. many employees of Wombat Motors drive the company's products
II. the power-steering defect cannot be fixed
III. potential accidents could affect Wombat Motor's reputation

(A) I only
(B) II only
(C) III only
(D) I and II only
(E) I and III only

13. Average scores on standardized tests have been dropping for the last decade. This is not the fault of the students. The dissolution of the nuclear family has created instablility for thousands of American children. And students need stability to fulfill their academic potential.

    Which of the following, if true, would most weaken the above statement?

    (A) In New Guinea, where fewer than 10% of all teenagers come from one-parent families, academic achievement is at an all-time high.
    (B) Many more people took the tests recently than took them in the last year in which the scores rose.
    (C) Fifty percent of all scholarship students at American colleges last year were from single-parent homes.
    (D) Students from single-parent homes have even less disposable income than was formerly thought.
    (E) Orphans tested the highest on standardized tests of any subgroup of students.

Questions 14–19

Strawberries are grown in California, Oregon, Washington, and Idaho.

Blueberries are grown in Nevada, Oregon, Washington, and Arizona.

Boysenberries are grown in California, Nevada, Utah, Washington, and Idaho.

Blackberries are grown in Arizona, Nevada, Utah, and Colorado.

Raspberries are grown in Arizona, Washington, Oregon, and California.

Gooseberries are grown in Oregon, Washington, Idaho, and Utah.

14. The berry that grows in the most states is
    (A) strawberry
    (B) blueberry
    (C) boysenberry
    (D) blackberry
    (E) all are the same

15. The state that has the most different kinds of berries growing in it is
    (A) California
    (B) Oregon
    (C) Washington
    (D) Nevada
    (E) Utah

16. If one wanted to grow boysenberries, gooseberries, and blackberries, then one should live in
    (A) Oregon
    (B) Arizona
    (C) Washington
    (D) Nevada
    (E) Utah

17. Which of the following must be true?

    I. Arizona is the only state to grow gooseberries but not boysenberries.
    II. Oregon is the only state to grow strawberries but not boysenberries.

    (A) I only
    (B) II only
    (C) I and II
    (D) either I or II but not both
    (E) neither I nor II

18. Blackberries can be grown in
    (A) Utah, where boysenberries cannot be grown
    (B) Nevada, where strawberries cannot be grown
    (C) California, where boysenberries cannot be grown
    (D) Washington, where blueberries cannot be grown
    (E) Arizona, where raspberries cannot be grown

19. If someone wanted to make preserves from both blueberries and blackberries that were freshly picked, then the person would have to live in
   (A) California or Utah
   (B) Oregon or Arizona
   (C) Arizona or Nevada
   (D) Washington or Colorado
   (E) Idaho or Utah

Questions 21–22

(1) Julie is 23 years old.
(2) Alice is not the youngest.
(3) Carol is not 25 years old.
(4) Julie is two years younger than Alice.
(5) Alice and Carol are three years apart.
(6) Carol is younger than Julie.
(7) Alice is not three years older than Julie.
(8) Julie is one year older than Carol.

20. Which of the following must be true?

   I. The difference in age between Alice and Julie is greater than the difference in age between Julie and Carol.
   II. Carol is younger than 22 years old.

   (A) I only
   (B) II only
   (C) I and II
   (D) either I or II but not both
   (E) neither I nor II

21. If another woman, Sheila, is younger than Alice but not older than Julie, then
   (A) she must be younger than Carol
   (B) she must be older than Carol
   (C) she is 24 years old
   (D) she could be the same age as Julie
   (E) she could be four years older than Carol

22. If a fifth woman, Jennifer, is as many years older than Julie as she is younger than Alice, then how many years older than Carol is Jennifer?
    (A) 1 year
    (B) 2 years
    (C) 3 years
    (D) 4 years
    (E) 5 years

23. When two dozen Fortune-500 chairpersons were interviewed, all agreed that business acumen and training were rarely important criteria for corporations to consider in their selection of executives to head important corporate divisions. Selection of divisional executives was based more on interpersonal and social qualities than on learned intellectual skills. In fact, some of the most productive divisional executives had little or no business training. Unhappily for corporations, however, executives with strong interpersonal talents are seldom, if ever, available for hire.

    In the above passage, the response of the chairpersons implies which of the following?

    (A) If a corporation believes that an executive has learned intellectual skills, it ought to consider that executive for a position as one of its divisional executives.
    (B) If a corporation determines than an executive has no business training, it ought not to consider that executive for an important divisional position.
    (C) If a corporation wants a particular executive for a divisional position, the corporation assumes that that executive will have the training and business skills to perform the necessary tasks.
    (D) If a corporation signs an executive to a divisional postion, that corporation probably believes the executive to have interpersonal and social skills.
    (E) If a corporation does not sign an executive to a divisional position, that executive does not have any interpersonal or social skills.

24. The profits in the United States from the sale of radios by the three largest Japanese manufacturers of electronics equipment last year represented 80% of the total profits earned by all American and foreign manufacturers. Yet 35% of the radios purchased in the United States last year were made by American manufacturers.

If the information above is true, which of the following can properly be concluded about the radios sold in the United States?

(A) Foreign manufacturers other than the Japanese had a large market share.
(B) Labor costs are higher in Japan than in other Asian countries that manufacture electronics products.
(C) Japanese manufacturers have a higher margin of profit than those of other countries.
(D) The Japanese increased their sales by selling at sharply discounted prices.
(E) Fifteen percent of the total profits from the sale of radios was earned by foreign manufacturers other than the three largest Japanese companies.

25. Mr. Tibbitts won't teach classes during the summer, and since he won't, neither will Ms. Mondragon. If Ms. Mondragon and Mr. Parnelli both decide not to teach classes during the summer, then Professor Revlon will have to teach summer classes, which will take him away from his administrative duties and will no doubt cause confusion in the administrative office. Therefore, Professor Revlon's actions will likely cause confusion in the administrative office.

Which of the following, if true, would allow the author to properly draw the conclusion expressed in the argument above?

I. Professor Revlon will not teach summer classes.
II. Ms. Mondragon will not teach summer classes.
III. Mr. Parnelli will not teach summer classes.

(A) I only
(B) II only
(C) III only
(D) I and II only
(E) I and III only

STOP. IF YOU FINISH BEFORE TIME IS CALLED, CHECK YOUR WORK ON THIS SECTION ONLY. DO NOT WORK ON ANY OTHER SECTION IN THE TEST.

SECTION VII: QUANTITATIVE ABILITY

Time: 30 Minutes
30 Questions

Quantitative Comparison

DIRECTIONS

In this section you will be given two quantities, one in column A and one in column B. You are to determine a relationship between the two quantities and mark

(A) if the quantity in column A is greater than the quantity in column B
(B) if the quantity in column B is greater than the quantity in column A
(C) if the quantities are equal
(D) if the comparison cannot be determined from the information that is given

Common Information:

Information centered above both columns refers to one or both columns.
All numbers used are real numbers.
Figures are intended to provide useful positional information, but are not necessarily drawn to scale and should not be used to estimate sizes by measurement.
Lines that appear straight can be assumed to be straight.

	Column A		**Column B**
1.	76.088		76.10
		$x + y = 0$	
2.	x		y
		Circle O has radius 1 unit	
3.	Number of units in area of circle O		Number of units in circumference of circle O

	Column A	Column B
	2.2 pounds in 1 kilogram	
4.	Number of kilograms in 50 pounds	Number of pounds in 50 kilograms

Questions 5–7 refer to the diagram.

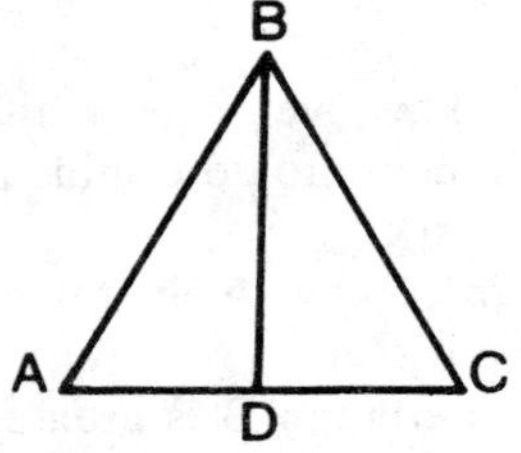

$\triangle ABC$ is equilateral
BD is a median

	Column A	Column B
5.	$\angle ABC + \angle BAC$	$\angle CDB$
6.	AD	DC
7.	AB + BD	BC

x and y are different prime numbers
x is even

	Column A	Column B
8.	xy	x + y

Questions 9–10 refer to the diagram.

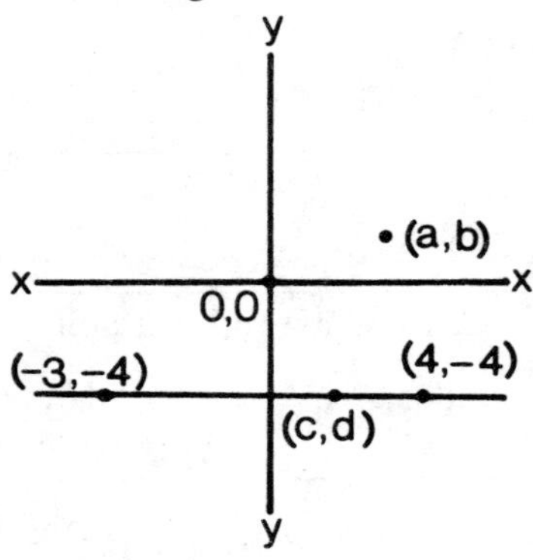

	Column A		Column B
9.	a		b
10.	c + d		a + b
		$x + y = 4$ $xy = 0$	
11.	x		y
12.	5^3		2^7
		$x^4 - 1 = 0$	
13.	x		x^2
		$x = \frac{4 - y}{y}$ $y \neq 0$	
14.	y		$\frac{4}{x + 1}$
		30¢ per pound tea X and 40¢ per pound tea Y were mixed to give 10 pounds of tea costing $3.60	
15.	Number of pounds of tea X		Number of pounds of tea Y

Math Ability

DIRECTIONS

Solve each problem in this section by using the information given and your own mathematical calculations. Then select the *one* correct answer of the five choices given. Use the available space on the page for scratchwork. NOTE: Some problems may be accompanied by figures or diagrams. These figures are drawn as accurately as possible, *except* when it is stated in a specific problem that the figure is not drawn to scale. The figure is meant to provide information useful in solving the problem or problems. Unless otherwise stated or indicated, all figures lie in a plane. All numbers used are real numbers.

16. The closest approximation of $\frac{69.28 \times .004}{.03}$ is

(A) .092
(B) .92
(C) 9.2
(D) 92
(E) 920

17. Mary will be y years old x years from now. How old will she be z years from now?

(A) $y - x + z$
(B) $y + x + z$
(C) $y + x - z$
(D) $y - x - z$
(E) $x + z - y$

18. What is the value of $3 + \cfrac{3}{3 + \cfrac{3}{3 + \cfrac{3}{3 + 3}}}$

(A) $3\frac{23}{27}$
(B) $3\frac{7}{9}$
(C) $3\frac{19}{27}$
(D) $3\frac{17}{27}$
(E) $3\frac{5}{9}$

19. If $6x - 3y = 30$ and $4x = 2 - y$, what is the value of $x + y$?

(A) 2
(B) −4
(C) −6
(D) −8
(E) −10

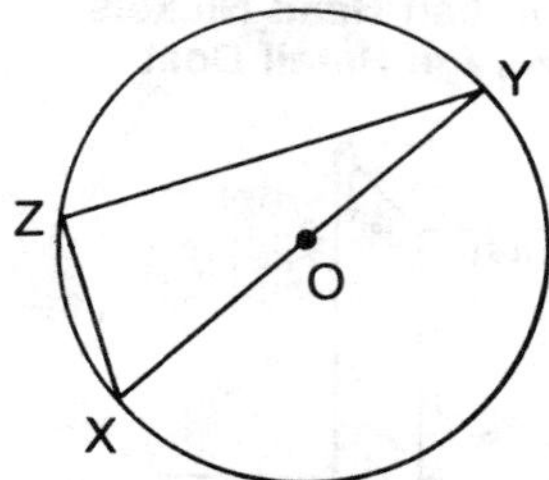

20. In circle O, OX = 8.5 and YZ = 15. What is the area of $\triangle XYZ$ in square units?
    (A) 127.5
    (B) 120
    (C) 60
    (D) 40
    (E) 30

Questions 21–25 refer to the graph on the following page.

21. Which of the following coin classifications represents the most coins?
    (A) large circulation
    (B) average circulation
    (C) average condition
    (D) fine condition
    (E) small circulation

22. If 10,000 uncirculated coins were available for sale, what would be the average cost per coin?
    (A) $9.01–$9.50
    (B) $9.51–$10.00
    (C) $10.01–$10.50
    (D) $10.51–$11.00
    (E) $11.01–$11.50

23. If 20,000 total coins are available for sale, how many of them would be from coins of average circulation?
    (A) 3500–5000
    (B) 5001–6500
    (C) 6501–8000
    (D) 8001–9500
    (E) 9501–11,000

U.S. Indian Head Nickels
Average Retail Cost

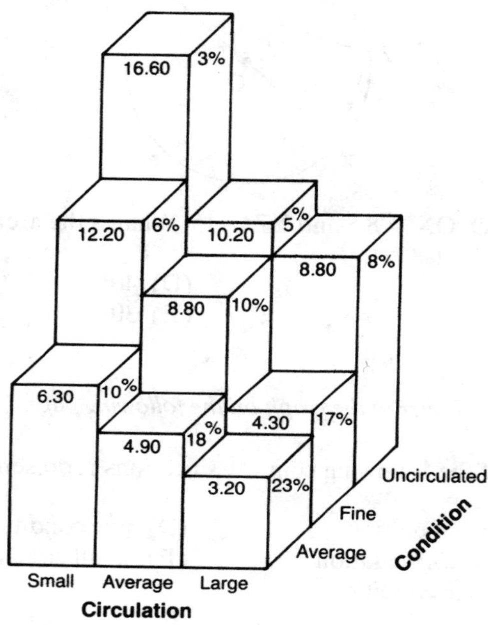

Percentages indicate percent of total coins available for sale.

Other numbers indicate average price of each coin.

24. If a coin collector who once collected only fine condition coins were to now collect both uncirculated and fine condition coins, the number of coins now available for her collection would represent an increase of approximately what percent over the number of coins formerly available?

(A) 16%
(B) 27%
(C) 33%
(D) 48%
(E) 66%

25. If 100 total coins are available for sale, how much more would a collector pay for all the average circulation coins of fine condition than for all the samll circulation coins of average condition?
(A) \$15
(B) \$25
(C) \$35
(D) \$63
(E) \$88

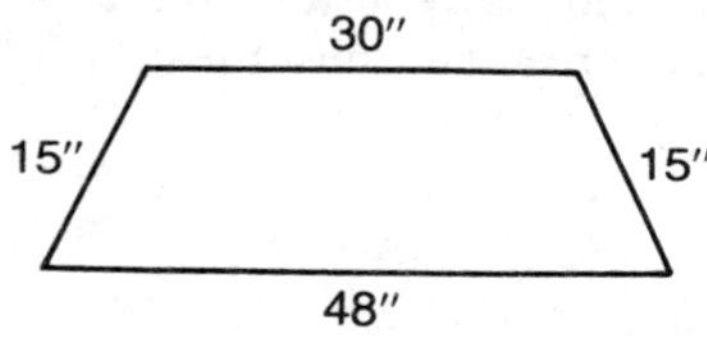

26. What is the area of the given trapezoid in square inches.
(A) 585
(B) 468
(C) 234
(D) 108
(E) cannot be determined

27. If $12 < 2x < 18$ and $-9 < 3y < 6$, then which of the following are true?

I. $3 < x + y < 11$
II. $-12 < y - x < -4$
III. $x > 7$

(A) I only
(B) III only
(C) II and III only
(D) I and III only
(E) I and II only

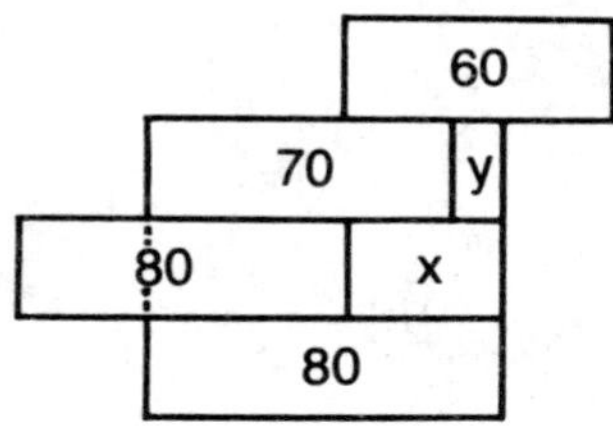

28. The horizontal length of each rectangle is marked within. What is the total horizontal length of $x + y$?
(A) 40
(B) 50
(C) 80
(D) 90
(E) cannot be determined

29. Which of the following is the largest?
    (A) half of 30% of 280
    (B) one-third of 70% of 160
    (C) twice 50% of 30
    (D) three times 40% of 40
    (E) 60% of 60

30. The product of x and y is a constant. If the value of x is increased by 50%, by what percentage must the value of y be decreased?
    (A) 50%
    (B) 40%
    (C) $33\frac{1}{3}$%
    (D) 25%
    (E) 20%

STOP. IF YOU FINISH BEFORE TIME IS CALLED, CHECK YOUR WORK ON THIS SECTION ONLY. DO NOT WORK ON ANY OTHER SECTION IN THE TEST.

SCORING PRACTICE TEST 2

ANSWER KEY

Section I Quantitative Ability	Section II Verbal Ability		Section III Analytical Ability	Section IV Verbal Ability	
1. A	1. B	31. A	1. D	1. E	31. D
2. D	2. B	32. A	2. D	2. A	32. A
3. C	3. E	33. B	3. A	3. B	33. D
4. A	4. B	34. B	4. E	4. E	34. C
5. A	5. B	35. C	5. D	5. D	35. D
6. D	6. C	36. C	6. E	6. A	36. B
7. B	7. D	37. E	7. B	7. D	37. A
8. B	8. D	38. B	8. D	8. E	38. B
9. D	9. C		9. D	9. B	39. C
10. C	10. D		10. C	10. A	
11. C	11. C		11. D	11. C	
12. A	12. B		12. E	12. C	
13. A	13. E		13. D	13. C	
14. B	14. A		14. A	14. D	
15. C	15. A		15. B	15. E	
16. A	16. B		16. B	16. D	
17. B	17. C		17. E	17. B	
18. B	18. B		18. D	18. D	
19. A	19. D		19. B	19. D	
20. B	20. B		20. B	20. C	
21. D	21. E		21. A	21. C	
22. B	22. B		22. B	22. B	
23. C	23. C		23. B	23. C	
24. C	24. A		24. E	24. B	
25. E	25. C		25. B	25. D	
26. D	26. D			26. D	
27. B	27. D			27. A	
28. B	28. A			28. C	
29. E	29. B			29. E	
30. C	30. E			30. D	

ANSWER KEY

Section V Quantitative Ability	Section VI Analytical Ability	Section VII Quantitative Ability
1. B	1. E	1. B
2. B	2. C	2. D
3. C	3. E	3. B
4. C	4. B	4. B
5. C	5. B	5. A
6. A	6. C	6. C
7. D	7. B	7. A
8. B	8. E	8. A
9. A	9. D	9. D
10. A	10. C	10. B
11. B	11. D	11. D
12. C	12. C	12. B
13. B	13. E	13. D
14. C	14. C	14. C
15. D	15. C	15. B
16. D	16. E	16. C
17. C	17. B	17. A
18. C	18. B	18. B
19. B	19. C	19. B
20. E	20. A	20. C
21. C	21. D	21. C
22. B	22. B	22. D
23. C	23. D	23. C
24. E	24. C	24. D
25. B	25. C	25. B
26. C		26. B
27. B		27. E
28. B		28. E
29. B		29. D
30. C		30. C

SCORE RANGE APPROXIMATORS

The following charts are designed to give you only an approximate score range, not an exact score. When you take the GRE General Test, you will have questions that are similar to those in this book; however, some questions may be slightly easier or more difficult. Needless to say, this may affect your scoring range.

Because one section of the GRE is experimental (it doesn't count toward your score), for the purposes of this approximation, do not count Section VII. Remember, on the actual test the experimental section could appear anywhere on your test.

Verbal Ability

To approximate your verbal score:

1. Total the number of questions you answered correctly in sections II and IV. No points are subtracted for incorrect answers.
2. Use the following table to match the total number of correct answers in those two sections and the corresponding approximate score range.

Number Right	Approximate Score Range
65–75	710–800
55–64	590–700
45–54	490–580
35–44	400–480
25–34	320–390
15–24	220–310
0–14	200–220

Average score is approximately 480.

Quantitative Ability

To approximate your quantitative score:

1. Total the number of questions you answered correctly in Sections I and V. No points are subtracted for incorrect answers.
2. Use the following table to match the total number of correct answers in those two sections and the corresponding approximate score range.

Number Right	Approximate Score Range
50–60	700–800
40–49	570–690
30–39	450–560
20–29	330–440
10–19	220–320
0–9	200–210

Average score is approximately 560.

Analytical Ability

To approximate your analytical score:

1. Total the number of questions you answered correctly in Sections III and VI. No points are subtracted for incorrect answers.
2. Use the following table to match the total number of correct answers in those two sections and the corresponding approximate score range.

Number Right	Approximate Score Range
40–50	700–800
30–39	560–690
20–29	410–550
10–19	240–400
0–9	200–230

Average score is approximately 540.

Remember, these are *approximate* score ranges.

ANALYZING YOUR TEST RESULTS

The charts on the following pages should be used to carefully analyze your results and spot your strengths and weaknesses. The complete process of analyzing each subject area and each individual problem should be completed for each practice test. These results should then be reexamined for trends in types of errors (repeated errors) or poor results in specific subject areas. THIS REEXAMINATION AND ANALYSIS IS OF TREMENDOUS IMPORTANCE TO YOU IN ASSURING MAXIMUM TEST PREPARATION BENEFIT.

VERBAL ABILITY ANALYSIS SHEET

SECTION II

	Possible	Completed	Right	Wrong
Sentence Completion	8			
Analogies	9			
Reading Comprehension	11			
Antonyms	10			
SUBTOTALS	38			

SECTION IV

	Possible	Completed	Right	Wrong
Sentence Completion	9			
Analogies	9			
Reading Comprehension	11			
Antonyms	10			
SUBTOTALS	39			
OVERALL VERBAL ABILITY TOTALS	77			

QUANTITATIVE ABILITY ANALYSIS SHEET

SECTION I

	Possible	Completed	Right	Wrong
Quantitative Comparison	15			
Math Ability	15			
SUBTOTALS	30			

SECTION V

	Possible	Completed	Right	Wrong
Quantitative Comparison	15			
Math Ability	15			
SUBTOTALS	30			
OVERALL QUANTITATIVE ABILITY TOTALS	60			

SECTION VII

NOTE: For this practice test, do not include Section VII in your overall Quantitative Ability score.

	Possible	Completed	Right	Wrong
Quantitative Comparison	15			
Math Ability	15			
TOTALS	30			

ANALYTICAL ABILITY ANALYSIS SHEET

	Possible	Completed	Right	Wrong
Section III	25			
Section VI	25			
OVERALL ANALYTICAL ABILITY TOTALS	50			

ANALYSIS: TALLY SHEET FOR PROBLEMS MISSED

One of the most important parts of test preparation is analyzing WHY! you missed a problem so that you can reduce the number of mistakes. Now that you have taken the practice test and corrected your answers, carefully tally your mistakes by marking them in the proper column.

REASON FOR MISTAKE

	Total Missed	Simple Mistake	Misread Problem	Lack of Knowledge
SECTION II: VERBAL ABILITY				
SECTION IV: VERBAL ABILITY				
SUBTOTALS				
SECTION I: QUANTITATIVE ABILITY				
SECTION V: QUANTITATIVE ABILITY				
SUBTOTALS				
SECTION III: ANALYTICAL ABILITY				
SECTION VI: ANALYTICAL ABILITY				
SUBTOTALS				
TOTAL VERBAL, QUANTITATIVE, AND ANALYTICAL				

Reviewing the above data should help you determine WHY you are missing certain problems. Now that you have pinpointed the type of error, take the next practice test focusing on avoiding your most common type.

COMPLETE ANSWERS AND EXPLANATIONS FOR PRACTICE TEST 2

SECTION I: QUANTITATIVE ABILITY

Quantitative Comparison

1. (A) Since both sides have the factors $2/5$ and $5/8$, you may eliminate them from each column. Now compare

   $3/7$ and $4/11$ by

   cross multiplying upward and you get (33) (28).

   $$\frac{3}{7} \times \frac{4}{11}$$

   Since 33 is greater than 28, $3/7 > 4/11$

2. (D) Substituting 0 for x, 1 for y, and 2 for z, gives

   (0) + (1) + (2)   (0)(1)(2)
   Therefore   3 > 0

   Now substituting −1 for x, 0 for y, and 1 for z gives

   (−1) + (0) + (1)   (−1)(0)(1)
   Therefore   0 = 0

   Since different values give different comparisons, the correct answer is (D).

3. (C) This is really an example of the distributive property of multiplication over addition. By multiplying (b + c)a you would get ab + ac.
   Therefore the correct answer is (C).

4. (A) Solving the equation

   $x\sqrt{.09} = 2$
   $x(.3) = 2$

   dividing by .3,

   $$\frac{x(.3)}{(.3)} = \frac{2}{.3}$$

$x = 20/3 = 6\frac{2}{3}$

Therefore $7 > 6\frac{2}{3}$

5. (A) To find the number of degrees in the interior angles of a pentagon use the formula $180 \times (n - 2)$, where n is the number of sides. Therefore $180 \times (5 - 2) = 180 \times 3 = 540$.

   $540° > 500°$

   Another method would be to draw the pentagon and break it into triangles connecting vertices, (lines cannot cross) as shown below.

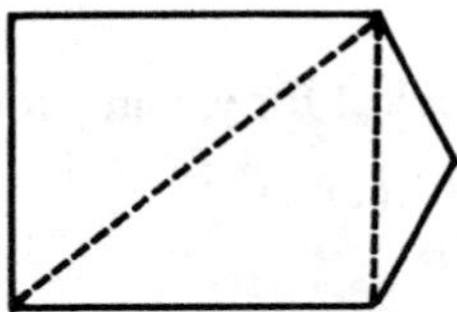

   Multiplying the number of triangles (3) by 180 (degrees in a triangle) gives the same result, 540°.

6. (D) Substituting $x = 0$ and $y = 1$

	$(x - y)^2$		$x^2 - y^2$
	$(0 - 1)^2$		$(0)^2 - (1)^2$
then	1	$>$	-1

   Now substituting $x = -1$ and $y = 0$

gives	$(-1 - 0)^2$		$(-1)^2 - (0)^2$
	$(-1)^2$		$(-1)^2$
then	1	$=$	1

   Since different values give different comparisons, then no comparison can be made.

7. (B) Finding a common denominator is not necessary here. Make a partial comparison by comparing the first fraction in each column; 1/71 is smaller than 1/65. Now comparing the second fractions that are being subtracted, 1/151 is greater than 1/153. If you start with a smaller number and subtract a greater number, it must be less than starting with a greater number and subtracting a smaller one.

8. (B) If a = b and a < c, then the following substitutions make the comparison simpler.

    2a   b + c
    a + a   b + c

    Since a = b, then

    a + b   b + c

    Now canceling b's from each column leaves a < c.

9. (D) The length of side AB is determinable by using the Pythagorean theorem, but since DC is not known, BC cannot be determined. Note that you cannot make a determination by measuring.

10. (C) ∠BAD = ∠ABD, for angles across from equal sides in a triangle are equal.

11. (C) Since there are 180° in a triangle and ∠BDC is 90°, the remaining two angles, ∠DBC and ∠BCD, must total 90°.

12. (A) AB + BC is greater than AC, since the sum of any two sides of a triangle is greater than the third side.

13. (A) Dividing the equation by 3 gives x − 4y = 12; now multiplying this by 2 gives 2x − 8y = 24. Therefore, column A is 24, which is greater than column B.

14. (B) Simplifying each column leaves

    $1/x^2$ $1/x^3$

    Now substituting simple fractions such as 1/2 gives

    $1/(1/2)^2$ $1/(1/2)^3$
    1/(1/4)   1/(1/8)
    4   <   8

    Column B will always be greater.

15. (C) Since triangle ABC is inscribed in a semicircle, angle C is 90°. Because there are 180° in a triangle, the sum of the

remaining angles, ∠CAB and ∠ABC, must total 90°. Therefore, the correct answer is (C) because 180 − 90 = 90.

Math Ability

16. (A) Multiply numerator and denominator by 12 (lowest common denominator).

$$\frac{12(2/3 - 1/2)}{12(1/6 + 1/4 + 2/3)} = \frac{8 - 6}{2 + 3 + 8} = 2/13$$

17. (B) Since XY = YZ = 10, then △XYZ is an isosceles △ and ∠X = ∠Z. ∠Y = 84°, since it forms a vertical angle with the given angle.

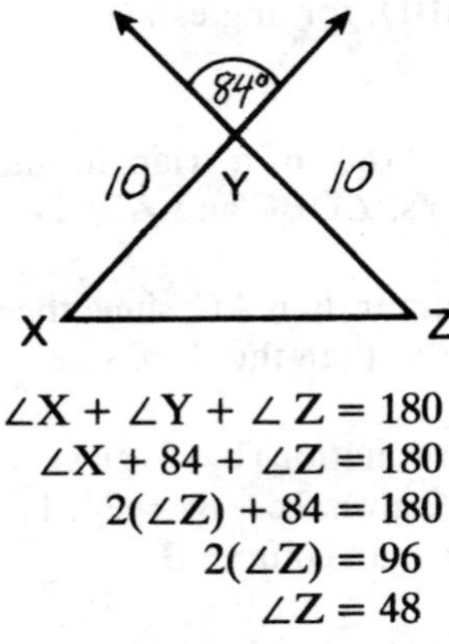

$$\begin{aligned} \angle X + \angle Y + \angle Z &= 180 \\ \angle X + 84 + \angle Z &= 180 \\ 2(\angle Z) + 84 &= 180 \\ 2(\angle Z) &= 96 \\ \angle Z &= 48 \end{aligned}$$

Hence the measure of ∠Z = 48°.

18. (B) If ⅔ of the container is full, there remains ⅓ of the container to fill. The time to fill ⅓ of the container will be half as long as the time needed to fill ⅔ of the container. Hence ½ (18 minutes) = 9 minutes.

19. (A) Since arc YXZ is a semicircle, its measure is 180°.

$$\begin{aligned} \text{arc XZ} &= \text{arc YXZ} - \text{arc YWX} \\ &= 180° - 100° \\ \text{arc XZ} &= 80° \end{aligned}$$

Since an inscribed angle = ½ (intercepted arc) we have

$$\angle XYZ = \tfrac{1}{2}(\text{arc } XZ)$$
$$= \tfrac{1}{2}(80)^\circ$$
$$= 40^\circ$$

Hence ∠XYZ has a measure of 40°.

20. (B) If the average of 9 numbers is 7, then the sum of these numbers must be 9 × 7, or 63.
If the average of 7 numbers is 9, then the sum of these numbers must be 7 × 9, or 63.
The sum of all 16 numbers must be 63 + 63, or 126.
Hence the average of all 16 numbers must be

$$126 \div 16 = \tfrac{126}{16} = 7\tfrac{14}{16} = 7\tfrac{7}{8}$$

21. (D) I and II only. In 1974, white students comprised 60%; other students comprised 20%; in 1976, white students comprised 40%; other students comprised 20%; in 1978, however, white students comprised 30% while other students also comprised 30%.

22. (B) In 1974, there were 60% white and 5% black students. Thus there were 12 times as many whites as blacks. Since there were 2000 whites in 1974, there were 2000/12 or 167 blacks.

23. (C) In 1976, there were 1000 white students. This was 40% of the total. Thus, the total must have been 2500.

24. (C) Whites declined from 80% to 30%, (50/80), a 62.5% decrease. Blacks increased from 5% to 15%, (10/5), a 200% increase. Mexican Americans increased from 5% to 25% (20/5), a 400% increase. Others increased from 10% to 30%, (20/10), a 200% increase.

25. (E) In 1974 there were 20% other and 60% white. Thus there were three times as many whites as others. Since there were 2000 whites, there were 666 other. In 1976, 40% white and 20%

other. Twice as many whites as other. Thus 500 other. Therefore, a decrease of 166.

26. (D) $\dfrac{(6!)(4!)}{(5!)(3!)}$

$$= \frac{(6 \cdot 5 \cdot 4 \cdot 3 \cdot 2 \cdot 1) \cdot (4 \cdot 3 \cdot 2 \cdot 1)}{(5 \cdot 4 \cdot 3 \cdot 2 \cdot 1) \cdot (3 \cdot 2 \cdot 1)}$$

$$= \frac{6 \cdot 4}{1} = 24$$

27. (B) Adding any two of three consecutive positive integers greater than 1 will always be greater than the other integer; therefore II is true. The others cannot be determined because they depend on values and/or the order of x, y, and z.

28. (B) If two points have coordinates (x_1, y_1) and (x_2, y_2), the distance, d, between these points is defined to be

$$d = \sqrt{(x_1 - x_2)^2 + (y_1 - y_2)^2}$$

Since E has coordinates $(-3, 5)$ and F has coordinates $(6, -7)$, the distance between E and F is

$$\begin{aligned} EF &= \sqrt{(-3 - 6)^2 + [5 - (-7)]^2} \\ &= \sqrt{(-9)^2 + (12)^2} \\ &= \sqrt{81 + 144} \\ &= \sqrt{225} \\ EF &= 15 \end{aligned}$$

29. (E) Perimeter = 10 feet
= (10)(12) inches
= 120 inches

Perimeter = $4s$(s = length of side)

$$4s = 120$$

$$\frac{4s}{4} = \frac{120}{4}$$

Area = s^2

$= (30)^2$

$= (30)(30)$

$= 900$ square inches

30. (C) Let x be the length of time Mr. Dinkle travels, then x + ½ is the time Mr. Smitherly travels. This gives the equation 50(x + ½) = 60x, to see when they will meet. Solving gives

$$\begin{aligned} 50x + 25 &= 60x \\ 25 &= 10x \\ 2.5 &= x \end{aligned}$$

Therefore, it will take Mr. Dinkle 2½ hours to overtake Mr. Smitherly. Since Mr. Dinkle starts at 8:30 A.M., he will overtake Mr. Smitherly at 11:00 A.M. Note that answers (A), (D), and (E) are not reasonable.

SECTION II: VERBAL ABILITY

Sentence Completion

1. (B) Working from the second blank first, notice that you are looking for a word coinciding with *thought.* Only *specter* is a type of thought (something that haunts or perturbs the mind), and along with it, *holocaust* (destruction by fire) makes good sense.

2. (B) Those who are *uncritical* of *regulation* would tend to hold *conventional* values. Along with this, *subsidization* (support) makes good sense.

3. (E) The correct answer is *conciliatory.* The sentence sets up a contrast situation with the word *but.* Truman tried to do something but ended up adopting a *tougher policy. Conciliatory* is the only choice which suggests a previous weaker approach.

4. (B) The answer is *vehement . . . acrimonious.* The signal words *controversial* and *more* and *more* suggest a conflict which increases or intensifies. The only pair which supports these context clues is *vehement . . . acrimonious.* Even if you are not certain of the definition of *acrimonious,* the other choices can be eliminated because none of them suggests the intensification of the controversy.

5. (B) The correct answer is *parsimonious.* The context provides a definition for the correct choice in *is more than economical.* The context also suggests the trait of being excessively frugal by the word *so.* Choices (C) and (D) would not apply because they mean poor and the aunt, we know, is wealthy. Choice (A) is not excessive. (E) does not fit with the exmple of washing paper plates.

6. (C) The correct answer is *still . . . media.* The phrase *in spite of* suggests an enduring situation, unchanged by competition. The second word is practically defined by the phrase *communication between advertisers and customers.*

7. (D) The second blank is a noun for which institutions must be *blamed,* so (A) cannot be right. The missing adjective must fit a primitivist view of human nature, and a view of humans as blameless. The only positive adjective is *benevolent.*

8. (D) In this case, the second blank is easier to fill because it is followed by a definition. *Differentiation* is *the recognition of different categories of people,* etc. *Stratification* which *does* imply the differences in rank which *differentiation* does not, is also appropriate.

Analogies

9. (C) The relationship here is one of opposites. *Ambiguous* (unclear or indefinite) is to *clear* as *synthetic* (false) is to *real.*

10. (D) The first term is an extralegal counterpart of the second. A *lynching* is an illegal form of *execution,* as *vigilante* (a member of an enforcement group organized without legal authority) differs from a *police officer.*

11. (C) The *larva* is the early form of an animal that undergoes structural changes, not merely growth, when it becomes an *adult*—for example, a *tadpole* and a *frog.*

12. (B) One meaning of the noun *extract* is excerpt, or *quotation. Forecast* and *prediction* are also alike.

13. (E) A *cupola* is a small structure built or resting on a *roof* (sometimes used as a belfry, lookout point, etc.) The *statue* on a *pedestal* is the closest parallel.

14. (A) A *felony* is a more serious crime than a *misdemeanor.* The analogy is the more serious *blunder* as opposed to *mistake.*

15. (A) The difficulty here is the meaning and part of speech of *fry.* The noun here means the young of fish, so the parallel is *lion* and *whelp.*

16. (B) As a *slothful* person is not likely to *overwork,* so a *mean* (stingy) person is unlikely to *overspend.*

17. (C) An *anachronism* is an error of time *period* where an object or event is represented in an era or period in which it does not belong. A *fallacy* is false reasoning, an error of *logic.*

Reading Comprehension

18. (B) The terms *indicates* and *suggestion* imply that theories described are only theories and not universally accepted. The passage calls DNA *the common denominator of all living things.*

19. (D) *Evolution* is to *species* in the same way as *bush* is to *branches.* Just as the branches of a bush reach out every which way in varying lengths, the results of evolution (forms of life, species) have devolved in irregular "branches." This is the main point of the second paragraph.

20. (B) Blue-green algae are the second step, emerging from bacteria.

21. (E) The passage presents sponges as evolving from rhizoflagellates, which came from green flagellates, which came from bacteria.

22. (B) Demand, as economists use the word, requires the relationship between price and the quantity demanded to remain unchanged. In both I and III the price has changed, rising in III and falling in I.

23. (C) The passage says the *demand shifts when there is a change in income, expectations, taste, etc., such that a different quantity of the good is demanded at the same price.* (A), (D), and (E) all involve a changing price, and (B) would reduce income so that demand would decrease.

24. (A) Intially, the passage emphasizes a distinction between *demand* and *quantity demanded,* concluding that *demand shifts when there is a change in income, expectations, taste, etc., such that a different quantity of the good is demanded at the same price.* This statement fits (A) precisely. All other choices include or allow for a changing price.

25. (C) This situation establishes a relationship between price and quantity which parallels the paragraph's explanation of the *law of demand.* This section discusses *the consumer's desire to get the "best buy"* and goes on to say that *if the price of good A increases, the individual will tend to substitute another good and purchase less of good A.* Since the appearance of a lower-priced breakfast drink makes orange juice more "expensive," in relation, the law of demand as so described would prevail.

26. (D) According to the law of diminishing marginal utility, as more units of a good are consumed, there is less utility or customer satisfaction (paragraph 3).

27. (D) The third paragraph distinguishes between *individual demand* and *market demand;* the former is exercised by a single person, whereas the latter is exerted by a group of individuals. With this distinction in mind, we may conclude that a group of individuals constitutes a market.

28. (A) The passage defines a number of important economic terms. Though it does question a popular misunderstanding (E), it does so only in the first paragraph. The passage does not deal with supply, (B), or marketing, (D).

Antonyms

29. (B) A *covenent* (*co* = together; *ven* = come) is a solemn mutual agreement. A *breach* is a violation of such an agreement.

30. (E) *Precarious* describes an uncertain, often dangerous, situation. The most nearly opposite is *certain.*

31. (A) *Contumacious* refers to defiance of authority. Its opposite is *compliant,* which refers to agreeing or giving in.

32. (A) *Wrangle,* a noun here, means a dispute or quarrel. The opposite is *concord,* harmony, agreement.

33. (B) *Tractable* (*tract* = to draw or pull) means easy to manage. Its opposite is *refractory,* which means difficult to manage, stubborn, obstinate. *Retractable* means capable of being withdrawn or denied.

34. (B) *Vapid* is often used to refer to talk which is extremely dull; it is quite the opposite of *engaging,* which suggests an "interesting" quality more strongly than any of the other choices.

35. (C) *Glib* refers to someone who speaks readily and easily. The opposite is *halting.*

36. (C) A *prototype* is an original, a model. The opposite here is *facsimile,* a copy or reproduction.

37. (E) *Plethora* generally means an overabundance; therefore, the opposite is *shortage. Modicum* is a possibility, but is not as extreme as *shortage.*

38. (B) The adjective *morbid* means unhealthy, diseased. Its antonym is *hale,* which means vigorous and healthy.

SECTION III: ANALYTICAL ABILITY

From the information for questions 1–6, these simple notes could be drawn:

RS or SR   ~~QW~~   V . . . T

1. (D) If *Victory* and *Terror* are screened the same day (obviously *Victory* first, since *Terror* cannot be screened prior to *Victory*), and if *Rats* and *Sam* are screened the same day according to the parameters of the schedule, that leaves two films (*Quest to Hope* and *Wellfleet*) to be screened over the remaining three days. Since these two films cannot be screened on the same day, exactly one day will have no film screening.

2. (D) *Terror* cannot be screened prior to *Victory*'s screening.

3. (A) If *Sam* is screened on Friday, then *Rats* must also be screened on Friday, since *Sam* and *Rats* are to be screened the same day. So if *Wellfleet* is also screened on Friday, that would mean three films are screened the same day, which does not conform to the parameters of the schedule.

4. (E) *Victory* cannot be screened on Saturday, since it must be screened prior to *Terror.*

5. (D) If *Victory* is screened on Sunday, it must be the first of two films screened that day, since *Terror* must be screened after it.

6. (E) *Victory* and *Terror* can both be screened the same day if *Victory* is shown first.

7. (B) *Sock* could not be in column 2 because it starts with *s. Stock* already starts with *s.*

8. (D) *Stove* could be added to column 4 because it starts with *s* and is five letters.

9. (D) Column 4 contains the word *strand,* which breaks the rule about having only five letters.

10. (C) III, *spill,* could not be added to column 1 because it starts with *s* (*still* already starts with *s*), and IV, *instill,* could not be added because it has seven letters.

11. (D) By inspection, we can see that each word in column 3 has two vowels.

12. (E) *Bill, dock, cream,* and *stow* do not violate any column rules and have no more than five letters.

13. (D) The passage is arguing that the rich are *not* treated unfairly. And if most of the money collected in taxes is used *to protect or enhance* wealth, the rich are the ones who profit from taxes after they have been collected.

14. (A) The conclusion is to follow the question *And why not?* That is, why should a farmer continue to resist conservation? Because water is cheap, and no rewards for conserving are offered.

15. (B) The commissioner is presented with a problem—a high crime rate—and the commissioner's reaction to it is to fight it by getting pay raises for city employees, which include the police. The commissioner therefore assumes that paying a police officer more will be instrumental in causing a lower crime rate.

From the information for questions 16–20, these notes can be drawn:

E . . . CF

D . . . AB

16. (B) In (A), Berti does not receive the ball from Ali. In (C), Fran does not carry the ball after Evan. In (D), Dani does not carry the ball before Ali. In (E), Cap does not pass the ball to Fran.

17. (E) If Dani carried the ball second, that leaves only Evan to carry the ball first.

18. (D) If Berti carried the ball fourth, then Cap and Fran must have carried the ball fifth and sixth.

19. (B) II only. Berti could not have been second because both Dani and Ali must carry the ball before Berti.

20. (B) If Berti passed the ball to Evan, then the order of carrying the ball must be: D, A, B, E, C, F.

From the information given for questions 21–22, the following chart may be constructed.

	Streets	*People On*	*People Get On*	*People Get Off*
	1	3		
Stop At	2		3	at least 1
	3			
	4			
Stop At	5			

21. (A) The van left First Street with three passengers aboard. At Second Street, three passengers got on the van. Since the van holds up to five passengers, at least one passenger must have gotten off the van at that Second Street stop to have allowed three passengers to board.

22. (B) II only. Since the van can hold up to five passengers, at least one passenger must have gotten off at the Second Street stop to accommodate the three passengers boarding there. Only II must be false; I and III could be true.

23. (B) Some of the other options may be true, but they cannot be inferred from this paragraph. The marked decline in the number of deaths since the act of suicide became more difficult to perform with household gas suggests that given more time to reflect, many would change their minds.

24. (E) The author uses the particular case of *little Jimmy Jones* to argue for the passage of the bond measure.

25. (B) The passage claims nothing but benefits from the changes, but the benefits have been to businesses, not to the individual consumer, whose rates have risen. Some of the other options neither support nor refute the argument of the passage.

SECTION IV: VERBAL ABILITY

Sentence Completion

1. (E) The best choice is *comparing . . . expectations.* The signal clues are *unknown world* and *careful to note.* The phrase *careful to note* suggests careful thought or *comparing,* while *unknown world* suggests a meaning in this sentence that is best fulfilled by the word *expectations.* In choice(B), the word *refuting* is negative and does not convey the intended meaning of *careful to note.*

2. (A) The *but* suggests that the first half of the sentence deals with a period before the recession when business is likely to be good, so either (A) or (C) is plausible. But the verb must be negative, so (C) can be eliminated.

3. (B) The use of *despite* with *staid appearance* suggests that the missing word must be unlike *staid.* The best choice is *volatile* (changeable, active).

4. (E) It makes good sense to conclude that a political institution would protect society from *external* forces—that is, those forces which threaten society as a whole. *Salient* (conspicuous, prominent) fits this meaning too.

5. (D) In this case, the second blank is easier to fill because it is followed by a definition; *relating the unfamiliar to the familiar by means of likeness* is a definition of *analogy.* Linking *analogical* with *interpreting,* we note that myths do indeed interpret nature, that is, the beginnings of cultures and societies.

6. (A) The signal word is *seamen. Circumnavigate* (sail around) is something only a seaman could no. None of the other choices has any relationship to either commerce or seamen.

7. (D) The best choice is *fail . . . operational.* The signal here is *cannot ________ to be impressed,* which should be a negative word, while the second choice should be a complement to *structural,* which is *operational.*

8. (E) The blank must be the opposite of *earthbound* and *materialistic.* The best choice, therefore, is *transcendental* (transcending material existence).

9. (B) The answer is *effect . . . conflict.* A cause and effect relationship is set up in this sentence with a negative term required for the second blank suggested by the term *bitter.*

Analogies

10. (A) In this problem, *candy* is a verb meaning to preserve with *sugar.* The analogous *pickle* is a verb meaning to preserve with *brine.*

11. (C) As a *helmet* is worn to protect the *head, goggles* are worn to protect the *eyes.* A *ring* is worn on the *finger,* but it is not the best answer because it is not worn for protection.

12. (C) One meaning of *domino* is a mask or a costume with a mask worn to a *masquerade.* The analogous *tuxedo* is the proper *prom* costume.

13. (C) The visibility of air is made *indistinct* (obscure) by *mist; light,* on the other hand, will make a scene glowing or *refulgent.*

14. (D) A very *enthusiastic* adherent to a cause is a *zealot,* as a very *lazy* man or woman is an *idler.*

15. (E) A *bellwether* is a leader of a *flock,* not merely a member. *Foreman* and *crew* is the closest analogy.

16. (D) A *bibliographer* (a student of editions, publications, authorship) is likely to do his or her work in a *library,* as a *teacher* is likely to work in a *classroom.*

17. (B) A *prolix* person is given to *verbiage* (wordiness); that is, the person is wordy or long-winded. The parallel is *fecund* (fertile) and *fertility.*

18. (D) A *wanton* life is licentious, an *ascetic* life, restrained. The analogy here is the opposition of *obstreperous* (boisterous) and *shy.*

Reading Comprehension

19. (D) The first paragraph explains that a universal Adam would involve all of the particulars of his class in his actions.

20. (C) According to Augustine, even a new-born would be guilty of the sin of Adam.

21. (C) The sins of the will are those which are pleasant at the moment, such as eating. Sins of pride, envy, or wrath are sins of the intellect.

22. (B) The second paragraph presents the notion of a good mind and evil body as Greek.

23. (C) The passage gives no information on the number of land lizards or on how the marine lizard divides its time.

24. (B) The passage suggests that land and sea lizards resemble one another. Since the sea lizard is said never to venture more than ten yards inland from shore, we can infer the land lizard lives further inland. If the sea lizard's feet are only partially webbed, it is unlikely that the land species has webbed feet.

25. (D) Since the lizard probably feeds at the sea bottom, the author has not observed its feeding habits. The second paragraph supports the two inferences.

26. (D) The passage suggests that the lizards feed on seaweed and that seaweed grows at some distance from the coast.

27. (A) In the second paragraph, the author refers to the *structure of its tail and feet* as evidence of its aquatic habits.

28. (C) Since the marine lizards would not flee into the water to escape the land predator, we can assume a land animal would be more successful than a marine predator.

29. (E) The passage deals with a specifc marine lizard, not with (B), herbivorous lizards in general. It says hardly anything at all about land lizards, (A).

Antonyms

30. (D) *Obsequious* means extremely submissive and polite (*ob* = upon; *sequor* = follow). The most nearly opposite is *rude.*

31. (D) *Bellicose* (*bell* = war) means inclined to fighting, hostile, quarrelsome. Its opposite, then, is *peaceful. Calm* is not correct because a calm person is not necessarily a nonhostile person.

32. (A) *Sporadic* means happening from time to time, not regular; the antonym here is *constant.*

33. (D) *Reserve* is reticence. The antonym here is *loquacity,* a noun meaning talkativeness.

34. (C) *Piquant* means pungent or flavorful. *Insipid* means without sufficient taste.

35. (D) *Insouciant* means carefree or without concern. *Concerned* is the nearest opposite.

36. (B) Here *spruce* is an adjective which means neat, trim, clean. The opposite is *squalid.*

37. (A) *Perfidy* means a breach of faith, or treachery. *Faithfulness* would be its opposite.

38. (B) *Palingenesis* means a transformation from one state to another. *Stablity* would be the opposite.

39. (C) *Hie* means to move with haste. *Saunter* is to linger or move slowly.

SECTION V: QUANTITATIVE ABILITY

Quantitative Comparison

1. (B) By inspection, if you multiply (.89/.919) × 57, this must be less than 57 (as you are multiplying 57 by a fraction less than 1). Therefore it must be less than 58. The correct answer is (B).

2. (B) Substituting -1 for x gives $(-1)^3 - 1 = -1 - 1 = -2$. Now trying -2 for x gives $(-2)^3 - 1 = -8 - 1 = -9$. It is evident that this phrase will always generate negative values if $x < 0$. Therefore, the correct answer is (B). The cube of a negative is negative. One less than a negative is negative. Any negative is less than 0.

3. (C) The prime numbers between 3 and 19 are 5, 7, 11, 13, and 17. The correct answer is (C), since there are 5 primes.

4. (C) To solve $a/6 = b/4$

   cross multiply, giving $4a = 6b$
   then divide by 2
   leaving $2a = 3b$

5. (C) $\overset{\frown}{AC} = 2(\angle B)$, since an inscribed angle is half of the arc it subtends (connects to).

6. (A) Since $\angle AOB$ is a central angle, it equals the measure of $\overset{\frown}{AB}$, and since $\angle ADC$ is outside the circle, but also intersects the circle at $\overset{\frown}{AB}$, it is less than half of $\overset{\frown}{AB}$. Therefore

   $\angle AOB > \angle ADC$

   Alternate method: The external angle AOB must be larger than either of the remote interior angles.

7. (D) This problem is best solved by inspection or insight. Since there are two variables in this single inequality, there are many possible values for x and y; therefore a comparison cannot be made.

8. (B) First set up the numbers for each side:

Number of inches in 1 mile	Number of minutes in 1 year
(12 inches in 1 ft) × (5280 ft in 1 mile)	(60 minutes in 1 hr) × (24 hrs in 1 day) × (365 days in 1 yr)
12 × 5280	60 × 24 × 365

Now dividing out, a 10 and 12 leaves

1 × 528	6 × 2 × 365
or 528	12 × 365

Column B is obviously greater.

9. (A) Area of circle with diameter 8 is computed by finding the radius, which is half of the diameter and substituting into this equation $A = \pi r^2$. Since the radius is 4, and π is about 3.14

$\pi (4)^2$	Area of square with
3.14 × 16	side 7 is
50.24	49

10. (A) Changing the form of column A by squaring 3 and multiplying it by 2 to get everything under the radical sign leaves the simple comparison $\sqrt{18} > \sqrt{17}$.

11. (B) Solving the systems of equations as follows by first multiplying the bottom equation by −5 gives

$5x + y = 2$
$-5x + -15y = -30$

Now adding equations leaves

$-14y = -28$

Therefore $y = 2$

Substituting $y = 2$ into the original second equation gives

	$x + 3(2) = 6$
then	$x + 6 = 6$
and	$x = 0$
Therefore	$x < y$

12. (C) Simplifying the complex fraction in column A as follows,

$$\frac{1}{1+\frac{1}{1+1/n}} = \frac{1}{1+\frac{1}{n/n+1/n}} = \frac{1}{1+\frac{1}{(n+1)/n}} = \frac{1}{1+\frac{n}{n+1}}$$

$$= \frac{1}{\frac{n+1}{n+1}+\frac{n}{n+1}} = \frac{1}{\frac{n+1+n}{n+1}} = \frac{1}{\frac{2n+1}{n+1}} = \frac{n+1}{2n+1}$$

An alternate method would involve substituting simple numbers into each expression.

13. (B) In quadrant II, all y values are positive and all x values are negative. Therefore, y will always be greater than x in quadrant II.

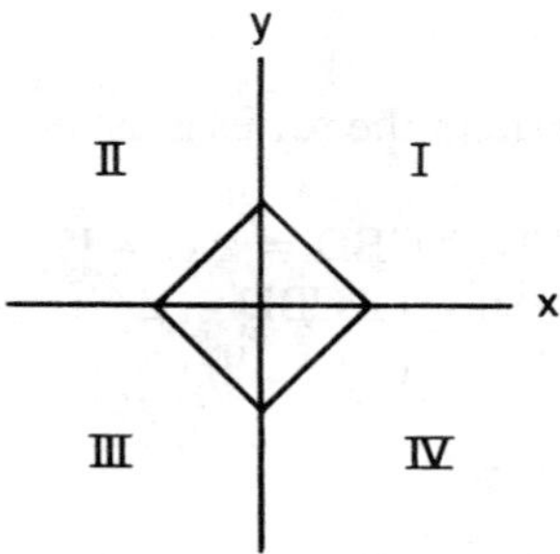

14. (C) Simplifying column A by following the rules for priorities of operations (powers, square root, multiply, divide, add, subtract) gives

$$5 + 4 \cdot 10^2 + 8 \cdot 10^3$$
$$5 + 4 \cdot 100 + 8 \cdot 1000$$
$$5 + 400 + 8000 = 8405$$

15. (D) We have not been given enough information to compare Jill and Joan.

Math Ability

16. (D) Solve for x, $2x - 5 = 9$
$$2x = 14$$
then $x = 7$

Now substitute 7 for x.

Hence $3x + 2 = 3(7) + 2$
$$= 21 + 2$$
$$= 23$$

17. (C) In the series, 8, 9, 12, 17, 24 . . .

$9 - 8 = 1$ $\quad 17 - 12 = 5$
$12 - 9 = 3$ $\quad 24 - 17 = 7$

Hence the difference between the next term and 24 must be 9 or
$x - 24 = 9$
and $x = 33$
Hence the next term in the series must be 33.

18. (C) Since BD = CD, $\angle CBD = \angle C = 19°$
Hence $\angle BDC = 180 - (\angle CBD - \angle C)$
$$= 180 - (19 + 19)$$
$$= 180 - 38$$
$$\angle BDC = 142°$$

then $\angle BDA = 180 - \angle BDC$
$$= 180 - 142$$
$$\angle BDA = 38°$$

Since AB = AD, $\angle ABD = \angle BDA = 38°$
Hence $\angle A = 180 - (\angle BDA + \angle ABD)$
$$= 180 - (38 + 38)$$
$$= 180 - 76$$
$$\angle A = 104°$$

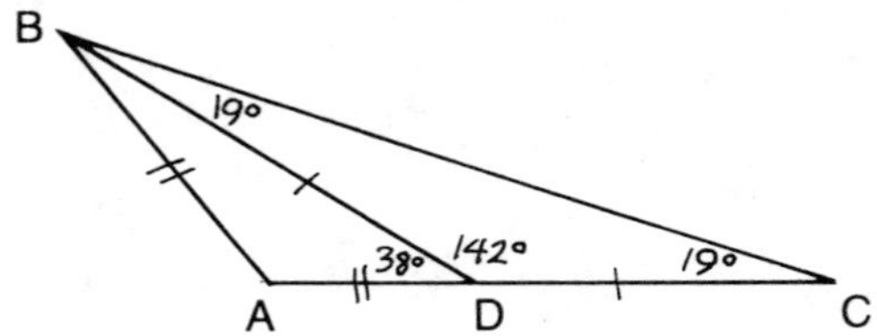

19. (B) Ratio of $\frac{3}{10}$ to $\frac{5}{8}$ = $(\frac{3}{10})/(\frac{5}{8})$
Multiply numerator and denominator by 40 (lowest common denominator).

$$\frac{40(\frac{3}{10})}{40(\frac{5}{8})} = \frac{12}{25}$$

Hence the ratio of $\frac{3}{10}$ to $\frac{5}{8}$ = $\frac{12}{25}$

20. (E) First change 2 hours into 120 minutes. (Always get a common unit of measurement.) Then dividing 120 by $\frac{2}{3}$ gives

$$\overset{60}{\cancel{120}} \times \frac{3}{\cancel{2}} = 180$$

The correct answer is (E), 180 items. Notice choices (A) and (B) are ridiculous answers.

21. (C) In 1970, housing was 25% of \$12,000, or \$3000. In that same year, medical expenses were 10% of \$12,000, or \$1200.

22. (B) In 1970, income spent on housing was 25% of \$12,000, or \$3000. In 1975, income spent on housing was 32% of \$16,000, or \$5120. The ratio is 3000 to 5120, or approximately 3 to 5.

23. (C) There was an increase from 18% to 22%. That is a 4% increase. Therefore a 4% increase from 18% is a 22% increase in the percent spent on food and drink.

24. (E) In 1975, entertainment was 7% of \$16,000, or \$1120. In 1970, entertainment was 7% of \$12,000, or \$840. So \$280 more was spent on entertainment in 1975 than in 1970.

25. (B) II only. Statement I cannot be inferred from the graph: savings in 1970 were 5% of \$12,000, or \$600, whereas savings in 1975 were 4% of \$16,000, or \$640. Statement II can be inferred from the graph: expenses for food and drink were a larger percentage of a larger total in 1975 than the corresponding figures in 1970. Statement III cannot be inferred from the graph: in 1970 "other" expenses comprised 35% of \$12,000, or \$4200. In 1975, "other" expenses comprised 23% of \$16,000, or \$3680.

26. (C) Since $\sqrt{mn} = 10$, $mn = 100$ and the possible values for m and n would be:

1 and 100	5 and 20
2 and 50	10 and 10
4 and 25	

Since none of these combinations yield $m + n = 50$, choice (C) is correct.

27. (B) Set up the problem as follows:

$$\frac{x + (2)}{x + 5 + (2)} = \frac{7}{12} \text{ or } \frac{x + 2}{x + 7} = \frac{7}{12}$$

By observation $x = 5$ since $\frac{5 + 2}{5 + 7} = \frac{7}{12}$

Substituting into the original fraction

$$\frac{x}{x + 5} \text{ gives } \frac{5}{5 + 5} = \frac{5}{10} = \frac{1}{2}$$

A longer method would have been to solve $\frac{x + 2}{x + 7} = \frac{7}{12}$ as follows:

Cross multiplying gives

$$12x + 24 = 7x + 49$$
$$5x = 25$$
$$x = 5$$

and then substitute in $\frac{x}{x + 5}$, or $\frac{5}{5 + 5} = \frac{5}{10} = \frac{1}{2}$

Alternate method: Subtract 2 from the numerator and denominator of $\frac{7}{12}$ and then reduce.

28. (B) Since $a = p + prt$

$$a - p = p + prt - p$$

$$a - p = prt$$

$$\frac{a - p}{pt} = \frac{prt}{pt}$$

$$\frac{a - p}{pt} = r$$

Hence
$$r = \frac{a - p}{pt}$$

29. (B) In parallelogram AEFG if all of the triangles have the same base, and they all meet at F (giving them all the same height), since the formula for area of a triangle is ½ × base × height, then they all have equal areas. Therefore the ratio of the area of triangle CDF to the area of triangle ABF is 1:1 and the correct answer is (B).

30. (C) Let x = first number
2x + 1 = second number
3x − 4 = third number
Since the average of the three numbers is 55, we have

$$\frac{x + (2x + 1) + (3x - 4)}{3} = 55$$

Multiplying both sides of our equation by 3, we have

$$x + (2x + 1) + (3x - 4) = 165$$

$$6x - 3 = 165$$

$$6x - 3 + 3 = 165 + 3$$

$$6x = 168$$

$$\frac{6x}{6} = \frac{168}{6}$$

$$x = \frac{168}{6}$$

x = 28 = first number
2x + 1 = 57 = second number
3x − 4 = 80 = third number
Hence the largest number is 80.

SECTION VI: ANALYTICAL ABILITY

From the information given for questions 1–6, this diagram can be drawn:

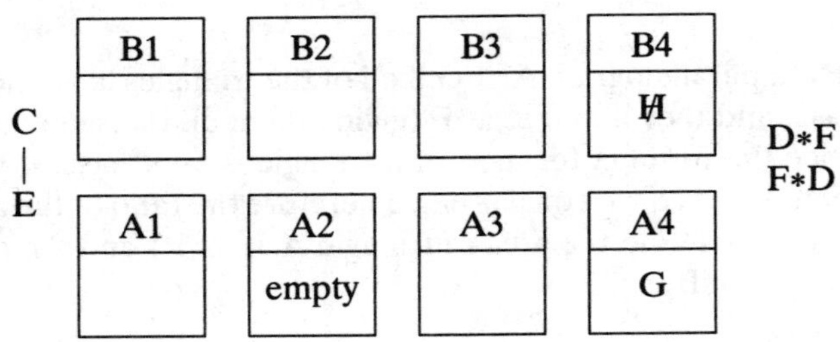

1. (E) If Davis sits in B3, seats A1 and B1 are the only seats remaining where Erkel can sit directly in front of Cabot. Therefore, since Forge cannot sit next to Davis, the only seat left for Forge is A3.

2. (C) If Harris and Erkel occupy A1 and A3, respectively, then Cabot must occupy B3. The diagram now looks like this:

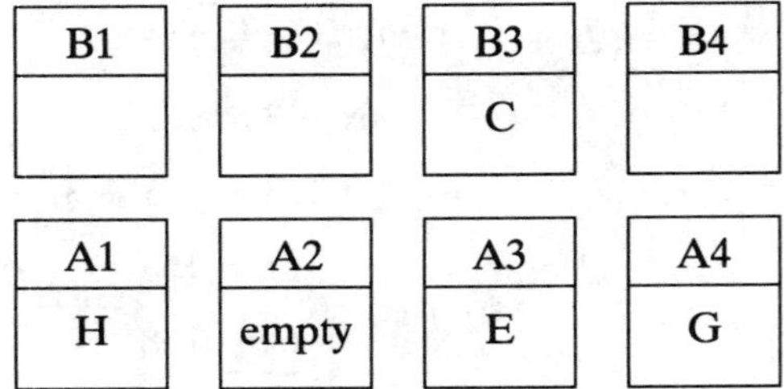

Since Davis cannot sit next to Forge,one of them must occupy seat B4.

3. (E) Since Erkel sits directly in front of Cabot, Erkel must sit in row A. Gabron sits in A4, also in row A.

4. (B) If Harris sits next to Gabron, Erkel and Cabot must sit in A1 and B1 respectively:

B1	B2	B3	B4
C			

A1	A2	A3	A4
E	empty	H	G

Since Forge does not sit next to Davis, seat B3 must be empty.

5. (B) Cabot will be sitting in either B1 or B3. If Cabot is in B1, then Harris must sit in B2. If Cabot is in B3, Harris can sit only in B2, since Harris does not sit in B4.

6. (C) If Forge sits in B3, the diagram looks like this:

B1	B2	B3	B4
		F	

A1	A2	A3	A4
	empty		G

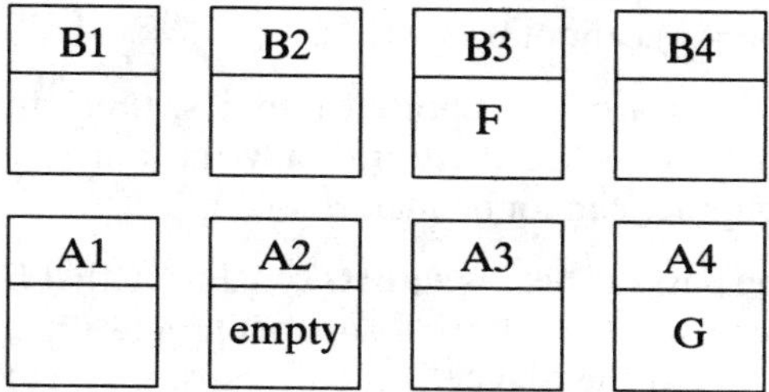

Now Erkel and Cabot must sit in A1 and B1, respectively:

B1	B2	B3	B4
C		F	

A1	A2	A3	A4
E	empty		G

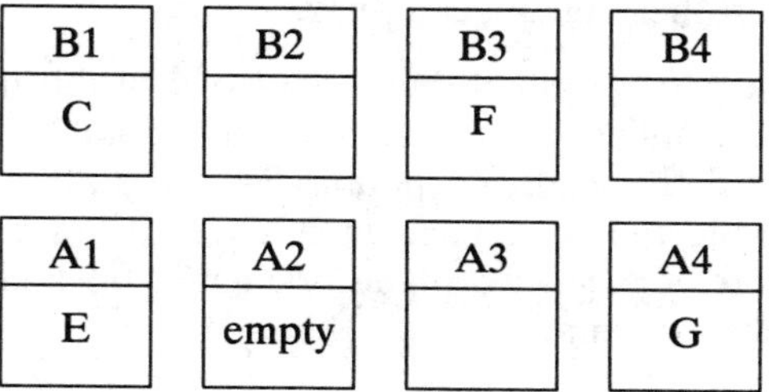

From the information given for questions 7–10, constructing a simple chart may be helpful:

___	___	___	___	___	___	___	___	7 brown
F	F	F	F	F	M	M	M	4 spotted

7. (B) Only II must be true. Since seven puppies are brown, the one nonbrown puppy could be either one of the males or one of the females. Therefore, I (All of the females are brown) is not necessarily true. Or the one nonbrown puppy could be male; therefore, only two male puppies are brown, so III (Three of the brown puppies are male) is not necessarily true. If four puppies are spotted, even if all three males are spotted, the fourth spotted puppy would be female. So only II must be true.

8. (E) Since there are five females and only four spotted puppies, all five of the females cannot be spotted.

9. (D) Since there are only four spotted puppies, all seven brown puppies cannot be spotted. Therefore, at least three of the brown puppies (7 − 4 = 3) cannot be spotted.

10. (C) If there are four spotted puppies, there must be four nonspotted puppies. Since there are only three male puppies, all four spotted puppies cannot be male.

11. (D) The passage begins with its conclusion that Biff is a great baseball player and then offers a supporting reason. If it takes a great player to lead the league in home runs, then Biff must be a great player, since he led the league in home runs.

12. (C) Only III is true. A diminished reputation in the marketplace could hurt the Wombat company.

13. (E) The passage establishes a chain of causality for academic success: stable families lead to stable children; stable children are able to fulfill their academic potential. And fulfilled academic potential is reflected by higher test scores. Choice (E) would weaken the statement, since orphans originate from homes in which neither parent is present.

With the information given for questions 14–19, a chart may be constructed.

	States							
Berry	CA	OR	WA	AR	NV	CO	ID	UT
Strawberry	X	X	X	—	—	—	X	—
Blueberry	—	X	X	X	X	—	—	—
Boysenberry	X	—	X	—	X	—	X	X
Blackberry	—	—	—	X	X	X	—	X
Raspberry	X	X	X	X	—	—	—	—
Gooseberry	—	X	X	—	—	—	X	X

14. (C) From the chart, it can be seen that boysenberries grow in five states.

15. (C) Washington has five varieties of berries.

16. (E) In Utah you can grow boysenberries, blackberries, and gooseberries.

17. (B) Oregon is the only state that grows strawberries but does not grow boysenberries.

18. (B) Blackberries grow in Nevada, but strawberries do not.

19. (C) Arizona and Nevada grow both blackberries and blueberries.

Questions 20–22 are answered by deduction. Since Julie is 2 years younger than Alice (4), and Julie is 23 years old, then Alice is 25. By statements 5 and 6 or by statement 8, Carol must be 22 years old. Therefore,

Carol is 22.
Julie is 23.
Alice is 25.

20. (A) I is true by substituting in the proper ages. Alice minus Julie is $25 - 23 = 2$, and this is greater than Julie minus Carol which is $23 - 22 = 1$. II is false since Carol is 22 years old.

21. (D) If Sheila is younger than Alice, she is younger than 25 but not older than Julie. She is then 23 or below. Sheila could therefore be the same age as Julie.

22. (B) If Jennifer is as many years older than Julie as she is younger than Alice, since Julie is 23 and Alice is 25, then Jennifer must be 24. So Jennier is 2 years older than Carol.

23. (D) The chairpersons suggest that the operative criteria for choosing an executive for a divisional position are interpersonal and social skills. All other criteria (for example, business acumen and training) are unimportant. Choice (E) is not necessarily true, as more than one divisional executive candidate with interpersonal and social skills may be considered for the same position with only one executive chosen. The executive(s) not chosen for that one position may be less qualified than the candidate chosen but nevertheless may have interpersonal and social skills.

24. (C) If the Japanese earned 80% of the total profits with only 65% of the total sales, they must have made more profit on each sale than their competitors.

25. (C) III only. The first sentence makes it clear that neither Mr. Tibbitts nor Ms. Mondragon will teach classes during the summer. However, nothing in the passage *assures* that Mr. Parnelli will also decide not to teach classes during the summer (. . . *if both Ms. Mondragon and Mr. Parnelli* . . .), and therefore we cannot conclusively deduce that Professor Revlon will teach classes during the summer. Only by knowing that Mr. Parnelli will not teach summer classes (III) do we then have all the pieces in place to conclude that Professor Revlon will teach summer classes and therefore cause confusion in the administrative office.

SECTION VII: QUANTITATIVE ABILITY

Quantitative Comparison

1. (B) The only difference in the two numbers occurs after the decimal points, where .10 (column B) is greater than .088 (column A).

2. (D) As the only condition for plugging in values for x and y is that together they must equal 0, the values for x and y may vary. For instance, both x and y may equal 0, in which case the answer would be (C). Or x may be 1 and y may be -1, in which case column A would be greater. Thus the answer is (D).

3. (B) The area of a circle $= \pi r^2$. So column A $= \pi(1^2) = \pi$. The circumference of a circle $= 2\pi r$. So column B $= 2(\pi)1 = 2\pi$.

4. (B) Column A $= 50 \div 2.2$, and column B $= 50 \times 2.2$.

5. (A) Since $\triangle ABC$ is an equilateral triangle, $\angle ABC = 60°$ and $\angle BAC = 60°$. So column A $= 120°$. Looking at $\triangle CDB$, $\angle CDB$

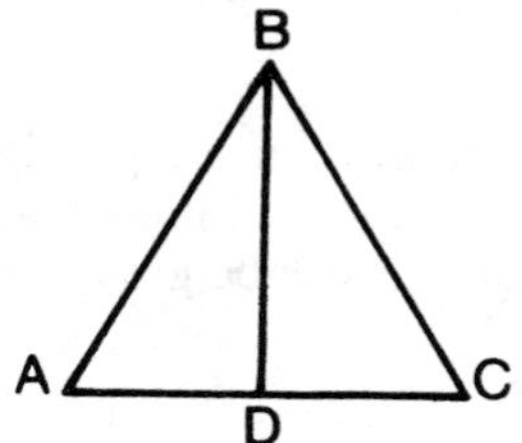

must be less than 120° because $\angle BCD$ already equals 60° and there is still another angle (CBD) in $\triangle CDB$.

6. (C) The definition of a median is that it divides the side it intersects into two equal parts.

7. (A) Since $\triangle ABC$ is equilateral, AB = BC. Thus AB + BD must be more than BC alone.

8. (A) 2 is the only even prime number. The lowest odd prime number is 3. So the least possible value of column A is 6, which would be more than column B, 5. Plugging in any other prime numbers will always give A greater than B.

9. (D) The values for a and b must be positive (because of the location in the upper right-hand quadrant. But we cannot be sure whether the x value (a) is greater than the y value (b), or vice versa. (Remember, unless the points plotted fall on a line, their location cannot be precisely pinpointed. We can know only the quadrant.)

10. (B) Point c,d falls on the $y = -4$ line before point 4, -4. So c is less than 4, and $d = -4$. So $c + d$ must be negative; a and b must both be positive because of their location in the upper right-hand quadrant.

11. (D) For xy to equal 0, either x or y must be 0. If $x = 0$, then $y = 4$. But if $y = 0$, then $x = 4$. There is no way of knowing which is which.

12. (B) $5^3 = 5 \times 5 \times 5 = 125$, and $2^7 = 2 \times 2 \times 2 \times 2 \times 2 \times 2 \times 2 = 128$.

13. (D) For $x^4 - 1 = 0$, then x^4 must equal 1; x, however, may then be $+1$ or -1. If $x = +1$, then columns A and B will be equal. But if $x = -1$, then column B will be greater than column A. So the answer is (D).

14. (C) Cross multiplying, we get

$$xy = 4 - y$$

$$xy + y = 4$$

$$y(x + 1) = 4$$

$$y = \frac{4}{x + 1}$$

15. (B) Since \$3.60 is closer to \$4.00, there must have been more 40¢ tea. Or let x equal the number of pounds of tea X and 10 − x equal the number of pounds of tea Y. Then

$$\begin{aligned} 30x + 40(10 - x) &= 360 \\ 30x + 400 - 40x &= 360 \\ -10x &= -40 \\ x &= 4 \end{aligned}$$

So there were 4 pounds of tea X and 6 pounds of tea Y.

Math Ability

16. (C) This problem is most easily completed by rearranging and approximating as follows:

$$\frac{69.28 \times .004}{.03} \cong 69 \times \frac{.004}{.03} \cong 69 \times .1 = 6.9$$

which is the only reasonably close answer to 9.2.

17. (A) Since Mary will be y years old x years from now, she is y − x years old now.
Hence z years from now she will be y − x + z years old.

18. (B) Start solving at the bottom right with the fraction 3/(3 + 3) and continue as follows:

$$3 + \cfrac{3}{3 + \cfrac{3}{3 + (3)/(3 + 3)}}$$

$$3 + \cfrac{3}{3 + \cfrac{3}{3 + 3/6}}$$

$$3 + \cfrac{3}{3 + \cfrac{3}{3\frac{1}{2}}}$$

$$3 + \cfrac{3}{3 + \cfrac{3}{\frac{7}{2}}}$$

$$3 + \frac{3}{3 + \frac{6}{7}}$$

$$3 + \frac{3}{3\frac{6}{7}}$$

$$3 + \frac{3}{\frac{27}{7}}$$

$$3 + \frac{21}{27}$$

$$3\tfrac{21}{27} = 3\tfrac{7}{9}$$

19. (B) We solve simultaneously

$$6x - 3y = 30$$
$$4x + y = 2$$

Multiply the bottom equation by 3 and add the two equations together.

$$\begin{array}{r} 6x - 3y = 30 \\ \underline{12x + 3y = \ \ 6} \\ 18x \qquad = 36 \end{array}$$

Thus $x = 2$
Substitute back to one of the original equations and we find that $y = -6$. Thus their sum is -4.

20. (C) $\triangle XYZ$ is inscribed in a semicircle and therefore $\angle Z$ is a right angle. Hence $\triangle XYZ$ is a right triangle and the Pythagorean theorem states

$$\begin{aligned} (XY)^2 &= (XZ)^2 + (YZ)^2 \\ (17)^2 &= (XZ)^2 + (15)^2 \quad \text{(XY is a diameter)} \\ 289 &= (XZ)^2 + 225 \\ (XZ)^2 &= 64 \\ XZ &= \sqrt{64} \\ XZ &= 8 \end{aligned}$$

Now to find the area ($\frac{1}{2}$ bh)

$$\tfrac{1}{2} \times 15 \times 8 = \tfrac{1}{2} \times 120 = 60$$

21. (C) Adding the percentages, the large circulation coins represent (23%, 17%, 8%), 48%, while the average condition coins represent (23%, 18%, 10%), 51%.

22. (D) The number of coins is irrelevant. Since 3%, 5%, and 8% add to 16%, we have the following:

16.60 × 3% plus 10.20 × 5% plus 8.80 × 8% = 1.712,

and 1.712/.16 = 10.70, which is the average price.

23. (C) There are (5%, 10%, 18%), 33% in this category. Thus 33% of 20,000 is 6600.

24. (D) The coin collector previously collected only fine condition coins, or a total of 17 + 10 + 6 = 33% of the coins available for sale. Now the collector collecting both fine and uncirculated adds another 16% (3 + 5 + 8) of the coins available for sale. Percent increase is found by dividing the change (in this case 16%) by the starting point (in this case 33%): 16 ÷ 33 is approximately 48%.

25. (B) Average circulation coins of fine condition represent 10% of the total of 100, or 10 coins, at $8.80 each, for a total price of $88. Small circulation coins of average condition represent 10% of the total of 100, or 10 coins, at $6.30 each, or a total price of $63. Therefore a collector would pay $25 more for all the average circulation coins of fine condition than for all the small circulation coins of average condition.

26. (B) Since the area of a trapezoid = $\frac{1}{2} \cdot h \cdot (b_1 + b_2)$, we need to find the altitude, h.
Draw altitudes in the figure as follows:

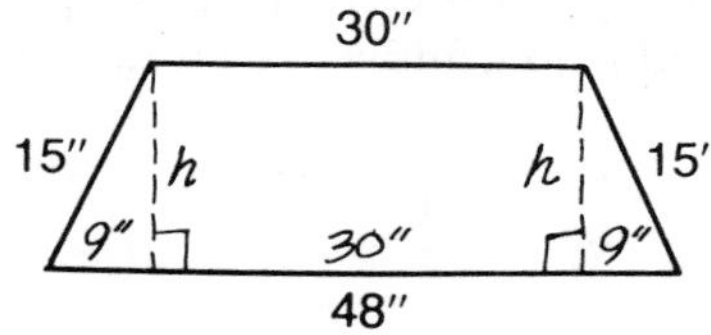

Since the triangles formed are right triangles, we use the Pythagorean theorem, which says

$$\begin{aligned} c^2 &= a^2 + b^2 \\ 15^2 &= 9^2 + h^2 \\ 225 &= 81 + h^2 \\ h^2 &= 225 - 81 \\ h^2 &= 144 \\ h &= \sqrt{144} = 12 \text{ inches} \end{aligned}$$

Hence the area of the trapezoid will be

$$\begin{aligned} \tfrac{1}{2} \cdot h \cdot (b_1 + b_2) &= \tfrac{1}{2} \cdot 12 \cdot (30 + 48) \\ &= (6)(78) \\ &= 468 \text{ square inches} \end{aligned}$$

27. (E) Divide the first inequality by 2 and we get $6 < x < 9$. Divide the second inequality by 3 and we get $-3 < y < 2$. If we add these two inequalities, we see that statement I is true. If we take these two inequalities and multiply the first by -1, we get $-6 > -x > -9$ or $-9 < -x < -6$. Now adding the two statements together, we get $-12 < y - x < -4$. So II is true.

28. (E) The length of x cannot be determined because there is no indication of the overlapping length of the rectangle to the left of x. If x cannot be determined, then x + y cannot be determined.

29. (D) Let us calculate the value of each:

(A) (.5)(.3)(280) = 42
(B) (.33)(.7)(160) = 36.96
(C) (2)(.5)(30) = 30
(D) (3)(.4)(40) = 48
(E) (.6)(60) = 36

30. (C) If x is increased by 50%, we can represent it by $\tfrac{3}{2}x$. We must multiply this by $\tfrac{2}{3}$ y in order to keep the product equal to xy. Since $\tfrac{2}{3}$ is a $\tfrac{1}{3}$ reduction, answer (C) is the correct response.

PRACTICE TEST 3

Section I:	Verbal Ability—30 Minutes; 38 Questions
Section II:	Analytical Ability—30 Minutes; 25 Questions
Section III:	Quantitative Ability—30 Minutes; 30 Questions
Section IV:	Quantitative Ability—30 Minutes; 30 Questions
Section V:	Verbal Ability—30 Minutes; 38 Questions
Section VI:	Analytical Ability—30 Minutes; 25 Questions
Section VII:	Quantitative Ability—30 Minutes; 30 Questions

ANSWER SHEET FOR PRACTICE TEST 3
(Remove This Sheet and Use It to Mark Your Answers)

SECTION I

1 Ⓐ Ⓑ Ⓒ Ⓓ Ⓔ
2 Ⓐ Ⓑ Ⓒ Ⓓ Ⓔ
3 Ⓐ Ⓑ Ⓒ Ⓓ Ⓔ
4 Ⓐ Ⓑ Ⓒ Ⓓ Ⓔ
5 Ⓐ Ⓑ Ⓒ Ⓓ Ⓔ

6 Ⓐ Ⓑ Ⓒ Ⓓ Ⓔ
7 Ⓐ Ⓑ Ⓒ Ⓓ Ⓔ
8 Ⓐ Ⓑ Ⓒ Ⓓ Ⓔ
9 Ⓐ Ⓑ Ⓒ Ⓓ Ⓔ
10 Ⓐ Ⓑ Ⓒ Ⓓ Ⓔ

11 Ⓐ Ⓑ Ⓒ Ⓓ Ⓔ
12 Ⓐ Ⓑ Ⓒ Ⓓ Ⓔ
13 Ⓐ Ⓑ Ⓒ Ⓓ Ⓔ
14 Ⓐ Ⓑ Ⓒ Ⓓ Ⓔ
15 Ⓐ Ⓑ Ⓒ Ⓓ Ⓔ

16 Ⓐ Ⓑ Ⓒ Ⓓ Ⓔ
17 Ⓐ Ⓑ Ⓒ Ⓓ Ⓔ
18 Ⓐ Ⓑ Ⓒ Ⓓ Ⓔ
19 Ⓐ Ⓑ Ⓒ Ⓓ Ⓔ
20 Ⓐ Ⓑ Ⓒ Ⓓ Ⓔ

21 Ⓐ Ⓑ Ⓒ Ⓓ Ⓔ
22 Ⓐ Ⓑ Ⓒ Ⓓ Ⓔ
23 Ⓐ Ⓑ Ⓒ Ⓓ Ⓔ
24 Ⓐ Ⓑ Ⓒ Ⓓ Ⓔ
25 Ⓐ Ⓑ Ⓒ Ⓓ Ⓔ

26 Ⓐ Ⓑ Ⓒ Ⓓ Ⓔ
27 Ⓐ Ⓑ Ⓒ Ⓓ Ⓔ
28 Ⓐ Ⓑ Ⓒ Ⓓ Ⓔ
29 Ⓐ Ⓑ Ⓒ Ⓓ Ⓔ
30 Ⓐ Ⓑ Ⓒ Ⓓ Ⓔ

31 Ⓐ Ⓑ Ⓒ Ⓓ Ⓔ
32 Ⓐ Ⓑ Ⓒ Ⓓ Ⓔ
33 Ⓐ Ⓑ Ⓒ Ⓓ Ⓔ
34 Ⓐ Ⓑ Ⓒ Ⓓ Ⓔ
35 Ⓐ Ⓑ Ⓒ Ⓓ Ⓔ

36 Ⓐ Ⓑ Ⓒ Ⓓ Ⓔ
37 Ⓐ Ⓑ Ⓒ Ⓓ Ⓔ
38 Ⓐ Ⓑ Ⓒ Ⓓ Ⓔ

SECTION II

1 Ⓐ Ⓑ Ⓒ Ⓓ Ⓔ
2 Ⓐ Ⓑ Ⓒ Ⓓ Ⓔ
3 Ⓐ Ⓑ Ⓒ Ⓓ Ⓔ
4 Ⓐ Ⓑ Ⓒ Ⓓ Ⓔ
5 Ⓐ Ⓑ Ⓒ Ⓓ Ⓔ

6 Ⓐ Ⓑ Ⓒ Ⓓ Ⓔ
7 Ⓐ Ⓑ Ⓒ Ⓓ Ⓔ
8 Ⓐ Ⓑ Ⓒ Ⓓ Ⓔ
9 Ⓐ Ⓑ Ⓒ Ⓓ Ⓔ
10 Ⓐ Ⓑ Ⓒ Ⓓ Ⓔ

11 Ⓐ Ⓑ Ⓒ Ⓓ Ⓔ
12 Ⓐ Ⓑ Ⓒ Ⓓ Ⓔ
13 Ⓐ Ⓑ Ⓒ Ⓓ Ⓔ
14 Ⓐ Ⓑ Ⓒ Ⓓ Ⓔ
15 Ⓐ Ⓑ Ⓒ Ⓓ Ⓔ

16 Ⓐ Ⓑ Ⓒ Ⓓ Ⓔ
17 Ⓐ Ⓑ Ⓒ Ⓓ Ⓔ
18 Ⓐ Ⓑ Ⓒ Ⓓ Ⓔ
19 Ⓐ Ⓑ Ⓒ Ⓓ Ⓔ
20 Ⓐ Ⓑ Ⓒ Ⓓ Ⓔ

21 Ⓐ Ⓑ Ⓒ Ⓓ Ⓔ
22 Ⓐ Ⓑ Ⓒ Ⓓ Ⓔ
23 Ⓐ Ⓑ Ⓒ Ⓓ Ⓔ
24 Ⓐ Ⓑ Ⓒ Ⓓ Ⓔ
25 Ⓐ Ⓑ Ⓒ Ⓓ Ⓔ

ANSWER SHEET FOR PRACTICE TEST 3
(Remove This Sheet and Use It to Mark Your Answers)

SECTION III

1 Ⓐ Ⓑ Ⓒ Ⓓ Ⓔ
2 Ⓐ Ⓑ Ⓒ Ⓓ Ⓔ
3 Ⓐ Ⓑ Ⓒ Ⓓ Ⓔ
4 Ⓐ Ⓑ Ⓒ Ⓓ Ⓔ
5 Ⓐ Ⓑ Ⓒ Ⓓ Ⓔ
6 Ⓐ Ⓑ Ⓒ Ⓓ Ⓔ
7 Ⓐ Ⓑ Ⓒ Ⓓ Ⓔ
8 Ⓐ Ⓑ Ⓒ Ⓓ Ⓔ
9 Ⓐ Ⓑ Ⓒ Ⓓ Ⓔ
10 Ⓐ Ⓑ Ⓒ Ⓓ Ⓔ
11 Ⓐ Ⓑ Ⓒ Ⓓ Ⓔ
12 Ⓐ Ⓑ Ⓒ Ⓓ Ⓔ
13 Ⓐ Ⓑ Ⓒ Ⓓ Ⓔ
14 Ⓐ Ⓑ Ⓒ Ⓓ Ⓔ
15 Ⓐ Ⓑ Ⓒ Ⓓ Ⓔ
16 Ⓐ Ⓑ Ⓒ Ⓓ Ⓔ
17 Ⓐ Ⓑ Ⓒ Ⓓ Ⓔ
18 Ⓐ Ⓑ Ⓒ Ⓓ Ⓔ
19 Ⓐ Ⓑ Ⓒ Ⓓ Ⓔ
20 Ⓐ Ⓑ Ⓒ Ⓓ Ⓔ
21 Ⓐ Ⓑ Ⓒ Ⓓ Ⓔ
22 Ⓐ Ⓑ Ⓒ Ⓓ Ⓔ
23 Ⓐ Ⓑ Ⓒ Ⓓ Ⓔ
24 Ⓐ Ⓑ Ⓒ Ⓓ Ⓔ
25 Ⓐ Ⓑ Ⓒ Ⓓ Ⓔ
26 Ⓐ Ⓑ Ⓒ Ⓓ Ⓔ
27 Ⓐ Ⓑ Ⓒ Ⓓ Ⓔ
28 Ⓐ Ⓑ Ⓒ Ⓓ Ⓔ
29 Ⓐ Ⓑ Ⓒ Ⓓ Ⓔ
30 Ⓐ Ⓑ Ⓒ Ⓓ Ⓔ

SECTION IV

1 Ⓐ Ⓑ Ⓒ Ⓓ Ⓔ
2 Ⓐ Ⓑ Ⓒ Ⓓ Ⓔ
3 Ⓐ Ⓑ Ⓒ Ⓓ Ⓔ
4 Ⓐ Ⓑ Ⓒ Ⓓ Ⓔ
5 Ⓐ Ⓑ Ⓒ Ⓓ Ⓔ
6 Ⓐ Ⓑ Ⓒ Ⓓ Ⓔ
7 Ⓐ Ⓑ Ⓒ Ⓓ Ⓔ
8 Ⓐ Ⓑ Ⓒ Ⓓ Ⓔ
9 Ⓐ Ⓑ Ⓒ Ⓓ Ⓔ
10 Ⓐ Ⓑ Ⓒ Ⓓ Ⓔ
11 Ⓐ Ⓑ Ⓒ Ⓓ Ⓔ
12 Ⓐ Ⓑ Ⓒ Ⓓ Ⓔ
13 Ⓐ Ⓑ Ⓒ Ⓓ Ⓔ
14 Ⓐ Ⓑ Ⓒ Ⓓ Ⓔ
15 Ⓐ Ⓑ Ⓒ Ⓓ Ⓔ
16 Ⓐ Ⓑ Ⓒ Ⓓ Ⓔ
17 Ⓐ Ⓑ Ⓒ Ⓓ Ⓔ
18 Ⓐ Ⓑ Ⓒ Ⓓ Ⓔ
19 Ⓐ Ⓑ Ⓒ Ⓓ Ⓔ
20 Ⓐ Ⓑ Ⓒ Ⓓ Ⓔ
21 Ⓐ Ⓑ Ⓒ Ⓓ Ⓔ
22 Ⓐ Ⓑ Ⓒ Ⓓ Ⓔ
23 Ⓐ Ⓑ Ⓒ Ⓓ Ⓔ
24 Ⓐ Ⓑ Ⓒ Ⓓ Ⓔ
25 Ⓐ Ⓑ Ⓒ Ⓓ Ⓔ
26 Ⓐ Ⓑ Ⓒ Ⓓ Ⓔ
27 Ⓐ Ⓑ Ⓒ Ⓓ Ⓔ
28 Ⓐ Ⓑ Ⓒ Ⓓ Ⓔ
29 Ⓐ Ⓑ Ⓒ Ⓓ Ⓔ
30 Ⓐ Ⓑ Ⓒ Ⓓ Ⓔ

SECTION V

1 Ⓐ Ⓑ Ⓒ Ⓓ Ⓔ
2 Ⓐ Ⓑ Ⓒ Ⓓ Ⓔ
3 Ⓐ Ⓑ Ⓒ Ⓓ Ⓔ
4 Ⓐ Ⓑ Ⓒ Ⓓ Ⓔ
5 Ⓐ Ⓑ Ⓒ Ⓓ Ⓔ
6 Ⓐ Ⓑ Ⓒ Ⓓ Ⓔ
7 Ⓐ Ⓑ Ⓒ Ⓓ Ⓔ
8 Ⓐ Ⓑ Ⓒ Ⓓ Ⓔ
9 Ⓐ Ⓑ Ⓒ Ⓓ Ⓔ
10 Ⓐ Ⓑ Ⓒ Ⓓ Ⓔ
11 Ⓐ Ⓑ Ⓒ Ⓓ Ⓔ
12 Ⓐ Ⓑ Ⓒ Ⓓ Ⓔ
13 Ⓐ Ⓑ Ⓒ Ⓓ Ⓔ
14 Ⓐ Ⓑ Ⓒ Ⓓ Ⓔ
15 Ⓐ Ⓑ Ⓒ Ⓓ Ⓔ
16 Ⓐ Ⓑ Ⓒ Ⓓ Ⓔ
17 Ⓐ Ⓑ Ⓒ Ⓓ Ⓔ
18 Ⓐ Ⓑ Ⓒ Ⓓ Ⓔ
19 Ⓐ Ⓑ Ⓒ Ⓓ Ⓔ
20 Ⓐ Ⓑ Ⓒ Ⓓ Ⓔ
21 Ⓐ Ⓑ Ⓒ Ⓓ Ⓔ
22 Ⓐ Ⓑ Ⓒ Ⓓ Ⓔ
23 Ⓐ Ⓑ Ⓒ Ⓓ Ⓔ
24 Ⓐ Ⓑ Ⓒ Ⓓ Ⓔ
25 Ⓐ Ⓑ Ⓒ Ⓓ Ⓔ
26 Ⓐ Ⓑ Ⓒ Ⓓ Ⓔ
27 Ⓐ Ⓑ Ⓒ Ⓓ Ⓔ
28 Ⓐ Ⓑ Ⓒ Ⓓ Ⓔ
29 Ⓐ Ⓑ Ⓒ Ⓓ Ⓔ
30 Ⓐ Ⓑ Ⓒ Ⓓ Ⓔ
31 Ⓐ Ⓑ Ⓒ Ⓓ Ⓔ
32 Ⓐ Ⓑ Ⓒ Ⓓ Ⓔ
33 Ⓐ Ⓑ Ⓒ Ⓓ Ⓔ
34 Ⓐ Ⓑ Ⓒ Ⓓ Ⓔ
35 Ⓐ Ⓑ Ⓒ Ⓓ Ⓔ
36 Ⓐ Ⓑ Ⓒ Ⓓ Ⓔ
37 Ⓐ Ⓑ Ⓒ Ⓓ Ⓔ
38 Ⓐ Ⓑ Ⓒ Ⓓ Ⓔ

ANSWER SHEET FOR PRACTICE TEST 3
(Remove This Sheet and Use It to Mark Your Answers)

SECTION VI

1 Ⓐ Ⓑ Ⓒ Ⓓ Ⓔ
2 Ⓐ Ⓑ Ⓒ Ⓓ Ⓔ
3 Ⓐ Ⓑ Ⓒ Ⓓ Ⓔ
4 Ⓐ Ⓑ Ⓒ Ⓓ Ⓔ
5 Ⓐ Ⓑ Ⓒ Ⓓ Ⓔ

6 Ⓐ Ⓑ Ⓒ Ⓓ Ⓔ
7 Ⓐ Ⓑ Ⓒ Ⓓ Ⓔ
8 Ⓐ Ⓑ Ⓒ Ⓓ Ⓔ
9 Ⓐ Ⓑ Ⓒ Ⓓ Ⓔ
10 Ⓐ Ⓑ Ⓒ Ⓓ Ⓔ

11 Ⓐ Ⓑ Ⓒ Ⓓ Ⓔ
12 Ⓐ Ⓑ Ⓒ Ⓓ Ⓔ
13 Ⓐ Ⓑ Ⓒ Ⓓ Ⓔ
14 Ⓐ Ⓑ Ⓒ Ⓓ Ⓔ
15 Ⓐ Ⓑ Ⓒ Ⓓ Ⓔ

16 Ⓐ Ⓑ Ⓒ Ⓓ Ⓔ
17 Ⓐ Ⓑ Ⓒ Ⓓ Ⓔ
18 Ⓐ Ⓑ Ⓒ Ⓓ Ⓔ
19 Ⓐ Ⓑ Ⓒ Ⓓ Ⓔ
20 Ⓐ Ⓑ Ⓒ Ⓓ Ⓔ

21 Ⓐ Ⓑ Ⓒ Ⓓ Ⓔ
22 Ⓐ Ⓑ Ⓒ Ⓓ Ⓔ
23 Ⓐ Ⓑ Ⓒ Ⓓ Ⓔ
24 Ⓐ Ⓑ Ⓒ Ⓓ Ⓔ
25 Ⓐ Ⓑ Ⓒ Ⓓ Ⓔ

SECTION VII

1 Ⓐ Ⓑ Ⓒ Ⓓ Ⓔ
2 Ⓐ Ⓑ Ⓒ Ⓓ Ⓔ
3 Ⓐ Ⓑ Ⓒ Ⓓ Ⓔ
4 Ⓐ Ⓑ Ⓒ Ⓓ Ⓔ
5 Ⓐ Ⓑ Ⓒ Ⓓ Ⓔ

6 Ⓐ Ⓑ Ⓒ Ⓓ Ⓔ
7 Ⓐ Ⓑ Ⓒ Ⓓ Ⓔ
8 Ⓐ Ⓑ Ⓒ Ⓓ Ⓔ
9 Ⓐ Ⓑ Ⓒ Ⓓ Ⓔ
10 Ⓐ Ⓑ Ⓒ Ⓓ Ⓔ

11 Ⓐ Ⓑ Ⓒ Ⓓ Ⓔ
12 Ⓐ Ⓑ Ⓒ Ⓓ Ⓔ
13 Ⓐ Ⓑ Ⓒ Ⓓ Ⓔ
14 Ⓐ Ⓑ Ⓒ Ⓓ Ⓔ
15 Ⓐ Ⓑ Ⓒ Ⓓ Ⓔ

16 Ⓐ Ⓑ Ⓒ Ⓓ Ⓔ
17 Ⓐ Ⓑ Ⓒ Ⓓ Ⓔ
18 Ⓐ Ⓑ Ⓒ Ⓓ Ⓔ
19 Ⓐ Ⓑ Ⓒ Ⓓ Ⓔ
20 Ⓐ Ⓑ Ⓒ Ⓓ Ⓔ

21 Ⓐ Ⓑ Ⓒ Ⓓ Ⓔ
22 Ⓐ Ⓑ Ⓒ Ⓓ Ⓔ
23 Ⓐ Ⓑ Ⓒ Ⓓ Ⓔ
24 Ⓐ Ⓑ Ⓒ Ⓓ Ⓔ
25 Ⓐ Ⓑ Ⓒ Ⓓ Ⓔ

26 Ⓐ Ⓑ Ⓒ Ⓓ Ⓔ
27 Ⓐ Ⓑ Ⓒ Ⓓ Ⓔ
28 Ⓐ Ⓑ Ⓒ Ⓓ Ⓔ
29 Ⓐ Ⓑ Ⓒ Ⓓ Ⓔ
30 Ⓐ Ⓑ Ⓒ Ⓓ Ⓔ

SECTION I: VERBAL ABILITY

Time: 30 Minutes
38 Questions

In this section, choose the best answer for each question and blacken the corresponding space on the answer sheet.

Sentence Completion

DIRECTIONS

Each blank in the following sentences indicates that something has been omitted. Considering the lettered words beneath the sentence, choose the word or set of words that best fits the whole sentence.

1. Editorial cartoonists cannot be successful unless they can _________ the consciences of their audience and stir up controversy.
   (A) assuage
   (B) tweak
   (C) dwarf
   (D) amuse
   (E) absolve

2. The Oxford research team was afraid that sensationalized television reports of its work on paranormal phenomena would undermine its academic _________.
   (A) responsibility
   (B) questioning
   (C) credibility
   (D) freedom
   (E) credulousness

3. Believing that to lead her people she must walk behind them, leaving them free to set their own course, the Nicaraguan president has restored _________ politics and renewed the _________ spirit.
   (A) economic . . . chauvinistic
   (B) environmental . . . ecological
   (C) conservative . . . legalistic
   (D) open-market . . . entrepreneurial
   (E) national . . . parochial

4. Along with a handful of other ________, the lawyer refuses to believe the evidence submitted by the FBI.
   (A) investigators
   (B) rationalists
   (C) regionalists
   (D) legislators
   (E) skeptics

5. Though the city's downtown area is extremely ________, many areas in the ________ have not yet been affected by the economic slump.
   (A) depressed . . . periphery
   (B) prosperous . . . suburbs
   (C) recessive . . . center
   (D) overcrowded . . . country
   (E) propitious . . . outskirts

6. Remarkably, the coastal wetland has been preserved in the midst of some of the state's ________ real estate.
   (A) undesirable
   (B) priciest
   (C) undeveloped
   (D) soggiest
   (E) unsaleable

7. The comedy ________ from the ________ of his huge size and the tiny voice with which he speaks his lines.
   (A) accrues . . . harmony
   (B) diminishes . . . opposition
   (C) extends . . . contrast
   (D) decants . . . junction
   (E) derives . . . incongruity

Analogies

DIRECTIONS

In each question below, you are given a related pair of words or phrases. Select the lettered pair that *best* expresses a relationship similar to that in the original pair of words.

8. EPIC : EPIGRAM ::
   (A) opera : lied
   (B) museum : exhibit
   (C) manuscript : illumination
   (D) column : pillar
   (E) newspaper : press

9. JANITOR : BUILDING ::
   (A) rider : horse
   (B) fisherman : fire
   (C) violinist : orchestra
   (D) ranger : forest
   (E) policeman : judge

10. CAPSTAN : CABLE ::
   (A) rod : reel
   (B) spool : thread
   (C) table : tablecloth
   (D) telephone : telegraph
   (E) rowboat : oar

11. COMPLAIN : SNIVEL ::
   (A) circle : wind
   (B) condole : slaver
   (C) grieve : sulk
   (D) equip : supply
   (E) hasten : expedite

12. CHECKERS : CHESS ::
   (A) tennis : soccer
   (B) field hockey : ice hockey
   (C) basketball : gymnastics
   (D) hearts : bridge
   (E) square : diamond

13. PATRIOT : CHAUVINIST ::
   (A) epicure : glutton
   (B) pessimist : cynic
   (C) taste : tang
   (D) candidate : incumbent
   (E) misanthrope : misogynist

14. THWART : ABET ::
   (A) unify : knit
   (B) strip : befit
   (C) lacerate : incise
   (D) savor : enjoy
   (E) murmur : caterwaul

15. BAROMETER : AIR PRESSURE ::
    (A) stethoscope : heartbeat
    (B) compass : circle
    (C) tachometer : blood pressure
    (D) anemometer : wind speed
    (E) hourglass : sand

16. SWINDLE : GUILE ::
    (A) commit : felony
    (B) believe : opinion
    (C) anticipate : foresight
    (D) invest : profit
    (E) argue : case

Reading Comprehension

DIRECTIONS

Questions follow each of the passages below. Using only the stated or implied information in each passage, answer the questions.

In clean air, the human lung capacity will increase for the first twenty years of life, then begin to decrease slowly. But in areas with heavy air pollution, lung capacity growth is slowed. Breathing high levels of ozone or of sulfur and nitrogen oxides lessens the growth of lung capacity and increases the speed of its deterioration in later life. Adults who spend all their lives in bad air may have as much as 75% less lung capacity than those who have lived in unpolluted air. The loss of both the large and small airways of the lungs, narrowed by the unclean air, results in the inefficient supply of oxygen to the organs of the body. The lungs do not recover over time, and the ozone of Los Angeles and the sulfates and hydrocarbons of industrialized eastern cities are equally pernicious. The victims of air pollution are unlikely to be aware of what they have lost; they are so accustomed to shorter breath and coughs that they vigorously deny that they have been affected at all.

17. Which of the following most accurately describes this passage?
    (A) a description of a specific experiment
    (B) a summary report of scientific findings
    (C) a recommendation for improving health
    (D) a confirmation of an earlier theory
    (E) a refutation of an earlier theory

18. According to the passage, the capacity of the human lung would be greatest if a person were
    (A) forty years old and had not been exposed to unclean air until the age of thirty
    (B) forty years old and had lived without exposure to unclean air
    (C) twenty years old and had lived without exposure to unclean air
    (D) twenty years old and had been exposed to unclean air for five years
    (E) ten years old and had been exposed for one year to heavy amounts of ozone

19. It can be inferred from the passage that denizens of areas with heavy air pollution have not been more active in attempting to improve air quality because
    (A) they fear the costs of cleaning the air may increase their taxes
    (B) the federal government does not encourage clean air vigorously enough
    (C) the dangers of air pollution have only recently been discovered
    (D) they are unaware of the harm unclean air has done
    (E) there are rivalries between local, state, and federal clean air agencies

20. According to the passage, middle-aged adults who have lived all their lives in a city with heavy air pollution from sulfur and nitrogen oxides may have

I. as limited a lung capacity as life-long residents of Los Angeles of the same age
II. lung capacity less than that of life-long residents of an industrialized city in Eastern Europe
III. significantly reduced oxygen supplied to their vital organs

(A) I only
(B) II only
(C) III only
(D) I and II only
(E) I and III only

The railroads played a key role in the settlement of the West. They provided relatively easy access to the region for the first time, and they also actively recruited farmers to settle there (the Santa Fe Railroad, for example, brought 10,000 German Mennonites to Kansas). The railroads are criticized for their part in settling the West too rapidly, with its resultant economic unrest. (After the Civil War the vast Great Plains area was settled all at once.) Of course there were abuses connected with building and operating the railroads, but it must be pointed out that they performed a useful service in extending the frontier and helping to achieve national unity.

The real tragedy of the rapid settlement of the Great Plains was the shameful way in which the American Indians were treated. Threatened with the destruction of their whole mode of life, the Indians fought back savagely against the white man's final thrust. Justice was almost entirely on the Indians' side. The land was clearly theirs; frequently their title was legally certified by a treaty negotiated with the federal government. The Indians, however, lacked the military force and the political power to protect this right. Not only did white men encroach upon the Indians' hunting grounds, but they rapidly destroyed the Indians' principal means of subsistence—the buffalo. It has been estimated that some 15 million buffalo roamed the plains in the 1860s. By 1869 the railroads had cut the herd in half, and by 1875 the southern herd was all but eliminated. By the middle of the 1880s the northern herd was also a thing of the past. Particularly galling to the Indians was the fact that the white man frequently killed the buffalo merely for sport, leaving the valuable carcass to rot in the sun.

The plains Indians were considered different from the Indians encountered by the English colonists on the Atlantic coast. Mounted on horses descended from those brought by the Spanish to Mexico many years before, typical plains Indians were fierce warriors who could shoot arrows with surprising accuracy while galloping at top speed. Although they quickly adapted themselves to the use of the rifle, the Indians were not equal to the firepower of the United States army and thus were doomed to defeat.

Theoretically, at least, the government tried to be fair to the Indians, but all too often the Indian agents were either too indifferent or corrupt to carry out the government's promises conscientiously. The army frequently ignored the Indian Bureau and failed to coordinate its policies with the civilians who were nominally in charge of Indian affairs. The settlers hated and feared the Indians and wanted them exterminated. This barbaric attitude is certainly not excusable, but it is understandable in the context of the times.

21. The author's attitude toward the treatment of American Indians by whites is one of
    (A) qualified regret
    (B) violent anger
    (C) strong disapproval
    (D) objective indifference
    (E) unfair bias

22. The author implies which of the following about the forces at work during the settlement of the Great Plains?
    (A) The federal government represented the moral use of law.
    (B) Justice was overcome by military firepower.
    (C) Attempts by the government to be fair were rejected by the Indians.
    (D) The settlers' hatred and fear was offset by the Indians' attempts at kindness.
    (E) The Indians and the white settlers shared a sporting interest in the hunting of buffalo.

23. Which of the following is concrete evidence that the white settlers did not need the buffalo for their own subsistence, as did the Indians?
    (A) More than half of the great buffalo herd had disappeared by 1869.
    (B) Nearly fifteen million buffalo were killed within twenty years.
    (C) Buffalo carcasses were left rotting in the sun by whites.
    (D) The railroad brought necessary food and supplies to the white settlers from the East.
    (E) The white settlers had their own hunting grounds separate from the Indians'.

24. What is the point of the comparison between plains Indians and the Indians encountered on the Atlantic coast?
    (A) The Atlantic coast Indians were not as abused by white settlers.
    (B) Because they were considerably better warriors than the Atlantic coast Indians, the plains Indians were a match for the United States military.
    (C) If Indians such as those on the Atlantic coast had populated the plains, there would have been no bloodshed of the white settlement.
    (D) The Indians encountered by English colonists posed no violent threat to the colonists.
    (E) The Atlantic coast Indians were unfamiliar with horses.

25. Which of the following characteristics of the passage suggests that the abuse of the Indians is a more significant topic for the author than the beneficial role of the railroads?
   (A) the statement that the railroads "are criticized for their part in settling the West too rapidly"
   (B) the amount of discussion devoted to the abuse of the Indians
   (C) the reliance on statistical details in both the first and second paragraphs
   (D) the very brief mention of the migration of German Mennonites
   (E) the perception that the achievement of national unity was one of the services that the railroad performed

26. The author of the passage would most likely disagree that
   (A) the United States government's policies towards the American Indians were shameful
   (B) the land that the Indians fought to retain belonged to them
   (C) numerous abuses were among the results of the railroads' rapid spread westward
   (D) some American Indian tribes used sophisticated weapons brought by settlers
   (E) the United States army could not be considered a friend of the American Indian

27. It can be inferred from the passage that the purpose of the Indian Bureau was to
   (A) try Indians who violated the laws of the new territory
   (B) establish reservations where the peaceful American Indians would live
   (C) assist with Indian affairs and policies of the government regarding the American Indian
   (D) bring to justice white settlers who treated the Indians in a savage or unlawful manner
   (E) assist the Indians in learning a new method of procuring food to rely less on buffalo meat

Antonyms

DIRECTIONS

Each word in CAPITAL LETTERS is followed by five words or phrases. The correct choice is the word or phrase whose meaning is most nearly *opposite* to the meaning of the word in capitals. You may be required to distinguish fine shades of meaning. Look at all choices before marking your answer.

28. DETER :
    (A) surpass
    (B) delay
    (C) encourage
    (D) exchange
    (E) hesitate

29. FLOCK :
    (A) disperse
    (B) repair
    (C) herd
    (D) avoid
    (E) moisten

30. EQUIVOCAL :
    (A) unequal
    (B) silent
    (C) untruthful
    (D) certain
    (E) autumnal

31. TRAVAIL :
    (A) fetters
    (B) repose
    (C) smear
    (D) illumination
    (E) remainder

32. BOMB :
    (A) inception
    (B) task
    (C) divot
    (D) storm
    (E) hit

33. PURITANIC :
    (A) controlled by hand
    (B) making fast
    (C) imposing
    (D) freewheeling
    (E) obtuse

34. TRUMPET :
    (A) fetch
    (B) glut
    (C) hone
    (D) idle
    (E) veil

35. FERVENT :
    (A) intermittent
    (B) parietal
    (C) bland
    (D) resonant
    (E) sublime

36. AGGREGATE :
    (A) part
    (B) stand-off
    (C) prism
    (D) seam
    (E) individuality

37. HAVOC :
    (A) mirth
    (B) construction
    (C) making light of
    (D) insouciance
    (E) fandango

38. AGGRIEVE :
    (A) hamper
    (B) gladden
    (C) repulse
    (D) satirize
    (E) rejoice

STOP. IF YOU FINISH BEFORE TIME IS CALLED, CHECK YOUR WORK ON THIS SECTION ONLY. DO NOT WORK ON ANY OTHER SECTION IN THE TEST.

SECTION II: ANALYTICAL ABILITY

Time: 30 Minutes
25 Questions

DIRECTIONS

The following questions or group of questions are based on a passage or set of statements. Choose the best answer for each question and blacken the corresponding space on your answer sheet. It may be helpful to draw rough diagrams or simple charts in attempting to answer these question types.

Questions 1–4

Eight antique airplanes are being considered for storage in two warehouses (East and West). The airplanes are single-wing (Dino, Kressna, Bonner, and Lear) and double-wing (Rickenbacher, Airheart, Orville, and Wilbur).

Neither of the two warehouses may go unoccupied.

The Dino and the Kressna may not be stored in the same warehouse.

The Lear and the Airheart are owned by the same pilot and must be stored together in the same warehouse.

The Dino and the Rickenbacher are serviced by the same mechanic and must be stored together in the same warehouse.

At least seven of the airplanes must be stored in the warehouses.

1. Which of the following could comprise the total storage of the East warehouse?
   (A) Kressna, Lear, Rickenbacher, Airheart, Orville, Bonner
   (B) Rickenbacher, Orville, Wilbur, Dino, Bonner
   (C) Rickenbacher, Airheart, Orville, Dino
   (D) Kressna, Lear, Orville, Dino. Bonner
   (E) Lear, Rickenbacher, Dino, Bonner

2. All of the following are suitable storage arrangements for the West warehouse EXCEPT
   (A) Kressna, Orville, Bonner
   (B) Kressna, Lear, Airheart, Orville, Wilbur, Bonner
   (C) Kressna, Lear, Airheart, Wilbur, Bonner
   (D) Kressna, Lear, Airheart, Orville
   (E) Kressna, Lear, Rickenbacher, Airheart, Bonner

3. If the Kressna is the only single-wing airplane stored in the East warehouse, which of the following must be true?
   (A) The East warehouse contains exactly two airplanes.
   (B) All the double-wing airplanes are stored.
   (C) Both warehouses each contain two double-wing airplanes.
   (D) Five or fewer airplanes are stored in the West warehouse.
   (E) At least three single-wing airplanes are stored.

4. Only the Dino and one other airplane are stored in the East warehouse. If the Kressna is stored, then the West warehouse must contain
   (A) the Kressna, Wilbur, Orville, and at least two more
   (B) the Kressna, Lear, Airheart, and at least two more
   (C) the Kressna, Airheart, Lear, Orville, but not the Wilbur
   (D) the Kressna, Wilbur, Lear, Airheart, but not the Orville
   (E) the Kressna, Wilbur, Lear, Airheart, and Orville

Questions 5–10

Ten students—Arnold, Brad, Charlotte, Danielle, Evan, Francine, Gabrielle, Hap, Ida, and Joshua—each choose one classroom assignment. There are four assignments from which to choose: Room Cleanup, Designing Bulletin Boards, Publishing the Class Newspaper, and Arranging Desks.

The Bulletin Boards group has one less student than the Room Cleanup group.

Arnold, Brad, and Charlotte do not join the Room Cleanup crew, individually or as a group.

None of the students joins the Arranging Desks group.

Danielle, Evan, and Francine do not design Bulletin Boards, individually or as a group.

Gabrielle, Hap, and Ida do not join the Newspaper staff, individually or as a group.

Joshua joins the Newspaper staff.

5. Which of the following is a list of students who could comprise the entire Newspaper staff?
   (A) Joshua, Brad, and Gabrielle
   (B) Joshua, Charlotte, and Francine
   (C) Joshua, Danielle, Evan, and Francine
   (D) Joshua, Brad, Charlotte, and Danielle
   (E) Joshua, Arnold, Charlotte, Francine, and Ida

6. Of those listed, what is the largest possible number of students who could serve on the Newspaper staff?
   (A) 6
   (B) 7
   (C) 8
   (D) 9
   (E) 10

7. If no other student except Ida is designing Bulletin Boards, which of the following students must have chosen Room Cleanup?
   (A) Danielle and Hap
   (B) Francine and Evan
   (C) Evan and Gabrielle
   (D) Hap and Francine
   (E) Gabrielle and Hap

8. If the Newspaper staff has one member, who of the following must have chosen Room Cleanup?
   (A) Arnold
   (B) Brad
   (C) Gabrielle
   (D) Danielle
   (E) Hap

9. If Gabrielle, Hap, and Charlotte are the only students designing Bulletin Boards, which three must be the only students who joined the Newspaper staff?
   (A) Arnold, Brad, and Joshua
   (B) Arnold, Danielle, and Joshua
   (C) Brad, Evan, and Joshua
   (D) Brad, Francine, and Joshua
   (E) Charlotte, Evan, and Joshua

10. If Arnold and Gabrielle are the only students designing Bulletin Boards, how many students must be publishing the Newspaper?
   (A) 2
   (B) 3
   (C) 4
   (D) 5
   (E) 6

11. Between 1980 and 1990, the number of divorces in the New England states increased by 20%. Therefore, the number of children in New England living in single-parent homes is probably 20% higher in 1991 than it was in 1981.

   All of the following, if true, would weaken the conclusion in the passage above EXCEPT

   (A) the number of marriages in the New England states between 1980 and 1990 decreased by 25%
   (B) between 1980 and 1990, the percentage of the New England population under 25 years old who moved to southern states increased by 20%
   (C) ninety percent of the American men who are divorced remarry in three years or less
   (D) fifty percent of the New Englanders who moved to Sunbelt states between 1980 and 1990 were single parents with one or more children
   (E) between 1980 and 1990, the number of adults living in New England remained unchanged

12. The true test of liberty is a willingness to grant it to those who would deny it to us.

    Which of the following best illustrates the idea in this quotation?

    (A) The Supreme Court denies an employer's right to prevent only female employees from engaging in work that exposes them to higher levels of lead.
    (B) The American Civil Liberties Union supports the rights of the Ku Klux Klan to hold a rally in Skokie, Illinois.
    (C) The Teamsters' Union supports a Republican candidate for governor who opposes higher taxes on Japanese imports.
    (D) The mayor opposes the call for the resignation of the chief of police in the wake of a drug-abuse scandal in the police department.
    (E) The Canadian government refuses to extradite to the United States an accused man whose conviction might result in capital punishment.

13. The city council is considering the so-called "hotel-room prison" law, which permits some people convicted of nonviolent crimes to serve their sentences on weekends in small suburban jails that often have many cells unused. The prisoners must pay up to $125 per day for the cells and their food. These fees go to support law enforcement throughout the city.

    All of the following arguments are likely to be used in support of this law EXCEPT

    (A) all people who are convicted of nonviolent crimes should be given a choice of when and where they serve their sentences
    (B) many jails and prisons are overcrowded already
    (C) parents serving sentences on weekends are able to work to support their families during the week
    (D) prisoners should share some of the cost of their imprisonment
    (E) the profits from this program will help to reduce crime throughout the city

Questions 14–17

An apartment building has eight floors with one apartment on each floor. Seven families—the Abrams, the Bakers, the Cabots, the DeLeons, the Elgars, the Fertittas, and the Grants— occupy each of the apartments, with one apartment vacant.

The number of floors between the Abrams and the Bakers is exactly the same as the number of floors between the Cabots and DeLeons.

The Elgars are on a floor immediately adjacent to the Fertittas.

The apartment on the bottom, the first floor, is occupied.

The Grants live on a lower floor than the Elgars.

14. Which of the following is a possible arrangement of families, from bottom floor to top floor?
    (A) vacant, Grants, Abrams, Cabots, Bakers, DeLeons, Elgars, Fertittas
    (B) Grants, Abrams, Elgars, vacant, Fertittas, Bakers, Cabots, DeLeons
    (C) Grants, Bakers, Abrams, Fertittas, Elgars, DeLeons, Cabots, vacant
    (D) Abrams, Bakers, Cabots, Grants, vacant, DeLeons, Elgars, Fertittas
    (E) Cabots, DeLeons, Elgars, vacant, Grants, Fertittas, Bakers, Abrams

15. If the Fertittas live on the second floor, which of the following must be true?
    (A) The top floor is vacant.
    (B) The Elgars live on the bottom floor.
    (C) The Grants live on the bottom floor.
    (D) The Bakers live on the top floor.
    (E) The vacant floor is not the top floor.

16. If the Abrams live on the sixth floor, the Bakers live on the seventh floor, and the Fertittas live on the fourth floor, which of the following must be true?

I. The Cabots live on the first floor.
II. The Elgars live on the fifth floor.
III. The DeLeons live on the second floor.
IV. The top floor is vacant.

(A) I and II only
(B) I, II, and III only
(C) II and III only
(D) II and IV only
(E) I, II, III, and IV

17. If the Abrams and Bakers live on the second and fourth floors, respectively, all of the following can be true EXCEPT
(A) the Cabots live on the sixth floor
(B) the DeLeons live on the third floor
(C) the Fertittas live on the seventh floor
(D) the Grants live on the first floor
(E) the Elgars live on the seventh floor

Questions 18–22

A botanical garden has four greenskeepers: Wilson, Xavier, Yussef, and Zachary. One or more of them must trim the greens each day, but none of them does so for two or more days in a row.

18. If Wilson, Xavier, and Yussef trim the greens working together three times from Monday through Friday, which of the following must be true?

I. Zachary trims the greens on Tuesday.
II. Zachary trims the greens on Wednesday.
III. Zachary trims the greens on Thursday.

(A) I only
(B) II only
(C) III only
(D) I and III only
(E) I, II, and III

19. Which of the following is possible during the period from Tuesday through Friday?
    (A) All four greenskeepers work together on Friday.
    (B) Three greenskeepers work together three of the four days.
    (C) Xavier works twice as many days as Yussef.
    (D) Zachary works three times as many days as Wilson.
    (E) Both Wilson and Zachary work three times as many days as Xavier.

20. If Wilson, Xavier, and Yussef work together on Monday, and Wilson, Xavier, and Zachary work together on Thursday, which of the following must be true?

    I. Zachary works alone on Tuesday.
    II. Yussef works alone on Wednesday.
    III. Yussef works alone on Friday.

    (A) I only
    (B) II only
    (C) III only
    (D) I and II only
    (E) I, II, and III

21. Suppose Wilson works alone on Wednesday, and exactly two greenskeepers work Monday, Tuesday, Thursday, and Friday, then it must be true that
    (A) the same two greenskeepers work Tuesday and Thursday
    (B) Yussef works with Wilson at least one day during the week
    (C) Xavier works exactly two days during the week
    (D) Zachary works with Wilson on Monday or Friday
    (E) the same two greenskeepers work Monday and Friday

22. If a fifth greenskeeper, Quincy, joins the staff and works only on Tuesday, during that same week of Monday through Friday, what is the maximum number of greenskeepers that can work on Wednesday?
    (A) 1
    (B) 2
    (C) 3
    (D) 4
    (E) 5

23. Students in the city's junior high schools have reported that their grades improved when they were permitted to listen to the radio while doing their school homework assignments. It therefore seems probable that school performance could be improved if radios with earphones were permitted during school study halls.

Which of the following statements, if true, would most weaken the argument above?

(A) Neither the teachers nor the parents of the students approve of their listening to the radio while doing their homework.
(B) Seventy percent of the city's high school students say they listen to the radio while doing their homework.
(C) Forty percent of the students who receive above-average grades in junior high school say they never listen to the radio.
(D) No libraries in the schools permit the use of radios, though many have audio equipment.
(E) Studies of teenage children show a correlation between the ability to solve problems and silence.

24. In the past year, the number of deaths of innocent bystanders killed by gangs has increased 25 percent. The number will not decline until the city council is willing to spend the money to increase the size of foot patrols in the neighborhoods plagued by this violence.

Of the following, the best criticism of the argument above is that the argument does not

(A) take into account the possibility of dealing with the gang problem by any means except foot patrols
(B) consider the possibility that, the bystanders were, in fact, not innocent
(C) differentiate between the innocent bystanders and other victims of gang violence
(D) take into account the fact that, regardless of anticrime efforts, a certain number of accidental deaths occur every year
(E) consider the other fiscal needs of the city that may be more important

25. Interviews with police and hospital emergency room workers have shown that 65% of them believe there is a significantly higher number of accidents on nights when the moon is full than on other nights. But statistical studies show that the number of accidents on nights when the moon is full is, in fact, lower than on other nights when weather conditions are similar.

Which of the following is the most logical completion of the paragraph above?

(A) The chances of the weather's being bad on nights of the full moon must be greater than on other nights.
(B) The statistical studies are probably in error.
(C) Legends about the sinister effects of the full moon go back thousands of years and must have an ultimate basis in fact.
(D) People will often believe an event has happened if they expect that event to happen.
(E) On nights of the full moon when the sky is overcast, the number of accidents is higher.

STOP. IF YOU FINISH BEFORE TIME IS CALLED, CHECK YOUR WORK ON THIS SECTION ONLY. DO NOT WORK ON ANY OTHER SECTION IN THE TEST.

SECTION III: QUANTITATIVE ABILITY

Time: 30 Minutes
30 Questions

Quantitative Comparison

DIRECTIONS

In this section you will be given two quantities, one in column A and one in column B. You are to determine a relationship between the two quantities and mark

(A) if the quantity in column A is greater than the quantity in column B
(B) if the quantity in column B is greater than the quantity in column A
(C) if the quantities are equal
(D) if the comparison cannot be determined from the information that is given

Common Information:
Information centered above both columns refers to one or both columns.
All numbers used are real numbers.
Figures are intended to provide useful positional information, but are not necessarily drawn to scale and should not be used to estimate sizes by measurement.
Lines that appear straight can be assumed to be straight.

	Column A		Column B
		$p = \pm 3$	
1.	$(p + 2)^2$		26
		$a > 0$ $b > 0$ $c > 0$	
2.	(3a)(3b)(3c)		3abc
3.	$(-10)^{100}$		$(-10)^{101}$

	Column A	Column B

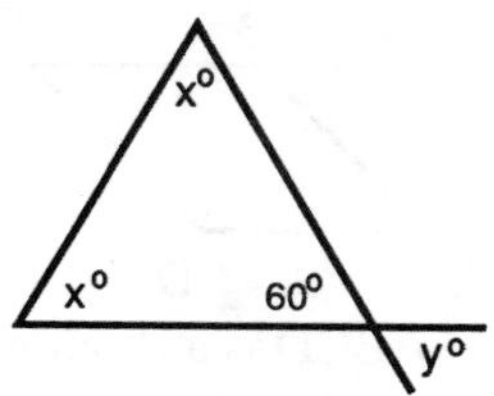

	Column A	Column B
4.	x°	y°
5.	$\frac{1}{19} - 1$	$\frac{1}{18} - 1$

Thirteen hundred subassembly units priced at 31¢ each are reduced for discount at a new price of 23¢ each.

	Column A	Column B
6.	Percent decrease in unit price of subassembly units	Percent decrease in number of subassembly units sold

Point O is the center of a circle which contains $\overparen{AB}$.
Point O does not lie on $\overline{AB}$

	Column A	Column B
7.	$\overline{AB}$	$\overparen{AB}$

Tom is 3 inches shorter than Dionne.
Joy is 4 inches shorter than Daniel.
Dionne is 1 inch shorter than Daniel.

	Column A	Column B
8.	Joy's height	Tom's height

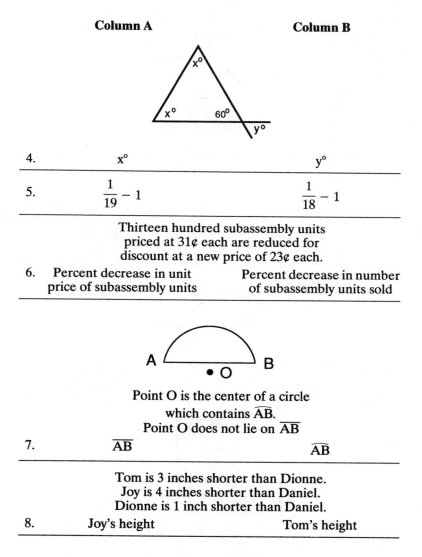

	Column A	Column B

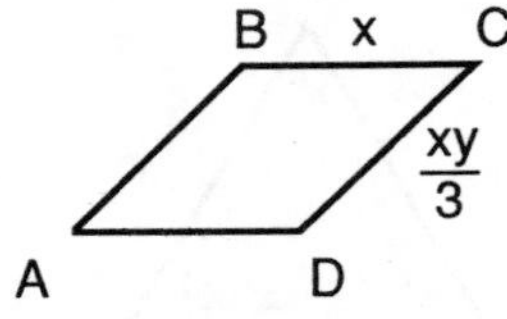

ABCD is a rhombus.

	Column A	Column B
9.	x	y

$0 < a < b < c < d$

	Column A	Column B
10.	$\frac{c}{d}$	$\frac{b}{a}$
11.	$\frac{10p + 20q}{3}$	$\frac{5p + 10q}{6}$

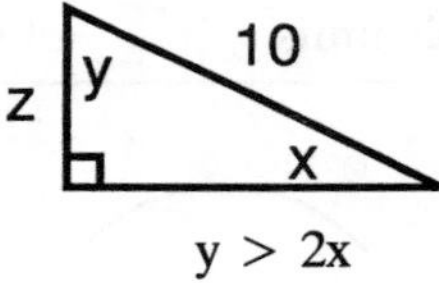

$y > 2x$

	Column A	Column B
12.	5	z
13.	$y^2 + 25$	$(y - 5)(y - 5)$

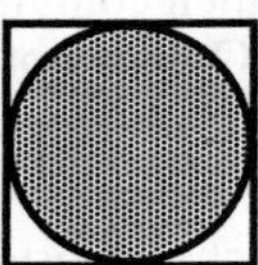

A noncompressible rubber ball exactly passes through a square hole, as shown above. The rubber ball is a perfect sphere. The diameter of the ball equals d.

	Column A	Column B
14.	The area of the hole	The perimeter of the hole

	Column A		Column B
		$z = 0$ $x = -y$	
15.	$10^x \cdot 10^y \cdot 10^z$		10^z

Math Ability

DIRECTIONS

Solve each problem in this section by using the information given and your own mathematical calculations. Then select the *one* correct answer of the five choices given. Use the available space on the page for scratchwork. NOTE: Some problems may be accompanied by figures or diagrams. These figures are drawn as accurately as possible, *except* when it is stated in a specific problem that the figure is not drawn to scale. The figure is meant to provide information useful in solving the problem or problems. Unless otherwise stated or indicated, all figures lie in a plane. All numbers used are real numbers.

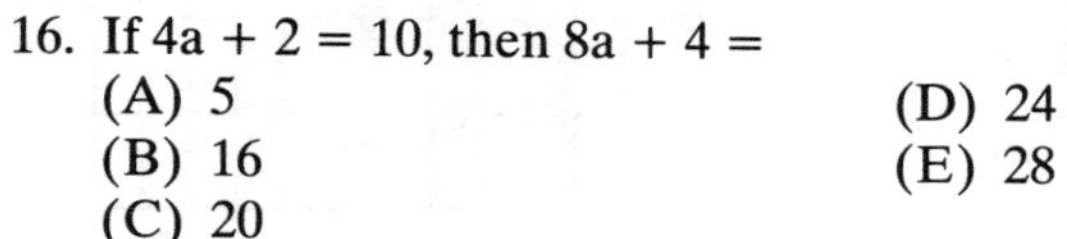

16. If $4a + 2 = 10$, then $8a + 4 =$
    (A) 5
    (B) 16
    (C) 20
    (D) 24
    (E) 28

17. An employee's annual salary was increased $15,000. If her new annual salary now equals $90,000, what was the percent increase?
    (A) 15%
    (B) $16\frac{2}{3}$%
    (C) 20%
    (D) 22%
    (E) 24%

18. $(4 + \frac{1}{2})(\frac{4}{9} + 2)$ equals what value?
    (A) $\frac{25}{9}$
    (B) $\frac{61}{18}$
    (C) 5
    (D) $\frac{74}{9}$
    (E) 11

19. If the area of a circular region exactly equals 4π square meters, which of the following is the circumference of that region?
(A) 2π meters
(B) 4π meters
(C) 6π meters
(D) 8π meters
(E) cannot be determined

20. If x, y, and z are consecutive negative integers, not necessarily in that order, which of the following may be true?
(A) $x + y > z$
(B) $xy < z$
(C) $z + y = y + x$
(D) $2x = (yz)/2$
(E) $x + y = z$

Questions 21–25 refer to the graphs.

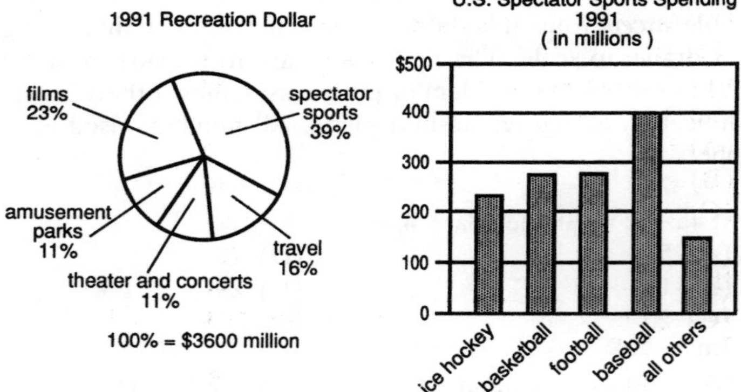

21. In 1991, Americans spent approximately how much more attending baseball games than attending ice hockey games?
(A) $400 million
(B) $280 million
(C) $230 million
(D) $200 million
(E) $170 million

22. In 1991, approximately how much more was the American attendance at films than at amusement parks?
(A) $430 million
(B) $620 million
(C) $720 million
(D) $830 million
(E) cannot be determined

23. In 1991, approximately how much more was spent by Americans on spectator sports than on travel?
(A) \$500 million
(B) \$850 million
(C) \$1150 million
(D) \$1250 million
(E) \$1450 million

24. Approximately what percent of the 1991 U.S. spectator sports dollar was spent on baseball?
(A) 10%
(B) 20%
(C) 25%
(D) 30%
(E) 39%

25. If, in 1992, the amount Americans spend on spectator sports reflects a percent increase of 33% over the 1991 figures, and the amount Americans spend on amusement parks in 1992 reflects a 10% decrease from their 1991 amusement park spending, then the ratio of American spending in 1992 at spectator sports to American spending at amusement parks would be approximately
(A) 72 to 1
(B) 36 to 1
(C) 5 to 1
(D) 3 to 1
(E) 2 to 1

26. If m is an integer such that $-5 < m < 2$, and n is an integer such that $-4 < n < 5$, what is the least possible value for $3m^2 - 2n$?
(A) −85
(B) −75
(C) −10
(D) −8
(E) 0

27. If P lies on $\widehat{ON}$ such that $\widehat{OP} = 2\widehat{PN}$ and Q lies on $\widehat{OP}$ such that $\widehat{OQ} = \widehat{QP}$, what is the relationship of $\widehat{OQ}$ to $\widehat{PN}$?
(A) 1/3
(B) 1/2
(C) 1
(D) 2/1
(E) 3/1

28. Tom can plow a field in 12 hours, but with Pat helping him they can plow the field together in 8 hours. If Pat works alone plowing for 12 hours, how long will it take Tom working alone to plow the remainder of the field?
    (A) 3 hours
    (B) 4 hours
    (C) $4\frac{1}{2}$ hours
    (D) 6 hours
    (E) $6\frac{2}{3}$ hours

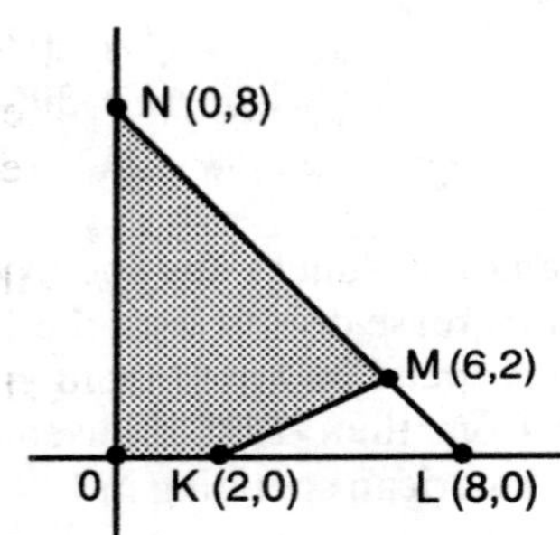

29. The area of the shaded region in the figure above is
    (A) 6
    (B) 12
    (C) 26
    (D) 32
    (E) 64

30. Three consecutive traffic signals each show either red or green. How many different arrangements of the three signals are possible? (Note: "red-red-green" is different from "green-red-red.")
    (A) 10
    (B) 9
    (C) 8
    (D) 7
    (E) 6

STOP. IF YOU FINISH BEFORE TIME IS CALLED, CHECK YOUR WORK ON THIS SECTION ONLY. DO NOT WORK ON ANY OTHER SECTION IN THE TEST.

SECTION IV: QUANTITATIVE ABILITY

Time: 30 Minutes
30 Questions

Quantitative Comparison

DIRECTIONS

In this section you will be given two quantities, one in column A and one in column B. You are to determine a relationship between the two quantities and mark

(A) if the quantity in column A is greater than the quantity in column B
(B) if the quantity in column B is greater than the quantity in column A
(C) if the quantities are equal
(D) if the comparison cannot be determined from the information that is given

Common Information:

Information centered above both columns refers to one or both columns.
All numbers used are real numbers.
Figures are intended to provide useful positional information, but are not necessarily drawn to scale and should not be used to estimate sizes by measurement.
Lines that appear straight can be assumed to be straight.

	Column A	Column B
1.	2	$\frac{7}{7}+\frac{6}{7}+\frac{2}{13}$
2.	$(.4)^2$	$(\frac{1}{2})^4$
3.	$66\frac{2}{3}$	66.66

	Column A		Column B

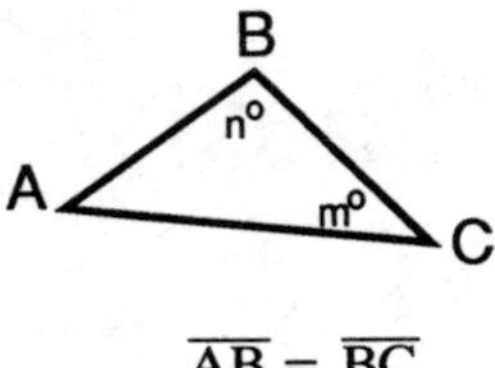

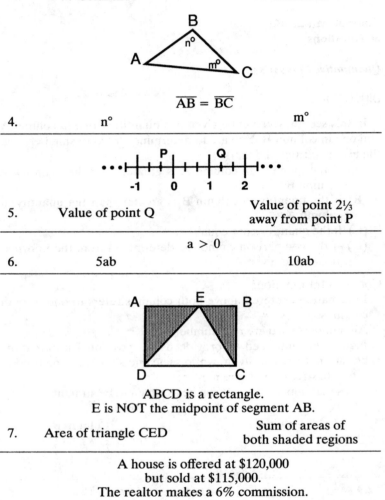

$\overline{AB} = \overline{BC}$

4.	n°	m°

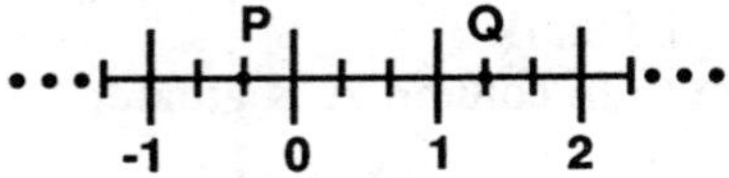

5.	Value of point Q	Value of point $2\frac{1}{3}$ away from point P

$a > 0$

6.	5ab	10ab

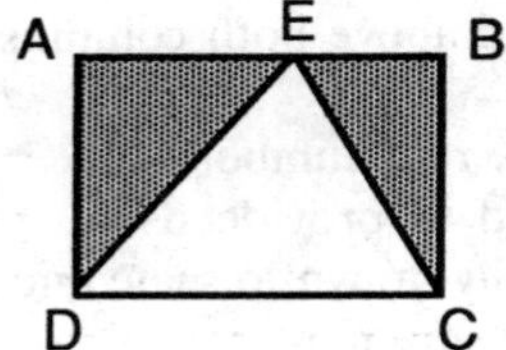

ABCD is a rectangle.
E is NOT the midpoint of segment AB.

7.	Area of triangle CED	Sum of areas of both shaded regions

A house is offered at $120,000
but sold at $115,000.
The realtor makes a 6% commission.

8.	Percent drop in price of house	Realtor's commission as a percent

Column A **Column B**

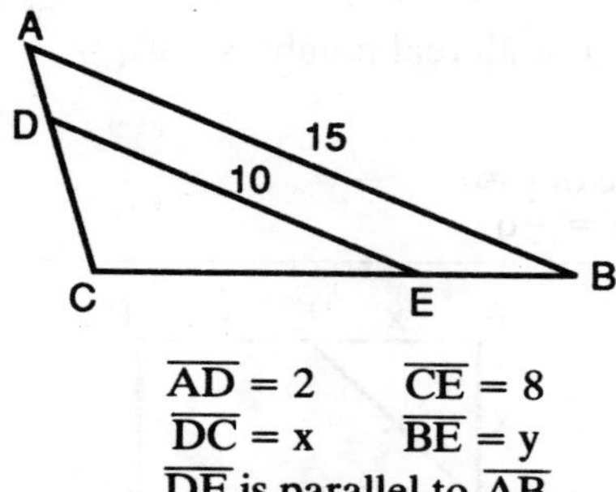

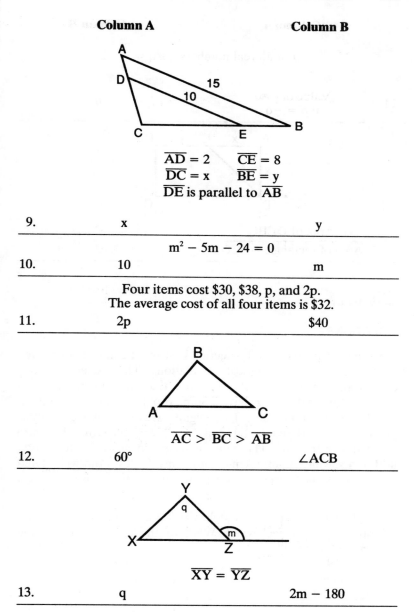

$\overline{AD} = 2$ $\overline{CE} = 8$
$\overline{DC} = x$ $\overline{BE} = y$
$\overline{DE}$ is parallel to $\overline{AB}$

9. x y

$m^2 - 5m - 24 = 0$

10. 10 m

Four items cost \$30, \$38, p, and 2p.
The average cost of all four items is \$32.

11. 2p \$40

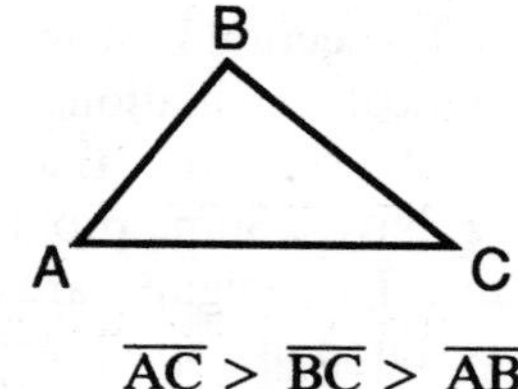

$\overline{AC} > \overline{BC} > \overline{AB}$

12. 60° ∠ACB

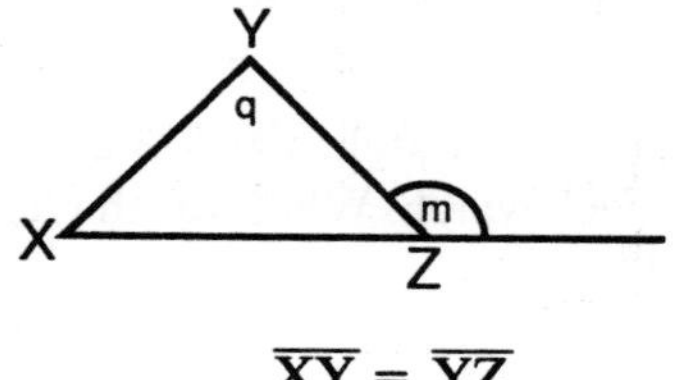

$\overline{XY} = \overline{YZ}$

13. q 2m − 180

	Column A	Column B
	For all real numbers, $p\#q = \frac{p^2}{q}$	
14.	Value of $p\#q$ if $p = -q$	q

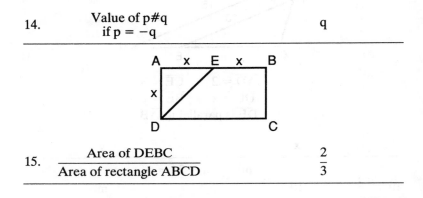

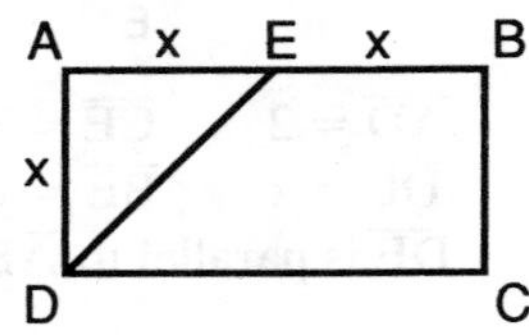

	Column A	Column B
15.	$\frac{\text{Area of DEBC}}{\text{Area of rectangle ABCD}}$	$\frac{2}{3}$

Math Ability

DIRECTIONS

Solve each problem in this section by using the information given and your own mathematical calculations. Then select the *one* correct answer of the five choices given. Use the available space on the page for scratchwork. NOTE: Some problems may be accompanied by figures or diagrams. These figures are drawn as accurately as possible, *except* when it is stated in a specific problem that the figure is not drawn to scale. The figure is meant to provide information useful in solving the problem or problems. Unless otherwise stated or indicated, all figures lie in a plane. All numbers used are real numbers.

16. A dealer purchased 85 watches at $23 each and sold then at a profit of $47 on each watch. What was the dealer's gross income on the watches?

(A) $1955
(B) $3995
(C) $5950
(D) $6800
(E) $6950

17. If x and y are integers such that $2 < y < 25$ and $5 < x < 13$, then the largest possible value of $(y/x) + (x/y) =$
(A) $\frac{1}{2}$
(B) 4
(C) $4\frac{1}{4}$
(D) 8
(E) 10

18. $$\frac{\frac{7}{10} \times 14 \times 5 \times \frac{1}{28}}{\frac{10}{17} \times \frac{3}{5} \times \frac{1}{6} \times 17} =$$
(A) $\frac{4}{7}$
(B) 1
(C) $\frac{7}{4}$
(D) 2
(E) $\frac{17}{4}$

19. If $3x + 2y = 10$, then $9x + 6y =$
(A) $3\frac{1}{3}$
(B) 15
(C) 25
(D) 30
(E) 35

20. Jane is six years older than Tom, and Tom is five years younger than Phillip. Chris is three years older than Tom. If Jane's age is expressed as J, what is the sum of the ages of Jane, Tom, Phillip, and Chris in terms of J?
(A) $4J - 10$
(B) $J - 9$
(C) $3J - 6$
(D) $4J + 12$
(E) $J + 14$

Questions 21–25 refer to the following figure.

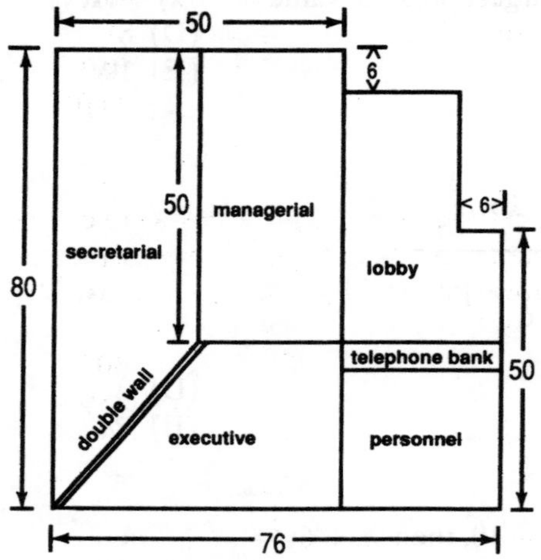

The figure above shows the floor plan of the ground floor of a commercial building.

Dimensions are in feet.

Thickness of walls should be ignored.

Except for the "double wall," all walls meet at right angles.

21. What is the area, in square feet, of the entire ground floor?
    (A) 5780
    (B) 6080
    (C) 6280
    (D) 6480
    (E) 6780

22. What is the perimeter, in feet, of the lobby?
    (A) 120
    (B) 126
    (C) 132
    (D) 136
    (E) 140

23. If the area of the telephone bank is 104 square feet, what is the area, in square feet, of the personnel division?
    (A) 625
    (B) 636
    (C) 666
    (D) 676
    (E) 696

24. If the wall separating managerial from executive measures 24 feet, how much more is the area, in square feet, of secretarial than executive?
(A) 460
(B) 510
(C) 580
(D) 760
(E) 1110

25. If the two exterior walls of the lobby were extended to conform to the rectangular dimensions of the rest of the ground floor, the total area of the lobby would be increased by approximately what percent?
(A) 15%
(B) 20%
(C) 25%
(D) 30%
(E) 35%

	3	
9	x	z
	y	

26. In the figure above, the sum of the values in the horizontal row equals the sum of the values in the vertical row. If z equals 5, what is the value of y?
(A) 1
(B) 3
(C) 5
(D) 11
(E) cannot be determined

27. If $ab \neq 0$, then $\frac{a + 8b}{8a} - \frac{a + 2b}{2a} =$

(A) $-\frac{3}{8}$

(B) $\frac{-3a + 16b}{8a}$

(C) 0

(D) $\frac{3a + 6b}{8a}$

(E) $\frac{10b}{8a}$

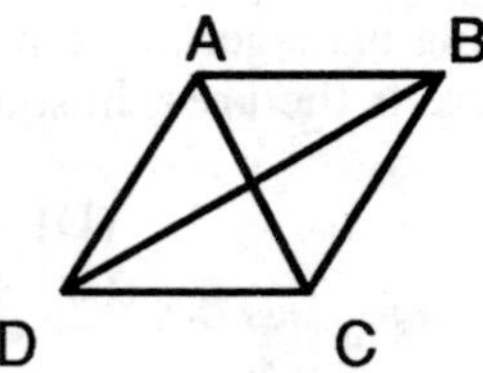

28. Rhombus ABCD has perimeter of 8, and diagonal AC equals 2. What is the area of ABCD?
(A) $\sqrt{3}$
(B) 2
(C) $2\sqrt{2}$
(D) $2\sqrt{3}$
(E) 4

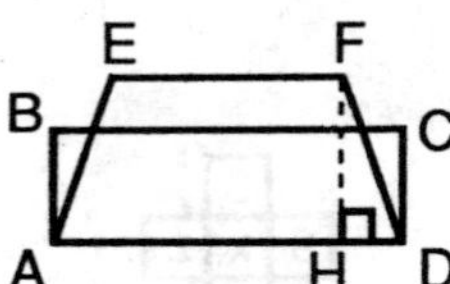

29. Rectangle ABCD and trapezoid AEFD have equal areas. If the ratio of $\overline{CD}$ to $\overline{FH}$ is 3 to 4, what is the ratio of $\overline{EF}$ to $\overline{AD}$?
(A) 1 to 2
(B) 2 to 3
(C) 3 to 4
(D) 4 to 3
(E) 3 to 2

30. Of 30 adults, exactly 15 are college graduates, exactly 10 are exchange students, and exactly 8 are multilingual. Only 3 college graduates are multilingual exchange students, and only 4 non-college graduates are multilingual exchange students. In this group, a person who is a college graduate may be both multilingual and an exchange student but not one or the other alone. How many of the 30 adults are not college graduates, multilingual, or exchange students?
(A) 4
(B) 5
(C) 6
(D) 7
(E) 8

STOP. IF YOU FINISH BEFORE TIME IS CALLED, CHECK YOUR WORK ON THIS SECTION ONLY. DO NOT WORK ON ANY OTHER SECTION IN THE TEST.

SECTION V: VERBAL ABILITY

Time: 30 Minutes
38 Questions

In this section, choose the best answer for each question and blacken the corresponding space on the answer sheet.

Sentence Completion

DIRECTIONS

Each blank in the following sentences indicates that something has been omitted. Considering the lettered words beneath the sentence, choose the word or set of words that best fits the whole sentence.

1. Unless the environmentalists can draft a more _________ proposal, the courts will disallow their proposition as too vague.
   (A) legal
   (B) restrictive
   (C) encompassing
   (D) specific
   (E) ecological

2. Heavy snows in the passes of the Pyrenees have seriously _________ rescuers trying to reach travelers surprised by the spring blizzards.
   (A) excluded
   (B) expedited
   (C) rappelled
   (D) assisted
   (E) hampered

3. It is difficult to take sides with either party since both of the combatants are so _________ to _________.
   (A) indifferent . . . evasion
   (B) reluctant . . . compromise
   (C) hostile . . . inteference
   (D) impenetrable . . . rhetoric
   (E) averse . . . expectation

4. The success of the English-Spanish simulcast must be _______ to Margo Quiroz, who interprets forty different news items in each nightly newscast.
(A) attested
(B) censured
(C) interpreted
(D) transliterated
(E) attributed

5. Time and time again, the power of the mob in Chicago has appeared to have been annihilated, but it has always _______ itself.
(A) reappeared
(B) eliminated
(C) returned
(D) regenerated
(E) exhumed

6. Slovenia's declared intention to _______ and Croatia's decision to _______ the conference aimed at preventing the breakup of the federation are twin blows to Yugoslavian unity.
(A) secede . . . boycott
(B) withdraw . . . foster
(C) divide . . . consolidate
(D) recede . . . avoid
(E) patronize . . . exclude

7. Walters and Torres _______ seven other candidates in the special election, but because neither _______ more than fifty percent of the vote, a runoff election will have to be held for the two of them.
(A) trailed . . . captured
(B) defeated . . . recaptured
(C) out-polled . . . garnered
(D) eliminated . . . reclaimed
(E) evaded . . . achieved

Analogies

DIRECTIONS

In each question below, you are given a related pair of words or phrases. Select the lettered pair that *best* expresses a relationship similar to that in the original pair of words.

8. OIL PAINTING : CANVAS ::
   (A) etching : acid
   (B) violin : bow
   (C) fresco : plaster
   (D) building : architecture
   (E) watercolor : brush

9. SPIDER : OCTOPUS ::
   (A) gibbon : salmon
   (B) locust : water beetle
   (C) coyote : dolphin
   (D) cheetah : lobster
   (E) oriole : ground hog

10. WRATH : IRATE ::
    (A) sloth : sleepy
    (B) gluttony : starving
    (C) pride : sullen
    (D) envy : craving
    (E) avarice : acquisitive

11. BREAKFAST : DINNER ::
    (A) lark : nightingale
    (B) stone : wood
    (C) tent : tepee
    (D) radar : sonar
    (E) realism : rationalism

12. WAIT : LURK ::
    (A) prowl : slink
    (B) expect : anticipate
    (C) service : repair
    (D) move : skulk
    (E) trot : canter

13. PINK : CLOTH ::
    (A) mortar : brick
    (B) weigh : anchor
    (C) weld : metal
    (D) card : wool
    (E) saw : board

14. ESSAY : SHORT STORY ::
    (A) symphony : concerto
    (B) biography : novel
    (C) acrylic : watercolor
    (D) comedy : burlesque
    (E) monologue : drama

15. TRIPTYCH : PANEL ::
    (A) triangle : hypotenuse
    (B) circle : arc
    (C) cathedral : nave
    (D) blossom : sepal
    (E) cheese : butter

16. SAVANNAH : VELDT ::
   (A) ulcer : eczema
   (B) forest : woodland
   (C) fathom : acre
   (D) falcon : condor
   (E) tundra : glacier

Reading Comprehension

DIRECTIONS

Questions follow each of the passages below. Using only the stated or implied information in each passage, answer the questions.

A. S. Byatt calls her book *Possession: A Romance* to claim the latitude, the freedom from minute fidelity to historical truth that Hawthorne believed distinguished the romance from the novel. Byatt's book tells two stories, one set in contemporary England and one in the Victorian era. Two twentieth-century academics meet and fall in love while trying to unearth the story of a secret love affair between a Victorian poet who resembles Robert Browning and a writer whose poems may remind modern readers of Emily Bronte and Emily Dickinson.

Byatt is a great ventriloquist and has reproduced many pages of the Victorian couple's letters, diaries, and poetry. Indeed, some modern readers may find the excerpts from the poetry too much of a good thing, and several of the poems run to genuine Victorian lengths. This challenging work is crammed with literary allusions, and in time a reader will see an eerie correspondence between the Victorian lovers and the modern man and woman who discover the secrets of the past.

17. The author's discussion of Byatt's *Possession: A Romance* can best be descibed as
   (A) argumentative
   (B) reserved and ironic
   (C) admiring with reservations
   (D) unqualifiedly enthusiastic
   (E) nonjudgmental

18. The author uses all of the following in discussing Byatt's book EXCEPT
    (A) personal opinion
    (B) literary comparison
    (C) definition of a term
    (D) rhetorical question
    (E) plot summary

19. The author probably uses the words "ventriloquist" and "reproduce" to suggest
    (A) the period accuracy of the Victorian sections
    (B) the unrealistic quality of the narrative
    (C) the lack of originality in the Victorian sections
    (D) the inferiority of the modern sections of the book
    (E) the book's use of literary allusions

20. The effect of the reference to the poetry's "genuine Victorian length" is to
    (A) stress the period accuracy
    (B) suggest the great length of the excerpts
    (C) indicate that the poetry is inferior to the prose
    (D) emphasize the tediousness of the poems
    (E) stress the superiority of the Victorian sections of the book

Because sharks are such ancient life forms, for many years scientists considered them primitive. But a growing body of research on sharks and their relatives portrays these creatures as behaving in ways far more sophisticated and complex than was thought possible. Scientists are documenting elaborate social behaviors among these fish, including never-before-witnessed mating rituals that seem to be based on electrical signals.

Compared to other fishes, shark have huge brains. Their brain-to- bodyweight ratio is more comparable to that found in birds and mammals than to other fishes. But because sharks are so difficult to study—they are dangerous, far-ranging, and usually inhabit murky waters—scientists only recently have accumulated enough data to even hint at their behavioral and sensory complexity. In one of the most surprising findings, a researcher discovered a new sense organ, located on top of certain sharks' heads. The organ is a sort of light-gathering "third eye" known in some prehistoric fishes, the lantern fishes, and at least one living reptile, the tuatara of New Zealand. Its precise function in the six-gilled shark is still uncertain, though sensing light at the deep depths to which they dive is most likely.

Sharks are literally covered in sense organs. Over the last two decades, researchers have found chemical receptor cells embedded inside sharks' teeth, in their throats, around the heads, and in pore-like openings on the skin. With no fewer than four separate sensory systems to detect chemicals in the water, sharks are able to detect amino acids in concentrations as low as one part per billion. Past researchers have documented that sharks also have good vision and can see in color; they have directional hearing, and although they cannot hear notes much above middle C, they can hear sounds below the threshold of human hearing.

But perhaps the most astounding sense possessed by sharks is their ability to sense electric fields. Sharks, skates, and rays—a group of closely related fishes collectively known as elasmobranchs—can detect fields so weak they cannot be measured by standard laboratory equipment. All live organisms, immersed in water, have a weak bioelectric field, a currect generated between biological membranes and the surrounding water. Elasmobranch fishes use electroreception to locate prey. Some scientists suspect that sharks, skates, and rays, sensing and interpreting the much larger voltage potentials created by salt-water currents moving through the earth's magnetic field, use this information to navigate.

Now it appears that electroreception may also play a key role in the mating system of sharks and the 1,000 other fishes in the same taxonomic group. The females use electroreception for some sort of social cues. Receptive females may be advertising their availability by congregating in large, highly visible, unburied piles; but unreceptive females, perhaps already pregnant, may use electroreception to locate other buried females to hide from amorous males in buried aggregation. Sharks and rays might purposely vary the information content of their electric fields to send different messages to one another. Field strength intensifies when the fishes open their mouths. Literally, "heavy breathing" could enhance a female's attraction.

21. The author refers to the shark's reputation as a primitive animal in order to
    (A) stress the evolutionary progress of the modern shark
    (B) question this opinion in the light of modern research
    (C) support an argument for the increased funding of scientific study of the shark
    (D) introduce the thesis of the passage
    (E) indirectly support the conclusions of earlier shark researchers

22. The complexity of the shark has been underestimated for which of the following reasons?

    I. Sharks are a very ancient life form.
    II. Sharks are dangerous.
    III. Sharks rarely live in clear waters.

    (A) II only
    (B) I and II only
    (C) I and III only
    (D) II and III only
    (E) I, II, and III

23. The passage compares the shark to all of the following EXCEPT
    (A) skates
    (B) a reptile
    (C) birds
    (D) rays
    (E) a dolphin

24. It can be inferred from the passage that female sharks hiding in groups from male sharks
    (A) could not be found if they were buried in the sand
    (B) could be discovered by a male shark using his "third eye"
    (C) would emit no bioelectric signals
    (D) would be easier to detect by electroreception than a female shark hiding alone
    (E) would open their mouths as often as possible

25. According to the passage, sharks may use their electroreceptive ability for all of the following EXCEPT
    (A) to locate prey
    (B) to navigate
    (C) to gather light
    (D) to locate other sharks
    (E) to locate breeding partners

26. Which of the following is most relevant to the research described in the passage?
    (A) Certain birds communicate by emitting cries pitched two octaves above middle C.
    (B) Certain migrating birds determine their location by detecting variations in the strength of the earth's magnetic field.
    (C) Migrating herds of wildebeest can reach their destination in spite of major changes in a landscape from one year to the next.
    (D) Some migrating birds and insects appear to arrive at the same place on exactly the same day year after year.
    (E) Dogs are capable of hearing sounds at pitches inaudible to human ears.

27. The author of the passage employs all of the following EXCEPT
    (A) personal opinion
    (B) questioning prior opinion
    (C) generalization
    (D) double meaning
    (E) comparison

Antonyms

DIRECTIONS

Each word in CAPITAL LETTERS is followed by five words or phrases. The correct choice is the word or phrase whose meaning is most nearly *opposite* to the meaning of the word in capitals. You may be required to distinguish fine shades of meaning. Look at all choices before marking your answer.

28. UNDAUNTED :
    (A) persistent
    (B) timorous
    (C) prepared
    (D) adventurous
    (E) somnolent

29. COALESCE :
    (A) separate
    (B) liquefy
    (C) improve upon
    (D) inflame
    (E) relax

30. CAPTIOUS :
    (A) eager
    (B) deprived
    (C) indulgent
    (D) free
    (E) anxious

31. SERVILE :
    (A) uninhibited
    (B) catlike
    (C) gauche
    (D) undivided
    (E) arrogant

32. DILATE :
    (A) still
    (B) widen
    (C) converse
    (D) contract
    (E) unify

33. SERRATED :
    (A) dull
    (B) conical
    (C) smooth
    (D) tender
    (E) open to the air

34. MACULATE :
    (A) undefiled
    (B) dried
    (C) hopeless
    (D) commonplace
    (E) severed

35. FEALTY :
    (A) insensitivity
    (B) unhappiness
    (C) torpor
    (D) indecision
    (E) infidelity

36. COGNATE :
    (A) ignorant
    (B) intestate
    (C) well-known
    (D) unrelated
    (E) inscrutable

37. REIN :
    (A) govern
    (B) release
    (C) dry up
    (D) muddle
    (E) insure

38. KUDOS :
    (A) reward
    (B) regrets
    (C) obloquy
    (D) freedom
    (E) glorification

STOP. IF YOU FINISH BEFORE TIME IS CALLED, CHECK YOUR WORK ON THIS SECTION ONLY. DO NOT WORK ON ANY OTHER SECTION IN THE TEST.

SECTION VI: ANALYTICAL ABILITY

Time: 30 Minutes
25 Questions

DIRECTIONS

The following questions or group of questions are based on a passage or set of statements. Choose the best answer for each question and blacken the corresponding space on your answer sheet. It may be helpful to draw rough diagrams or simple charts in attempting to answer these question types.

Question 1–6

Six actors (Al, Brandon, Charlie, Dusty, Earvin, and Francine) perform scenes at a showcase talent presentation. Every scene has four characters except scenes 1 and 3, which have three characters each.

Each character is played by one of the actors.

There are five scenes.

During each scene the actors not performing work the lights.

Each actor performs in three scenes, but the three scenes cannot be consecutive.

Each actor works lights for exactly two scenes, but they cannot be consecutive.

1. Assume Charlie and Earvin work lights during scene 1. Which of the following must be true?
   (A) Earvin and Charlie perform in scene 5.
   (B) Earvin and Dusty perform in scene 4.
   (C) Earvin and Charlie perform in scene 4.
   (D) Earvin performs in scenes 3 and 4.
   (E) Charlie performs in scenes 3 and 4.

2. If Brandon, Charlie, and Francine perform in scene 1, which of the following groups could perform in scene 2?
   (A) Brandon, Charlie, Dusty, and Francine
   (B) Al, Brandon, Charlie, and Francine
   (C) Al, Charlie, Dusty, and Francine
   (D) Al, Dusty, Earvin, and Francine
   (E) Charlie, Dusty, Earvin, and Francine

3. Assume Al, Brandon, and Dusty perform in scene 1. If Brandon, Dusty, and Earvin perform in scene 3, any of the following could perform in scene 4 EXCEPT
   (A) Al
   (B) Brandon
   (C) Charlie
   (D) Dusty
   (E) Earvin

4. Suppose Brandon and Dusty perform in scene 4, and Al, Dusty, and Earvin perform in scene 1. Each of the following could perform in scene 3 EXCEPT
   (A) Al
   (B) Brandon
   (C) Charlie
   (D) Francine
   (E) Earvin

5. Suppose Brandon, Charlie, and Dusty perform in scene 1. If Al, Charlie, and Dusty perform in scene 3, the actors performing scene 2 must be
   (A) Al, Brandon, Charlie, and Francine
   (B) Al, Brandon, Dusty, and Francine
   (C) Al, Brandon, Earvin, and Francine
   (D) Brandon, Charlie, Earvin, and Francine
   (E) Brandon, Dusty, Earvin, and Francine

6. Assume that Al, Charlie, and Dusty perform in scene 1. If Dusty is included in the performers for scene 2, who must perform in scene 4?
   (A) Al
   (B) Brandon
   (C) Charlie
   (D) Dusty
   (E) Francine

7. The observation of groups of chimpanzees living together in the wild has shown than when the number of adult males in a group is more than six, but less than ten, dangerous and sometimes fatal fights are common. But when the number is more than ten, or less than six, fighting is very rare. Therefore zoos must be required to limit the size of chimpanzee groups to six or fewer male adults.

The conclusion of the passage above makes which of the following assumptions?

(A) that chimpanzees will behave the same in a zoo as in the wild
(B) that with fewer than six males in a group, chimpanzees will fight infrequently
(C) that a group with fewer than six male chimpanzees will be safer
(D) fighting among chimpanzees is not determined by the number of adult males
(E) with more than ten males in a group, chimpanzees will be overcrowded

8. Apples are classified by increasing size in five grades, from one to five. The price of apples increases with the grade. If an apple has a grade of three or higher, it will cost more than thirty-nine cents per pound.

If the above statements are true, which of the following must also be true?

(A) An apple with the grade of two will cost less than thirty-nine cents per pound.
(B) An apple with the grade of one will cost less than thirty-nine cents per pound.
(C) Some apples cost less than thirty-nine cents per pound.
(D) An apple with a grade of three may cost thirty-nine cents per pound.
(E) An apple with a grade of four will cost more than thirty-nine cents per pound.

9. **If the effect is what causes the cause to become a cause, then the effect, not the cause, should be treated as origin.**

   If this statement is accepted, which of the following statements will be true?

   (A) The cause and the effect are identical.
   (B) There is no such thing as cause and effect.
   (C) The pinprick causes the pin.
   (D) Heavy rains are the cause of floods.
   (E) The lightning will follow the thunder.

Questions 10–13

A chef working at a Mr. Eggs franchise is preparing Mr. Eggs' famous giant breakfast omelettes. These omelettes require not only the finest grade AA eggs, but also at least two of the following specially prepared ingredients: tomatoes, diced ham, onions, mushrooms, cheese, and shrimp. These ingredients are measured in cups. When the chef cooks an omelette, she must follow Mr. Eggs' strict recipes:

She can never use onions and mushrooms in the same omelet.

For every cup of diced ham, she must also use a cup of mushrooms, but if mushrooms are used, she does not have to use diced ham.

If cheese is included in the omelet, the number of cups she uses must be greater than the total number of cups she uses for all the other specially prepared ingredients combined in that omelet.

For every cup of tomatoes used, she must use two cups of onions.

No omelette uses all of the specially prepared ingredients.

She cannot use any ingredients other than the ones listed above.

10. Which of the following combinations of ingredients can never be used together?
    (A) tomatoes and diced ham
    (B) tomatoes and onions
    (C) tomatoes and cheese
    (D) tomatoes and shrimp
    (E) cheese and shrimp

11. If one more cup of onions is added to the following ingredients, which of the following would conform to a Mr. Eggs recipe?
    (A) eggs, 2 cups onions, 1 cup mushrooms, 3 cups cheese, 2 cups shrimp
    (B) eggs, 2 cups diced ham, 1 cup onions, 4 cups cheese, 3 cups shrimp
    (C) eggs, 1 cup diced ham, 1 cup onions, 1 cup cheese, 2 cups shrimp
    (D) eggs, 1 cup tomatoes, 2 cups onions, 2 cups cheese, 1 cup shrimp
    (E) eggs, 1 cup tomatoes, 1 cup onions, 5 cups cheese, 1 cup shrimp

12. Which complete recipe below conforms to the restrictions of a Mr. Eggs omelette?
    (A) eggs, 3 cups onions, 3 cups tomatoes
    (B) eggs, 2 cups diced ham, 2 cups tomatoes
    (C) eggs, 1 cup tomatoes, 1 cup cheese
    (D) eggs, 4 cups mushrooms, 4 cups diced ham
    (E) eggs, 5 cups cheese, 5 cups diced ham

13. Of the following, which one ingredient could be added to ingredients already containing two cups onions and one cup cheese to make it conform to a Mr. Eggs omelette?
    (A) 2 cups cheese
    (B) 2 cups onions
    (C) 1 cup mushrooms
    (D) 1 cup diced ham
    (E) 1 cup tomatoes

Questions 14–19

Seven automobiles (an Acura, a Buick, a Chevrolet, a Dodge, an Edsel, a Ferrari, and a Jeep) are parked in a parking lot having ten spaces, equally spaced, numbered 1 through 10 from north to south.

The Acura is as far away from the Buick as the Chevrolet is from the Dodge.

The Ferrari is parked next to the Edsel.

Space 1 is always filled; spaces 8 and 9 are always empty.

14. If the Jeep is parked in space 1, the Buick is parked in space 5, and the Acura is parked in space 10, which of the following spaces must be empty?
    (A) 1
    (B) 2
    (C) 3
    (D) 4
    (E) 6

15. From north to south, which of the following is a possible order of parked automobiles?
    (A) Dodge, Chevrolet, Ferrari, Edsel, Acura, Buick, Jeep, empty, empty, empty
    (B) Dodge, Ferrari, Chevrolet, Edsel, Acura, Jeep, Buick, empty, empty, empty
    (C) Buick, Dodge, Jeep, Chevrolet, empty, Edsel, Acura, Ferrari, empty, empty
    (D) Chevrolet, Ferrari, Edsel, Acura, Buick, Jeep, empty, Dodge, empty, empty
    (E) Ferrari, Edsel, Dodge, Acura, Buick, Jeep, Chevrolet, empty, empty, empty

16. Assume the Acura is parked in space 3 and the Buick is parked in space 5. Which of the following could be true?
    (A) The Dodge is parked in space 7.
    (B) The Chevrolet is parked in space 1.
    (C) The Dodge is parked in space 10.
    (D) The Chevrolet is parked in space 6.
    (E) The Chevrolet is parked in space 9.

17. If the Acura is parked in space 1, the Ferrari is parked in space 2, and the Chevrolet is parked in space 4, which of the following must be true?

I. The Buick is parked in space 7.
II. The Dodge is parked in space 10.
III. The Edsel is parked in space 6.

(A) I only
(B) II only
(C) III only
(D) I and II only
(E) I, II, and III

18. Suppose the Jeep, Acura, and Chevrolet are parked in spaces 5, 6, and 7, respectively, and the Buick is parked less than four spaces north of the Dodge. Which of the following must be true?
(A) Space 10 is empty.
(B) The Edsel is parked in space 1.
(C) The Ferrari is parked in space 1.
(D) The Dodge is parked in space 4.
(E) The Buick is parked in space 3.

19. Which of the following CANNOT be true?
(A) The Ferrari is parked space 1.
(B) The Edsel is parked in space 10.
(C) The Dodge is parked in space 3.
(D) The Buick is parked in space 2.
(E) The Acura is parked in space 5.

Questions 20–22

Six musical songs play on a tape during lunch hour at a department store. The songs' performing artists are Sinatra, Joel, Rankin, Holiday, Cole, and McCartney, not necessarily in that order.

Holiday's song is immediately before McCartney's song.

Sinatra's song is immediately after the song sung by Rankin.

Cole's song is neither first nor second on the tape.

Joel's song comes exactly three songs after Cole's song.

20. If a customer enters the store as Holiday's song is ending, stays only through the next song, and then leaves as Cole's song begins playing, which of the following must be true?
(A) Holiday's song is first on the tape.
(B) McCartney's song is third on the tape.
(C) Cole's song is fourth on the tape.
(D) Rankins's song is fifth on the tape.
(E) Sinatra's song is sixth on the tape.

21. If Rankin's song is first on the tape, which of the following performers' songs must be playing immediately before Cole's?
(A) Holiday
(B) McCartney
(C) Rankin
(D) Sinatra
(E) Joel

22. If Sinatra's song is fifth on the tape, which of the following performers' songs must be playing immediately before Cole's?
(A) Holiday
(B) McCartney
(C) Rankin
(D) Sinatra
(E) Joel

23. Environmentalists are concerned about dry-cleaning solvents such as perchloroethylene which can harm the skin, pollute the air, and contaminate ground water. They are also hostile to plastic bags and wire coat hangers, which often end up in landfills. They recommend our buying clothes that will not require dry-cleaning, for example those made of cotton or linen.

Which of the following, if true, most seriously weakens the argument made in this paragraph?

(A) Most of the detergents used to wash natural fabrics cause environmental damage.
(B) A decline in the sale of wood could seriously undermine the economy in New Zealand.
(C) More costly chemicals that do not have the dangerous side effects of perchloroethylene are in use in Europe.
(D) The availability of landfills in the most populous states will be exhausted in five years.
(E) The manufacture of nylon and rayon depends upon the availability of certain petrochemicals.

24. After six months of intensive television watching, at the end of the Iraqi war, seventy-five percent of the Americans who supported the war mistakenly believed that the United States had made clear its intention to support Kuwait militarily before the Iraqi invasion. Seventy-seven percent did not know that Israel still occupied any lands of its Arab neighbors. This same large percentage of the American people has been watching at least two hours of television news every day for six months and claims to believe that the United States army should be used to restore the sovereignty of any illegally occupied country.

Which of the following is the most appropriate conclusion of this paragraph?

(A) It seems clear that the Americans approve only of wars they believe they will win.
(B) For those who believe that television news watchers will be well informed, these results must be grimly disillusioning.
(C) The Iraqi war was a just war undertaken by a principled government against an illegal occupation.
(D) This proves that we can know only what we wish to know.
(E) The army's rating have never been higher.

25. If we reduce the tax on capital gains on the sale of stocks, investors who have capital gains will sell their stocks and the result will be a much higher amount of taxable capital gains. Stock brokers will earn more, so income tax revenues will increase. Both the government and the taxpayer will be better off.

This argument is based on which of the following assumptions?

(A) The increased income from capital gains taxes will be equal to or greater than deductions for capital losses.
(B) There will be a rise in the prices of stocks producing capital gains.
(C) Only a small percentage of the nation's taxpayers will be affected by a reduction in taxes on capital gains.
(D) The capital gains tax is unfair to taxpayers on the higher end of the tax scale.
(E) Investors are reluctant to sell stocks because of the tax on capital gains.

STOP. IF YOU FINISH BEFORE TIME IS CALLED, CHECK YOUR WORK ON THIS SECTION ONLY. DO NOT WORK ON ANY OTHER SECTION IN THE TEST.

SECTION VII: QUANTITATIVE ABILITY

Time: 30 Minutes
30 Questions

Quantitative Comparison

DIRECTIONS

In this section you will be given two quantities, one in column A and one in column B. You are to determine a relationship between the two quantities and mark

(A) if the quantity in column A is greater than the quantity in column B
(B) if the quantity in column B is greater than the quantity in column A
(C) if the quantities are equal
(D) if the comparison cannot be determined from the information that is given

Common Information:

Information centered above both columns refers to one or both columns.
All numbers used are real numbers.
Figures are intended to provide useful positional information, but are not necessarily drawn to scale and should not be used to estimate sizes by measurement.
Lines that appear straight can be assumed to be straight.

	Column A	**Column B**
1.	4.7498	$4\frac{3}{4}$
2.	$\frac{9}{11}$	$\frac{11}{13}$
	$x > 0$	
3.	$x + \frac{x}{2}$	$x - \frac{x}{2}$

	Column A		Column B
		$abc > 0$	
4.	$c(a + b)$		abc
5.	Distance traveled by an airplane going 200 miles per hour		Distance traveled by an airplane going 190 miles per hour
		$6x + 18y = 12$	
6.	$x + 3y$		2

(x,y) P x 0

7.	x	y
8.	$(.18)^{100}$	$(1.8)^{10}$

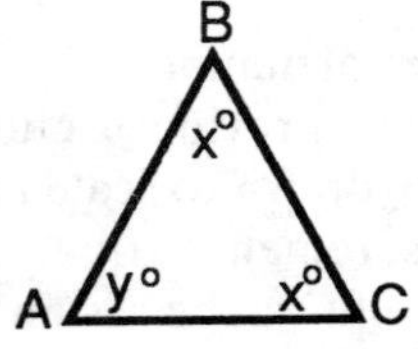

9.	AB		BC
		$x^2 + 2x + 1 = 0$	
10.	$(x + 1)(x + 1)$		$(x - 1)(x - 1)$

	Column A	Column B

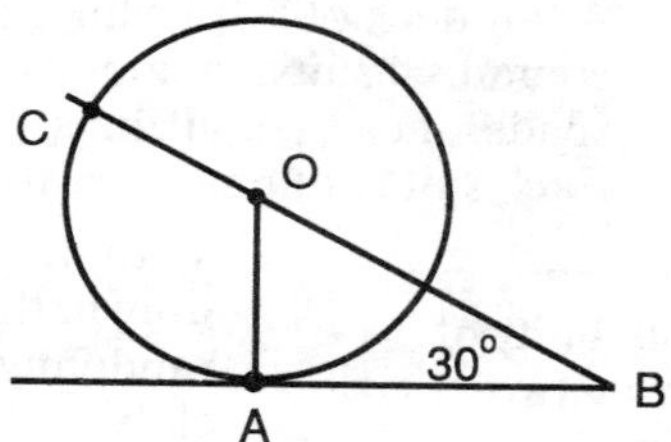

O is center of circle
AB is tangent to circle O

	Column A	Column B
11.	$\frac{1}{2}\widehat{AC}$	$\angle AOB$

$x > y > 0$
x and y are integers

	Column A	Column B
12.	$\frac{(x+y)^x}{x}$	$\frac{(x+y)^y}{y}$
13.	Circumference of circular region C with diameter d	Perimeter of rectangular region R with length 2d and width d

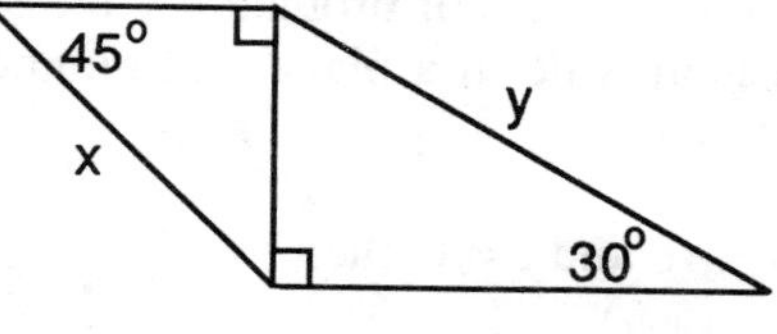

	Column A	Column B
14.	x	y

	Column A	Column B
	A fair deck of 52 playing cards contains 4 suits: diamonds, spades, hearts, and clubs. Each suit contains 13 cards.	
15.	Without replacing any cards drawn, the probability of randomly drawing two diamonds in a row	Without replacing any cards drawn, the probability of randomly drawing a heart, a club, and a spade, but not necessarily in that order

Math Ability

DIRECTIONS

Solve each problem in this section by using the information given and your own mathematical calculations. Then select the *one* correct answer of the five choices given. Use the available space on the page for scratchwork. NOTE: Some problems may be accompanied by figures or diagrams. These figures are drawn as accurately as possible, *except* when it is stated in a specific problem that the figure is not drawn to scale. The figure is meant to provide information useful in solving the problem or problems. Unless otherwise stated or indicated, all figures lie in a plane. All numbers used are real numbers.

16. If $x + y = m + rt$, and $r \neq 0$, then $t =$

(A) $\frac{x + y + m}{r}$

(B) $x + y + \frac{m}{r}$

(C) $x - y + \frac{m}{r}$

(D) $\frac{x - y}{r} - m$

(E) $\frac{x + y - m}{r}$

17. A third-grade class is composed of 16 girls and 12 boys. There are 2 teacher-aides in the class. The ratio of girls to boys to teacher-aides is
(A) 16:12:1
(B) 8:6:2
(C) 8:6:1
(D) 8:3:1
(E) 4:3:1

8	1	6
3	5	7
4	9	2

18. The figure above consists of 9 small squares and is called a "magic square" because the total of the numbers added horizontally, vertically, or diagonally are all equal. If the total of the two diagonal rows are subtracted from the total of the three horizontal rows, the result obtained will equal
(A) two-thirds a diagonal row
(B) three-halves a diagonal row
(C) any vertical row
(D) double a horizontal row
(E) one-half a horizontal row

19. If $3x = -9$, then $3x^3 - 2x + 4 =$
(A) -83
(B) -71
(C) -47
(D) -17
(E) 61

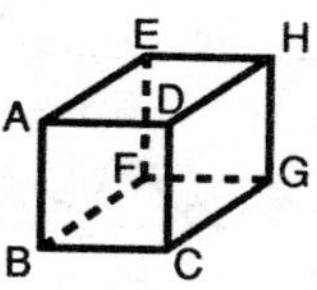

20. In the figure above, AB is one edge of a cube. If AB equals 5, what is the surface area of the cube?
(A) 25
(B) 100
(C) 125
(D) 150
(E) 300

Questions 21–25 refer to the following graphs.

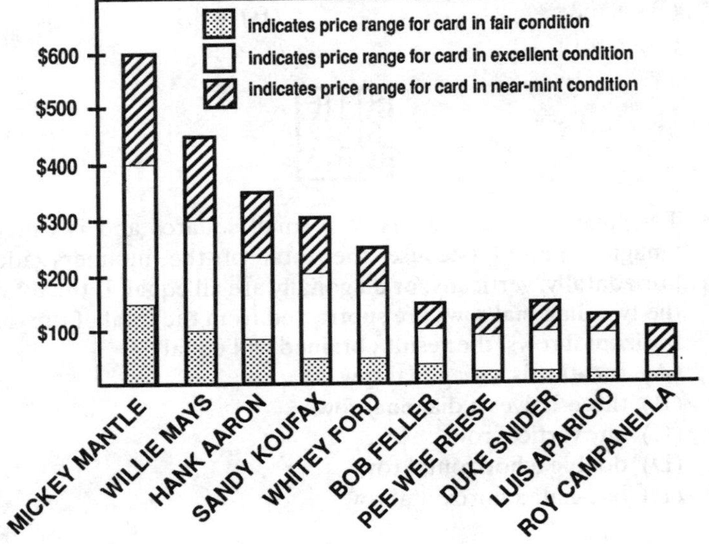

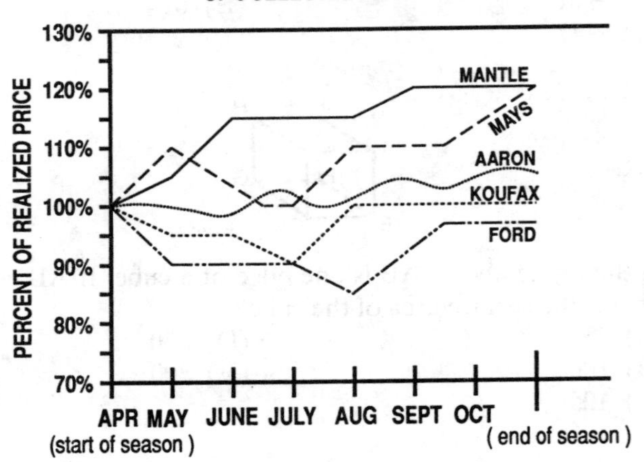

21. At the start of the 1991 season, the price range realized for a 1956 Bob Feller card in excellent condition was
(A) $100 to $200
(B) $100 to $150
(C) $50 to $100
(D) $30 to $100
(E) $0 to $30

22. The price range realized in September for a near-mint-condition Mickey Mantle card was
(A) $150 to $400
(B) $400 to $600
(C) $440 to $660
(D) $480 to $720
(E) $600 to $800

23. At the start of the season, which of the following cards had the greatest ratio of near-mint-condition range to excellent-condition range?
(A) Willie Mays
(B) Whitey Ford
(C) Bob Feller
(D) Duke Snider
(E) Roy Campanella

24. What was the difference in price realized anytime during the 1991 season between the highest-priced excellent-condition Willie Mays card and the highest-priced near-mint-condition Hank Aaron card?
(A) $7.50
(B) $10.00
(C) $12.50
(D) $30.00
(E) $60.00

25. Which of the following can be inferred from the graphs above?

I. Any price realized during the 1991 season for a near-mint-condition Sandy Koufax card would be enough to purchase one each of fair-condition cards of Whitey Ford, Bob Feller, Pee Wee Reese, Duke Snider, Luis Aparicio, and Roy Campanella.

II. The 1990 end-of-season price for a near-mint-condition Whitey Ford was less than its start-of-season price.

III. The highest price realized during the 1991 season for an excellent-condition Bob Feller is less than the lowest price realized during the 1991 season for a near-mint-condition Pee Wee Reese.

(A) I only
(B) II only
(C) III only
(D) I and II only
(E) II and III only

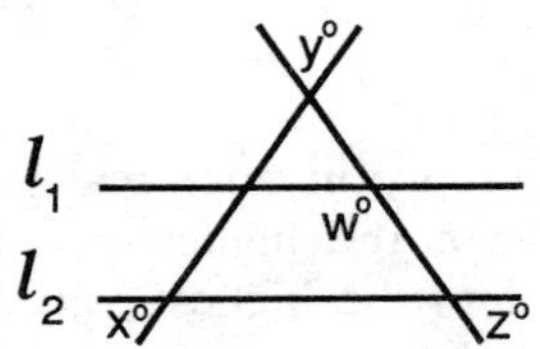

26. If $l_1 \parallel l_2$, x = 60°, and w = 2z, then y + z =
(A) 60°
(B) 90°
(C) 120°
(D) 180°
(E) cannot be determined

27. If # is a binary operation such that a#b is defined as $\frac{a^2 + b^2}{a^2 - b^2}$ and $(a^2 - b^2 \neq 0)$, then what is the value of a#b if 2a = b and a ≠ 0?
(A) $1\frac{1}{3}$
(B) $\frac{3}{5}$
(C) $-\frac{1}{2}$
(D) $-\frac{3}{5}$
(E) $-1\frac{2}{3}$

28. Tom is filling a bathtub with hot and cold water. The hot water running by itself would exactly fill the tub in 40 minutes. The cold water running by itself would exactly fill the tub in 20 minutes. With the plug out, it takes 30 minutes to empty a full tub. Tom accidentally leaves the plug out of the tub. When Tom checks on the tub 30 minutes after turning on the hot and cold water, he finds the tub
(A) empty
(B) one-third full
(C) one-half full
(D) two-thirds full
(E) overflowing

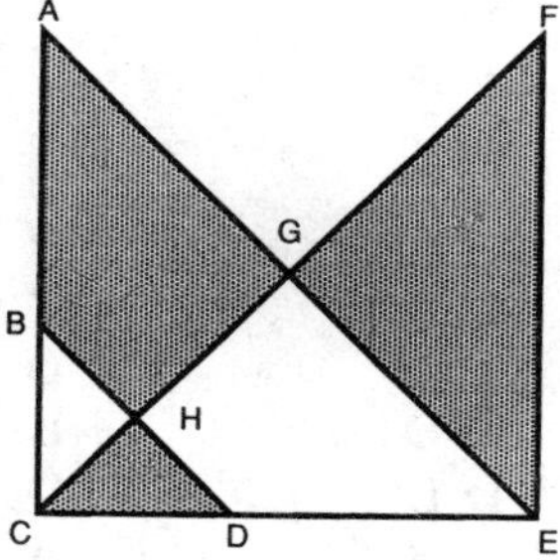

29. In the figure above, AE ∥ BD, AC ∥ FE, AC ⊥ CE, and BD ⊥ CF. H is the midpoint of BD. What is the ratio of the shaded area to the unshaded area?
(A) 1/2
(B) 2/3
(C) 4/3
(D) 3/2
(E) 2/1

30. If x + y forms an integer z that is greater than 0 and not divisible by 3, and if x is an even integer, which of the following CANNOT be values of y?

I. $\frac{2z}{3}$ II. $2z+1$ III. $\frac{z}{2}$

(A) I only
(B) II only
(C) III only
(D) I and II only
(E) II and III only

STOP. IF YOU FINISH BEFORE TIME IS CALLED, CHECK YOUR WORK ON THIS SECTION ONLY. DO NOT WORK ON ANY OTHER SECTION IN THE TEST.

SCORING PRACTICE TEST 3

ANSWER KEY

Section I Verbal Ability	Section II Analytical Ability	Section III Quantitative Ability	Section IV Quantitative Ability
1. B	1. B	1. B	1. B
2. C	2. E	2. A	2. A
3. D	3. E	3. A	3. A
4. E	4. B	4. C	4. D
5. A	5. B	5. B	5. D
6. B	6. B	6. D	6. D
7. E	7. E	7. B	7. C
8. A	8. D	8. C	8. B
9. D	9. A	9. D	9. C
10. B	10. D	10. B	10. A
11. C	11. E	11. D	11. C
12. D	12. B	12. A	12. A
13. A	13. A	13. D	13. C
14. E	14. C	14. D	14. C
15. D	15. C	15. C	15. A
16. C	16. D	16. C	16. C
17. B	17. A	17. C	17. C
18. C	18. D	18. E	18. C
19. D	19. C	19. B	19. D
20. E	20. E	20. E	20. A
21. C	21. C	21. E	21. A
22. B	22. C	22. E	22. E
23. C	23. E	23. B	23. D
24. D	24. A	24. D	24. C
25. B	25. D	25. C	25. D
26. A		26. D	26. D
27. C		27. C	27. A
28. C		28. D	28. D
29. A		29. C	29. A
30. D		30. C	30. D
31. B			
32. E			
33. D			
34. E			
35. C			
36. A			
37. B			
38. B			

ANSWER KEY

Section V Verbal Ability		Section VI Analytical Ability	Section VII Quantitative Ability
1. D	31. E	1. A	1. B
2. E	32. D	2. D	2. B
3. B	33. C	3. E	3. A
4. E	34. A	4. B	4. D
5. D	35. E	5. C	5. D
6. A	36. D	6. D	6. C
7. C	37. B	7. A	7. B
8. C	38. C	8. E	8. B
9. B		9. C	9. D
10. E		10. A	10. B
11. A		11. E	11. C
12. D		12. D	12. A
13. E		13. A	13. B
14. B		14. E	14. B
15. A		15. A	15. B
16. B		16. D	16. E
17. C		17. D	17. C
18. D		18. A	18. C
19. A		19. B	19. B
20. B		20. A	20. D
21. B		21. D	21. D
22. D		22. B	22. D
23. E		23. A	23. E
24. D		24. B	24. A
25. C		25. E	25. A
26. B			26. C
27. A			27. E
28. B			28. E
29. A			29. E
30. C			30. A

SCORE RANGE APPROXIMATORS

The following charts are designed to give you only an approximate score range, not an exact score. When you take the GRE General Test, you will have questions that are similar to those in this book; however, some questions may be slightly easier or more difficult. Needless to say, this may affect your scoring range.

Because one section of the GRE is experimental (it doesn't count toward your score), for the purposes of this approximation, do not count Section VII. Remember, on the actual test the experimental section could appear anywhere on your test.

Verbal Ability

To approximate your verbal score:

1. Total the number of questions you answered correctly in Sections I and V. No points are subtracted for incorrect answers.
2. Use the following table to match the total number of correct answers in those two sections and the corresponding approximate score range.

Number Right	Approximate Score Range
65–75	710–800
55–64	590–700
45–54	490–580
35–44	400–480
25–34	320–390
15–24	220–310
0–14	200–220

Average score is approximately 480.

Quantitative Ability

To approximate your quantitative score:

1. Total the number of questions you answered correctly in Sections III and IV. No points are subtracted for incorrect answers.
2. Use the following table to match the total number of correct answers in those two sections and the corresponding approximate score range.

Number Right	Approximate Score Range
50–60	700–800
40–49	570–690
30–39	450–560
20–29	330–440
10–19	220–320
0–9	200–210

Average score is approximately 560.

Analytical Ability

To approximate your analytical score:

1. Total the number of questions you answered correctly in Sections II and VI. No points are subtracted for incorrect answers.
2. Use the following table to match the total number of correct answers in those two sections and the corresponding approximate score range.

Number Right	Approximate Score Range
40–50	700–800
30–39	560–690
20–29	410–550
10–19	240–400
0–9	200–230

Average score is approximately 540.

Remember, these are *approximate* score ranges.

ANALYZING YOUR TEST RESULTS

The charts on the following pages should be used to carefully analyze your results and spot your strengths and weaknesses. The complete process of analyzing each subject area and each individual problem should be completed for each practice test. These results should then be reexamined for trends in types of errors (repeated errors) or poor results in specific subject areas. THIS REEXAMINATION AND ANALYSIS IS OF TREMENDOUS IMPORTANCE TO YOU IN ASSURING MAXIMUM TEST PREPARATION BENEFIT.

VERBAL ABILITY ANALYSIS SHEET

SECTION I

	Possible	Completed	Right	Wrong
Sentence Completion	7			
Analogies	9			
Reading Comprehension	11			
Antonyms	11			
SUBTOTALS	38			

SECTION V

	Possible	Completed	Right	Wrong
Sentence Completion	7			
Analogies	9			
Reading Comprehension	11			
Antonyms	11			
SUBTOTALS	38			
OVERALL VERBAL ABILITY TOTALS	76			

QUANTITATIVE ABILITY ANALYSIS SHEET

SECTION III

	Possible	Completed	Right	Wrong
Quantitative Comparison	15			
Math Ability	15			
SUBTOTALS	30			

SECTION IV

	Possible	Completed	Right	Wrong
Quantitative Comparison	15			
Math Ability	15			
SUBTOTALS	30			
OVERALL QUANTITATIVE ABILITY TOTALS	60			

SECTION VII

NOTE: For this practice test, do not include Section VII in your overall Quantitative Ability score.

	Possible	Completed	Right	Wrong
Quantitative Comparison	15			
Math Ability	15			
TOTALS	30			

ANALYTICAL ABILITY ANALYSIS SHEET

	Possible	Completed	Right	Wrong
Section II	25			
Section VI	25			
OVERALL ANALYTICAL ABILITY TOTALS	50			

ANALYSIS: TALLY SHEET FOR PROBLEMS MISSED

One of the most important parts of test preparation is analyzing WHY! you missed a problem so that you can reduce the number of mistakes. Now that you have taken the practice test and corrected your answers, carefully tally your mistakes by marking them in the proper column.

REASON FOR MISTAKE

	Total Missed	Simple Mistake	Misread Problem	Lack of Knowledge
SECTION I: VERBAL ABILITY				
SECTION V: VERBAL ABILITY				
SUBTOTALS				
SECTION III: QUANTITATIVE ABILITY				
SECTION IV: QUANTITATIVE ABILITY				
SUBTOTALS				
SECTION II: ANALYTICAL ABILITY				
SECTION VI: ANALYTICAL ABILITY				
SUBTOTALS				
TOTAL VERBAL, QUANTITATIVE, AND ANALYTICAL				

Reviewing the above data should help you determine WHY you are missing certain problems. Now that you have pinpointed the type of error, focus on avoiding your most common type.

COMPLETE ANSWERS AND EXPLANATIONS FOR PRACTICE TEST 3

SECTION I: VERBAL ABILITY

Sentence Completion

1. (B) The missing verb must mean something that will parallel *stir up*. Of the five choices, only *tweak* (to irritate, pinch) will fit.

2. (C) The correct noun must be something that sensational television coverage would undermine in a university setting. The best choice here is *credibility*, or believability.

3. (D) The correct words must be consequences of the freedom described. Both *open-market* and *entrepreneurial* suggest the absence of government interference.

4. (E) The last half of the sentence describes a reluctance to believe—the action of a *skeptic*.

5. (A) The first adjective should describe the effects of an economic slump; the missing noun is contrasted with the downtown. Though (B), (D), and (E) are plausible, only (A) has a proper adjective as well.

6. (B) The adverb *remarkable* makes clear that the survival of the wetland is surprising, so the real estate must be valuable.

7. (E) The use of *huge* and *tiny* suggests that the noun cannot be (A) or (D). Of the three remaining options, the most logical is clearly (E).

Analogies

8. (A) The *epic* is a long narrative poem; the *epigram* is a short, usually witty or satiric poem. Both are forms in which poetry is composed. *Opera* and *lied* are musical forms for the voice. *Opera* is normally a much larger (and longer) form than the *lied* (or song).

9. (D) The *janitor* is the person in charge of the maintenance of *building* property. The parallel here is a *ranger* who is responsible for the *forest.*

10. (B) A *capstan* is the apparatus on ships around which a *cable* (or hawser) is wound, like a very large *spool* with the *cable* as its *thread.*

11. (C) To *snivel* is to whine or fret in a tearful manner, to *complain* with more unpleasant connotations. The relationship of the two verbs can be compared to *grieve* and *sulk* in which the second verb adds a suggestion of sullen ill-humor.

12. (D) Both *checkers* and *chess* are board games, but the moves and strategy in *chess* are more complex. Both *hearts* and *bridge* are card games, with the latter the more complex.

13. (A) Until the late twentieth century, the usual meaning of *chauvinist* was a fanatical *patriot.* The best parallel is an *epicure,* a person fond of pleasure in eating and drinking, and the excessive eater, drinker, a *glutton.*

14. (E) The two verbs are opposites, like *murmur* (to make a low, indistinct sound) and *caterwaul* (to howl shrilly).

15. (D) A *barometer* is an instrument for measuring *air pressure* as an *anemometer* is an instrument for measuring *wind speed.* A *stethoscope* is a listening not a measuring device.

16. (C) *Swindle* is a verb (to deceive, to trick), while *guile* is a noun describing the craft of one who *swindles.* Someone with *foresight* is able to *anticipate* as someone with *guile* is able to *swindle.*

Reading Comprehension

17. (B) The passage summarizes findings about the effects of several kinds of unclean air on the human lungs throughout a lifetime. No mention is made of the earlier theories, and insofar as the passage makes a recommendation for health improvement, it does so obliquely.

18. (C) The passage places the beginning of the decrease in lung size at twenty. Exposure to unclean air at any age decreases lung capacity.

19. (D) The passage describes the victims of air pollution as unaware of the damage they have suffered. It is reasonable to infer that they would be more active if they were more conscious of their loss.

20. (E) Both the damage from ozone and industrial pollutants and the reduction in oxygen supply are specific details in the passage. Eastern Europe is not mentioned.

21. (C) Although the author does not express violent anger, the characterization of the treatment of the Indians as a *tragedy* and the pronouncement that the whites' behavior was *barbaric* certainly express strong disapproval.

22. (B) Although justice was on the Indians' side (second paragraph), *the Indians were not equal to the firepower of the United States army.* Each of the other choices contradicts information in the passage.

23. (C) This is evidence that the whites killed buffalo for sport rather than for subsistence. The disappearance of the buffalo herd is not, of itself, evidence that the buffalo did not provide subsistence to the whites.

24. (D) The point of comparison is that the Atlantic coast Indians were not fierce warriors like the plains Indians. Thus they did not pose any kind of violent threat.

25. (B) Three of the four paragraphs of the passage are devoted to discussing the abuse of the plains Indians. The "weight" which the author gives to this topic suggests its significance.

26. (A) The author states that the government itself *tried to be fair* but that the *agents'* indifference or corruption failed the American Indians.

27. (C) According to the final paragraph of the passage, *the Indian agents were either too indifferent or corrupt to carry out the government's promises conscientiously. The army frequently ignored the Indian Bureau and failed to coordinate its policies with the civilians who were nominally in charge of Indian affairs.* Choices (B) and (D) may be historically correct but cannot specifically be inferred from the passage.

Antonyms

28. (C) To *deter* is to discourage; its antonym is to *encourage.*

29. (A) Here, *flock* is a verb meaning to assemble in a flock; to *disperse* is an antonym.

30. (D) The adjective *equivocal* means uncertain, undecided, doubtful; an opposite is *certain.*

31. (B) The noun *travail* means toil, hard labor; its opposite here is *repose.*

32. (E) A *bomb* is American theatre terminology for a failure, the opposite of *hit.*

33. (D) The adjective *puritanic* means excessively strict in morals. The most nearly opposite choice here is *freewheeling.*

34. (E) The verb *trumpet* means to announce loudly, to proclaim. The opposite here is *veil.*

35. (C) The adjective *fervent* means ardent, intensely felt, the opposite of *bland.*

36. (A) As a noun, *aggregate* means a total or whole, the antonym of *part.*

37. (B) The noun *havoc* means ruin or devastation, the opposite of *construction.*

38. (B) To *aggrieve* is to cause grief or injury to, the opposite of *gladden.* There is a a difference between *grieve* and *aggrieve.*

SECTION II: ANALYTICAL ABILITY

From the information given for questions 1–4, the following notes can be made:

~~DK~~ AL DR

1. (B) Since the Dino must be stored with the Rickenbacher, choices (A) and (D) are not possible. Since the Lear must be stored with the Airheart, choices (C) and (E) are not possible.

2. (E) Since the Rickenbacher must be stored with the Dino, choice (E) is not suitable.

3. (E) If the Kressna is the only single-wing airplane stored in the East warehouse, then the two pairs that must be stored together (Dino and Rickenbacher, Lear and Airheart) will be stored in the West warehouse (since at least seven airplanes are stored). Since the Lear and the Dino are two single-wings, at least three single-wings are stored.

4. (B) If only the Dino and one other airplane are stored in the East warehouse, that other airplane stored with the Dino is the Rickenbacher. That means the other pair—the Lear and the Airheart—must be stored in the West warehouse along with the Kressna said to be stored and at least two more to bring the total airplanes stored to at least seven.

From the information given for questions 5–10, the following diagram can be drawn:

1 less than RC Bulletin Boards	Room Cleanup	Newspaper
~~D~~ ~~E~~ ~~F~~	~~A~~ ~~B~~ ~~C~~	~~G~~ ~~H~~ ~~I~~ J

5. (B) Choices (A) and (E) are not possible because neither Gabrielle nor Ida join the Newspaper staff. Of the remaining choices, (C) and (D) are not possible because they each comprise four students, leaving six students for both Room Cleanup and Bulletin Boards. With six students, it is not possible for Bulletin Boards to have one less student than Room Cleanup.

6. (B) The largest possible number of students on the Newspaper staff are all but Gabrielle, Hap, and Ida—seven—which leaves two for Room Cleanup and one for Bulletin Boards.

7. (E) If only Ida designs Bulletin Boards, then Gabrielle and Hap must have chosen Room Cleanup, since they didn't join the Newspaper staff.

8. (D) If only one student joined the Newspaper staff, that student was Joshua. Therefore, Danielle, Evan, and Francine, since they do not design Bulletin Boards, must have chosen Room Cleanup.

9. (A) If Gabrielle, Hap, and Charlotte are the only students designing Bulletin Boards, since Arnold and Brad do not join the Room Cleanup crew, Arnold, Brad, and Joshua must be on the Newspaper.

10. (D) If Arnold and Gabrielle are the only students designing Bulletin Boards, and Bulletin Boards has one less than Room Cleanup, there must be three students on Room Cleanup. That leaves five students publishing the newspaper.

11. (E) The passage does not consider a number of variables such as the number of children of divorced parents, if any, the stablity of the population of New England, the number of remarriages among the divorced. Only choice (E) does not seriously call the conclusion into doubt.

12. (B) Only the Ku Klux Klan here is an example of a group that would deny liberty to others but which has been granted its liberty by the supporting American Civil Liberties Union.

13. (A) The first choice argues that all nonviolent criminals be offered this choice, but the law speaks only of *some.* Presumably, there are many crimes, even nonviolent ones, that should not be punished so leniently.

14. (C) Choice (A) has the vacant floor on the bottom. Choices (B) and (E) do not have the Elgars and the Fertittas on adjacent floors. Choice (D) does not have the same number of floors between the Abrams and Bakers as between the Cabots and DeLeons.

15. (C) If the Fertittas live on the second floor, the Elgars must live on the third floor (on a floor adjacent to the Fertittas) so that the Grants can live on the first floor (a lower floor than the Elgars).

16. (D) II and IV only. If the Abrams live on the sixth floor, the Bakers on the seventh floor, and the Fertittas on the fourth floor, a diagram can be drawn:

8
7 B
6 A
5
4 F
3
2
1

Since the Bakers live on an adjacent floor to the Abrams, so must the Cabots live on an adjacent floor to the DeLeons. That leaves floors 1 and 2 or floors 2 and 3 for the Cabots and DeLeons (or DeLeons and Cabots).

8		
7 B		
6 A		
5		
4 F		
3	C/D	
2	D/C	C/D
1		D/C

Either way, the Elgars must be adjacent to the Fertittas, and the Grants must be on a floor lower than the Elgars:

8		
7 B		
6 A		
5 E		
4 F		
3	C/D	G
2	D/C	C/D
1	G	D/C

The Elgars will definitely be on the fifth floor, and the top floor will be vacant.

17. (A) If the Cabots were to live on the sixth floor, then the DeLeons would have to live on the eighth floor so that the number of floors between the Abrams and Bakers equals the number of floors between the Cabots and DeLeons. But if floors 2, 4, 6, and 8 are taken by these four families, the Fertittas and the Elgars won't be able to live on adjacent floors.

18. (D) I and III only. Information in the question states that Wilson, Yussef, and Xavier work together three times from Monday through Friday. The only way this can happen such that none of them works two or more days in a row is:

Monday	*Tuesday*	*Wednesday*	*Thursday*	*Friday*
W X Y	—	W X Y	—	W X Y

This leaves the remaining greenskeeper, Zachary, to trim the greens on Tuesday and Thursday.

19. (C) During the period from Tuesday through Friday, it is possible that Xavier works twice as many days (2) as Yussef (1). It is not possible for all four greenskeepers to work together on a given day, since on the day before/after, none of them could work. Nor is it possible for any greenskeepers to work three times as many days as another, since this would mean working three out of the four days (Tuesday–Friday) which would require working two consecutive days.

20. (E) I, II, and III. From the information in the question:

Monday	*Tuesday*	*Wednesday*	*Thursday*	*Friday*
W X Y	—	—	W X Y	—

Since no one may work two consecutive days, Zachary must work alone on Tuesday, and Yussef must work alone on Wednesday and Friday.

21. (C) If Wilson works alone on Wednesday, and exactly two greenskeepers work Monday, Tuesday, Thursday, and Friday, then:

Monday	*Tuesday*	*Wednesday*	*Thursday*	*Friday*
—	—	W	—	—
—	—		—	—

Notice that no matter who works Tuesday and Thursday, Wilson must be one of the two greenskeepers who works on Friday:

Monday	*Tuesday*	*Wednesday*	*Thursday*	*Friday*
W	—	W	—	W
—	—		—	—

If Zachary works on Monday, then Yussef and Xavier must work on Wednesday. But if Yussef works on Monday, then Zachary and Xavier work on Tuesday. Or Xavier could work on Monday, and Zachary and Yussef will work on Tuesday. The same is true for Thursday and Friday. In all cases, Xavier, Yussef, and Zachary each work exactly two days.

22. (C) If Quincy works only on Tuesday, then:

Monday	*Tuesday*	*Wednesday*	*Thursday*	*Friday*
—	Q	—	—	—

If all four remaining greenskeepers work on Wednesday, then no greenskeeper can work on Thursday (since Quincy works only on Tuesday). So the maximun number of greenskeepers that can work on Wednesday is three.

23. (E) Only choice (E) introduces a fact strictly relevant to the argument that listening to the radio will improve school performance. This fact contradicts the argument based on student claims.

24. (A) The argument focuses narrowly on a single solution to a complex problem.

25. (D) This conclusion attempts to explain the inconsistency between what many believe is true and conflicting statistical studies.

SECTION III: QUANTITATIVE ABILITY

Quantitative Comparison

1. (B) Plugging in each value for p in column A, if $p = +3$, then $(p + 2)^2 = (5)^2 = 25$. Plugging in -3 for p gives $(-3 + 2)^2 = (-1)^2 = 1$. In either case, column B, 26, is greater.

2. (A) Multiplying column A gives $(3a)(3b)(3c) = 9abc$. Since a, b, and c are all positive values, 9abc will always be greater than 3abc.

3. (A) A negative number multiplied an even number of times will yield a positive product. A negative number multiplied an odd number of times will yield a negative product. Since column A will be positive and column B will be negative, A is greater.

4. (C) In the triangle, one angle is 60°. Therefore, the remaining two angles must sum to 120° (since the total degree measure in any triangle is 180°). Since the two angles are each x, they then are equal and each is 60°. Y is the vertical angle of 60°. Since vertical angles are equal, y also equals 60°. So $x = y$.

5. (B) In both columns, the same number, 1, is being subtracted. Therefore, the column which is greater can be determined simply by comparing the "starting" values. The column with the larger "starting" value (the number being subtracted from) will yield the larger remainder. Since $1/18$ is larger than $1/19$, column B is greater. (That both remainders are negative does not affect the relationship.)

6. (D) Since no information is given regarding the change in numbers of units sold, not enough information is given to determine column B.

7. (B) The shortest distance between two points is a straight line. Therefore, arc AB must be greater than line segment AB.

8. (C) Begin by assigning a value to one of them, for example:

Dionne = 10. Now, since Tom is 3 inches shorter than Dionne, Tom must equal 7. Since Dionne is 1 inch shorter than Daniel, Daniel must equal 11. Since Joy is 4 inches shorter than Daniel, Joy must equal 11 − 4 = 7. Joy and Tom are equal.

9. (D) Since ABCD is a rhombus, all sides are equal. Therefore, $x = (xy)/3$. Solving, first cross multiply:

$$3x = xy$$

Canceling x's from each side: $y = 3$. However, knowing that y equals 3 tells nothing about the value of x.

10. (B) Since a, b, c, and d are each greater than 0, they are therefore positive. In column A, the denominator is greater than the numerator, so the fraction equals less than 1. In column B, the numerator is greater than the denominator, so the fraction equals more than 1. Therefore, column B is greater.

11. (D) If p and q each equal 1, then column A equals 10 and column B equals 2½. But p and q may each possibly equal 0, in which case the value of each column would be 0, and so the columns would be equal. Therefore, a definite relationship cannot be determined.

12. (A) If angle y were equal to 2x, then in the triangle, y would be 60° and x would be 30°. In a 30°-60°-90° triangle, z would be half 10, or 5. However, since y is more than twice x, x cannot be 30°; it must be less than 30°. Therefore, side z must be less than half 10, or less than 5.

13. (D) If y is 0, columns A and B each equal 25, and so the columns could be equal. However, if y is 1, then column A equals 26 and column B equals 16. No definite relationship can be determined.

14. (D) The distance across the hole equals the distance across the ball, which is the ball's diameter. Each side of the hole therefore equals d (the ball's diameter). So the perimeter of the hole = 4d. The area of the square equals d times d, or d^2. Which is greater, 4d or d^2? If $d = 4$, column A equals column B.

However, if d equals any value other than 4, the columns are not equal. So no definite relationship can be determined.

15. (C) To multiply similar bases with different exponents, retain the base and add exponents:

$$10^x \times 10^y \times 10^z = 10^{(x+y+z)} = 10^{(x+y)} = 10^0 = 1$$

Therefore, both columns are equal.

Math Ability

16. (C) One may answer this question by solving:

$$\begin{aligned} 4a + 2 &= 10 \\ 4a &= 8 \\ a &= 2 \end{aligned}$$

Now, plugging in 2 for a:

$$\begin{aligned} 8a + 4 &= \\ 8(2) + 4 &= 20 \end{aligned}$$

A faster way of solving this is to see the relationship between the quantity 4a + 2 (which equals 10) and 8a + 4. Since 8a + 4 is twice 4a + 2, the answer must be twice 10, or 20.

17. (C) Percent increase = change/starting point. If the employee's salary was increased \$15,000 to \$90,000, then the starting salary was 90,000 − 15,000 = 75,000. Therefore,

percent increase = 15,000/75,000 = 1/5 = 20%

18. (E) First work within parentheses:

$$\left(4 + \tfrac{1}{2}\right) = \left(4\tfrac{1}{2}\right) = \left(\tfrac{9}{2}\right)$$
$$\left(\tfrac{4}{9} + 2\right) = \left(2\tfrac{4}{9}\right) = \left(\tfrac{22}{9}\right)$$

Now, multiply these quantities, canceling where possible:

$$\left(\frac{9}{2}\right)\left(\frac{22}{9}\right) = \frac{22}{2} = 11$$

You could also have used decimals and approximated the values as 4.5 and 2.5 (4/9 is approximately .5), realizing that the answer will be slightly less.

19. (B) If the area of the circular region equals 4π, then

$$A = \pi r^2$$
$$4\pi = \pi r^2$$
$$4 = r^2$$
$$2 = r$$

Now, using the formula for circumference of a circle:

$$C = 2\pi r$$
$$C = 2\pi(2)$$
$$C = 4\pi$$

20. (E) Since x, y, and z are consecutive negative integers, try plugging in values to test each choice. For example, x, y, and z could equal -1, -2, and -3 (not necessarily in that order) or, for that matter, -8, -9, and -10. Only choice (E) may be true, and that will occur if x equals -1, y equals -2, and z equals -3.

21. (E) According to the bar graph, in 1991, Americans spent approximately $400 million to watch baseball and approximately $230 million to watch ice hockey. The difference between these two figures is $170 million.

22. (E) The graphs show number of dollars spent, not attendance. No information is given for numbers in attendance. Since one cannot assume that admission prices are the same for films and amusement parks, the answer cannot be determined.

23. (B) In 1991, spectator sports was 39% of the American recreation dollar and travel was 16% of the recreation dollar. This is a difference of 23%, or a little under one-quarter, of the entire amount. Since one-quarter of the entire amount ($3600 million) is $900 million, the difference is slightly under $900 million, or $850 million.

24. (D) Adding all the bars gives the total for spectator sports spending: $230 (ice hockey) + $280 (basketball) + $280 (football) + $400 (baseball) + $150 (all others) = $1340 million. Baseball is $400 million out of $1340 million, or approximately 30%.

25. (C) If, in 1992, spectator sports spending shows a percent increase of 33%, that's almost exactly a one-third increase. So the 39% would rise another 13% (one-third of 39) to 52%. If amusement park spending in 1992 shows a percent decrease of 10%, it will drop one-tenth of its 1991 figure: one-tenth of 11% is about 1%. So amusement park spending drops from 11% to 10%. The 1992 ratio of spectator sports spending to amusement park spending will then be approximately 52 to 10, or about 5 to 1.

26. (D) If m and n are integers, the least possible value for $3m^2 - 2n$ may be found by assigning the value of 0 for m (therefore, $3m^2 = 0$) and then assigning the largest integer possible for n. Since $-4 < n < 5$, the largest possible integer for n is 4. Therefore:

$$3m^2 - 2n = 3(0)^2 - 2(4) = 0 - 8 = -8$$

27. (C) Assign values on $\overparen{ON}$ such that $\overparen{OP} = 2\overparen{PN}$: $\overparen{OP}$ could equal 2 and $\overparen{PN}$ could equal 1. If Q lies on $\overparen{OP}$ such that $\overparen{OQ} = \overparen{QP}$, then $\overparen{OP}$ (2) is divided in half. So $\overparen{OQ} = 1$, and $\overparen{QP} = 1$. So the relationship of $\overparen{OQ}$ to $\overparen{PN}$ is 1 to 1.

28. (D) First determine Pat's rate alone by using the equation:

$$\frac{1}{\text{Tom's rate}} + \frac{1}{\text{Pat's rate}} = \frac{1}{\text{rate together}}$$

$$\frac{1}{12} + \frac{1}{p} = \frac{1}{8}$$

$$\frac{1}{p} = \frac{1}{8} - \frac{1}{12}$$

$$\frac{1}{p} = \frac{3}{24} - \frac{2}{24}$$

$$\frac{1}{p} = \frac{1}{24}$$

$$\text{so } p = 24$$

Now you know that Pat's rate alone is 24 hours. So if Pat works alone for 12 hours, he will have plowed exactly half the field. If Tom alone can plow the entire field in 12 hours, he can plow half the field in 6 hours.

29. (C) First find the area of the larger triangle. Its base is 8, and its height is 8, so its area is ½ base × height = ½(8)(8) = 32. Now find the area of the small triangle: its base is 6, and its height is 2, so ½ base × height = ½(6)(2) = 6. Now, subtract the small triangle from the large triangle to find the shaded area: 32 − 6 = 26.

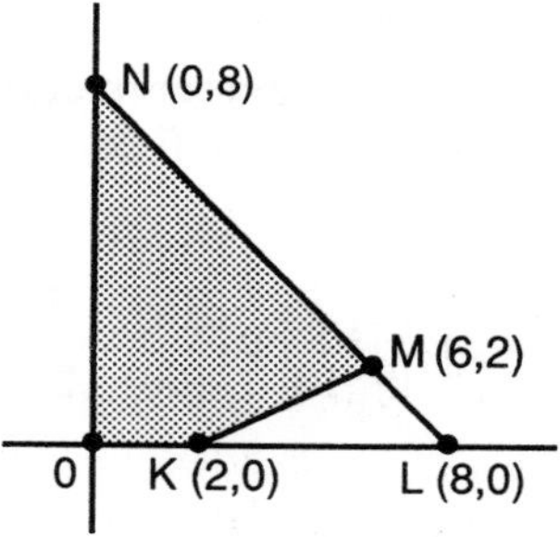

30. (C) There are 8 different arrangements, as follows:

red-red-red
green-green-green
red-green-green
green-red-green
green-green-red
green-red-red
red-green-red
red-red-green

SECTION IV: QUANTITATIVE ABILITY

Quantitative Comparison

1. (B) The first two fractions in column B sum to $1\frac{6}{7}$. Therefore, the question is simply how does $\frac{2}{13}$ compare to $\frac{1}{7}$? If $\frac{2}{13}$ is less than $\frac{1}{7}$, then column B is less than column A. If $\frac{2}{13}$ is greater than $\frac{1}{7}$, then column B is greater than column A. A fast way to compare two fractions is to cross multiply up:

$$\underset{\textcircled{14}}{} \qquad\qquad 13$$

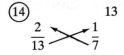

$$\frac{2}{13} \times \frac{1}{7}$$

The greater product is above the greater fraction. Since 14 is greater than 13, $\frac{2}{13}$ is more than $\frac{1}{7}$, so column B equals more than 2.

2. (A) Column A is:

$$\left(\frac{4}{10}\right)\left(\frac{4}{10}\right) = \frac{16}{100} = \frac{4}{25}$$

Column B is:

$$\left(\frac{1}{2}\right)\left(\frac{1}{2}\right)\left(\frac{1}{2}\right)\left(\frac{1}{2}\right) = \frac{1}{16}$$

Since $\frac{4}{25}$ is greater than $\frac{1}{16}$, column A is greater.

3. (A) $\frac{2}{3} = .666666\ldots$

So column A $= 66.666666\ldots$ and
column B $= 66.660$

Column A is greater.

4. (D) Since $\overline{AB} = \overline{BC}$, $\angle A = \angle C$. But no information is given for $\angle B$. So no relationship can be determined between n and m.

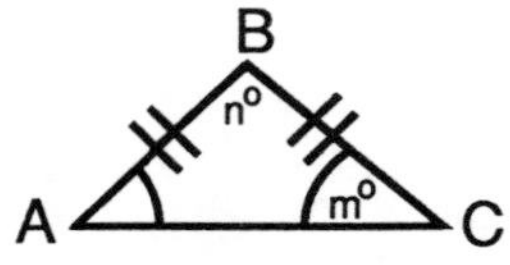

5. (D) The value of point Q is $1\frac{1}{3}$. But the value of the point $2\frac{1}{3}$ away from Q may be either $-2\frac{2}{3}$ or 2. So it could be either greater or less than Q. No relationship can be determined.

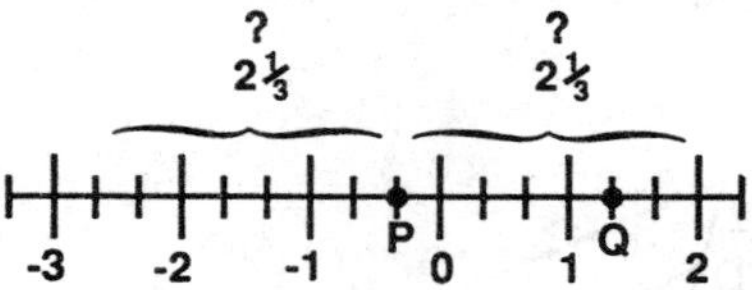

6. (D) The value for b could be 0, which would make column A equal to column B. Or b could be positive, which would make column B greater than column A. No relationship can be determined.

7 (C) It does not matter that E is not the midpoint of $\overline{AB}$. The area of $\triangle DEC$ equals ½(base)(height) = $\frac{1}{2}(\overline{DC})(\overline{AD})$. Notice that this area is half the area of the rectangle, which leaves the other half as the shaded regions.

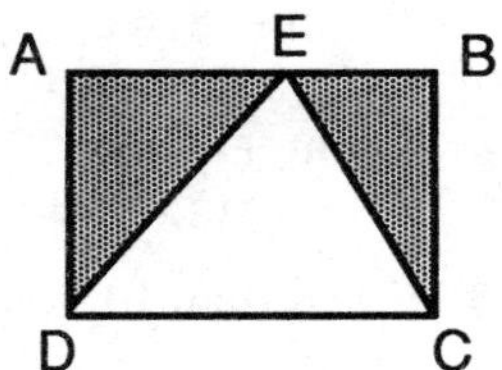

8. (B) Column A is the percent drop in price, which is:

$$\frac{\text{change}}{\text{starting point}} = \frac{5{,}000}{120{,}000} = \frac{5}{120}$$

Since $\frac{5}{100}$ is 5%, $\frac{5}{120}$ is less than 5%. Since column B is 6%, column B is greater.

9. (C) Since $\overline{DE} \parallel \overline{AB}$, $\triangle DCE$ is similar to $\triangle ACB$. Therefore, since $\overline{AB}$ is 50% greater than $\overline{DE}$, $\overline{CB}$ is 50% greater than $\overline{CE}$, so y must equal 4. Similarly, $\overline{AC}$ is 50% greater than $\overline{DC}$, so $\overline{DC}$ must equal 4. So x = y.

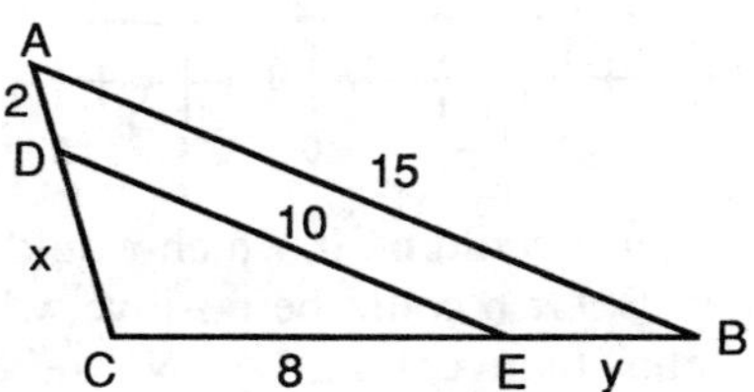

10. (A) First factor:

$$m^2 - 5m + 24 = 0$$
$$(m - 8)(m + 3) = 0$$

Now set each equal to 0:

$$m - 8 = 0$$
$$m = 8$$
$$m + 3 = 0$$
$$m = -3$$

Since both 8 and −3 are less than 10, column A is greater.

11. (C) if the average cost of four items is \$32, the items total $4 \times 32 = \$128$. So:

$$30 + 38 + p + 2p = 128$$
$$68 + 3p = 128$$
$$3p = 128 - 68$$
$$3p = 60$$
$$p = 20$$

Therefore, 2p = \$40. The columns are equal.

12. (A) Since $\overline{AB}$ is the smallest side of the triangle, then its opposite angle, ∠ACB, is the smallest angle. The smallest angle must be less than 60° because if the smallest angle were equal to 60°, the three angles would sum to greater than 180°, which isn't possible. So column A is greater.

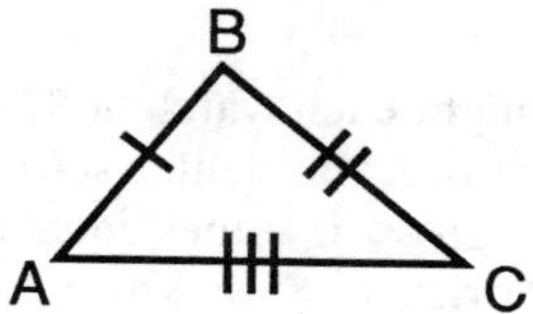

13. (C) Since $\overline{XY} = \overline{YZ}$, their opposite angles are equal. Lets call them each x:

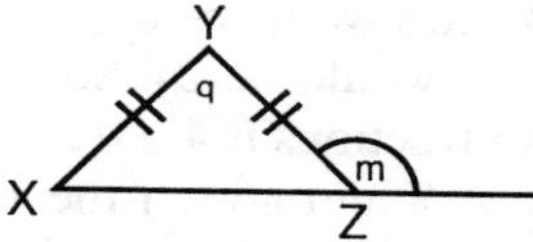

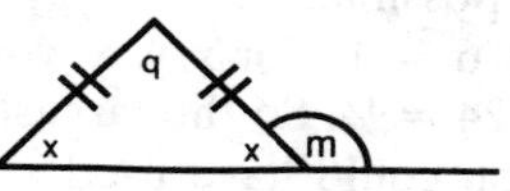

Plugging in any value for x, say 40°, then

$$q = 100°$$
$$m = 140°$$

Therefore, column A = 100° and column B = 280° − 180° = 100°. The columns are equal.

14. (C) for all numbers, $p\#q = \frac{p^2}{q}$

Then, if $p = -q$,

$$p\#q = \frac{(-q)^2}{q} = \frac{q^2}{q} = q$$

Both columns are equal.

15. (A) The area of DEBC is ¾ the area of ABCD, or:

$$\frac{\text{area DEBC}}{\text{area ABCD}} = \frac{3 \text{ units}}{4 \text{ units}} = \frac{3}{4}$$

Column A is greater.

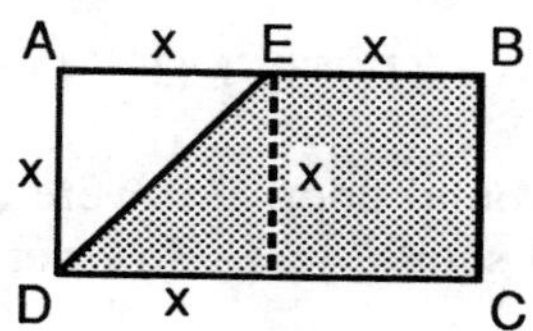

Math Ability

16. (C) The dealer bought each watch at \$23 and made a profit on each of \$47. Therefore, the dealer sold each watch for \$23 + \$47 = \$70. The gross income equals number of watches multiplied by unit price, or 85 × \$70 = \$5950.

17. (C) To obtain the largest sum of (y/x) + (x/y), make the numerators as large as possible and the denominators as small as possible. So for x/y, y would be 24 and x would be 6. So y/x = 24/6 = 4. For x/y, x would be 6 and y would be 24. So x/y = 6/24 = ¼. So the largest sum of both fractions is 4 + ¼ = 4¼. You could have used x = 12 and y = 3 and gotten the same answer.

18. (C)

$$\frac{\dfrac{7}{{}_{2}\cancel{10}} \times \dfrac{{}^{1}\cancel{14}}{1} \times \dfrac{{}^{1}\cancel{5}}{1} \times \dfrac{1}{\cancel{28}_{2}}}{\dfrac{{}^{2}\cancel{10}}{{}_{1}\cancel{17}} \times \dfrac{\cancel{3}^{1}}{\cancel{5}_{1}} \times \dfrac{1}{\cancel{6}_{2}} \times \dfrac{\cancel{17}^{1}}{1}} = \frac{\dfrac{7}{4}}{\dfrac{2}{2}} = \frac{\dfrac{7}{4}}{1} = \frac{7}{4}$$

19. (D) Notice that (9x + 6y) is exactly three times (3x + 2y). Therefore, (9x + 6y) equals three times 10, or 30.

20. (A) *Jane:* Jane = J.

Tom: Since Jane is six years older than Tom, Tom is six years less than Jane, or Tom = J − 6.

Chris: Since Chris is three years older than Tom, add three to Tom to get Chris's age.
Chris = J − 6 + 3 = J − 3.

Phillip: Tom is five years younger than Phillip, so Phillip is five years older than Tom. So add five to Tom to get Phillips's age. J − 6 + 5 = J − 1.

The sum of their ages is:

$$J + (J - 6) + (J - 3) + (J - 1) = 4J - 10$$

21. (A) The entire ground floor, if it were a rectangle, would be 76 × 80, or 6080 square feet. However, the lobby is slightly

"indented," so the total area will be slightly less than 6080. The only reasonable answer is (A), 5780.

22. (E) To find the measurements of the lobby, side A is found by subtracting 50 (along the top) from 76 (along the bottom). Side A is 26. Side B is found by subtracting 6 (at the top) from 50. So B is 44. Notice that sides D + E equal 44 as well. Side C is similar to A minus 6, or 26 − 6 = 20. So adding along the edge: 26 + 44 + 20 + 44 + 6 = 140. (Don't forget the 6 feet between D and E, which was given.)

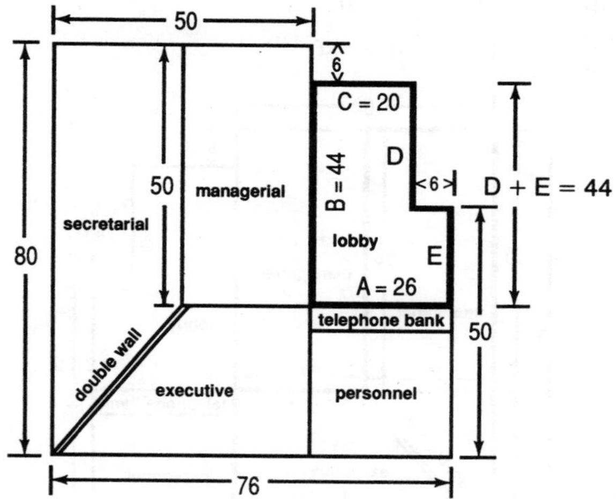

23. (D) If the area of the telephone bank is 104 square feet, then since the length of the telephone bank is 26 feet, its width must be 104/26 = 4 feet. Since managerial is 50 feet wide, plus the 4 for the telephone bank, that leaves 26 for personnel. So personnel is 26 × 26 = 676 square feet.

24. (C) If the wall separating managerial from executive is 24 feet, that leaves secretarial's width to be 50 − 24 = 26 feet. So the area of secretarial (a trapezoid) is

$$\frac{(b_1 + b_2)}{2}(h) = \frac{80 + 50}{2}(26) = 65(26) = 1690$$

The area of executive (a trapezoid) is

$$\frac{(b_1 + b_2)}{2}(h) = \frac{50 + 24}{2}(30) = 37(30) = 1110$$

So $\quad 1690 - 1110 = 580$

Or you might have quickly realized that the triangular areas of secretarial and executive are equal and figured only the remaining rectangular area in this way:

secretarial: $50 \times 26 = 1300$
executive: $30 \times 24 = 720$

$1300 - 720 = 580$

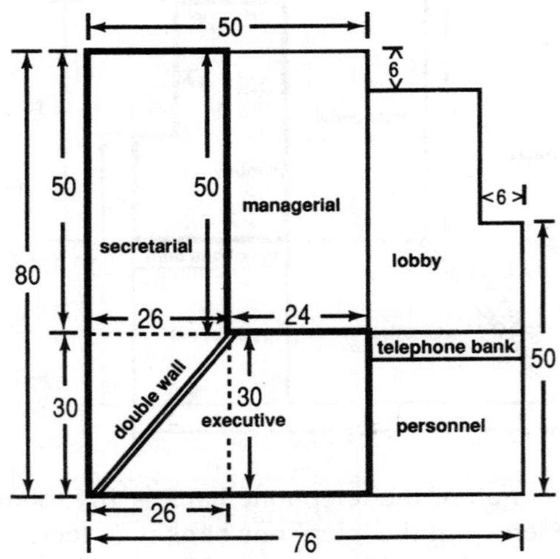

25. (D) The present area of the lobby can be found by visualizing the lobby as two spaces as shown on the next page:

Therefore, the top part is $20 \times 24 = 480$. The bottom part is $26 \times 20 = 520$. So the lobby's present area is 1000. If its exterior walls were to conform to the rectangular dimensions of the rest of the ground floor, the lobby would be $26 \times 50 = 1300$, an increase of 300. Percent increase is change/starting point = 300/1000 = 30% increase.

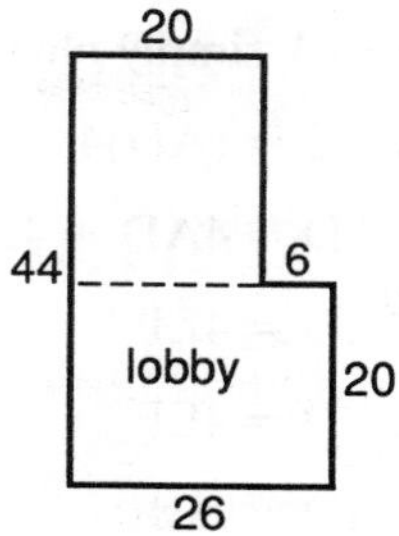

26. (D) Since horizontal = vertical then

$$3 + x + y = 9 + x + z$$

If z equals 5, and canceling x's from each side:

$$3 + y = 9 + 5$$
$$y = 9 + 5 - 3$$
$$y = 14 - 3$$
$$y = 11$$

27. (A) Using 8a as common denominator:

$$\frac{a + 8b}{8a} - \frac{a + 2b}{2a} = \frac{a + 8b}{8a} - \frac{4a + 8b}{8a} = \frac{-3a}{8a} = -\frac{3}{8}$$

28. (D) If rhombus ABCD has a perimeter of 8, each side is 2. If diagonal AC equals 2, then triangles ABC and ACD are equilateral triangles. Diagonal BD therefore bisects AC and forms perpendicular angles. Each of the smaller triangles are 30°–60°–90° triangles with sides 1, $\sqrt{3}$, 2. Since the area of one small triangle is ½bh = ½(1)$\sqrt{3}$, then all four triangles sum to $2\sqrt{3}$.

29. (A) Setting the areas equal to each other:

$$(AD)\,(CD) = \frac{(AD) + (EF)}{2}\,(FH)$$

$$2(AD)\,(CD) = (AD)\,(FH) + (EF)\,(FH)$$

Since CD to FH is 3 to 4, simply plug in 3 for CD and 4 for FH:

$$2(AD)3 = (AD)4 + (EF)4$$

$$6AD = 4AD + 4EF$$

$$6AD - 4AD = 4EF$$

$$2AD = 4EF$$

$$AD = 2EF$$

Since AD is twice as big as EF, the ratio of EF to AD is 1 to 2.

30. (D) Using Venn diagrams, we may diagram as shown.

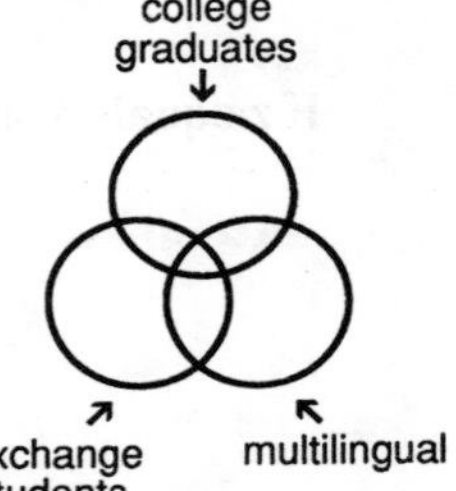

The 3 college graduates who are multilingual and exchange students will occupy the space contained by all three circles.

college graduates
3
exchange students
multilingual

The 4 non-college graduates who are multilingual and exchange students will occupy the space contained by multilingual and exchange student, but not contained by college graduate.

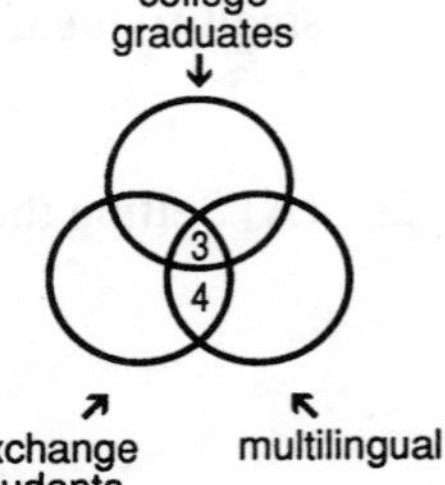

Since there is a total of 15 college graduates, add so that the sum of the college graduates equals 15.

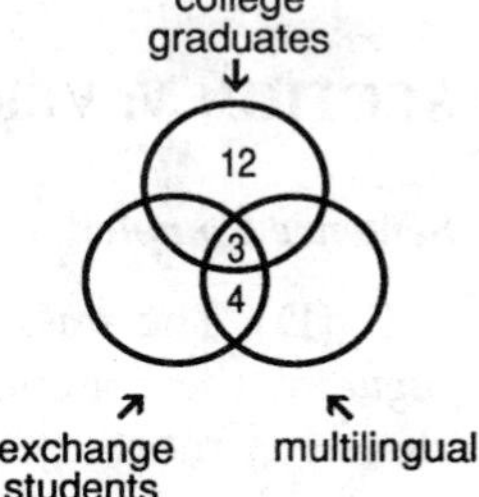

Since there is a total of 10 exchange students and a total of 8 multilingual, add as above.

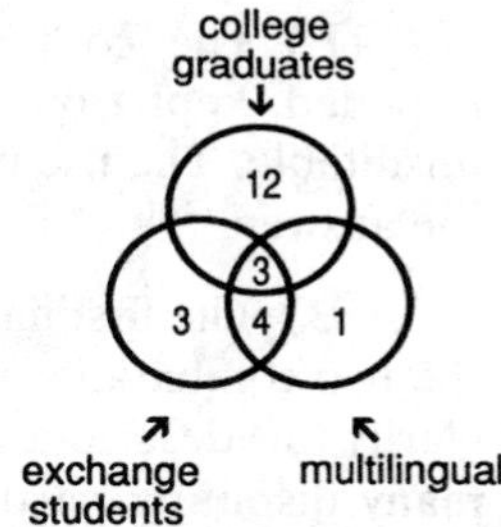

The total number of adults is 30. Since 23 are contained in our three circles (college graduates, multilingual, and exchange students), seven therefore are *not* graduates, multilingual, or exchange students.

SECTION V: VERBAL ABILITY

Sentence Completion

1. (D) The missing adjective is defined as the opposite of *too vague* by the completed sentence. Though (B) is possible, the best choice is more *specific. Restrictive* means limiting or tending to restrict, but the context calls for *specific,* that is, explicit or definite.

2. (E) The context indicates the missing verb should mean impeded, kept from moving freely. (B), (C), and (D) are clearly unsuitable. The use of the adjective *seriously* eliminates *excluded* as the answer.

3. (B) The first half of the sentence presents the choice between the two combatants as difficult. Choices (A), (D), or (E) would not clarify this description. Both (B) and (C) are plausible, but because many disputing parties would object to *interference,* choice (B) is preferable.

4. (E) The context requires a transitive verb used with the preposition *to* meaning assign or ascribe. Choices (B), (C), and (D) do not fit these requirements. Choice (A), *attested,* is used with *to* but means to certify or make clear.

5. (D) The *but* indicates the power has not been annihilated, so the verb that is missing must indicate a rebirth and be used with *itself.* (A) and (C) are not used with the pronoun; (B) has the opposite of the required meaning; and though (E) is possible, (D) is clearer.

6. (A) The two verbs must both (twin blows) indicate a divisive action. The words *foster, consolidate,* and *patronize* do not fit, while choice (D) is marred by the use of *recede,* which means to move back, not to withdraw from.

7. (C) The sentence makes it clear that the first missing verb should indicate a success in the election, and the second should mean received. Choices (A) and (E) do not indicate a win, while *recaptured* in (B) and *reclaimed* in (D) are faulty because of the prefix *re.*

Analogies

8. (C) The *canvas* is the surface on which the *oil painting* is painted. Similarly, a *fresco* is painted on wet *plaster.*

9. (B) The *spider* and the *octopus* are eight-legged animals of land and sea. The *locust* and *water beetle* are six-legged animals of land and sea. The leg count of the animals in the other options is not parallel.

10. (E) The noun *wrath* is the consequence of the disposition described by the adjective *irate.* Similarly, an *acquisitive* person is guilty of *avarice.*

11. (A) The nouns describe meals, one of the morning, one of the evening. The *lark* is conventionally presented as a dawn singer, while the *nightingale* is associated with evening or night. While it is true that *dinner* can also describe a midday meal, no answer choice provides a morning/midday option.

12. (D) The second of the two verbs adds sinister overtones to the action of the first verb. *Move* and *skulk* (to move in a stealthy manner) are similarly related.

13. (E) To *pink* is to cut with a saw-toothed edge. The analogy is to *saw* a *board.*

14. (B) An *essay* and a *short story* are both short prose works, nonfiction and fiction. Similarly, a *biography* and a *novel* are both prose works, nonfiction and fiction, but they are longer works.

15. (A) A *triptych* is a hinged set of pictures or carvings with three *panels.* The *hypotenuse* is one of three sides of a *triangle.*

16. (B) *Savannah* and *veldt* are nearly synonyms, a flat, open, grassland. The *forest-woodland* analogy is the closest.

Reading Comprehension

17. (C) The passage is admiring (*great ventriloquist, challenging*) with a minor reservation about the length of some of the poetry.

18. (D) There is no rhetorical question in the passage. The four other techniques are employed.

19. (A) The passage wishes to praise the accuracy of the Victorian excerpts and *ventriloquist* and *reproduce* both suggest this precision.

20. (B) The sentence calls the excerpts possibly *too much of a good thing* and genuinely Victorian in length.

21. (B) The purpose of the passage is to describe the complexity of the shark revealed by modern researchers.

22. (D) Shark study has been slowed because the sharks are so dangerous and live in murky waters.

23. (E) All of the comparisons except to a dolphin occur in the passage.

24. (D) All organisms have a bioelectric field, so the male shark would be able to find many sharks more easily than one. They congregate to make it more difficult for the male to grasp one, not to make detection more difficult.

25. (C) The *third eye* is the light-gathering organ.

26. (B) The sharks' sensing the voltage created by currents moving through the earth's magnetic field is at least tangentially relevant to choice (B).

27. (A) The passage is objective. It uses the other techniques, including the double meaning in *heavy breathing.*

Antonyns

28. (B) To daunt is to make afraid. *Undaunted* means fearless. The opposite here is *timorous,* fearful.

29. (A) To *coalesce* is to grow together, to unite. The antonym is to *separate.*

30. (C) *Captious* means quick to find fault, carping. The opposite here is *indulgent.*

31. (E) *Servile* means submissive, humbly yielding, the opposite of *arrogant.*

32. (D) To *dilate* is to expand, to swell. The antonym is to *contract.*

33. (C) This adjective means with a sawlike edge; a leaf or a knife may be *serrated.* The opposite is *smooth.*

34. (A) The adjective *maculate* means defiled, impure, the opposite of immaculate or *undefiled.*

35. (E) *Fealty* is loyalty or allegiance; the opposite is *infidelity.*

36. (D) The adjective *cognate* means related to, having the same quality or origin. The opposite here is *unrelated.*

37. (B) To *rein* is to guide, control, or slow. The best antonym here is to *release.*

38. (C) *Kudos* is a singular noun meaning glory, fame, or prestige. The opposite of *kudos* is *obloquy,* censure.

SECTION VI: ANALYTICAL ABILITY

1. (A) If Charlie and Earvin work lights during scene 1, they both perform in scene 2. Since every actor performs in a total of three scenes (but not consecutive), Charlie and Earvin will each be in scenes 2, 3, and 5 or in scenes 2, 4, and 5. So they both will definitely be together in scene 5.

2. (D) If Brandon, Charlie, and Francine perform in scene 1, then Al, Dusty, and Earvin work lights during scene 1. Therefore Al, Dusty, and Earvin must perform in scene 2, since they cannot work lights two consective scenes. Only choice (D) includes Al, Dusty, and Earvin.

3. (E) From the information in question 3, this diagram can be drawn:

```
(1) A  B  D
(2) ?  ?  ?  ?
(3) B  D  E
(4) ?  ?  ?  ?
```

Since Charlie, Earvin, and Francine worked lights during scene 1, they must perform in scene 2, and since Al does not perform in scene 3, he also must perform in scene 2.

```
(1) A  B  D
(2) C  E  F  A
(3) B  D  E
(4) ?  ?  ?  ?
```

So you know that Earvin performs in scenes 2 and 3. Since he cannot perform in a third consecutive scene, he cannot perform in scene 4.

4. (B) From the information in question 4, this diagram can be drawn:

(1) A D E
(2) ? ? ? ?
(3) ? ? ?
(4) B D ? ?

Since Brandon, Charlie, and Francine worked lights during scene 1, they must perform in scene 3:

(1) A D E
(2) B C F ?
(3) ? ? ?
(4) B D ? ?

Since Brandon performs in both scene 2 and scene 4, he cannot perform in scene 3.

5. (C) From the information in question 5, this diagram can be drawn:

(1) B C D
(2) ? ? ? ?
(3) A C D

Since Al, Earvin, and Francine worked lights during scene 1, they must appear in scene 2:

(1) B C D
(2) A E F ?
(3) A C D

Since Charlie and Dusty perform in scenes 1 and 3, neither of them can perform in scene 2. That leaves Brandon as the final performer in scene 2.

6. (D) From the information in question 6, this diagram can be drawn:

(1) A C D
(2) ? ? ? D
(3) ? ? ?
(4) ? ? ? ?

Since Brandon, Earvin, and Francine work lights in scene 1, they must perform in scene 2:

(1) A C D
(2) B E F D
(3) ? ? ?
(4) ? ? ? ?

Since Dusty cannot perform in three consecutive scenes, Dusty must work lights for scene 3 and then must perform again in scene 4.

7. (A) The conclusion of the passage concerns how the chimpanzees should be treated in a zoo and assumes that behavior in the wild and in the zoo are related. None of the other options alludes to the zoo, and the most plausible alternatives, (B) and (C), may be true, but *infrequently* or *safer* are less certain than the assumption of (A).

8. (E) The statement does not say what a grade one or two apple will cost; it says only that grade threes cost more than thirty-nine cents. If a grade four apple costs more than a grade three, it must cost more than thirty-nine cents.

9. (C) The cause (the pin) is here a cause because of the effect (the pinprick), and so the effect (the pinprick) is treated as the origin of the cause (the pin). They are not identical, and they both exist, though not in the relation we expect.

10. (A) Using tomatoes requires using onions; using diced ham requires using mushrooms. But onions and mushrooms can never be used together.

11. (E) Adding another cup of onions will make twice as many cups of onions as of tomatoes, which is required when tomatoes are used. Choices (B) and (C) contain diced ham but no mushrooms, which are required with diced ham. Choices (A), (B), (C), and (D) do not have more cups of cheese than the total cups of other specially prepared ingredients.

12. (D) Choices (A), (B), and (C) contain tomatoes without twice as many cups of onions. Choice (E) contains diced ham without mushrooms.

13. (A) At least one more cup of cheese must be added so that the number of cups of cheese is greater than the total number of cups of all other specially prepared ingredients.

14. (E) From the information in question 14, this diagram can be drawn:

1 Jeep
2
3
4
5 Buick
6
7
8 empty
9 empty
10 Acura

The number of spaces between the Acura and Buick equals the number of spaces between the Chevrolet and Dodge, so the Chevrolet and Dodge must be in spaces 2 and 7. And the Ferrari and the Edsel must then be parked next to each other in spaces 3 and 4, leaving space 6 empty.

1 Jeep
2 Chevrolet/Dodge
3 Edsel/Ferrari
4 Ferrari/Edsel
5 Buick
6
7 Dodge/Chevrolet
8 empty
9 empty
10 Acura

15. (A) Choices (B) and (C) do not have the Edsel parked next to the Ferrari. Choices (D) and (E) do not have the same number of spaces between the Acura and Buick as between the Chevrolet and Dodge. Additionally, choices (C) and (D) do not have both the eighth and ninth spaces empty.

16. (D) Since the Chevrolet is as far from the Dodge as the Acura is from the Buick (one space between), neither the Chevrolet nor Dodge can be in spaces 1, 7, or 10 (remember, spaces 8 and 9 are empty). But the Chevrolet can be in space 6 if the Dodge is in space 4.

17. (D) From the information in question 4, this diagram can be drawn:

1 Acura
2 Ferrari
3
4 Chevrolet
5
6
7
8 empty
9 empty
10

Since the Edsel must be next to the Ferrari, the Edsel must be in space 3. So option III is incorrect. Since the Acura must be as far from the Buick as the Chevrolet is from the Dodge, the Buick can be only in space 7 and the Dodge in space 10.

18. (A) Using the information in question 18, a diagram can be drawn:

1
2
3
4
5 Jeep
6 Acura
7 Chevrolet
8 empty
9 empty
10

Since the Buick is as far from the Acura as the Dodge is from the Chevrolet, the Buick must be parked in a space immediately before the Dodge. Remembering to leave two spaces together for the Edsel and Ferrari indicates that the Buick and Dodge could be in spaces 1 and 2 respectively, or in spaces 3 and 4 respectively. Whichever way, space 10 will be empty.

19. (B) The Edsel cannot be parked in space 10, since space 9 is empty and the Edsel is parked next to the Ferrari.

From the information given for questions 20–22, the following chart can be drawn:

		C			J	RS
1	2	3	4	5	6	HM
¢	¢					

20. (A) If the customer enters as Holiday's song is playing, stays through one song, and then hears Cole's song, since Cole's song is third, Holiday's song must be first.

21. (D) If Rankin's song is first, Sinatra's must be second, and Holiday and McCartney must be fourth and fifth respectively, with Joel last.

22. (B) If Sinatra's song is fifth, then Rankin's is fourth, leaving Holiday-McCartney as first/second.

23. (A) If the laundering of the clothes made of natural fabrics like cotton also causes environmental damage, the avoidance of dry-cleaning is undermined.

24. (B) The paragraph focuses upon the group of television watchers whose ignorance has proven invincible. The concern of the paragraph is not so much attitudes toward war as it is the effect of television news watching.

25. (E) The argument of the passage is that lower capital gains taxes will increase the sale of stocks on which investors have realized capital gains. The assumption here is that these investors are not taking profits now because of the tax on capital gains.

SECTION VII: QUANTITATIVE ABILITY

Quantitative Comparison

1. (B) Since $4\frac{3}{4}$ is equivalent to 4.75, column B is greater.

2. (B)Converting each fraction to a decimal (dividing numerator by denominator) gives .82 for column A and .84 for column B. A faster way to compare two fractions is to cross multiply up:

$$\begin{array}{ccc} 117 & & 121 \\ \frac{9}{11} & \times & \frac{11}{13} \end{array}$$

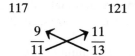

The larger product (121) is above column B, so column B is greater.

3. (A) First eliminate the equal values of x from each side, leaving (x/2) in column A and −(x/2) in column B. The information centered between the columns indicates that x is positive. Plugging in any positive value for x will result in column A being positive and column B being negative. So column A is greater.

4. (D) Since $abc > 0$, you could start by plugging in 1 for each of a, b, and c. So column A will equal $c(a + b) = 1(1 + 1) = 2$; column B will equal $abc = (1)(1)(1) = 1$. So column A is greater. Now plug in a different set of numbers such that $abc > 0$, for example, 10 for each of a, b, and c. Now column A will equal $c(a + b) = 10(10 + 10) = 200$; column B equals $abc = (10)(10)(10) = 1000$. Now column B is greater. Since we find two different relationships when we use different values, no definite relationship can be determined.

5. (D) Since no information is given for the amount of time each of the airplanes was traveling, no determination can be made about their distances traveled. You cannot assume that each airplane traveled the same amount of time.

6. (C) The information centered between the columns shows that $6x + 18y = 12$. Notice that the quantity in column A, $x + 3y$, exactly equals $\frac{1}{6}$ of $6x + 18y$. Therefore, column A equals $\frac{1}{6}$ of 12, or 2. Since column B equals 2, the columns are equal.

7. (B) The coordinates of point P are x, y. Since the x coordinate is to the left of the origin, x is negative. The y coordinate is above the origin, so y is positive. Therefore, column B is greater than column A.

8. (B) In column A, a fractional value (a value less than one) is multiplied by itself many times. So its value becomes increasingly smaller. (For example, $\frac{1}{2} \times \frac{1}{2} = \frac{1}{4}$; $\frac{1}{4} \times \frac{1}{2} = \frac{1}{8}$, and so forth.) In column B, a number greater than 1 is multiplied by itself; its value grows larger. So column B is greater.

9. (D) In a triangle, equal angles have equal opposite sides. Therefore, AB = AC. But no information is given about angle y, and so no relationship can be drawn regarding side BC.

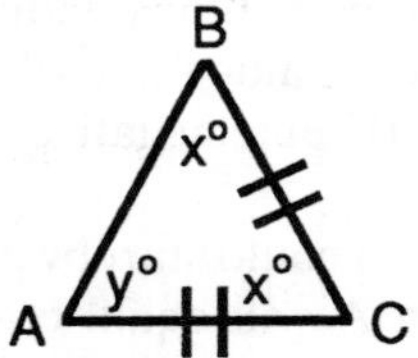

10. (B) Solving the information centered between the columns:

$$x^2 + 2x + 1 = 0$$
$$(x + 1)(x + 1) = 0$$

So
$$x + 1 = 0$$
$$x = -1$$

Plugging in -1 for x in each column gives:

column A:
$$(x + 1)(x + 1) =$$
$$(-1 + 1)(-1 + 1) =$$
$$(0)(0) = 0$$

column B:

$$(x - 1)(x - 1) =$$
$$(-1 - 1)(-1 - 1) =$$
$$(-2)(-2) = 4$$

So column B is greater.

11. (C) Since AB is tangent to circle O, ∠OAB = 90°. Since the total interior degrees of any triangle is 180°, in triangle OAB, ∠AOB must equal 60°. Since COB is a straight line, ∠COA equals 120°. Since a central angle equals the amount of arc it intersects, $\widehat{AC}$ also equals 120°. So ½ AC = 60°, and the columns are equal.

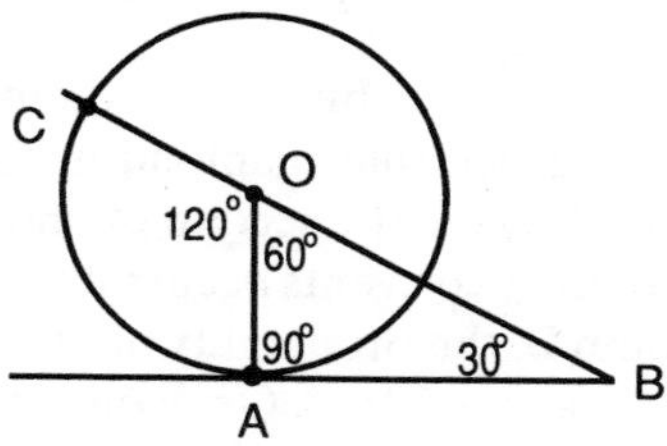

12. (A) Plug in values for x and y such that $x > y > 0$. For example, let $y = 1$ and $x = 2$. Then column A equals

$$\frac{(2 + 1)^2}{2} = \frac{9}{2}$$

Plugging in the same values in column B gives:

$$\frac{(1 + 2)^1}{1} = 3$$

Using these values, column A is greater. Using other values such that $x > y > 0$ will always give the same relationship. Column A is greater.

13. (B) In column A, the circumference of a circle = πd, or slightly greater than 3d (since $\pi \cong 3.14$). In column B, the perimeter of rectangle =

$$2l + 2w = 2(2d) + 2(d) = 6d$$

So column B is greater.

14. (B) Assume that the side shared by each of the triangles equals 1. Therefore, the triangle on the left, a 45°-45°-90° triangle, has sides in the ratio of 1-1-1$\sqrt{2}$. So x = $\sqrt{2}$. The triangle on the right is a 30°-60°-90° triangle, which has sides in the ratio of 1-$\sqrt{3}$-2. Therefore, y = 2. Column B is greater than column A.

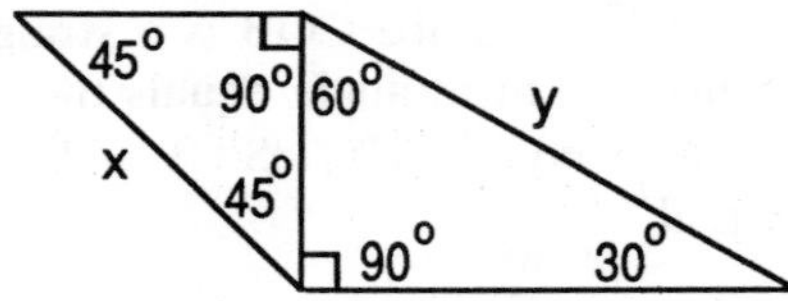

15. (B) in column A, the probability of randomly drawing the first diamond is 13/52. Since that diamond is now out of the deck, the probability of drawing the second diamond is now 12/51. So the probability of the two events occurring together is (13/52) × (12/51). In column B, the probability of first randomly choosing a heart, club, or spade is 39/52. Once one of those three suits is chosen, the probability of choosing one of the remaining two suits is 26/51. Finally, the probability of choosing the third suit is 13/50. So the probability of the three events occuring together is (13/52) × (12/51) × (13/50).

Column A	**Column B**
$\frac{\not{13}}{\not{52}} \times \frac{12}{\not{51}}$	$\frac{39}{\not{52}} \times \frac{\not{26}^{13}}{\not{51}} \times \frac{\not{13}}{\not{50}_{25}}$

Canceling across columns, 12 is left in column A, and (39/25) × 13 is left in column B. Since, in column B, 13 is multiplied by a number greater than 1, B is greater.

Math Ability

16. (E) If $x + y = m + rt$, solving for t:

$$x + y - m = rt$$

$$\frac{x + y - m}{r} = \frac{rt}{r}$$

$$\frac{x + y - m}{r} = t$$

17. (C) Girls to boys to teacher-aides are in proportion 16 to 12 to 2. Reduced to lowest terms, 16:12:2 equals 8:6:1.

18. (C) Since all rows are equal, subtracting two rows from three rows gives a result of one row, either vertical, horizontal, or diagonal.

19. (B) First solving $3x = -9$, $x = -3$. Now plug into $3x^3 - 2x + 4$:

$$3x^3 - 2x + 4 =$$

$$3(-3)^3 - 2(-3) + 4 =$$

$$3(-27) + 6 + 4 =$$

$$-81 + 6 + 4 = -71$$

20. (D) Since one edge of the cube is 5, all edges equal 5. Therefore, the area of one face of the cube is (5) (5) = 25. Since a cube has 6 equal faces, its surface area will be (6) (25) = 150.

21. (D) The range for excellent condition (white part of the bar) for Bob Feller's card extends from \$30 to \$100.

22. (D) In September, a Mantle card realized 120% of its start-of-season price. The price range at the start of season for a near-mint Mantle card was \$400 to \$600. Therefore, increasing its range by 20% would indicate a new range of \$480 to \$720.

23. (E) Roy Campanella had a greater range for near-mint condition ($50 to $100, or a range of $50) compared to the range for excellent condition ($20 to $50, or $30). Campanella is the only card whose near-mint-condition range exceeded its excellent-condition range.

24. (A) An excellent-condition Willie Mays card had a top price of $300 at the start of the season and realized 120% of its price at the end of the season. So its highest price for such a condition card was $360. A near-mint-condition Hank Aaron card started the season with a top price of $350 and reached 105% of its price in October, or $367.50. So the difference in highest prices of these condition cards was $750.

25. (A) I is true. At its lowest price, a near-mint Sandy Koufax card realized 90% (in July) of $200, or $180. The top prices for fair-condition cards of Whitey Ford, Bob Feller, Pee Wee Reese, Duke Snider, Luis Aparicio, and Roy Campanella were $50, $30, $25, $25, $20, and $20, respectively, which equals $170.

II is false. No information is given about end-of-season 1990 prices.

III is false. The highest price realized for an excellent-condition Bob Feller was $100, whereas the lowest price for a near-mint-condition Pee Wee Reese was under $100.

26. (C) Since $l_1 \parallel l_2$, the corresponding angles formed on lines l_1 and l_2 are equal:

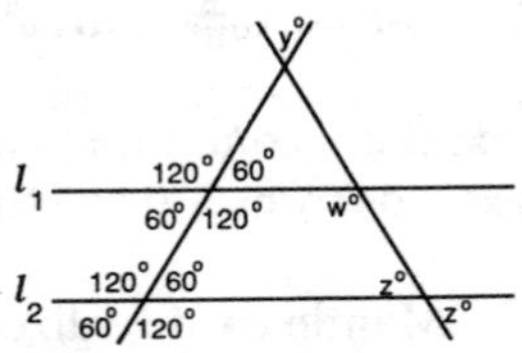

In any quadrilateral, the sum of interior degrees equals 360°. Therefore, $\angle w + \angle z = 180°$. If $w = 2z$, $\angle w = 120°$, and $\angle z = 60°$. Therefore:

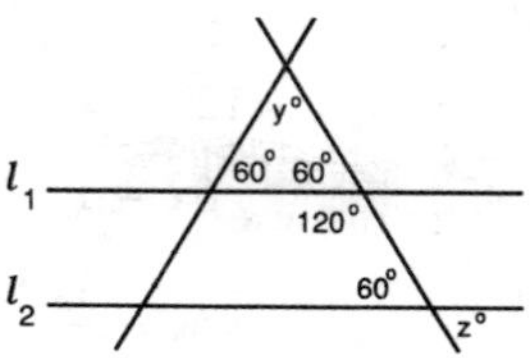

$\angle y = 60°$ (since there are 180° in a triangle). So the sum of $y + z = 60° + 60° = 120°$.

27. (E) The value of a#b =

$$\frac{a^2 + b^2}{a^2 - b^2}$$

If 2a = b, plug in 2a for b:

$$\frac{a^2 + (2a)^2}{a^2 - (2a)^2} = \frac{a^2 + 4a^2}{a^2 - 4a^2} = -\frac{5a^2}{3a^2} = -\frac{5}{3} = -1\tfrac{2}{3}$$

28. (E) The cold water alone fills the tub in 20 minutes. Since the plug is out, exactly this amount of water drains in 30 minutes. But since the cold water stays on for another 10 minutes, as the full tub of cold water is draining, the cold tap adds 10 minutes more of cold water. This equals water to fill half the tub, and this water won't drain. In addition, the hot water tap is on for 30 minutes, allowing it to produce hot water to fill the tub ¾ full (since the hot water would fill the tub in 40 minutes). Since ½ tub + ¾ tub equals more than 1 tub of water (in addition to the 1 tub being drained), Tom will return to find the tub overflowing. Working the problem mathematically would look like this:

$$\frac{1}{20} + \frac{1}{40} - \frac{1}{30} = \frac{1}{x}$$

$$\frac{6}{120} + \frac{3}{120} - \frac{4}{120} = \frac{1}{x}$$

$$\frac{9}{120} - \frac{4}{120} = \frac{1}{x}$$

$$\frac{5}{120} = \frac{1}{x}$$

$$5x = 120$$

$$x = \frac{120}{5}$$

$$x = 24 \text{ minutes}$$

Therefore, the tub would be filled in 24 minutes. Since Tom returned in 30 minutes, the tub would be overflowing.

29. (E) If $AC \perp CE$ and $AC \parallel FE$, then $\angle ACE$ and $\angle CEF$ are right angles. If $BD \perp CF$ and $AE \parallel BD$, then all angles formed at points G and H are right angles. Since H is the midpoint of BD, BH = HD, and therefore CH is not only a median perpendicular to its opposite side, but also an angle bisector. Angles FCE and FCA are therefore each 45°. Similarly, angles CAE and EFC are also each 45°. So there are three equal 45°-45°-90° triangles: triangles FGE, CGE, and AGC. Flipping the shaded quadrangle ABHG into its equal space GHDE shows that two of the equal triangles are shaded, and one is not. Therefore, the ratio of shaded area to unshaded area is 2 to 1.

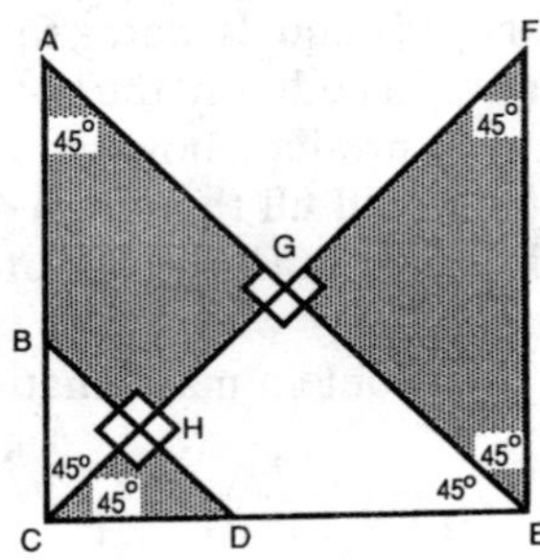

30. (A) Only I cannot be a value of y. Options II and III can be values of y. Since x + y forms an integer z, set up the equation x + y = z. Now plug in values according to the information in each option and in the question (z is an integer greater than 0 and not divisible by 3; x is an even integer):

I—Plugging in values for z: If z is 1, y would be $\frac{2}{3}$—not an integer and therefore not possible. If z is 2, y would be $\frac{4}{3}$—again, not possible. z cannot be 3, since 3 is divisible by 3. If z is 4, y would be $\frac{8}{3}$—not possible. You'll notice that since z cannot be a multiple of 3, all of the values of y obtained by plugging in integers other than multiples of 3 are non-integers. So I, $(2z)/3$, cannot be a value of y. I is true.

II—If z is 1, y is $2z + 1$, or 3. If $x + y = z$, then $x + 3 = 1$, so x is -2, which is an even integer. This option, $2z + 1$, is a possible value of y. II is false.

III—If z is 4, then y is $z/2$, or 2. Since $x + y = z$, then x will equal 2, which is an even integer. So $z/2$ is a possible value of y. III is false.

FINAL PREPARATION: "The Final Touches"

1. Make sure that you are familiar with the testing center location and nearby parking facilities.
2. The last week of preparation should be spent primarily on reviewing strategies, techniques, and directions for each area.
3. Don't *cram* the night before the exam. It's a waste of time!
4. Remember to bring the proper materials to the test—identification, admission ticket, three or four sharpened Number 2 pencils, a watch, and a good eraser.
5. Start off crisply, working the ones you know first, and then coming back and trying the others.
6. Be sure to mark an answer for each question because THERE IS NO PENALTY FOR GUESSING.
7. Mark in reading passages, underline key words, write out information, make notations on diagrams, take advantage of being permitted to write in the test booklet.
8. Make sure that you are answering "what is being asked" and that your answer is reasonable.
9. Using the TWO SUCCESSFUL OVERALL APPROACHES is the key to getting the ones right that you should get right—resulting in a good score on the GRE.

TAKING THE GRE ON COMPUTER

Educational Testing Service now offers candidates the option of taking a "computerized adaptive" version of the GRE. This exam is similar to the paper-and-pencil GRE in some respects, but it differs in other important ways. Like most alternatives in life, it has both advantages and disadvantages of which you may wish to become aware.

Advantages of the Computerized GRE

- **You have convenience in scheduling.**

  You are no longer restricted to taking the exam only on its prescribed paper-and-pencil test dates, just four times per year. You can now arrange to take the computerized GRE whenever a test site near you has an opening. In some instances, you may be able to register by telephone, using a VISA or MasterCard credit card, and take the exam the next day.

- **You can immediately know your test scores.**

  Immediately after taking the exam you have a choice:

  You can know your test scores within minutes, or

  You can cancel your test scores, in which case your test is not scored, but a record of your having taken the GRE unscored is recorded (unscored) in the files of Educational Testing Service. This notation becomes part of your GRE file.

- **You have a choice in whether to take breaks.**

  You may, if you wish, decide not to take breaks when they are offered, but rather continue on to the next section.

- **You can have as much scratch paper as you need.**

  In the pen-and-pencil GRE, you must make do with the space available in your test booklet for scratch work. In the computerized GRE, you are provided with scratch paper and can get more as is detailed below.

- **You may have less trouble marking your answer choice.**

  Clicking on one bubble among the four or five choices appearing on the screen *may* be less trouble than transferring your answer to the proper bubble among hundreds of bubbles on the machine-scored answer sheet of the paper-and-pencil GRE.

- **You can practice on a computer.**

  If you're considering taking the exam on computer, it may make sense to *practice* on a computer. You can do that by using a computerized test-preparation product like *Cliffs StudyWare for the GRE* (available at most software outlets and college bookstores). You'll find that, while the computerized test-preparation system is not exactly the same as the actual computerized exam, there are enough similarities to make such an approach worthwhile.

Disadvantages of the Computerized GRE

Taking the computerized GRE has a number of significant disadvantages besides its additional cost. (Presently, the fee is over $90.) The disadvantages are described among the items below, and some strategies for dealing with these disadvantages are suggested.

What You Should Know

- **Check-in time.**

  You'll be given a check-in time of approximately a half hour before your official test time. For example, if your test time is 9 A.M., you will likely be asked to arrive at 8:30 A.M.

- **The computer tutorial.**

  The computer tutorial is one of the reasons for the early check-in time. It allows you to gain familiarity with

  using a mouse
  selecting answer choices
  using the testing prompts
  scrolling through long passages

  If you are even slightly familiar with a Macintosh or PC Windows™ system, you will be comfortable with the GRE computerized format. In fact, double clicking is never necessary. A single click on a selected prompt button always activates whatever action you choose. In addition to clicking on individual answer choices for question items, you will have buttons for requesting help for mouse choices, showing or hiding the amount of time left in a section (except when you are within five minutes of the end of a section, in which case the running time always appears), and quitting the exam.

  If you are familiar with using a computer mouse, you will no doubt work through the tutorial in less than thirty minutes. If so, you will be asked if you would like to begin the test immediately. If you would, you can choose to do so. In the computerized GRE, unlike the paper-and-pencil exam, there is no unnecessary waiting period to accommodate all the other test takers' reading of the directions, filling in of personal information, and so forth. If *you* are ready to start after the computer tutorial, *you* can begin.

- **Your desk space.**

  Before electing to begin your GRE, rearrange your desk space to optimize your work style. For instance, when you are seated in the test carrel, you'll initially find a keyboard immediately in front of you. After you work with the computer by hitting "return" or "enter" on the keyboard, the computer program will then ask you to use the mouse and pad. From that point on, you'll never use the keyboard again, so get it out of your way! Move it to the back of the desk, reposition the mouse and pad so that you can comfortably maneuver the mouse, and place your scratch paper and pencils wherever on the desk they will be most convenient for you to use.

- **Your lamp.**

  You may find a small lamp on your desk, and it may be turned on. Before beginning the test, determine whether the light is helpful for you in doing your scratch work or whether the lamp simply produces ambient light which makes it harder to read the computer screen. If you don't need or want the lamp on, feel free to turn it off.

- **Scratch paper.**

  When the test administrator seats you, you will be given several pencils and about five or six pieces of standard-size paper (8½″ × 11″) to use for scratch work. These pages must be surrendered at the end of the exam, and they possibly will not be sufficient to work through all the sections of the test. Don't feel compelled to cramp all your work for the entire GRE on these half-dozen sheets. After you've finished a section, you can, without losing valuable testing time, raise your hand and indicate to the test administrator that you need more scratch paper. After new scratch paper is provided, you can then activate the "start" button to begin the next section.

- **Directions.**

  Just as on the paper-and-pencil GRE, reading the directions for each question type constitutes part of your testing time and thus lessens the amount of time you have to answer the questions in that section. Ensure that you fully understand the directions for each question type *before* going in to take the test so you can minimize any time reading them during the exam.

- **Eliminating answer choices.**

  A powerful strategy for efficiently taking standardized multiple-choice tests is the elimination strategy (explained on page 10 of this book). Unfortunately, at present the computerized program does not permit GRE candidates to use this strategy on the actual screen of the computerized GRE. (Some practice computer programs do allow the user to "cross out" choices on the screen; the computerized GRE, however, at the time this book went to press, does not.) Therefore, in order to use this effective strategy, you'll have to either (1) quickly write the choice letters (that is, A, B, C, D, and E) all at once onto your scratch paper and cross them out as you eliminate possibilities or (2) write them crossed out one by one as you realize they are incorrect on the screen. Moving back and forth from your scratch paper to the screen is not only troublesome but also possibly too time consuming and distracting. You might consider placing your scratch paper on the screen immediately alongside the choices given and gently marking on your scratch paper adjacent to each choice. At this time, administrators have not declared this procedure to be against the rules; they may, however, do so in the future. It may also be uncomfortable to work "against" the screen in this fashion. Use your best judgment. But as the elimination strategy is particularly important for the analytical and verbal sections, you'll want to be prepared for this disadvantage if you take the GRE on computer.

- **Dealing with diagrams.**

  You may also need to redraw diagrams because the computerized GRE does not permit marking on them (to note equal angles, write in values for parts of geometric figures, circle the particular amounts required for a chart question which are listed among other possible values, and so forth). Don't hesitate to redraw diagrams carefully if marking them will help you answer the question.

- **Scrolling.**

  Some reading passages are quite long and require much scrolling to move from beginning to end and back. Some quantitative problem sets require you to refer to a number of different charts or graphs for one question, but only one chart may be viewed on the screen at any one time. Be aware of this disadvantage so you aren't suddenly surprised by the inconvenience during your test section.

- **The "plus-minus" strategy, or skipping.**

  On the adaptive computerized GRE, you cannot skip questions and return to them later. Each question must be answered before you are allowed to move on to the next question, and you may never return to a question once you have registered your answer and chosen to move on. You can, however, record an answer and then reconsider it by not clicking on the "move to the next question" button. But once you click the "move" button, your answer to that question has been registered, that question disappears, and the next one appears.

- **The "adaptive" test.**

  The computerized GRE is what's called an "adaptive" test. Simply put, this means that all GRE candidates will not be answering the same test items. Based on the computerized program, your answer to a particular question will send you either to more difficult questions or to easier questions, depending upon whether you answer correctly or incorrectly. The administrators of Educational Testing Service apparently believe that this process allows them to assess more accurately your level of skill in each of the different areas (quantitative, verbal, and analytical). As you answer more difficult questions correctly, they move you to a higher level of difficulty and determine with more precision this higher skill level than they would have had they given every candidate the same question set. Likewise, if you answer certain questions incorrectly, they move you to an easier set and thus can make more precise determination of your skills at that easier level.

  Whether or not you agree with this procedure, one thing is clear. Early questions of each question-type set, which on the paper-and-pencil test are among the easiest, will likely now be of middle-of-the-road difficulty and may possibly take on greater importance because they will help establish your particular skill level. Before you take your first section of the computerized GRE, make sure you are adequately "warmed up" and ready to go because once you answer these important initial questions, you can't go back and recheck your work!

- **Item ordering.**

As you may know, or will soon learn upon reading this *Cliffs GRE Preparation Guide,* the GRE has established certain orders of questions within sections. For instance, the quantitative section has typically consisted of an initial set of fifteen Quantitative Comparison questions followed by fifteen Math Ability questions. The middle five items of the Math Ability questions are typically chart or graph questions. Similarly, established orders within sections exist for the analytical question types (Analytical Reasoning and Logical Reasoning) and the verbal question types (Antonyms, Analogies, Sentence Completion, and Reading Comprehension). The computerized GRE appears to scramble the orders within sections. For example, you may have two or three Quantitative Comparison questions, then a few Math Ability questions, then back to several Quantitative Comparison questions, and so on. Hence, it is especially important that you are thoroughly familiar with the requirements and strategies for each question type in a section and can easily move back and forth among them without losing your focus as to what the directions require.

- **Canceling your score.**

At the termination of your GRE, you will have the option of receiving your three scores (quantitative, verbal, and analytical) or canceling your score. On the paper-and-pencil exam, answering only half the questions correctly on the verbal section typically would result in a score slightly higher than 400. However, on the "adaptive" computerized GRE, answering only half the questions correctly may result in a much higher (or perhaps lower) score, depending upon which of the questions (easy or hard) were answered. For example, if the first sets are answered correctly, the program automatically moves you to a higher level of difficulty and, with that move, into a higher score even though you may subsequently have less success answering the tougher questions that follow. The point is that you should not automatically presume that if you cannot answer correctly, say, an "average" number of questions, you will necessarily get a "below-average" score. The number of questions answered correctly and their equivalent scaled scores on the paper-and-pencil GRE do not necessarily correlate with those of the adaptive computerized

GRE! Be aware of this if, at the end of the test, you are considering canceling your score.

- **Scheduling a test date.**

To schedule an appointment to take the computerized GRE, you may call a test center number (a list is available from Educational Testing Service) or the Sylvan National Registration Center at 1-800-967-1100 during regular business hours. For answers to questions about the Computer-Based Testing Program, you may contact Graduate Record Examinations, Computer-Based Testing Program, Educational Testing Service, P.O. Box 6000, Princeton, New Jersey 08541-6000.

UPDATE: ANALYSIS OF EXPLANATIONS

Recently, a new analytical question type, or rather a variation of an old question type that the GRE used a number of years ago, has appeared occasionally on the exam. While these questions may be used only in experimental sections at this point, there is no way to be certain whether a section is experimental or not, so you should be aware of this type of question and how to attack it.

Ability Tested

These questions test your ability, in assessing explanations, to read closely and carefully and understand logical relationships which are expressed or implied.

Basic Skills Necessary

No knowledge of formal logic is required, but you must be able to understand all details of the material presented and identify shades of meaning, inferences, and interrelationships.

Directions

Analysis of Explanations can have two answer choices (A, B), three choices (A, B, C), or four choices (A, B, C, D). The following sets of questions and analysis are based on the two-choice format that has recently been presented in the information bulletin.

A fact situation and a result are followed by two types of questions with following statements. Evaluate each statement in relation to the question asked about it, the fact situation, and the result.

Each statement is to be considered separately from the other statements. For this set, choose (A) if your answer is "yes." Choose (B) if your answer is "no."

Analysis

The key to doing well here is thoroughly understanding the intent of the two types of questions that follow each situation/result passage.

Question 1:

Is the following statement, if true, relevant to some possible adequate explanation of the result? A statement is relevant to an explanation if it *either* supports or weakens that explanation.

Notice these points:

- Note the words *if true.* Assume that all statements given are true.
- Note the words *relevant to some possible adequate explanation.* The statement need not *be* an explanation for the result; it need only be *relevant to* such an explanation.
- Note that a relevant statement may *either support* or *weaken* an explanation of the result. A statement, then, is *irrelevant* if it logically has no bearing on whether the result did or did not occur.

Question 2:

Could the following statement, if true, provide the basis for an adequate explanation of the result? An adequate explanation for this purpose does not need to be complete in all details.

Notice these points:

- Note the words *if true.* Assume that all statements given are true.
- Note that the statement must *provide the basis for an adequate explanation. Unlike* the first set of statements, these statements must be more than relevant to the explanation; they must provide a basis for it in order for you to answer *yes.*

- Note that the *adequate explanation . . . does not need not be complete.* In other words, the statement need not cover every detail in leading to the result. It must only logically have to do with explaining why the result might have occurred. Note that, *unlike* the first set of statements, these statements **may not weaken** the likelihood of the result; they may only strengthen it in order for you to answer *yes*.

Suggested Approach with Samples

Set 1

Situation:

In a highly contested race for the city council, the incumbent councilman Arthur Jones is opposed by political newcomer Mary Evans in the well-to-do Oakdale district of the city. If she wins, Ms. Evans will become the only conservative member of the city council and will join the five liberal male councilmen who are running unopposed in the other districts. In her campaign, Evans is concentrating on issues of education, the elderly, and the excessive city property taxes on large, single-family homes. The Oakdale district has been proposed as the site of a new state prison, which Evans opposes.

Result:

Mary Evans was elected to the city council by a very large majority of votes.

Question:

Is the following statement, if true, relevant to some possible adequate explanation of the result? A statement is relevant to an explanation if it *either* supports or weakens that explanation.

1. Councilman Arthur Jones has always opposed building a state prison in the Oakdale district.

2. The five city council members from other districts declined to take part in a televised debate on the issue of prison construction.

3. Both local and national women's groups supported the candidacy of Mary Evans.

Question:

Could the following statement, if true, provide the basis for an adequate explanation of the result? An adequate explanation for this purpose does not need to be complete in all details.

4. The city council recently raised taxes on residential property for single-family homes assessed at more than $200,000.

5. After this election, Arthur Jones was charged with and acquitted of irregularities in his campaign financing.

6. Throughout the city, high school students have been bused to schools in other districts for many years.

Answers:

1. (A) This information is relevant because it *weakens* a possible explanation that Ms. Evans won because of her opponent's opposition to the prison construction. If both opposed the prison, Jones's opposition cannot be the reason for her victory.

2. (B) This statement is irrelevant because the election in question was confined to the Oakdale district, and we do not have any information about the participation of Evans and Jones.

3. (A) This information is relevant because it suggests Ms. Evans's appeal to women voters and the possibility of her having received financial support to conduct her campaign.

4. (A) This statement adequately explains the result of the election as a taxpayer revolt. The details of the passage make clear that Oakdale would have many homes whose taxes were raised, and Jones, as a member of the council, would be held responsible.

5. (B) This statement makes no reference to the situation before or during the election. If Jones was not accused until after the election, the charge would not explain what occurred in the voting, the result.

6. (B) Although Evans is interested in education, there is nothing in the passage to suggest that busing is an issue or that Jones and Evans take different sides on the issue.

Set 2

Situation:

Having to spend thousands of dollars each year removing graffiti from traffic signs and walls, the city of Walden has passed a law forbidding the sale of markers and spray paint to anyone under the age of eighteen. The number of police cars on the streets has been increased, and a public campaign to encourage parents to supervise their teenage children more carefully has been undertaken. The proposed curfew to keep the teenage children off the streets after nightfall was narrowly defeated in a public referendum.

Result:

The city's expense for graffiti removal had not declined but had slightly increased at the end of the year after the law had passed.

Question:

Is the following statement, if true, relevant to some possible adequate explanation of the result? A statement is relevant to an explanation if it *either* supports or weakens that explanation.

1. None of the towns adjacent to Walden have ordinances against the selling of spray paints.

2. The number of crimes of all kinds has increased substantially in the year.

Question:

Could the following statement, if true, provide the basis for an adequate explanation of the result? An adequate explanation for this purpose does not need to be complete in all details.

3. In order to avoid a strike of its maintenance workers, the city of Walden increased their salaries by twenty-two percent this year.

4. Law enforcement costs in several nearby cities are similar to those in Walden.

Answers:

1. (A) If none of the nearby towns refuse to sell spray paint to teenagers, the youth of Walden can buy their materials nearby, and the law will be ineffectual.

2. (A) If increased crime places greater demands on the time of police officers, there will be less time to enforce laws against vandalism.

3. (A) The increased costs for graffiti removal may be due to the higher salaries for workers, who will now have to be paid more to keep up to the level of work in the former year.

4. (B) The cost of law enforcement in nearby cities does not explain the rise in the cost of graffiti removal in Walden. This information has no clear relevance to the situation.